LIBRARY LIT. 3 – The Best of 1972

edited by
BILL KATZ
and
JANET KLAESSIG

The Scarecrow Press, Inc.
Metuchen, N. J.   1973

ISBN 0-8108-0613-4
Library of Congress Catalog Card Number 78-154842

Copyright 1973 by The Scarecrow Press, Inc.

CONTENTS

Introduction v
Acknowledgments viii
PROLOGUE: Social Responsibility and the Library
   Press (William R. Eshelman) 1

PART I: LIBRARIES AND LIBRARIANS
The Premise of Meaning (Archibald MacLeish) 20
Turnstiles in the Library? (William Cole) 26
Public Facilities--A Memoir (Bette Howland) 33
Association Agonies: Life with ALA (Eric Moon) 58
Libraries Are for Librarians: A View from the
   Editor's Chair (Gerald R. Shields) 71
The Literate Profession (D. E. Gerard) 76
A Librarian's First Loyalty (W. G. K. Duncan) 85
From Reaction to Interaction: The Development of
   the North American University Library
   (Samuel Rothstein) 102
Functions and Organization of a Rural Library
   System (F. A. Sharr) 111
Library Life in Middle America (Arthur Plotnik) 121

PART II: TECHNICAL SERVICES/READERS' SERVICES
Williams & Wilkins v. The U.S. (Ralph R. Shaw) 140
Cataloging-In-Publication: Will It Succeed?
   (Margaret C. Brown) 172
Of Mice and Lions and Battleships and Interlibrary
   Things (R. H. Blackburn) 181
The Serials Librarian and the Journals Publisher
   (Huibert Paul) 194
The Cataloger's White Knight? MARC
   (Hillis L. Griffin) 204
From Information Science to Informatics: A
   Terminological Investigation (Hans Wellisch) 212
Bibliography Old and New (Herman W. Liebert) 249
George Smith and the DNB (Anonymous) 264

PART III: COMMUNICATION AND EDUCATION

The Making of the New York Times Book Review
  (Thomas Weyr) 276
Concerned Criticism or Casual Cop-outs?
  (Patricia Glass Schuman) 306
Crisis Information Services to Youth: A Lesson for
  Librarians? (Carolyn Forsman) 317
American Children's Classics: Which Will Fade,
  Which Endure? (Sara Innis Fenwick) 341
Time for Decision: Library Education for the
  Seventies (Andrew H. Horn) 353
New Trends in Higher Education: The Impact on the
  University Library (Richard W. Lyman) 367
The Sobering Seventies: Prospects for Change
  (Ellsworth Mason) 377
The Qualities of a Book, The Wants of a Dissertation
  (Robert Plant Armstrong) 391

PART IV: THE SOCIAL PREROGATIVE

The Great East Hampton Library Mess
  (Dwight Macdonald) 406
Revealing Herself (Janet Sternburg) 422
Senior Power! (Peggy O'Donnell) 437

Notes on Contributors 447

INTRODUCTION

Representing the third annual effort at library literature made easy, this is a collection of 30 "best" articles published in magazines between November 1971 and November 1972. The purpose is to acknowledge the good work in the field and to offer librarians and students a painless, even pleasant overview of libraries and librarianship.

How are the articles selected? There are no mechanical standards, although some effort is made to identify areas of particular interest. Approximately 200 library oriented magazines are searched for likely candidates. A number of general periodicals are examined, too. The result is a group of some 100 or so articles which are gradually cut back to a manageable size by the editors and the jury. It is worth mentioning that several entries were suggested by readers of the previous collections. Readers are asked to submit potential winners for next year. Yes, these collections will continue until such time as an individual or coteries of librarians discover another formula for aesthetic conscience.

The faculty of "appreciating" what constitutes a good or best article is hardly limited to the participants in the present assemblage. Everyone can be, and usually is, his or her own judge of what constitutes style, content, originality, scholarship and wit. Detecting these attitudes is not difficult, although finding published illustrations is quite another matter. Which is to say that the articles collected here are all the more impressive because of the commonplaceness of much of what passes for library literature. Obviously, no reader is going to agree entirely with what should be excluded or included--the judges had difficulty enough doing that--but presumably the essence of the best material published in 1972 is represented by the judges' choices.

Some critics rightly take the view that the choices are limited in that they ignore articles in non-English publications. And in this they are quite correct. Admittedly, any collection of library articles which ignores most of Western Europe, as well as a good proportion of the globe, is wanting. The solution is to publish articles in Spanish, German, French, Russian and so on; but even in this international age one must honestly ask how many readers would be able to get past the common words. The other answer is to offer translations, and while not impossible, it presents certain technical and editorial difficulties which are beyond the scope of the present work. One of these years the situation should be corrected, although for now all that can be done is to acknowledge the presumable gap. Parenthetically, the major English and Canadian magazines are dutifully examined, as are the translation journals. The result, then, is not simply limited to American writers.

Anyone who has taken the trouble to follow the course of this series will note a number of weak, yet possibly meaningful trends. A sample of 90 articles is hardly scientifically adequate, but to compromise the theory of objectivity it can be said that the library world is growing weary of social issues, is more inclined these days to concentrate on the possible in the individual library. (The "proof" is the fact that the first compilation had eight entries under "The Social Prerogative." The second had four, and now we are down to three.) Less obvious is the apparent movement away from purely technological issues, as witnessed by the decline in articles under "Technical Services." This time around, in fact, "technical processes" is deleted in favor of "readers' services." One may counter that both the social and the technological are with us, but grow less apparent in this collection because they are tending to become more and more repetitive, less and less original. Also, to be sure, not only the judges have grown weary of the same authors over and over again promising the impossible, or threatening the fall of libraries. Whether these conclusions are more illusions than fact is unimportant, perhaps even wrong, yet disciplines do change and these collections offer at least an opportunity to square reality (whatever that may be) with all too readily assumed myths and time-worn clichés.

A case in point is the article about the Chicago Public Library by Bette Howland. Much of what she says does more to explain the real malaise than the statistically damning report of Lowell Martin, namely, <u>Library Response to Urban Change</u> (Chicago: American Library Association, 1969). Both, to be sure, have their place, and Martin is unquestionably one of the true masters of the meaningful survey, but the cardinal point is that the seeker after goodness must be many voiced, not exclusively a professional librarian.

No one was a better example of individual opinion than Ralph Shaw who devoted a whole lifetime to assessing, and usually finding wanting, the library profession. In many respects he was the conscience of us all, and it is with considerable regret that his death deprives us of ever considering one of his articles again. Fortunately, though, the entry here is one of his best, certainly one of his more meaningful, scholarly and thoughtful contributions.

Which brings up a final point. Impertinent as any evaluation of this or that must be, it does seem necessary particularly in terms of library literature. One may ask by what authority the editors and judges take custody of the community's values. The answer is: absolutely none, except we elected one another to discharge a not always pleasant task because we, and many of the readers and writers, think library literature is important and deserving of something more than derision. Many librarians, and particularly students, are systematically discouraged by forced reading of inadequate, anti-intellectual, downright distasteful documents which are passed as "literature." What prompts an otherwise sane inoffensive teacher to assign such readings is quite beyond the present introduction, as is the barely understandable encouragement librarians give their fellows who write neither well nor wisely, but none of us is going to plead guilty to such sins. And at the expense of being self-appointed judges, we give you the present best articles of 1972.

William A. Katz
Janet Klaessig
Albany, New York
December 1972

ACKNOWLEDGMENTS

Jurors: The editors wish to thank the jurors who carefully selected the 30 articles represented here: Lillian N. Gerhardt, editor, School Library Journal; Janet D. Bailey, editor, Special Libraries; Arthur Curley, director, Montclair Public Library, N.J. and editor, New Jersey Libraries; and Eric Moon, president, Scarecrow Press.

Editors and Authors: A word of thanks to the editors of the magazines who were kind enough to allow reprinting; and to the authors whose works are honoring this anthology and the literature as a whole.

Consultants: The editors wish also to thank those many librarians who so generously suggested entries for consideration. There are simply too many names to list individually, so we take this opportunity to thank one and all in the name of better library literature.

Finally, will any reader who has a candidate for the best of 1973 please send me the necessary citation. Please do it at any time between now and November 1, 1973. A post card will do. To: Bill Katz, Library School, State University of New York, Albany, N.Y. 12203.

PROLOGUE

SOCIAL RESPONSIBILITY AND THE LIBRARY PRESS*

William R. Eshelman

Since 1968, mostly through the activity of the American Library Association's Social Responsibilities Round Table, there has come more and more frequently a call for advocate-librarians. Groups such as "Librarians for 321.8" and the "Congress for Change" have also prodded ALA and pricked the conscience of the profession. While the library press dutifully reported on these happenings, it also engaged in some editorial soul-searching: was its role merely to report, or to report and comment, or to advocate in its turn and thus be among the leaders of the profession?

The most dramatic--some would say melodramatic--example of an act of social responsibility by a library periodical was undoubtedly the issue of Library Journal that carried on its cover, in a gold frame, a portrait of Senator Barry Goldwater. It ran on the eve of Goldwater's election race for the presidency--the October 15, 1964, issue. The editorial in that issue drew much fire from readers, even from those who thought extremism in the defense of liberty was a vice; many, of course, thought it completely beyond the pale for LJ to endorse a candidate for the presidency of the United States. It was defended, however, by John Dawson, prominent ALA councilor and later member of the Executive Board. He pronounced the editorial "most temperate and reasoned," and went on to say "I'm glad you made a dent in the 'lamentable record of unnecessary neutrality.' "1

Despite the comments of some other readers, Eric Moon's editorial was indeed well within the scope of professional responsibility. It began by quoting from the platforms of both parties, and for both the 1960 and 1964

---

*Reprinted by permission from the January 1972 issue of Wilson Library Bulletin. Copyright 1972 by The H. W. Wilson Company. First delivered as a speech at Dalhousie University, School of Library Science, Feb. 14, 1972.

Prologue 3

campaigns: in 1960 there were genteel promises and platitudes, while in 1964 the platforms were in complete agreement--neither mentioned libraries at all. Next, the editorial gave a run-down on the voting records of Mr. Goldwater and Mr. Johnson (and their running mates), citing the Library Services and Construction Act, the Higher Education Facilities Act, the National Defense Education Act, and the Economic Opportunity Act. It summarized: "On these four crucial pieces of legislation, each of which has, or can have, a vital impact on library service in this country, the position of at least three of the four candidates is crystal clear." LJ thereupon took an editorial stand by endorsing Lyndon Johnson: "We feel that we have a strong responsibility to speak out on an election in which the candidates offer us 'a clear choice' on the future direction and health of library service in the United States."[2]

Some readers took drastic action. One wrote, "My subscription for the Library Journal expires in 1964 and it will not be renewed."[3] Another, Maurice D. Walsh, at a meeting in Little Rock, Arkansas, a few days after the editorial appeared, tried to persuade the Southwestern Library Association Conference to censure LJ's publishers, the R.R. Bowker Co., for endorsing a presidential candidate. John Anderson, then of the Tucson, Arizona, Public Library, spoke against the Walsh motion, and it was tabled.[4]

One states-righter observed: "Senator Goldwater advocates not less but more aid for education and libraries. Where will the extra money come from? From taxes raised by the states and kept at home."[5] Another reader misunderstood the cover completely, thinking LJ had endorsed Goldwater. Still another noted, "I would bet that more than half the recipients never did read the editorial this time--and most will therefore conclude LJ perversely backs BG."[6] One wrote, "I immediately tore this cover off (carefully discarding the magazine) and proudly displayed the photograph in our window."[7] And another stated, "You may be sure that this issue of LJ awaits our attention FACE DOWN on our desks."[8]

In 1968, Mr. Walsh noted that LJ had backed no candidate, and wrote inquiring about their plans: "Will the two unendorsed presidential candidates' pictures share a cover or will they be honored in separate issues?" LJ confessed to being "desperately neutral" in 1968, having given up the idea of endorsing Snoopy (whom they found to be weak on law and order), and likewise Pat Paulsen (who was unclear on foreign relations).9

Advocacy Journalism

There are perhaps three basic approaches to the editorial task, and all are to be found in the library press. First, and most common, is to present no editorial opinion at all, merely publishing what is available and, if an author's statements border on the controversial, pointing out that the publisher bears no responsibility. Most of the State library association journals fall into this category, as do the magazines published by State libraries. Second is the grand tradition in journalism, which calls for "objectivity" and a dispassionate tone in the reporting of the news, with an editorial page to carry articles of opinion or commentary. LJ under Eric Moon's editorship exemplified this approach, as did the Wilson Library Bulletin under John Wakeman and, in a different way, when edited by Stanley Kunitz. Some State association journals also have editorials (Alabama Librarian, California Librarian), as does the regional PNLA Quarterly--but few if any published by State libraries allow editorial opinion. The third approach is sometimes called "advocacy journalism," and is a comparative newcomer to the field. No library periodical has adopted this philosophy (with the possible exception of New Jersey Libraries under Arthur Curley), although all three national journals occasionally--especially when reporting ALA conferences--exhibit its features.

The rationale for advocacy journalism is similar to the arguments for greater social responsibility on the part of librarians. Every reporter has a point of view, the argument runs, and cannot escape some coloring of his story no matter how hard he tries to be objective. Granting that, it is therefore better to admit one's biases frankly, so that the reader is alerted and can make allowances. Truth emerges, then, from conflicting or complementary accounts of the same event. A virtue of this approach, the advocates of advocacy journalism say, is that the reader is not lulled into a false sense of having gotten the facts when, indeed, no one account can possibly present them without bias.

Arguments against this kind of journalism seem to come down to "projection," in the psychological sense. The reader who believes in objective reporting cannot imagine that an advocate journalist will play fair with the facts, once having admitted his own bias. There are, however, two correctives to the misuse of advocacy journalism, both under the reader's control. If a publication very often fails to provide a balanced account of the facts prior to making editorial comment, the reader may reject the publication completely. If it only occasionally transgresses, the reader has the option of righting the balance by reading an account in another journal. By far the best way to evaluate reporting is when chance includes the reader as a witness or participant in an event. Then the advocate journalist's point is made for him, since a witness or participant rarely agrees with any reporter's account of something he has himself seen and is likely to find fault with all accounts he reads.

Just as advocate-librarians see as one advantage the counteracting of the drab stereotype with a dash of human enthusiasm, the advocate-journalists believe that writing with a viewpoint makes for livelier, more readable prose. The reading of objective reporting, each set of facts carefully balanced by an opposing set (and sometimes, one suspects, the opposing set is strengthened just to give the appearance of balance)--such reporting seems as much of an opiate as television. But more important, advocacy journalism puts the reader in the judge's seat--before coming to a conclusion, the other side should be heard.

Now regardless of the editorial approach, the editor usually has the prerogative of selection. With the national journals, at least, the editor can hint at his personal beliefs through giving space to some developments and allotting less space (or none) to others. The motto of The New York Times--"All the News that's Fit to Print"--allows a good deal of latitude. In the case of the Harrisburg 7 (which involves two librarians as witnesses), the one million readers of the Times did not learn of the use of a government informer until two weeks after the Los Angeles Times had run a long piece of investigative reporting and analysis. In fact, there was a virtual blackout of the news on this case in the New York metropolitan area, unless one looked at papers other than the Times. The Bergen County (N. J.) Record, for example, picked up the L. A. Times' story and ran a shortened version the next day--thus beating their big brother across the Hudson by a half month. In April, 1971, WLB carried an account of the case which later was the basis for a resolution passed at the ALA meeting in Dallas.

An Early Instance

The distinguished poet and man of letters Stanley Kunitz, when he was editing WLB (1927-1943), used a version of the traditional journalistic method. What little news was reported was given straight, and the editorial page was rigorously non-controversial. But in his selection of articles, Kunitz managed to interject some "think" pieces among the litter of practical hints, tips, and small success stories, which had made WLB the most widely read magazine in the profession.

Few librarians recall, I suspect, the very modern-sounding article published by editor Kunitz in 1938, written by Bernard Berelson: "The Myth of Library Impartiality; an Interpretation for Democracy."[10] A quote will give the flavor of it:

> Librarianship must pay more attention to [the] educational program than to the methodology and mechanics which now intrigue it. Librarians must be better trained in the social sciences and in adult education. Most important, librarians must administer forums, reading groups, discussion groups, lectureships, etc., for informal guidance. They must give wide publicity to material on social questions.... It is time, I think, for the library to forsake the genteel tradition.

Almost a year later, editor Kunitz published a reply to Berelson by Bernard Fry, who wrote:

> If the study of human affairs can be reduced to a lucid science in which finality can be reached, the exercise of partiality no longer involves arbitrary selection but becomes merely the simple choice between the socially good as against the socially bad, as one chooses between "intelligence and stupidity." Controversies agitating the public mind supposedly would be deflated to a point where the "facts" could be determined; hence, the role of the librarian becomes that of a teacher who "encourages" the patron to think and act on the basis of demonstrated truth.[11]

But, Mr. Fry continues, in the social sciences no such precision is possible, leaving the reader to infer that Berelson's

Prologue 7

case has been demolished. Berelson replied, of course, and editor Kunitz had an interesting exchange of ideas although he took no editorial stand himself.

In the interim, Marion S. Scandrett contributed a resounding denunciation of librarians, with the title, "Mr. Berelson's Lost Cause."[12] She castigated the profession as "neither socially curious nor intellectually alert," citing four grounds for this judgment. First, the professional literature, "when not actually ungrammatical, ... is repetitious, circuitous, dull." Second, she noted a distaste for controversy among librarians: "It is news when a library meeting produces sparks." Next, the profession's lack of interest in evolving a philosophy--"Oncoming librarians look quizzically at a man or woman who after a life-time of service cannot pass on to his juniors a clear statement of his objectives and philosophy which has given them point. Devotion, like patriotism, is not enough, and the old generalities no longer convince." And last, she accused librarians of a "wavering faith in democracy." "They feel confidence," she continues, "in common people only when they appear individually, as suppliants before a desk. The same people, as sitdown strikers, as union members, as the unemployed, as WPA workers, even in the same building, find small place in the librarian's consciousness, and only a vague place in his sympathies."

And later, in the same article, Ms. Scandrett sounded a note that some librarians still have not heard:

> What is wrong with unions if they are incompatible with professionalism in general? What is wrong with librarianship that to preserve standards it must remain aloof from one of the most compelling social movements of the modern world? Is it true, as many honest students of social problems believe, that professional and trade groups, each being workers, have enough traits in common to render their common strength essential to the democratic survival of both?

But if editor Kunitz only selected articles, and took no editorial stand himself, how does one explain Jesse Shera's considered judgment, recollected in tranquility? Dean Shera says:

> To our full buoyancy of youth, the WLB gave a

generous share of hope, and joy, and aspiration.
It was then only emerging from the chrysalis of a
house organ, and it may not have been a great
national force, even among the slender output of
library journals. But with Stanley Kunitz at its
head, it was a rallying point for a group of
youngsters who were in hot revolt against tradition.[19]

Perhaps WLB was a rallying point not because of its
editorial stance, but because editor Kunitz, for those young
librarians who knew him, served to sharpen their own perceptions and offered his own poetic insights. And then there
was that famous editorial, which doubtless had great impact
because it was so unusual. The year was 1936, and Kunitz
took a look at the upcoming ALA conference in Richmond,
Virginia, and unleashed his eloquence. His editorial page
was called "The Roving Eye," and for May, 1936, was titled,
"The Spectre at Richmond":

To the librarians assembled, or preparing to
assemble, at Richmond:
I bring you greetings and my best wishes for the
success of your conference. The program that has
been arranged for you is a varied one, from addresses on such broad and compelling themes as
"Objectives of the Library Profession" to more particularized dissertations on "Microphotography" and
"Methodology Used in Compiling a Bibliography in the
Field of Agricultural Economics." There is even to
be a paper with the teasing title, "So What?" One
subject, however, I have failed to find in the program. It is not slated for official discussion. Yet
I dare say that none of you will be able to shake your
mind free from it for long. It will be a spectre
haunting the halls.
I refer to your shockingly cruel and feudal policy
with respect--or should I say, "with disrespect"--to
Negro librarians at the conference. Let me quote
from the "semi-official" letter sent to some of your
professional colleagues--those whose skins are more
highly pigmented than others':

Because of the traditional position of the South in
respect to mixed meetings it seems necessary to
have the position of the American Library Association and its committees made known. It is also

advisable to suggest to Negro librarians the conditions they should expect to find in Richmond during the conference.

These are the "conditions" at Richmond, corresponding, it would seem from the language of the letter, with the "position" of the A. L. A. (italics [underlines] are my own):

> The American Library Association has obtained the promise from the John Marshall and Jefferson Hotels that Negro delegates to the conference may use the same entrance as the white delegates and will be received and housed in the same manner during the conference meetings. <u>This does not mean that Negro delegates may obtain rooms and meals at these hotels</u> as this is forbidden by Virginia laws. All delegates will also use the main entrances to the Mosque auditorium where the general sessions will be held. <u>Those meetings which are a part of breakfasts, luncheons or dinners are not open to Negroes</u>, who may, however, attend sessions which are followed by meals, provided they do not participate in the meals. <u>Provisions will be made to seat Negroes in the front right hand section of the main floor of the auditorium</u> during the general sessions. This same section is reserved for them at the large group meetings and round tables at the hotels.

In brief, Negro librarians will be segregated throughout the conference: they will not be permitted to attend meetings where food is served.

Unless you believe that Negroes are incapable of being insulted, you must agree with me that a minority group of the A. L. A. has been greatly offended. If you permit this organized insult to pass unchallenged, there is but one conclusion to be made: that American librarians do not, in their hearts, care for democracy or for the foundation principles of decent and enlightened institutions. No elegant platform phrases of devotion to the idea of a free and equal society or to the theory of liberty can be sufficient to obviate that conclusion.

You may say, as assuredly will be said, in defence of the Negro policy at the conference, that it is merely conforming with the laws of Virginia. To this I reply that there is a higher law ... and that we have forty-eight States in the Union. Other organizations make a practice of convening only in communities where their own standards of eligibility and respectability are honored. An association of American professional men and women cannot go into convention part white and part black without doing violence to the best thought and the highest hope of our national life.

For the culture of Virginia, mother of much that is noblest in our American heritage, I have a profound respect. Will a Virginian rise to tell me that his culture is not broad enough or deep enough to tolerate the Christian spectacle of black and white librarians meeting together in free fellowship and dining at a common table? Interracial student meetings, I am informed, have been held before in the South, where all delegates have eaten together. Unless the clock turns backward, the South will welcome more of these meetings, will multiply them, where the bread of tolerance is broken and shared.

Along with my greeting, then, I bring you the burden of responsibility for action. "The trusteeship of truth is a serious responsibility," wrote the Vice-Chancellor of Birmingham University a few months ago in rejecting Heidelberg's invitation to participate in the celebration of its five hundred and fiftieth anniversary.... "Cooperation can be purchased at too dear a price if one of the parties surrenders the first principles of a free life.... Treachery to truth and betrayal of the conditions in which alone truth can be saved and promoted are a breach of trusteeship, the consequences of which may be irreparable."

You have your trusteeship. What do you propose to do with it?[14]

The Spectre Finally Exorcised

Curiously enough, a quarter-century later, the spectre at Richmond theme united the editors of WLB and LJ in a renewed assault on segregation, not just in library associations but in library service to Negroes. John Wakeman and Eric Moon, both Englishmen, had recently assumed the editorships of the two independent national journals. Both WLB, in September, 1960, and LJ the following December, ran articles and editorials on the segregated

Prologue 11

libraries still extant in the South. The two editors differed on the adequacy of ALA's social responsibility, with Wakeman taking the kinder view. (But the first affirmative action even he can cite is the moving of the 1954 ALA conference from Miami Beach to Minneapolis; the Richmond spectre walked 18 years before, in 1936.)

Both editors called on ALA to provide legal service, and Mr. Moon even went so far as to question whether it was proper to make federal funds available to segregated libraries.

As editor of the California Librarian, I followed up the LJ and WLB editorials, suggesting in my January, 1961, editorial that "ALA should sponsor or conduct a survey of libraries in the South to define the problem: how many libraries have quietly integrated? How many remain segregated?"[15] Further, the editorial admonished the northern States not to feel too smug about the matter, and recommended that the California Library Association look into segregation in libraries with the same seriousness that characterized the much-admired Fiske report on censorship.

In the May, 1961, WLB, editor Wakeman published a mini-symposium on the topic of segregation by four Negro librarians, Dean Virginia Lacy Jones (Atlanta University), Milton S. Byam (Brooklyn Public), Spencer G. Shaw (Nassau Library System), and Miles M. Jackson (Hampton Institute).[16] Here it came out that ALA had not been so effective as Mr. Wakeman assumed when he wrote his September, 1960, editorial, quoting the ALA Bulletin: "The North Carolina Negro Library Association was formally dissolved by its members on November 4, 1955, in order to facilitate designation of the North Carolina Library Association as the ALA chapter in North Carolina."[17] Editor Wakeman assumed that the other State associations in the South were likewise integrated, but Dean Jones pointed out that even six years later, in 1961, she could not be a member of the Georgia Library Association.

There followed an editorial in the ALA Bulletin, by Samray Smith, on the general topic of segregation in libraries, but it stood in striking contrast to the thrust of editors Wakeman and Moon. The official journal of the association undertook to spell out not ALA's stand on segregation but why ALA "is not doing and cannot now do some of the things demanded of it."[18] In the following issue,

Eli Oboler made a new demand: "If ALA 'was not designed to do and by its present nature and structure cannot do' those things which its membership want it to do as relates to segregation, then the major and urgent and vital task for the Association now is to change the nature and structure of ALA to conform to its membership's wishes."[19]

Efforts continued by some ALA members to lay to rest the spectre at Richmond. In 1962, the Intellectual Freedom Committee submitted a call for action to eliminate discrimination within ALA's own membership, but the Executive Board delayed. In the spring of 1963, John Berry, editor of The Bay State Librarian, charged that eleven of the libraries in the South which had just received the Dorothy Canfield Fisher Award were still segregated. Mr. Berry's editorial was based on a response to a query he had sent to the Southern Regional Council, but he did no direct verification with the libraries.[20] His method brought him little but condemnation. For example, LJ took him to task: "Is it responsible editorial practice to ask a question, loaded with dynamite as this one is, without first making an attempt to check the facts with the individual libraries involved, with the State library agencies or with ALA?"[21] Richard K. Burns, director of one of the accused libraries (Falls Church, Virginia), was sensitive to Mr. Berry's intent:

> We regret that we should be accused without being asked or investigated. The writer of the editorial was, of course, careless and wrong. It appears that he was looking for an argument. For my part, however, I'm not too unhappy about it. Although erroneous in its facts, the editorial does ask a serious question, and asks it seriously. I prefer this to the countless editorials which are spineless in spirit, based on empty ideals, and achieve only their pointless effect, which appear again and again in our professional journals.[22]

By 1964, following the disaster of the ALA Access Study and its dismemberment by the Board of the Library Administration Division, the association finally got its policies pretty much in order. Four State library associations had been excluded from chapter status by ALA; they were: Alabama, Georgia, Louisiana, and Mississippi. The next task was to implement the policies fully, and at St. Louis, E. J. Josey pointed out that no elected officer of ALA and no staff member should ornament those sub-standard

Prologue

associations by appearing or speaking at their conferences. The next year, thanks to President Robert Severence, the Alabama Library Association managed not only to begin integration but also arranged that all members could attend the conference, eat, and be housed in Mobile. Mr. Josey was admitted to the Georgia Library Association's membership, and Louisiana applied for ALA chapter status, affirming that their former discriminatory practice had been ended. The spectre at Richmond was finally being exorcised.

During the mid-sixties, only one of the three national library periodicals maintained an editorial page; LJ's best are gathered together in Library Issues: the Sixties. The ALA Bulletin occasionally ran a page labeled "Editorial," but it contained such things as a plea for names of librarians suitable for committee appointment, or a bland comment on a conference somewhere. With John Wakeman's return to England, WLB was gradually turned into a journal of intellect, along the lines of Harper's or the Atlantic. Under the editorial hand of Kathleen Molz, it published articles by writers such as Susan Sontag, Ralph Ellison, Karl Shapiro, and Benjamin De Mott; polemicists Murray Kempton, Dwight Macdonald, and Carey McWilliams; and scholars Jacques Barzun and Allan Nevins. Like Stanley Kunitz, editor Molz confined her advocacy to the selection of articles and writers. Controversy almost disappeared from WLB's pages, except for Miss Molz's own articles, such as the "Report from Pikeville, Kentucky."

The forces for change were gathering, however, and erupted at the 1968 ALA conference in Kansas City. There Dorothy Bendix, Ken Duchac, and Tom Walker spearheaded the organization of the Social Responsibilities Round Table, an implicit recognition that the Junior Members Round Table had become moribund. No longer did JMRT have the vigor or impact it had when Jesse Shera and his colleagues were at the helm. Prior to the Atlantic City conference the next year, a group of young activists met in Washington, D.C., in a "Congress for Change." They brought many resolutions to the ALA conference the following week, opposing ABM's, Chicago as an ALA meeting place, and the Vietnam war, while favoring change in ALA, financial support of intellectual freedom and sanctions for offenders, and recruitment of librarians from minority groups.

In 1968 also, a new generation of editors for the three national library periodicals began to appear. Gerald

R. Shields, former editor of the Ohio Library Association Bulletin took over the ALA Bulletin. Later that year, WLB passed into my hands when Kathleen Molz took a position at the U.S. Office of Education. And, at the year's end, Eric Moon left LJ to the young man he had recruited on the basis of his editing of The Bay State Librarian, John N. Berry, III. All three new editors had tried their hands at State association journals, each of which had been recognized by the Library Periodicals Award, jointly sponsored by ALA and The H. W. Wilson Company.

Gerald Shields, whose ALA Bulletin was cited by Eric Moon as "by far the most obviously improved library periodical in the United States,"[23] has now accomplished a revitalization of that journal. He re-established a true editorial page, initiated many new departments and columns, and got from the ALA Publishing Board a policy statement which allows unusual editorial freedom--the editor can disagree with official ALA actions.

At LJ, most policies continue from Eric Moon's tenure in the editor's chair, and indeed only Pat Schuman is new on the LJ/SLJ team. Lillian Gerhardt, new editor of SLJ (having moved up from the editorship of the "Book Review"), may bring some changes, but it is too early to discern new directions clearly. One trend, often stated as a desideratum by Mr. Moon, may be emerging at SLJ: less dependence on articles from the field and more on those written by the staff. A recent issue of SLJ (January 1972) had no fewer than three staff-written articles.

At WLB, the former accent on big name writers had been reduced, although there are still a few.[24] No so many issues are focused on a single theme, but the Library Trends sort of thing has continued. Significant among the choice of themes, however, is the emphasis on the socially-responsible: "Library Outreach" (May 1969); "Libraries and the Spanish-Speaking" (March 1970); "When Is a Social Issue a Library Issue?" (September 1970); and "Our Other Customers" (January 1971). And WLB even turned its children's number toward a current topic, "Sex and the Single Child" (October 1971). Further, despairing of ever getting articles from the silent majority in libraryland, WLB contracted for a series of columns from Col. James Hillard titled "Right of Center."

All of the Big Three national library periodicals

Prologue

serve their readers fairly well in reporting the news. LJ, with more than twice the number of pages of either of the others, tries to be comprehensive. WLB aims at selectivity, and tries to dig beneath the stories in the press releases by interviewing at least one of the principals. When Ellis Hodgin was fired by the Martinsville, Virginia, Public Library board because as a parent he had filed suit against the public schools for teaching religion, LJ had a reporter at Hodgin's side the next day. And the editors of both WLB and LJ attended his trial, held in the spectre-haunted city of Richmond, in order to report at first hand. In the Joan Bodger case in Columbia, Missouri, both Gerald Shields and I made numerous telephone calls to interview principals, and WLB's report was based on these plus a first-hand account by a former member of the history department faculty at MU.[25]

In the selection of articles to be published, the national library press attempts to give broad coverage to all points of view. The state association journals, the publications of State libraries, and even the regional journals have less to choose from and hence find it more difficult to provide balance. But an examination of Library Literature reveals that the new subject headings, "Librarians--social responsibilities" (1968), "Librarians--political activities" (1969), and "Libraries and social and economic problems" (1964), have entries from all levels of the library press, and a fairly wide geographic distribution. The heading, "Librarians--social responsibilities," peaked numerically in 1969 with 15 items, and held steady in 1970 and 1971 with 12 items in each of those years. A brand new heading, "Discrimination in employment," was just established last February; there are five entries already.

No article dealing with the library press and social responsibilities could fail to mention Synergy, the very imaginative and lively publication of the Bay Area Reference Center in San Francisco. The national library press has reprinted articles from Synergy, and has gotten ideas from it to develop into articles for the librarians of the nation. In addition to its articles, usually staff-written, it carries useful departments, such as the one which updates standard reference works.

In England, the only periodical that seems responsive to social concerns is The Assistant Librarian, although the New Library World seems about to join it. In both editorials and in selection of news, the AL has spoken forthrightly, and drawn much comment from its readers. Recently, AL carried a comprehensive account of the Reizia Palatnik imprisonment in the USSR, and upcoming is an account of libraries in Ulster.

The library press in Canada apparently feels little called upon to include much controversy, or perhaps there is little to include. The Canadian Library Journal has no editorial page, nor does BCLQ, Ontario Library Review, or APLA Bulletin. Much of the news, of course is carried in Feliciter, but without editorial comment.

Both LJ and American Libraries maintain separate departments for news and editorial matter, while WLB's "The Month in Review" uses the device of the editors' initials after each item that contains both reporting and comment. All three journals tend to mix comment with reportage when it comes to reports of ALA and other library conferences, but the pieces do carry initials or by-lines for attribution. The newest thing in the library press in the LJ Hotline, a weekly newsletter edited by Karl Nyren, associate editor of LJ. In its search to seem exciting--at least in the first few issues--it has aroused the ire of many librarians, and errors of fact appear on virtually every page. Similarly, for one of its "Vigilante of the Month" awards, WLB made the error of not checking with the library director, thinking that a long interview with the assistant director would suffice. That way lies the credibility gap.

Again, when LJ ran, under the guise of an article, a piece by Daniel Fader lauding his newly published microfilm collection--published, curiously, by University Microfilms, which, even more coincidentally, is a member of the Xerox education group, along with LJ and Bowker--some readers must have lifted an eyebrow.[26] That way lies the credibility gulch. And when LJ used its editorial page to plug and justify its new LJ Hotline,[27] some thought that Mr. Berry might have found issues to editorialize about--or rename the column.

If to be judged socially responsible the library press must simply report and comment on the happenings in the field, it would seem that such a performance were only good journalism. But if the call for social responsibility is one involving the total editorial thrust, including spurring the profession to higher levels of sensitivity, then it is something

Prologue

more. Should the library press just give the facts? Should it give facts plus occasional editorials? Or should it heed the admonition of Coleridge: "O! it is the relation of the facts--not the facts, friend."28

References

1. Library Journal, 89 (Nov. 1, 1964) p. 4234.
2. Ibid., 89 (Oct. 15, 1964) pp. 3926-7.
3. Ibid., 89 (Nov. 1, 1964) p. 4234.
4. Ibid., 89 (Nov. 15, 1964) p. 4490.
5. Ibid., p. 4448.
6. Ibid., 89 (Nov. 1, 1964) p. 4234.
7. Loc. cit.
8. Library Journal, 89 (Nov. 15, 1964) p. 4448.
9. Ibid., 93 (Dec. 1, 1968) p. 4459.
10. Wilson Bulletin for Librarians, 13 (Oct. 1938) pp. 87-90.
11. Wilson Library Bulletin, 14 (Sept. 1939) pp. 52-5.
12. Wilson Bulletin for Librarians, 13 (Feb. 1939) pp. 398-400.
13. Wilson Library Bulletin, 36 (Sept. 1961) p. 69.
14. Wilson Bulletin for Librarians, 10 (May 1936) pp. 592-3. The force of the editorial may be judged by the following statement, which appeared in the next issue: "Since there has been some curiosity as to whether my remarks last month on the segregation of Negroes at conferences of the American Library Association ("The Spectre at Richmond") represent the viewpoint of the publishers of the Wilson Bulletin, I have been asked to explain that my observations in this department of commentary on the contemporary scene are invariably founded on my personal views and that The H. W. Wilson Company, as a corporation, has no opinions whatever to express on this controversial matter. The invitation to readers to dissent in print from my views is a standing one."
15. California Librarian, 22 (Jan. 1961) pp. 23-4.
16. Wilson Library Bulletin, 35 (May 1961) pp. 707-10.
17. Ibid., 35 (Sept. 1960) pp. 63-4.
18. ALA Bulletin, 55 (June 1961) p. 485.
19. Ibid., (July-August 1961) p. 608.
20. The Bay State Librarian, 53 (April 1963) pp. 9-10.
21. Library Journal, 88 (July 1963) pp. 2644-7.
22. Loc. cit.
23. Library Journal, 94 (Nov. 15, 1969) p. 4106.

24. E.g., Nat Hentoff, Ray Bradbury, Robert Russell, Lloyd Alexander, Francis Keppel, Henry Steele Commager.
25. Wilson Library Bulletin, 44 (Nov. 1969) pp. 266-77.
26. Library Journal, 96 (April 15, 1971) pp. 1330-2.
27. Ibid., (Nov. 15, 1971) p. 3705.
28. Samuel Taylor Coleridge, Anima Poetae, (London, 1895), quoted in: Norman Fruman, Coleridge, The Damaged Archangel, (N.Y.: Braziller, 1971) p. 3.

Part I

LIBRARIES AND LIBRARIANS

THE PREMISE OF MEANING*

Archibald MacLeish

What is a collection of books? Which can be reversed to read: what is a book in a collection?--a book to a library?--to a librarian? Is it merely the unit of collection, a more or less fungible (as the lawyers put it) object made of paper, print and protective covering that fulfills its bibliographical destiny by being classified as to subject and catalogued by author and title and properly shelved? Or is it something very different? Is it still a book? Is it, indeed, something more now than a book, being a book selected to compose with other books a library? But, if so, what has it become?

When he was seventy-four years old the Cretan novelist Nikos Kazantzakis began a book. He called it Report to Greco, Greco being, of course, the older and even more famous Cretan who painted the Burial of Count Orgaz and other canvases. Report is the operative word in this title: Kazantzakis thought of himself as a soldier reporting to his commanding officer on a mortal mission--his life. "I collect my tools: sight, smell, touch, taste, hearing, intellect.... I call upon my memory to remember, I assemble my life from the air, place myself soldier-like before the general and make my report.... For Greco is kneaded from the same Cretan soil as I and is able to understand me better than all the strivers of past and present. Did he not leave the same red track upon the stones?"

Well, there is only one Report to Greco, but no true book--no book truly part of a true library--was ever anything else than a report. Shakespeare used a different--and, being

---

*This essay is adapted from an address delivered at the opening of the Scott Library at York University in Toronto, fall 1971, and was first published in American Scholar, Summer 1972. Reprinted by permission.

Shakespeare, a better--metaphor but it comes to the same thing. Lear speaks it to Cordelia at that sunshine moment toward the play's end before the deluge of the dark. They will go off, says Lear, the two of them, to their prison cell and "take upon's the mystery of things/As though we were God's spies." All poems worthy to be preserved as poems are written so--by God's spies beneath the burden of the mystery--and so are all other gathered writings of whatever kind however we may classify them, whether as fictions or as science, as history or philosophy or whatever. A true book is a report upon the mystery of existence; it tells what has been seen in a man's life in the world--touched there, thought of, tasted.

But it does more, too, as Kazantzakis' *Report* does more: it interprets the signs, brings word back from the frontiers, from the distances. Whether it offers its news in a live voice or is left, like Emily Dickinson's snippets of paper tied up with loops of thread, to be found by an astonished sister afterward in a little drawer, it speaks of the world, of our life in the world. Everything we have in the books on which our libraries are founded--Euclid's figures, Leonardo's notes, Newton's explanations, Cervantes' myth, Sappho's broken songs, even the vast surge of Homer--everything is a report of one kind or another and the sum of all of them together is our little knowledge of our world and of ourselves. Call a book Das Kapital or The Voyage of the Beagle or Theory of Relativity or Alice in Wonderland or Moby Dick, it is still what Kazantzakis called his book--what Shakespeare intended by that immortal metaphor--it is still a "report"--upon the "mystery of things."

But if this is what a book is in a library, then a library, considered not as a collection of objects that happen to be books but as a number of books that have been chosen to constitute a library, is an extraordinary thing. It is not at all what it is commonly supposed to be even by men who describe themselves as intellectuals--perhaps I should say particularly by men who describe themselves as intellectuals. It is not a sort of scholarly filling station where students of all ages can repair to get themselves supplied with a tankful of titles; not an academic facility to be judged by the quantity of its resources and the promptness of its services. On the contrary it is an achievement in and of itself--one of the greatest of human achievements because it combines and justifies so many others. That its card catalogues and bibliographical machinery are useful no one doubts: modern scholarship would be impossible without them. That its housing and safekeeping arrangements are vital, essential, necessary goes without saying. But what is more important in a library than anything else--than everything else--is the fact that it exists.

For the existence of a library, the fact of its existence, is, in itself and of itself, an assertion--a proposition nailed like Luther's to the door of time. By standing where it does at the center of the university--which is to say at the center of our intellectual lives--with its books in a certain order on its shelves and its cards in a certain structure in their cases, the true library asserts that there is indeed a "mystery of things." Or, more precisely, it asserts that the reason why the "things" compose a mystery is that they seem to mean: that they fall, when fathered together, into a kind of relationship, a kind of wholeness, as though all these different and dissimilar reports, these bits and pieces of experience, manuscripts in bottles, messages from long before, from deep within, from miles beyond, belonged together and might, if understood together, spell out the meaning which the mystery implies.

For the point is that without the implication of meaning, which is to say the premise of meaning, there can be no mystery anywhere. The dark is not mysterious: it is merely dark. Even the greatest of physicists, even Einstein himself, when he wished to speak of the universe as science observes it, spoke of it as standing before us "like a great, eternal riddle." And a riddle, needless to say, even a scientist's riddle, even a scientist's eternal riddle, even a scientist's eternal riddle of the dimensions of the universe, is something which, by hypothesis, exists to be solved.

It is this fact--the fact of the library's implicit assertion of the possibility of meaning--which provides the drama of the dedication of a new library in a world like ours. Whatever the opening of a library may have been back in the days of Mr. Carnegie's kindness when all good Scots believed that reading resulted in understanding and the rest of the world believed the Scots--whatever the opening of a new library may have been in those days there is a taste of irony about it now and more than a stir of drama. Our world--at least that part of our world which we call the West--no longer hopes for meanings. Even the philosophers, whose goal was once what they called A Final Explanation, concern themselves these days with something less--with a process. And as for the intellectuals, more numerous as confidence in the intellect declines, their shuttling caravan has almost come to rest at the last oasis on the road to Prester John--the sandy spring of the absurd. Their leaders may desert them. Ionesco himself, author of The Bald Soprano, may regret the disappearance of meaning from the world. But the caravan holds firm beneath the dying date trees. "There was a time, long, long ago," says Ionesco, "when the world seemed to man to be so charged with meaning that he didn't have time to ask himself questions ... The whole world was like a theater in which the elements, the forests, the oceans, the rivers, the mountains and the plains, the bushes and each plant played an incomprehensible role that man tried to understand, tried to explain to himself ... Exactly when," says Ionesco, "was the world emptied of substance, exactly when were the signs no longer signs?" To which the caravan responds with a single voice that there was a time long, long ago when Ionesco's answer to all those draughty questions would have been "Who cares?" Certainly the caravan doesn't care. Meanings went out for it with Hiroshima. All that's left us is absurdity. Unless you count despair.

But if Ionesco's complaint is out of fashion, what shall we say of the Great Affirmation spelled out in almost visible letters above the door of a new library? Those Reports to Greco on its shelves exist in a relationship which implies that the library's business is relationship. But the generation the library is to serve has been raised in the belief that what matters is not the relationships which compose our lives but something very different--something called relevance--the relevance of each aspect of existence to ourselves. Not the weft and weave that surrounds us, the mystery of things, the riddle of the universe, the implicitness of meaning, but an immediate identification of each thing with each self on the assumption that there is no meaning and that only self is real. Love, for example, which is all relationship, total relationship, infinite connection, is made relevant by turning it to sex which is connection and nothing more. Death, which was once, in the old world of relationship, the perspective of everything, the distance that turns the mountains blue, becomes relevant by becoming conclusion: not even exit--just an end.

And life itself, once that infinite possibility, that prison cell where the defeated king could take upon himself and his mild daughter the vastness of our human wonder, is made a prison cell and nothing more--the ultimate relevance--in a solitary and absurd confinement where nothing, not even Godot, ever comes and nothing answers but the idiot whimper of self-pity.

Oh, there is drama enough on this occasion, irony enough, but which way truly does the irony cut? Is it the library's implicit assertion of the immanence of meaning that has become ridiculous in our fuddled time, or is it the tired caravan of intellectual fashion stumbling toward the Mountains of the Moon? I do not know the answer but I know something that can learn the answer. I know that meaninglessness is just as much a matter of belief as meaning. The caravan of the intellectuals would have you think that someone has discovered meaninglessness out there beyond us in the desert--in the infinities of space--and brought it home like a phoenix egg to prove the world is void. Nothing could be more childish. Meaninglessness, like meaning, is a conclusion in the mind, a reading, an interpretation.

And science--honest science--knows it. Jacques Monod, the French biochemist who sees living beings as chemical machines that construct themselves out of chemical chance, concludes that the process of life is blind and man an accident. But he reaches this conclusion, as he himself acknowledges, by way of his belief in theories of quantum mechanics in which other scientists, Einstein among the lot, are unable to believe. "A mutation," writes M. Monod, "is in itself a microscopic event, a quantum event, to which the principle of uncertainty consequently applies." But to Einstein the consequence does not apply because the assumption is unsound. Einstein, as Gerald Holton puts it, was a scientist "fighting for a causal physics" who assumed "a rational God of causal laws who would not play dice with the universe." Whether Einstein's assumption is right or M. Monod's, is not, perhaps, for us, and certainly not for me, to say, but one thing is clear even to a scientific illiterate like myself: the issue between M. Monod and Einstein, or between their positions, is an issue of belief. Einstein makes that clear enough. Quantum physics was to him a "false religion." And he said so. In so many words.

It would be helpful to us, with a library to open and a question to answer, if there were an Einstein of the world of letters to match that explicit Einstein in the world of science. For it is in the world of letters that the contemporary taste for meaninglessness has presented itself most flagrantly as something more than a taste, more than an opinion: as an established fact to be accepted with despair. And it is in the world of letters that this masquerade can do most damage. Critics may pursue the meaningless relentlessly, as they may pursue anything else that moves, without damage to their reputations or themselves. And playwrights, ambiguous reporters, may make their fortunes by it--they have. But the poor devil of a poet lives by meanings if he lives at all. Relationship is all he has to work with: that <u>analogie</u> <u>universelle</u> which Baudelaire discovered in the poems of two thousand years and which the poems not yet written still must seek. For the poet, the novelist--the artist in letters--to assert the meaninglessness of the world is the ultimate act of human folly, the act that ridicules itself. Even if the "principle of uncertainty" were established to the satisfaction of all science and M. Monod were right in his finding that no "master plan" exists for the construction of his "chemical machines," man would still exist. And it is precisely man who, through his arts, through his thought, through his Reports to Greco, has constructed meanings over millennia of time, whether the universe has confirmed them or not. Job's demand for justice was shouted down by the voice from the whirlwind but Job, because he was a man, took back his life and lived it notwithstanding.

No, it is not the library, I think, that has become ridiculous by standing there against the dark with its books in order on its shelves. On the contrary the library, almost alone of the great monuments of civilization, stands taller now than it ever did before. The city--our American city at least--decays. The nation loses its grandeur, becomes what we call a "power," a Pentagon, a store of missiles. The university is no longer always certain what it is. But the library remains: a silent and enduring affirmation that the great Reports still speak, and not alone but somehow all together--that, whatever else is chance and accident, the human mind, that mystery, still seems to mean.

TURNSTILES IN THE LIBRARY?*

William Cole

The heart of the New York Public Library has always seemed to me to be Room 315.

Many years ago, when I first entered the library and asked where I should go to look something up, I was told "Room 315." Well, it seemed silly to call it a room; it was more a place, an acreage. And I still never enter it without being awed by its spacious dignity and air of no-nonsense utility.

The heart of the heart of Room 315 is the Information Desk, a 700-square-foot enclosure within which work 20 busy librarians--11 men and nine women--each of whom is particularly skilled in ready reference. To work on the Desk is the ultimate for any librarian who is attracted to research; it is to a librarian what working at Bellevue would be to a young doctor, such is the range, variety and volume. The Desk, this card-file-lined room and the adjacent reading rooms are under the direction of James G. Tobin, a quietly efficient man in his early sixties, whose title is Chief of the General Research and Humanities Division.

About 2,000 people pass through Room 315 daily. There are no guided tours; but many New Yorkers, such as myself, looking for something impressive to show out-of-town visitors, will parade them through this three-story-high room with its ornate ceiling into the still more impressive Reading Rooms, which extend for two whole city blocks. (The Reading Rooms--North Hall and South Hall--are really one long room divided by a book delivery area.)

But it is Room 315 itself, and more specifically its Information Desk, that has always fascinated me. The mind boggles at the information these librarians can make available to the man-from-the-street. Here is a room lined

---

*Reprinted from The New York Times Book Review, March 26, 1972, by permission. Copyright (c) by The New York Times Company.

Libraries and Librarians

with 10,000 card trays, containing 10 million cards. In this room and the adjoining ones are 40,000 reference books available on open shelves. And all this is backed up by seven floors of stacks, holding 2-1/2 million books, one of which can (ideally) be put into a reader's hands in 20 minutes.

There are four librarians "up front" at the Desk at any given moment. Each is an hour at this post, handling an average of 30 questions, and is then rotated with the other librarians. When not up front, the librarians are assigned other positions within the enclosure. One stint is answering telephone queries, about 150 daily; this used to figure much larger in their schedule until last year, when the nearby Mid-Manhattan Library established a separate telephone reference room which handles about 1,000 calls daily. Now the questions that come to the Desk are only those fielded to them by Mid-Manhattan, questions they are not equipped to handle.

Another assignment is answering mail queries from the public, from scholars and from other libraries; these letters range from a request for the text of James Whitcomb Riley's "The Passing of the Backhouse" to aid in tracking down a 13th-century manuscript. You will always find one librarian working on a "snag," as Mr. Tobin calls it; these are extremely tough questions that the librarians look on as challenges. They admit that they don't always get their man, but almost always. And then a great deal of time is taken up with ordering books, the point being to keep the research library as up-to-date as possible; someone is always poring over catalogues, book-trade publications and library listings from all over the world.

The librarians up front are the ones on the firing line. Their customers come in waves:

At one moment the four librarians will be standing four abreast behind the Desk, one tapping his pencil absently, another two exchanging a few words, the fourth catching a glance at a literary review. Then, the next moment, they'll be beseiged, with readers lining up behind one another impatiently.

Most of the questions are routine: Someone filled out a call slip wrong, forgot to put down an asterisk or a plus sign or filled out a slip for a book that is to be found only in one of the library's specialized collections. Others can't quite remember the title of a book or got it a bit wrong--the librarians still remember a request for Darwin's "Oranges and Peaches." Many want information on the city's social services, on schools or biographical information about an author. The librarians are trained not so much to answer questions as to point the reader in the direction of a reference tool that will.

Over the years Mr. Tobin has found that the books most likely to be stolen or mutilated are those containing hard, practical information. Outstanding victims are such titles as "Practice for the Armed Forces Tests," "Hotel and Motel Red Book," "Resumés that Get Jobs" (easier to tear out a page than to copy a whole resumé) and "The Foundation Directory." These, even for quick, on-the-spot consultation at the Desk, have to be signed for. The librarians keep their reference books up-to-the-minute. The day after Padraic Colum died, I happened to pick up "Twentieth Century Writing" at the desk. It fell open to his biography; and the day, month and year of his death had already been neatly penciled in. Snooping among the ready reference books, I was surprised to see "The Joy of Cooking" over the telephone reference desk. Sure, they use it; someone has lost a recipe, or run out of an ingredient in mid-recipe, and what should he substitute?

There are 300 to 400 books within the enclosure available to the librarians for "stand-up" questions. These are supplemented by what Mr. Robin calls the "scrapbox." This is a file of Manila folders, each of which pertains to frequently-asked questions. Looking through it, I came across folders for "Water Dowsing," "The Bible," "Phobias," "Peace Symbols," "Draft" (which contained, among other things, a pamphlet called "Manual for Draft-Age Immigrants to Canada"). The librarians really get to know what the fads and current concerns of the public are, and have recently built up files on organic food, communes, astrology, parapsychology, group therapy and, happily, ecology and urban planning.

It is only in recent years that the library schools have originated courses in the handling of reader's questions. What's the quickest way to really find out what a reader wants to know? Some readers are reluctant to come to the point and will begin with a general question, such as, "How are the catalogue files arranged?" The librarians train themselves to do a "quick take." "A reader asks, 'Do you have anything on pattern-cutting?' and I have to figure is he after dress patterns or sheet-metal patterns? If the question is about Indians, is he after American Indians or India Indians?" There are a certain number of pests, and some lonely people who just want some human communication.

The librarians are asked to hold each questioner down to a maximum of five minutes. "Sometimes that's hard to do," said one librarian. "I get interested in the subject and want to find out more about it myself." There is an air of genteel camaraderie within the enclosure; if the librarians notice that someone up front is having trouble with a reader who is a time-waster or is hard to understand, they'll come to his assistance. They share 12 languages among them, and one recalls the case of a reader she simply couldn't understand. After a few minutes of this non-communication, she asked, "Pardon me, sir, but what is your language?" "Lingwitch! Lingwitch!" he burst out, "Inklitsch!"

One day, after browsing around the room looking at the catalogue, I had a question of my own. "Why," I asked Mr. Tobin, "under all those headings for 'World War,' is there nothing for World War I? It's all World War II!" "Well," he replied, "at the time of World War I, we didn't know it was World War I. You'll find it under 'European War'."

Over the years, the librarians have noted down some of the more unusual, even looney, questions that come to them. Some are poignant: "Is there a law in New York City where a child can become unrelated to his parents if they don't like each other?" Some have an eerie logic about them: "If self-preservation is the first law of nature, what's the second?" and "Can you give me a list of historical characters who were at the right place at the right time?" Others stagger the imagination: "Can mice 'throw up'?" and "Does the female human being belong to the mammal class?" Yet others are little comic dramas:

    Q. "What is the natural enemy of the duck?"
    A. "I don't quite understand your question."
    Q. "Well, I have this swimming pool, and a flock of ducks landed on it. I went out and waved a broom at them, but they just looked at me and quacked. I want to know what kind of animal I can get who's their natural enemy."

And this hysterical monologue which came in over the phone:

> Q. "How do I put up wallpaper? I have the paper, I have the paste. What do I do next? Does the paste go on the wall or on the paper? I've tried both, and it doesn't seem to work."

As is true of any other public facility, a certain number of eccentrics can be found in Room 315. Derelicts come in out of the cold; young men find it a place for pick-ups; occasionally a real crazy has to be ejected. I suppose the passing thousands represent as good a cross section of New York as you'd find anywhere. I watched the people for a half hour one afternoon: There's an elderly man in a three-piece-suit whose secretary is helping him go through a file; over in the corner are two bearded poets I know huddled over a file drawer working on a poetry anthology; through the door comes a handsome, bra-less girl whose appearance untracks half the research in the room; there's a nattily-dressed black man carrying a dispatch case and a tennis racquet; there's a young man wearing what seems to be a horse blanket. Every kind of fashion can be seen, from mod to mess.

Mr. Tobin tells me that there is a kind of seasonal migration observable; Christmas, when the schools are out, is the maddest time, a time for the serious researcher to stay away. In the fall the fashion academy students come in droves; at midyear gray-clad young men from the police academy come in pairs, like nuns. In the late spring the college instructors and young professors appear, full of beans for their summer projects, knowing they must publish early lest they perish.

Over the years, the librarians get to notice the "regulars," outstanding among whom is Mr. Norbert Pearlroth. Mr. Pearlroth is the researcher for the syndicated feature, "Believe It or Not," and should qualify for inclusion in it himself, having been in the library almost every day for the past 50 years. I spoke with this record-holder, who is a spry 74, with white hair and black eyebrows. "When they cut down on the open days, it was catastrophe for me," he said. "I used to come in seven days a week." Mr. Pearlroth always sits at the same table in the South Hall. "You can tell where I am because I always put the reading light out, I prefer to read by natural light." A good testimony from a man who doesn't wear glasses.

Mr. Pearlroth is the only man I ever heard of who researches by serendipity. Shortly after 10 in the morning, he enters Room 315 and selects a file drawer at random, preferring one that is already out and sitting on a table. He then goes rapidly through the cards, selecting, with what he calls a second sense, a dozen books that sound promising. It doesn't really matter what language they're in--he reads a dozen. He puts the call slips in, three at a time, during the morning, and sets to work. When I visited his reading table, he was surrounded by a dozen books, each of which either had "Kirch ..." as the beginning of its title or whose author was named Kirch. He'd been in a "K" file. In German there was a book on poisons, one on noted Berlin women and a long treatise on the Swiss town of Kirchberg.

There were nine books in English, including a history of the Roan Schools and a book on whales. "I average 24 books a day--I don't eat lunch--and I'm lucky if I find three usable items." Occasionally he gets stuck in a book, to his annoyance--usually a book about World War I, in which he served in the Austrian Army. He finds local histories the most promising mines, and travel books by Frenchmen, who seem to have a flair for the strange and unusual. Travel books by South Americans are useless. "Too much about churches," he says. His technique is to skim rapidly, paying particular attention to pictures, the most interesting of which he had reproduced in the Photographic Services Room at the end of each day. He figures he has gone through 7,000 books a year, making a grand total of 350,000 books. What does Mr. Pearlroth do when he goes home at night? "Sometimes I read."

Another regular was a woman who earned the distinction of having worked her way methodically through every one of the 10,000 card trays in Room 315. She was after every listed French translation of American works. This woman always worked at a particular seat in the South Hall, near the French reference books, and claimed squatter's rights to it. If she found anyone else in her seat, she firmly asked them to move.

And then there's Timothy Dickinson, a young Englishman who is in the way of being a professional polymath. I had met him socially a couple of times and thought of him as a kind of ambulatory encyclopedia. Mention any subject, particularly history or literature, and he would come forth with dates, places, incidents and a list of secondary sources. The indelible impression that this makes on people is reinforced by his individualistic style: striped trousers, what appears to be a morning coat, and pince-nez. Mr. Dickinson is frequently to be found in the library doing freelance research for publishers of scholarly reprints and reference books. The librarians know him, of course, and when I asked them whether or not he put many questions to them, the reply was, "Not really--but sometimes he's very helpful to us. He's given us some good leads."

It's easy to see that the librarians in Room 315 take pride and pleasure in their work. They are genuinely pleased when they can supply an answer to a question; and the harder the question, the more pleasure. They weren't really offended by the wording of a question that one of them remembers from last year: "Is this the place where I ask questions I can't get the answers to?"

PUBLIC FACILITIES--A MEMOIR*

Bette Howland

The most popular volume in the branch library was the medical dictionary. Heavy, dated, it had to be retrieved from a locked glass case, had to be consulted on the premises. The borrowers, coughing behind their hands, concealed avid worries about their health. But the causes for concern were all too obvious: those racking coughs, hoarse whispers; open sores oozing serum, limbs swollen with purple pressures; eyes rimed with yellow matter, crumbs. One woman I observed over some months had something the matter with her nose. From the nose it progressed to her eye. Nose, eye were being eaten away by some inner acid. The other eye cheerful enough. A feisty type she was, short and energetic, big bony elbows and a corn-cob pipe. At last she began to wear a bandage. One wondered what this bandage could be concealing that must be yet more terrible. Leprosy? That's what I would always think of: one's vocabulary of suffering is so limited. Maybe that's why these people were boning up. But what was the use of pondering these pages? It can only have excited fresh anxieties, deeper fears. The medical dictionary was returned without comment. Miss Rose, the Reference Librarian, would take back the germy, contaminated thing and lock it up again. Lock it up and then--she couldn't help it, kindly as she was, with her loud rude voice and her knocking heels--she'd sneak back to the john and scrub her hands with green soap.

I lived in the neighborhood, a few blocks walk from the branch, and saw a lot of this. There is more than urban poverty in Uptown. The population is heavily Appalachian, American Indian, and these people bring a special rural desolation. The city blight extends to natural objects; the streaked grime of melting snow--characteristic of

---

*Reprinted from Commentary, by permission; copyright 1972 by the American Jewish Committee.

Chicago buildings in winter--can be seen here even on the
faces. Also Puerto Rican, black, Mexican, Korean, pen-
sioned-off Jew, coexisting without racial strife. Rebellion
was a private and individual matter. Uptown runs east to
the lakefront, so it is bounded by fancy buildings, motel
architecture. Early in the morning, salesmen who have
breakfasted in cozy coffee-shops will be seen cruising its
dismal streets in their big cars, loaded with racks and
sample cases. The same thing happens again in early afternoon, the leisurely hours of businessmen's lunch. These
are the times when the younger and prettier girls ply their
trade, during commercial hours, working a conventional
shift. It's only the old warhorses who come out at night.
Heavy, cold-skinned legs covered with bruises. These
bruises are like the old woman's bandage--not a matter for
the curious. Conjecture is inadequate, but this is standard:
this is how you tell a whore in Uptown. Mountain children
dance barefoot in the snow. The public pay phones are
much in use here; in drugstores, lobbies, you overhear
the most intense, private conversations. "Oh yeah, who's
threatening who?" says a thin girl in haircurlers into the
receiver, while a toddler clings to her slacks. "Suck my
box, that's what you can do." On a street corner, next to
an empty newsstand, a couple of men and a woman are
warming their hands over a trashcan fire. Gaunt, dingily
cold; the woman's shins are naked. She wears a babushka,
sunglasses, and a split fur jacket. "This neighborhood is
really going to the dogs," she is saying, loudly, wanting
people to hear ... the undesirable elements? Who can they
be? But all this means is that everyone is conscious of
degradation in Uptown. Everyone has the right to object.
"I'll drink to that," says one of the men, wiping the mouth
of the snug pint-flask as it passes around.

   But Chicago winters are not all bad. Sometimes it
gets cold, really cold, 10 or 15 below. An icy extermina-
ting cold, sweeping down from the north like a moral force.
Dung freezes in the street; germs drop dead; vermin
starve. It strikes at corruption; breathing seems less in-
jurious. The air is pure and full of truth. Walking down
Argyle Street, Broadway, on my way to the library, I was
in a position to appreciate this especially.

   The reason I was working for the library is somewhat obscure, but I'll tell you. This was a special new
program for what they called internes, or technicians--I
forgot the particular quasi-scientific designation. It didn't

really matter; for me, the appeal was that you could work half-time. And with the Public Library, half really meant half: 18-3/4 hours--half the 37-1/2 hour week. Benefits accumulated at half-rate; half the vacation time, half the sick pay, half the insurance coverage, and so on. They were nervously precise about all this; but, once again, I was in a position to appreciate. I've had a lot of part-time jobs in my life.

In fact, I was always looking for part-time work, lesser commitments. Like most struggling writers, I wanted to avoid putting my heart and soul into anything; I was saving myself--my Serious Self--my Spiritual Powers, my Best Energies. O ye of little faith! Also, of course, this is a female trait, or it was, anyway, before the great crest of Women's Liberation. So I got it both ways. All the women I knew worked at such jobs, around libraries, universities, social agencies; or else, were on the lookout for them. And the way you could tell such a job was simple: it was understood that it was not _serious_. There was always some catch. The pay was smaller too--but this limitation was the real compensation. "It's not a _real_ job," that's what you always heard. One's true abilities, one's inner ardors, were not expended, were still intact. Everyone was secretly keeping herself for better things.

I was, incidentally, a divorcee (vulgar word) with two young children, and had to work. Which is only to say that I had my role cut out for me; it was a struggling, ungraceful role, so I struggled ungracefully. And all this was really baffling to me.

Had it not been for the medical dictionary, there would have been little traffic at our Reference Desk. Borglum Branch was not very busy. A sort of club of elderly gentlemen competed daily for possession of _Barron's_ and the _Wall Street Journal_. If you didn't have today's, yesterday's would do. Miss Rose kept these papers in the right-hand drawer, smelling of peppermints. She herself smelled of bath oil, a surge of pine. A thin elderly spinster with uneven hems and furiously powdered cheeks. Friendly, the permissive type. (Mrs. Speer, the Head Librarian, was the other, the watch-dog type; censorious in her judgments. Hence the lurid books in locked cases.) Maybe Miss Rose kept these papers in the drawer just so she could have an excuse to open it once in a while, exchanging a warm remark. "How are you today, Mr. Adorno?" She knew them all by name. A grittily poor neighborhood, the most despairingly poor in the city; but the financial papers were in great demand, and the old men in their baggily empty coats, with their Woolworth's spectacles, trembled when they asked: eying the drawer. For the patrons--the regulars, the same ones who showed up every day--were familiar with our procedures, knew them better than we did. Indeed, any departure troubled them; they had a strong sense of the appropriate, and were particularly strict about the rule of silence. They knew their rights. There was something wrong with the fan-belts in our blower system; it made gentle, trifling noises, palpitating and fluttering. The regulars complained of the distraction, an impropriety--it detracted from the mood. Miss Rose herself had a loud self-betraying voice and heels like circus snare drums. A novel situation: the regulars used to tell <u>her</u> to be quiet. This was supposed to be a library, wasn't it? People were supposed to shut up? She went gallantly back and forth, elbows locked with books, followed by frowns, clicking tongues. "For shame! It's not ladylike," one gray-haired old lady would whisper to me, shaking her head. "It's not <u>refined</u>." The old lady wore gym shoes and her fur coat was fastened with diaper pins. " 'Her voice was ever soft and low, / An excellent thing in woman.' Pass it on," she'd say. She herself seemed peculiarly vociferous.

    But Miss Rose also had her admirers. Mr. Cohen had been asking her out to dinner for years. Tall, in his hat and heavy coat, he was another of our regulars, sat every day in the same chair at the same varnished oak table. Armchairs were provided, sunnier spots in front of large plate windows; but the regulars scorned these--too casual, maybe. Their habits were more rigorous. They were not here for browsing, that had to be understood. For them the library was an alternative to idleness. Old ladies, speedy in sneakers, in fur coats fallen on evil days--standard dress on Broadway that winter; narrow men from queues at day-labor agencies, fingering back numbers of magazines; pensioners poring over the market reports with trembling hands. The fascination with the stock market of these impoverished old men always seemed brutal to me, like the preoccupations of the diseased with the medical dictionary. But who knows what fantasies of wealth and power were fluttering in those ribcages? Sickness, failure, old age, neglect: you got the impression these were temporary reversals--the utilities disconnected, the heat cut off--one could live with such interruptions. The thin pages--of

Barron's air-mail edition especially--rattled like tissue paper in the musty quiet.

Let us speak frankly. Where are these people to go? There are no clean well-lighted places. Bus stations are too sorrowful, with their dead television sets coming to life twenty minutes for a quarter. The all-night movies, where ushers used to nudge your shoulder if you snored too loudly, have converted to porno-houses and charge too much. One mourns their passing. I am thinking in particular of the Clark Theater, once the most illustrious of such institutions. For the Clark served Art too, these facts were inseparable; odors of winos' holey socks mingled powerfully with the dust of Desenex in college-boys' sneakers. Open twenty hours out of twenty-four; tickets were cheap; the double-bill changed daily. Another thing that was changed very often was the seats. The customers moved in and out of them with strange restlessness. Watching <u>Grand Illusion</u>, <u>The Thirty-Nine Steps</u>, you couldn't help taking this in out of the corner of your eye. Eyes sliding, oily surfaces in the emulsive light. Under folded jackets, in hidden laps, hands are reaching; slowly, with painful efforts at concealment-- very distracting--uncoupling zippers. In the same way the little old ladies in the balcony timidly peel their candy bars. The Ladies Gallery is an invention of the Clark--"For Ladies Only." But it is not only for the fainthearted. Some of the women straddle their seats boldly; two seats, three seats: a shopping bag on either side. And the shopping bags get noisier as they get emptier.

Sometimes a man gets into the Ladies Gallery, possibly by mistake. But as far as the ladies are concerned, it's intentional. They give him looks that could kill. All up and down the rows, in their hearts they are jabbing him with hat-pins--no longer handy, alas. Some day the worm will turn, the righteous will be justified, the meek will inherit the earth. But for now there sits a man in the Ladies Gallery, an unholy hairy-legged intruder. When the usher arrives, he'll throw him out.

The fellow next to you jerks his head back, sets himself against his seat. A few small defenseless whimpers --then a grunt, a noise of very minor satisfaction. But the tension goes. He fumbles, rises at once--jacket folded over his arm. Off to look for another seat. His place is taken immediately, but this is a more familiar type. The Clark Street panhandler with upturned collar, sugared whiskers.

He loosens his shoelaces, stretches out his legs. His chin
sags to his chest; his head bobs freely; with a loud,
snickering snore, it drops on your shoulder.

    On Saturday nights there was the motorcycle crowd,
boots, hairy chests, crosses, earrings. The gobs from
Great Lakes, pea-coats three deep in the lobby. But these
don't matter, they can go elsewhere. Maybe that hasn't
changed anyhow. Its most loyal customers the Clark has
deserted forever. On the last night before this reform a
brawl broke out on the darkened floor. A drunk got noisy,
crashed a bottle, startled wielding its jagged neck. The
situation was intimidating. Finally a lanky black man rose
calmly from his seat and pointed a gun. "You get out," he
told the drunk, waving the gun at him. It was very dark
of course, hard to see; but in the flickering light all the
movie aficionados recognized the weapon, its steely gleam.
We weren't Humphrey Bogart fans for nothing. "I's fixing
to concentrate. Drop you bottle, man." It was an Orson
Welles festival, <u>The Magnificent Ambersons</u>. Bustles,
ostrich plumes, and Joseph Cotten. The black man sat.
The drunk, disarmed, left readily. Other patrons followed
in droves. Outside in the lobby he was lynched by the
mob--his peers, other winos, panhandlers, senior citizens
with umbrellas. These were the ones who had the real
beef: where would they go tomorrow?

    There remain the neighborhood branches of the
public library, overheated rooms and yellow-varnished
tables. The library is really the same sort of institution,
assuming a responsibility to the cultured and the rejects--
sometimes the same--the old-fashioned derelict, the harm-
less eccentric, the pensioned poor. What about the Christian
Science Reading Room, you say? But that's just the point:
a few newspaper racks, preachy pamphlets, this is arid
stuff. It lacks the one thing indispensable: the dramatic
element. Even the el stations are better than this; in
Uptown they were certainly preferred. Turnstiles, traffic,
mind-throttling trains darkening overhead; newspapers,
magazines, exotic jungle covers--but here you get into private enterprise, and browsing is risky.

    Picture then the Chicago Public Library, the down-
town edifice, distantly resembling Fort Dearborn. But its
massive staircases are Italian marble, glowing with an inner
whiteness. The auditorium a Civil War Museum, full of
artillery, heavy cannon. The same theme upstairs in the

Libraries and Librarians

vast high-ceilinged gloom of reading-rooms; crossed swords, seals, flags draped everywhere. Guardposts, kiosks, flank the turnstile entrances--and the doors to the public lavatories. Stationed in hollow marbled corridors. Funny business goes on in libraries, everybody knows that. It's got something to do with all those stacks, the dark heavy books. Their presence is somber and primary. You are reminded that Reason is a human passion, like any other, an instinct, a drive. It is not strange that people respond in its temples with primitive gestures, flashing switchblades, unzipping flies. No, the public library is much closer to the Clark Theater than it is to the Christian Science Reading Room. And bars, flophouses, disqualify themselves at the other extreme. For the connection is not haphazard; it must be intimate, necessary, this mingling of serious things, the High and the Low, Art and Despair. The public libraries of great cities are among the last institutions remaining for the socialization of these quiet dissenters. This is one of the unavowed, but truest functions. It is even more evident in the branch libraries, outposts flung beneath the elevated tracks of the great provincial city. Here you sense the exile. And the least deviant among these are in fact employed by the institution, and serve the rest.

Mrs. Speer was nearing retirement. With some relief. Wrapped round her head the gray braids were harried, wisps escaping. She had pale, mistreated eyes. The rimless glasses go without saying; likewise, the tailored suits-- under which, less severe with herself, she wore frilly blouses, the flimsiest nylon. Very revealing, and the buttons were always coming undone. An odd mixture this, dishabille and desiccation. Her breath was stale and strong-- almost desperately so, reaching out to you, her essence.

Borglum Branch was losing customers continuously, and--at a more alarming rate--books. There were two schools of philosophy in the public library. One was that it existed for the sake of circulating books. The other was that it existed for the sake of preserving them. With any bureaucracy in the public service, this is what it all boils down to, eventually. Mrs. Speer belonged to the public-enemy school.

Anyone who pushed through those glass doors was immediately suspect. Even patrons returning books were eyed with mistrust: we were given orders to ask for their library cards. Just in case. Pasted above the check-out machine, where you could keep your eye on it while you stamped the cards and stuffed the pockets, was a list of defaulters: card-holders who owed hundreds of dollars in overdue fines, delinquent books. Names like Rockett J. Squirrel, Hedy Lamarr, J. Edgar Hoover. The public-enemy theory is not outright error, not downright contemptible.

Mrs. Speer's efficacy as a supervisor may have been judged in terms of circulation numbers--books outgoing, active, revitalizing, indicating that the library was a live force in the community. But in her own heart she knew that the public had to be protected from itself. These were not borrowers, they were thieves! And the ones who were not thieves, mutilators. Bindings loose, pages missing, pictures defaced; mustaches, pubic hair, scribbled in with ball-point pen. Also telephone numbers, shopping reminders. Read in steamy bathtubs, under dripping submarine sandwiches. And people had wept over these books, rent their nails, torn their hair. Of other traces of temporary human habitation, artifacts, I won't speak. The books had to be preserved. At some branches, the big Webster's dictionary was bolted and chained; things had gone that far.

And all this was in Mrs. Speer's breath.

A man was hurrying in, a great armload of books up to his chin. Through the glass doors you could see his car double-parked in the street. "Ask to see his library card," Mrs. Speer whispered sharply. For she knew I didn't like to do this and kept an eye out when I worked behind the desk. And now she had spotted him coming and moved in, her breath as close to me as her elbow. More prodding. Together we watched the man struggling through two sets of doors, puffing as hard as the engine--wheezing outside into wintry air. He hoisted all his books onto the desk and started away, unburdened.

"May I see your card?"

Taken aback, he reached distractedly for his pocket. "How come? What for? Nothing's wrong?" Angry with me, fumbling through his billfold.

"Because this lady standing right next to me is my boss, and she just told me to ask you."

Wise guy. It wasn't kind. I was lazy and proud, a difficult combination. And Mrs. Speer was definitely not a a bad sort; it was just that years of working as a public servant had made her peculiar. There is a certain socialized insanity in these categories. Schoolteachers used to have it. Once I read a note posted on the bulletin board in the high-school principal's office; it was from a teacher who had retired, gone to live on a chicken farm. I had been in her English class. We read Ivanhoe. That is, she read it aloud to us, sitting behind the desk in her smock, her cheek in her hand. Her crimped white head. On her desk, under her desk, piled on top of windowsills, along radiators, from head to foot in her closet, were stacks of colored notebooks, theme papers. They were all on Ivanhoe. These theme papers were a requirement; the colored notebooks too--no grade issued without one. But everyone knew how grades were distributed in Miss Bozzich's class: "Neat" girls got E's; girls who wore blue-jeans, G. Short boys, F; boys with long legs, protruding from the childish seats, failed invariably. There was no appeal. All classes were the same. Each day before her reading began, someone had to get up and tell "the story thus far." As we progressed into the story, these daily résumés naturally got longer. Besides, we had caught on; some of us were deliberately long-winded. By the time Miss Bozzich started to read, the bell would ring. We had reached a point of impasse. I remember the close print, the thick rough paper, the name of dark Rebecca.... But we stopped on page 98. Next semester it would begin all over again. "My little chickens are so nice and polite--so well-behaved; much more grateful than my students ever were," she had written in her note.

Anyway, after the double-parked man, my services were not often required at the desk. But Mrs. Speer already had her chickens. These were the new books, stacked on the long table in the back room in tall neat rows. On top of each pile, a note: "Do Not Disturb, J. Speer." Mrs. Speer was cataloguing these books, and whenever she could she'd go into the back and shut the door. This was her retreat. The books already on the shelves may have been used, grubby, touched by too many hands; but these books confronted her in all their original splendor. The room was fragrant with their newness. Mrs. Speer loved these books, loved them apparently as physical objects. This was something else you discovered in libraries; there were those who read books, and then there were those whose attachment to them was of another order altogether. I can't say what the nature of this attachment was. But one thing for sure: all

the shipments of new books that came into Borglum went
straight into the back room. And they tended to stay there.
A virgin forest. No one else was allowed to touch them;
and if, through necessity, you had to budge a stack or two--
for they mounted up on the typing table, the files, the
chairs, you couldn't get through--then there were those
notes, warning you that here was a Secret Order, not to be
imperiled.

   The thing was, the cataloguing had already been done
at the Downtown Library. The books came carded, pocketed,
and numbered, and all that remained for the branches to do
were a few perfunctory clerical tasks. At one time, the
cataloguing had been indeed the special office of the Head
Librarians; but now they had been freed from such musty
associations, ordered out of their dry cubbyholes, to put
themselves--in other words--into circulation. This was the
idea; not Mrs. Speer's idea at all. She had put up with
this new dispensation for a time, until her husband died.
This had happened not long ago, and shortly thereafter she
had made the simple readjustment necessary to her sanity.
She had simply resumed cataloguing.

   The cards that came with the books were disregarded,
she started the whole job afresh, from scratch. Did she
get the same results? Who knows? For the trouble with
this, as with most individual solutions, was that things were
against her. There really was too much to do. And the
steeper the piles sprouting under the thick oak legs, the
more she pondered. The intricacies of cataloguing seemed
to multiply--refracted, like prisms, rainbows. She talked
about her "problems," the "tough nuts" she had to crack.
Was a volume on Colonial Furniture--History? Handicraft?
Art? Was Horticulture a Science or a Hobby? You see?
She had lost her nerve for making such fundamental decisions.

   Some of this Miss Rose had told me; some of it
Mrs. Speer told me herself, for when I first came she
intended to have me help her with the cataloguing, she confessed that she needed help badly--her breath desperate as
usual. But this task had been promised also to my predecessor, an M.A. fresh out of library school; she never
got to do it. So the young woman had made a point of telling me. And cataloguing was her specialty! Her field of
academic concentration! Perhaps Mrs. Speer did not trust
such avidity. I presented the opposite case. Mrs. Speer

saw that I had no lively interest, was not keen for the complexities. Also, she didn't care for my typing, which was as rapid as a machine-gunner and riddled with errors. Flack flack flack. She was afraid of it! Listening to those brutal noises, her pale glance would fuse behind her rimless glasses. So Mrs. Speer could not trust me either, a totally accurate instict. The time had not come for her to surrender. She could not relinquish her task; nor, what it amounted to, the books. She may have been protecting them in this way, delaying the inevitable process of attrition, despoliation--borrowing, mutilation, theft.

She put off giving me my instruction; the subject dropped, disappeared altogether. But this was what usually happened. The library technician (interne) was a semi-professional, semi-clerical position; you were supposed to do everything, make yourself useful, fill in the gaps. But employees were Civil Service, fingerprinted in City Hall; people already had their places, their allotted tasks, and did not wish to share them. It threatened their own role in the institution. What with one thing and another, it was proving difficult to find a spot for me at Borglum.

Beebee, sitting on her high stool at the circulation desk, hunched over in characteristic bad posture, was not less protective of her overdue notices than Mrs. Speer was of her books. Strange, but in the library employees themselves were forbidden to read, it was against the rules. Which was why Beebee was always hunched over like that, a passionate book-worm, passionately concealing the pages of some contraband book in her lap. Glancing down at it possessively as her fingers riffled the files. She wouldn't let anyone look over her shoulder. But when she did this-- when she glanced down--you could see the slovenly, dandruffy part in her strong black hair. Beebee was like dark Rebecca; that is, she had certain vital characteristics: that black hair, the white sharply-modeled nose, heavy Sephardic eyes. But Beebee was terribly untidy. Coarse wires straggled from her bun. Her gums--the kind that played a prominent role in her smile--were rimmed with dried blood, her teeth furred with green moss. Beebee lived at home and had a boyfriend named Henry who was not Jewish. This was the dilemma, the present interest, the focus, the drama of her life. Henry would meet her at the library--meetings proscribed and rare--very tall, thin in the face, with long big teeth and foggy glasses. His hair was inconsequential. After they said hello, that was it; they never seemed to need

another word. Henry in gym shoes would sprawl across the
counter on baseball-jacket sleeves, gazing after Beebee,
hunched busily on the high stool, her striking and disorderly
head ducking over the files. From time to time she'd lower
her white elbows to her lap, sink her chin into her hands,
and gaze back. This collapsed Henry. Their slumped
shoulders heaved a loud, prolonged sigh.

    This was our current even too; what we talked
about over coffee break in the <u>back</u> back room. Sitting
round the chrome-legged dinette. Should Beebee leave home
and marry Henry? Defy her parents? Deny her faith?
What if Henry converted?--he looked convertible. Etc.
Listening to our advice, sipping sweet tea through green
teeth, Beebee grew evasive and dreamy. Her dark, high-
crested glance had a certain remoteness. She liked to have
us talking about her life, didn't want to end the discussion
too abruptly; still, she was a private and secretive soul.
Most of us kept our lunch in the refrigerator, but Beebee
kept hers in her locker; and she went in and out of this
locker as jealously, possessively, as she dipped into her
files--fines, overdue notices, privileged information.
She'd slam the tin door if you caught her. Probably she
had nothing more terrible hidden in there than some books;
but books, come to think of it, were the worst thing you
could hide. In a library. The pall of suspicion hung over
us all. We were surrounded by temptation, breathing books.

    The clandestine had a natural appeal for Beebee. It
was actually Miss Rose who took the more pressing interest
in her plight, for Miss Rose had a story of her own. In
college she had been engaged to an interne; drafted as a
medic, he had been killed in the war. And after Stanley
was killed ... "Well after Stanley was killed, I knew I'd
never find another man as good. 'What's the matter with
you?' my mother would say. 'You're too particular.'
Well I couldn't help being particular. After Stanley."

    Her elbows, planted on the formica top, were
steeped in bracelets--these bangles had a way of sliding
up her thin arms. Her light blue eyes were flush with the
level of the teacup, brimming over behind horn-rims. I
may as well get it over with, the whole description; the
peering near-sighted expression, the bold nose, the (sometimes) hennaed hair. Beads, powder, taffeta skirts, fumes
of pine--all this loosely assembled; when Miss Rose tucked
in her blouse, her slip would pop out; when she hiked up

her slip, something else would give. She bought her clothes
in the gloomiest shops on State Street, under the darkest influences of the el-tracks; bounty signs posted all over the
place announcing that shoplifters will be prosecuted; mirrors
--like hub-caps--spying down from every corner. If you
catch sight of your face in such a mirror, distorted, spoon-
shaped, you look like a criminal. But how could Miss Rose
ever look like a criminal? Who could make such a mistake?
When she discarded her glasses, her face was defenseless
altogether. Once it greeted me thus from behind her desk,
weakly beaming: cocked to one side; fresh powder, thick
as flour, but carnation pink, an inflammatory hue; and she
was mischievously sucking on a peppermint. What was this
all about? I had mentioned that a friend--male--would be
picking me up at work, and Miss Rose had made herself
presentable. It touched me. Garish? Loud? Yes, I suppose so; offense is the best defense; the vulgarity was
there. It hurt. It has to be mentioned. But after all it
was just there. It was an accident.

    This was not the first time I had heard such a story.
Sister Grace, my ex-husband's aunt, had converted to the
Episcopal Church so she could become a nun; her lover
had been killed in the First World War, and she wished to
dedicate herself. There was a parallel; the same motivation, a removal from the mainstream. Sister Grace's convent occupied a lovely big house on Brattle Street in Cambridge; the nuns were always polishing the lustrously dark
stairs. They had cats, and a black cook named Cleopatra.
Was she a good cook? That I can't tell you. Seated at
lunch, at the long table laid with linen, crystal, silver nap-
kin rings, the long leaded windows trailing shadows of ivy,
I found I couldn't taste the food: it was all too institutional.
In their idleness, the nuns doted on the cats, imitated
them; now they made cats' tongues, licking cream. Bland
faces, white surplices, gray habits; and many aged women
boarded with them, their mothers. It seemed that the
mothers of these nuns lived to a ripe old age. The widows'
securities helped to support the convent; all this New England gentility was on its last legs. But Sister Grace was
one of their real mainstays, a nurse specializing in terminal
cases. In her spare time looking after other elderly nuns
and their even more elderly mothers. They had problems;
they fainted in Filene's basement, they fell off subway platforms in Mass. Square. Sister Grace would tell you; a
fine old woman, drawing herself rigid and upright, fixing
her gaze on a far corner as if she were reading off a chart.

Broken heads, hips, colostomy bags. She dealt in misfortunes. Miss Rose, being Jewish, had chosen the bookish way. After Stanley? But there was no after.

    I would urge Miss Rose to take Mr. Cohen up on his offer. "Why not go out with him? He looks presentable. He seems like a gentleman."

    "Oh yes," Miss Rose would say, hastily affirmative. After all, he was her suitor! "Mr. Cohen is certainly a gentleman. A gentleman of the old school. A very fine man."

    "So? How come? What's a dinner? No lifetime commitment."

    It seemed that she liked to be teased in this way. On such cold nights, waiting at her bus stop--she was afraid to stand alone on the dark, chill, sharp corner--she would allow it, anyway. Safe to talk when her bus was coming. Looking out after the vague lights that would come dipping up to the curb. People were always urging Miss Rose. If she took a certain exam and passed it, she could become a Head Librarian herself. No routine promotion, this was a leap, and her salary would increase considerably. Everyone thought she should do it. But Miss Rose was afraid to take this exam, she shuddered at the thought of it, the very mention sent her fluttering. And it must have been mentioned with some regularity, since this had been going on by now for years. Like Mr. Cohen.

    She shrugged. "After Stanley...."

    "Oh Miss Rose! You know that's a lot of baloney!"

    Her eyes lit up. She cocked her head to one side in its fluffy angora cap, peeling off her glove to get at her bus fare. She always carried the change in her knitted mitt. "Yes," she said cheerfully, "I guess it is. Yes, I know it." And climbed aboard in her galoshes.

    How could the tall, politely bespectacled Mr. Cohen, keeping an eye on IBM, Bunker-Ramo, and Xerox, but having all his money in a mattress somewhere, or possibly even in the lining of his coat--it looked bulky enough--how could he compete with a dead man, a war hero? And a doctor on top of it? How disappointed he looked whenever he saw me

Libraries and Librarians 47

sitting at her desk! Presenting himself faithfully, laying his hat across his chest:

"No Miss Rose tonight?"

It was not that Miss Rome needed or desired assistance any more than anyone else; but she was softer than anyone else, more vulnerable, she had to give in. That was how I had finally ended up spending most of my 18-3/4 hours at the Reference Desk--the one place in all that moribund, underused facility where there really was the least to do. This was the backwater of backwaters, and one became preoccupied with its significant facts. The fan-belts; the <u>Moody's Guides</u>, <u>Commodities and Futures</u>. The Children's Library was in another wing, a totally autonomous sector, a brighter, more spacious room with its low tables. And Mrs. Endlin pasted colorful book-jackets and snow scenes on her bulletin board, kept a jar of candy canes on her desk. She had right instincts. Plump, red-haired, her vital juices still flowing. Her breath was sweet. It was as if dealing with children had kept her healthy--saner. But her cactus plants were doing badly, they looked gray.

We had our flurries of activity. On Friday afternoons, invariably, there would be some barroom bet to settle. It was payday, and workmen having a few beers in a nearby tavern would fall into aimless arguments. World records, batting averages, the age of the Pope, the name of President McKinley's assassin. This meant a delegation: three, four solid laboring men, shouldering their way in a body, asking here and there and directed at last--mistrustful, unconvinced--to the Reference Desk. These presentations used to remind me of scenes in old movies, when such heavy naturalism was still in vogue, in which the striking workers confronted the boss, swivelling behind his big desk. These was suspicion here, too, there was a kind of hostility. They were still hot under the collars of their lumber-jackets.

"We want to see a copy of 'If.' 'If' by Rudyard Kipling. It's a poem. 'If you can keep your wits when all about you....' "

"It's 'head,' stupid."

"It's 'wits,' nit-wit. Wits."

"It's 'head,' " I said.

Wrong move.

"Oh yeah?"

They all glared at me. They were not going to be patronized. Even the man who had his money on "head" was against me, seemed about ready to change his mind.

"Can you show us in a book?"

Did I think they were going to take my word for it, just because I was sitting behind a desk? It was just that for me it was always easier to rattle these things off; the truth being that I didn't know where to find anything. But that would never do. They weren't going to take anybody's word--except Kipling's. Proof they were after, the evidence had to be produced. Sometimes they would make a copy on the duplicating machine; money changed hands.

Also bound to put in his appearance at least once a week: a big Sterno-breathed man, bareheaded, towing a little boy. The kid very small, hanging on by his mittens; and his nose was running. But they had the same way of standing, straddle-legged, buttoned up in their pea-coats; the same crew-cuts, revealing the same long bumpy skulls. The kid's bumpier, more tender; you could see the furrows and worries of his scalp through pale fuzz. His face as pale, unoriginal.

This man always had a quotation for me to look up.

"Let's have a copy of 'The Face on the Barroom Floor.' Just the last line--" he would add impatiently-- "I know the rest."

He had me there.

He pointed to the shelves: "It should be in this one over here: Beloved Hymns and Popular Verse."

The next time, what? "Let's see--I think it's that line from Thoreau. About marching to the footsteps of a different drummer. It's in Walden, but it might be easier for you to find it in Bartlett's."

Becoming familiar, you see, with my limitations.

I never figured out what this was all about. Did he want to test me and trip me, or just to make sure he kept me on my toes? I, me, being here not an individual but an entire institution. Maybe he visited other branches too? It's possible. A one-man citizens' committee, self-appointed in his rounds. Confronting me, big and rough and fortified with alcohol against the cold like a vigilante. The little boy, expressionless, licking his clear, shining lip. They qualified as regulars.

It was strange that the one outstanding fact of life in our library--the fact that so many of our patrons were regulars, more faithful than any of us (some certainly put in as many hours)--was never mentioned. It was unmentionable. More ordinary patrons took out books, swelled our credit, kept us in business. Regulars of course never took out any books; what for? they didn't need to. "She's very good with the old people," I heard Mrs. Speer saying once into the phone--a conversation about Miss Rose's promotion. She meant: the regulars; but she did not know that that was what she meant. Our real business, our real function, this went unacknowledged. And what about those Board of Directors meetings downtown, in the immense flag-draped room with its black cannons that had boomed over Gettysburg? Plans were being drawn up, funds sought, for the expansion of the Main Library building. It was a limestone white elephant, but it couldn't be torn down; it could only be surrounded. Architects submitted fanciful sketches: malls, trees, glass walls surmounting the old gray bulging stones. Did anyone ever get up at such meetings and say: "Do you think the bums from Clark Street will go for this? After all, they're the ones who spend the most time here. And what about the old ladies with the shopping bags? If we make the place look like Saks Fifth Avenue, will they feel at home?"

Popkin, a thin old man, scrawny-necked, in a long coat which reached to his ankles--a peculiar shade of naval blue--went in and out of the stacks in a rapid shuffle. A timid soul, singleminded, turning neither left nor right, with his matted white head, shuffling headlong, tiptoeing forward with a book, some precious volume, always tucked under his elbow, nestling in his armpit. He was hatching it. Miss Rose told me he was a poet. But what if you said, "But Miss Rose--have you ever noticed that Popkin comes every day? the whole day? day and night? that tiptoe shuffle?" What would happen if you said this? And what about Judge Brady. A big, open-faced man with an impressively white mane of hair; not a real judge, of course, but he had the more primary qualifications. Stern and impassive, a pillar of dignity, easing himself down in his chair at the varnished oak table--a sturdy oak himself--about to preside. Over what? Why always that chair? Or tidy little Mr. Adorno, eyes hugely magnified, with a bright polished smile, teeth regular, alight in his apple face. He was eighty, as he was always saying, always asking me to read aloud for him notes he had scribbled to himself. Listening, all teeth and eyes: nodding, Yes, yes, that's right. What was? My transcription? His thoughts? Or something else entirely.

And then the tall, straight, gray old woman who dropped in every day to use the bathroom. Gray?--from head to foot: gray hair, gray face, gray coat, gray dress; and finally, a pair of laced-up combat boots. She stayed in long; you could hear the toilet flushing--but continuously, endlessly; it went on without let-up. It was, almost, a natural phenomenon. Yellowstone. Niagara Falls. The water, rushing hoarsely, was being sucked straight into the earth. What could she be up to? But no one else could get in there. One simply had to wait until she decided to emerge, dripping wet--long and thin and gray as a wet-mop--and sloshing out of the door in her thicksoled boots. What about pneumonia? an old woman going about drenched in the cold. But it may have been a health regimen--her own--some people take cold showers. Was she perhaps doing her laundry in the john? Or dunking her feet, some kind of physical therapy? Whatever--she seemed to survive. This activity titillated; roused a few eyebrows, a few glances of wild surmises; but that was all. Our business was books--checking them in, stamping them out, cataloguing, shelving. Minding our own business. At Borglum the level of tolerance for individual variations was very high. It had to be, the facts were too peculiar. And this--a wondering glance at the bathroom door, emitting its awesome, unmistakable noises--this was the closest we ever got to acknowledging any of that other business. For this was the one thing that could not be tolerated: to have characterized the services of the public library in this way.

Miss Rose, second-in-command, took charge when Mrs. Speer was not there, which meant she had to close up

most late nights. Such responsibility worried her wretchedly.
She was no authoritarian, not a bossy bone in her body.
She'd go knocking about in noisy agitation, heels clattering,
dragging kitetails of lace petticoat. Perhaps she hoped to
rout everyone with this noise? Or was she concealing the
pounding of her heart? There were always some patrons
who objected. Surly, looking at the clock: "What do you
mean, it's closing time? It's five to nine." When the
page-boy--Alfonse, a tall, stooping, black high-school boy
of a downcast and moody disposition; or so he seemed,
shoving the heavy cart, always behind a barricade of books--
when Alfonse came loping and trundling through the reading
room, dumping books on his cart in his dangerously off-hand
way and warningly dimming the lights, it was taken as a
personal insult. Why not? It was a personal insult. The
regulars had as much right to the premises as we did--
squatters' rights.

The heavy-shouldered, unshaven man, slouching on
his elbows, pressing the heels of his hands into his eyes.
This one always came with a companion, another gaunt
familiar type of the neighborhood, a mass of dry hair, hag-
gard fur. But all this haggardness, hair, still attracted the
eye; its color was gone, not its wild vitality. She had
been a great beauty, squandered powerful gifts, that was the
impression she created; her chair thrust back, her fur coat
flung open, legs crossed, raw-boned, raw-boned and bare.
When the time came, she'd shake her friend's shoulder.
But others, alone, could not be persuaded so gently; shaken
by the shoulder, they might not take it so kindly. If they
were asleep, you never knew--as in the legends of the
Islanders, their souls off, wandering, might not have time
to return.

But Miss Rose could rise to the occasion:

"If you don't go quietly," she'd say, her voice forced
and violently tremorous, "then--well then--we'll just have to
get the page-boy to throw you out!"

Alfonse's dark eyes lustrously widened. He was
extraordinarily tall, but thin as a rail, with long reticent
hands and feet--and no inclination for being drawn out in
this way. Stooping behind his barricaded cart. This was
a bouncer? At such times we were conscious of our lack
of manpower.

This was another fact of life in a branch library.
There was an unspoken rule: none of the staff could leave
at night until all of us were ready. We would assemble at
the desk in our wraps (I was reminded of the terminology
of kindergartens, cloakrooms, fire-drills), waiting to depart
together. This was protocol. And it was like a drill;
Miss Rose, timid, would test all the doors again and again;
the lockers, the cashdrawer, even the bathroom: was anyone hiding? One has fantasies about being forgotten in such
places at night--public facilities, museums, even department
stores. Once at the zoo I walked into the lion house after
closing time; the door had been improperly locked, sprang
open. The long gallery was deserted, and from dark cages,
behind thick bars, the big cats were already talking to each
other. Their powerful growls rolling down the cavernous
hall like thunder. They knew. And one sensed something
like this about the library at night, when we waited to leave
the darkened building; gloomy and depopulated with all its
brooding stacks of books. If you were left alone with them,
would they talk back to you?

When Miss Rose had locked the front doors, she
would lock them again. Fingers stiff in knitted gloves
fumbling with the keys. At last she would fling them down
the brass mouth of the Book Depository--a final precaution.
She never transported these keys with her. What if she
took that famous exam and passed it?--that's what she was
afraid of. Then what would she do? It was enough to have
to worry about locking up on these nights! The fluffy angora
head peering down the dark slot, just to make sure....
Done with formalities. Now it was time to hurry, waving
goodbye, going our separate ways at the corner; and as we
dispersed, remembering the grimness of the neighborhood.
A general observation, but there were particulars. Beebee
had been followed to her el station a couple of nights by one
of our patrons. Her departing figure, in flats and babushka,
kept turning, looking backward.

We all knew who this was, a young man in a leather
jacket. He was slight, fair, with ridges of kinky blond hair;
pale eyes, bony orbs; a preponderant forehead. And he had
a nervous tic of the jaw; you could see the muscles leaping
under his skin. It seemed that he took out books on remedial
reading--a laudable enterprise--and sometimes he sat and
studied them. But one foot never stopped tapping under the
table; one blue-jeaned knee jerked constantly up and down.

As soon as Beebee saw him, she climbed off her high stool and concealed herself behind the tall hedge of the circulation desk. He kept shifting in his seat, glancing over there. He'd reach deep inside his leather jacket, draw out a straight shiny object, a fountain pen perhaps? Crouching over as if to write. Then the kinky blond head looked all around, the eyes darted in their corners, the muscles jumped in his cheek. He'd slip the object back. Someone might be eavesdropping on his thoughts, that's what it looked like; reading his mind in every random twitch.

But who could be eavesdropping on him? Not at this table. Judge Brady, unbending even over his books, sat erect, reading at a distance through his magnifying glass. Another man dozed on folded arms. As for the gray-haired old lady with the diaper pins in her coat, it was Miss Rose she had her eye on--fiercely waiting to pounce on her. What could that loud person be up to now? Approaching the table, very pink in the face, heels battering, rapid, noisier than ever?

No sooner had Miss Rose leaned over to speak to the young man than he bounded up--so suddenly, violently, that his chair crashed over backward. His clenched fists struck the table.

"You godddamned lousy Jews. You're always telling people what to do!"

"If you're going to talk that way," said Miss Rose, thickly, her heart at once in her throat--"If you won't keep your voice down--"

"Fucking niggers and Jews! That's all you've got in here anyhow. And you think you're running the whole goddamned show."

"Such language," the old lady whispered. "But you hear everything these days."

There was a murmur throughout the room. The financial pages stopped rustling. For a moment, all you could hear were the fan-belts, flimsy, fainthearted. A violation of the library's inalienable silence. But the young man had all the attention now. And he knew it; zipping his jacket up smartly with a jerk of the chin, methodically

picking up his books. His swivelling eyes were taking it all
in. "I'll be back," he said--announced, looking all around,
addressing the whole room now, his audience. "And I'm
going to fix you lousy Jews if it's the last thing I do."

"Oh yeah? Why don't you start right now then?"

It was Mr. Cohen, rising, drawing himself up to his
full height and slamming his hat on his head.

"Oh yeah?" This was Mr. Adorno. He shoved his
chair back with a deliberate, threatening thud. All over the
room chairs were scraping, tottering. The old pensioners,
rising; sleepers, waking. The young man tossed down his
books and put up his fists. He began to back off, cautious,
elbows gripping his chest.

They were closing in; gaunt men, baring their arms.
Mr. Adorno, with his big soft eyes and bright teeth, kept
grinning, thumbing his nose. Popkin's timid, frothy white
head peeped in and out as he tiptoed round and round with
his rapid shuffle. They all seemed merely to be skipping
round, for that matter; like boxers from the past, bantam-
weights, keeping their guard up, shifty moving targets.
Politely almost; an old-fashioned match, with their old-
fashioned rules. You could see their enemy's eyes darting
behind his knuckle-ridges. Not quite believing this. Only
Judge Brady stood firm, feet planted, one arm doubled up
in front of the other and arching his back in a stand-offish
way. A most honorable, upright John L. Sullivan, Gentle-
man Jim. The Marquis of Queensberry himself!

Miss Rose tugged at Cohen's coat-sleeve, but he
shook her off.

"He started it."

They were waiting for him to swing first; he did--
an arm shot out, jerked back. The old women gasped.
This was for real! Then Cohen took his swing--very wide,
spinning himself halfway about under the weight of his own
long arm in its heavy sleeve--and the young man ducked
easily and crouched again. Taunting now, jerking his
twitching jaw, flexing his shoulders in the leather jacket.

The situation was serious. Even worse, it was
sensitive. We weren't so much worried that the fellow

would land a punch and hurt anyone--though his knuckles were sharp, might damage an old face. But what if one of these old guys should have a heart attack and drop right on the spot? All this fancy footwork, crowding toward the enemy; such excitement was dangerous. But no one dared to say this. Mortal injury? yes, but there was something more touchy, more serious, with these old men especially. It seemed to me that this was the influence of the Six-Day War last spring. Cohen, the other old Jews in their overcoats, saw themselves suddenly as warriors, men of that strong arrogant race they were breeding these days in the desert. And maybe the rest of the old men, not Jews, felt something of this. Why shouldn't they? They were equally aroused; weak, counted out, they had had enough too. The worms were turning, the meek were inheriting the earth.... And you couldn't interfere with them. You couldn't, at such a moment, bring to their attention the fact that they really were old and feeble. Judge Brady's firm face was congested and purple. And Mr. Adorno! Such bright ferocity--at eighty! The gaunt man in his shirtsleeves (his once heavy frame!) was coughing; lungs wheezing. All that the timid librarians were worried about was protecting them from themselves.

"Do something, Alfonse! Do you think I ought to call the police?" This was the last thing Miss Rose would ever do.

"What are you waiting for? Break it up."

"You may need the inhalator squad instead."

But somehow they had managed to surround him; a skinny arm grabbed his collar, a heavy coat-sleeve hooked his belt. They pinned his arms. "Let's show him the door, boys," Judge Brady shouted, and they hustled him out-- jerking, kicking, the kinky blond head, bony orbs, swivelling.

"Kikes! Crazies! Niggers! Bums! That's all you've got!"

They ran him into the street. He disappeared. Very soon the police arrived, partners, a low-slung heavy-set pair in fur-collared jackets. They were wiping their caps dry. For it had started to snow, and clots of the stuff slid from collars and brawny leather shoulders, dripped and melted all around them.

They put their caps on again. "What's the trouble?"

It was past nine, but none of the regulars had left, and no one had asked them to. Now everyone started talking at once; everyone had a complaint, an injury. The old lady clicked her tongue as she knotted her plastic rain-bonnet under her chin. Such language! In a library! Where you had a right to expect some consideration! Miss Rose, under compulsion, forced herself to repeat the young man's words. The old men told of a knife. And Beebee--who had not yet poked her black head out from behind the counter-- reported being followed.

But the cops, listening to all this, were more and more and more unmoved. Their eyes grazed slowly on one old face and on another--the aged kooks in their shabby coats, abominable smelly furs, weakly indignant. Big deal! This arousing incident bored them completely. They looked toward each other. You could see what they thinking: Kikey Cohen? Nigger Alfonse? What's to get excited? Facts, just facts. They and the young man were in significant agreement. For the second time that night, the unmentionable came close to being, humiliatingly, mentioned.

They held up their hands. "Okay, cool it everybody."

"And here's Judge Brady. And he'll tell you. He saw the knife."

Judge Brady had gone outside to watch. To watch what? Now he came in to report.

"Is he really a judge?" asked one of the policemen, forgetting about the knife and for the first time lifting his eyes, showing a flicker of interest. He turned round respectfully.

"It's snowing so hard you can't tell much!" The big white-haired old man was full of breath-puffing, snow-stamping enthusiasm. He blew his nose and hastened out again.

The cop turned back. "Will you push the buzzer and let me in?" He wanted to use the bathroom.

"Give us another call if this fellow shows up again."

As a matter of fact, the young man continued to hang around Borglum, in his familiar leather jacket. He was eventually arrested, locked up; he had a history. But this didn't matter now.

The cops left then and we locked up. It was snowing forcefully. Not one of your fresh, swirling paperweight versions; not the pelt of dreamy white Xmases; but a wet cutting sleet. The north wind was blowing it all horizontally. It grappled with clutched coat-collars; the streets were already covered with the stuff. All those gym shoes in that peroxide slush! Judge Brady and Mr. Adorno appointed themselves to escort Beebee to her el train. Others trudged off; the street lights were melting. Mr. Cohen, trying to touch his hat in the slashing sleet, asked Miss Rose if he could see her home. She demurred--she would always demur. But, after all, tonight was different; it was time for a little charity. She consented to be walked to her bus stop. He grasped her elbow, she pinched his thick sleeve; and they bowed their heads to the snow.

ASSOCIATION AGONIES: LIFE WITH ALA*

Eric Moon

I'm going to ramble a bit about library associations. I'm not going to get hung up with definitions and altercations about what is or is not a professional association. That's library school lawyer rhetoric, academic garbage, a waste of time. The only substantive question is whether our associations are doing the job we want them to do--indeed, whether they can do it.

I am concerned most particularly about ALA. A man (unless he be a consultant or a rogue) should talk about what he knows best. I'm going to start off with a medley of quotations to set the scene, the theme, the tenor of what is to follow.

Quote I (on Special Libraries Association): "If the sixty-second annual conference of SLA is to have an overall meaning, it does not lie in its meaningless theme, 'Design for Service: Information Management,' but in the death of a concern--the merger (with ASIS)--that has already drained energy which might have been better used. For however well the merger might have served the association members themselves and reduced somewhat the schizophrenic anxieties of librarian/information scientists, it would have made little difference in service to the library user."

Quote II (on the Medical Library Association): "The 1,400 librarians who gathered in New York ... for the seventieth annual meeting of the Medical Library Association may, collectively, have known more than any one doctor about the treatment of physical diseases, but the group still entered its septuagenarian era suffering from those afflictions common to all library associations: professional identity crisis and organizational obsolescence."

---

*Reprinted by permission of the American Library Association from American Libraries, February 1972. First delivered as a speech at Dalhousie University, School of Library Science, Oct. 4, 1971.

Quote III (on the Canadian Library Association): "The theme was 'Reorganization, Recruitment, and Results.' It had a ring of desperation to it: CLA must restructure and revitalize itself or it will lose both present and potential members. Some would have added 'rehash' to these three Rs, because CLA has covered this ground many times before--without results."

Quote IV (on the American Library Association): "If more ALA members now realize that real power in the association is beyond their grasp--Dallas also proved to them that you can still apply effective pressure, and in time, achieve rhetorical goals. This appeared to be especially true if all you wanted was an expression of ALA sentiment on a current issue, and it wouldn't cost any money."

Quote V (also on ALA): "Dissent and disenchantment counterpointed the week's events, with school librarians seriously considering terminating their ALA ties while the college and university librarians set up August 31, 1972 as their federation or forget it day. Trustees, too, entertained independence, with the urban group making the loudest noise and then agreeing to stay on for a while to help the other trustees get the courage to strike off on their own."

Those five quotations come from the pens of four different writers, writing in the "big three" American library periodicals (LJ, WLB, AL) about the meetings this summer of four different library associations.

If, collectively, they seem to you to present a picture of confusion, desperation, chaos, you read them correctly. The library associations are, without exception, in a mess, trying to find a direction, a purpose; trying to understand what their members really want (and generally to find ways to tell them it's impossible); trying to find a role for themselves in a society which is changing faster than ever they knew how; trying to survive a battery of pressures they have never faced--perhaps never seen--before.

But if it is all a mess, it is a healthy one, in my opinion. At least the associations have been knocked off the dead center of the status quo. Some bullets of concern have riddled the armor of complacency and left it yawning with holes of doubt and uncertainty. The reason that words like restructuring and new directions pervade every meeting of every association is that there is, finally, an awareness that change is no longer desirable but mandatory--or the associations will die or be replaced. I also think the chaos is healthy because the library paste that has held the associations together--membership inertia--is finally coming unstuck.

While the realization is dawning, however, that the associations must change drastically, must gear themselves up to deal with a world and a membership which are both vastly different from those of 1876 (or even 1945), the big question which hangs over the association scene, as the bomb does over us all, is whether a structure and a purpose which will hold everything together can be found quickly enough, before the friction and the forces burn and blast the remnants of a century of dedicated, if not always inspired, effort into a cloud of ashes.

Let's look, then, at ALA, which is better and worse, in various respects, than most of the other library associations, to see if we can discern where some of the problems lie and what, if anything, can be done about them.

Morality Gap

It may be almost a cliché, but I have to say that the most powerful force which is making the gothic pillars of the library associations tremble is morality. This is a problem that our associations share with many of the most basic and prestigious institutions in society: the schools and universities, government and the courts; science and the church; many of the other professions, beginning with the most prestigious (hitherto) of them all, medicine. The gulf between word and deed in all these arenas seems not only to have become more apparent today but it is being challenged and questioned as rarely, perhaps never, before.

Now I do not mean to set up any simple, black-and-white dichotomy in which the establishment (i.e., the oldies) are all immoral, and the turks (i.e., the kids) are all snow-white and virtuous. I do mean to suggest, though, that many of those who grew up through the years of the Depression and World War II, the years when material comfort and prosperity were major, urgent, and difficult goals, have an understandable survival complex, and thus an armament in which expediency and a deliberate (i.e., slow) rate of change are honored and well-used weapons. Many of the younger librarians, like other young people--and, let it be said, a goodly number of oldies, too--do not see materialism and survival as synonymous, and they can get so hung-up on principle that expediency can appear downright immoral.

What I'm talking about may make better sense if we examine a few prominent specifics, vis-à-vis ALA. Perhaps the most holy sacred cow in the ALA stable is the association's legislative program and its Washington Office. It is understandable that it should be so. Remember that prior to 1956 federal aid to libraries, for all intents and purposes, just didn't exist. From the first passage of the Library Services Act that year, literally hundreds of millions of federal money (and a few million more from other sources, stimulated by that flow) have poured into library coffers across the land. Libraries owe most of that manna to ALA, to a hard-working and exceptionally able lobbying staff, and to the number one priority which the association has given to that effort. There was no doubt of the need, and no doubt either than in this area ALA has produced, and produced big. Can there be room for criticism, then? Yes, there can.

It is a fact of life--still, but it was even more so in the late fifties and early sixties--that the real power in Congress lay in the cotton- and tobacco-stained palms of southern committee chairmen. So, too, did the fate and continued health of library legislation. It was no coincidence, nor any real reflection of the concentration of need, that the early emphasis in the Library Services Act was on rural library development. Nor is it any coincidence that today, when the screamingly obvious crisis in libraries is in the big cities, federal aid to city libraries is still, proportionately, pathetic.

That fact of life is also why pressure was brought to bear, heavily and rapidly, on me and on my friend John Wakeman at the Wilson Library Bulletin when, very early in the sixties, we decided to expose the silent hypocrisy of the racial situation in U.S. librarianship. Not only were discrimination and outright segregation rife in libraries-- most evidently but not exclusively in the South--but ALA was nestling under its wing a number of state associations, several of them as chapters of the parent association, which were themselves segregated. Wakeman and I were urged to cool it because too much noise about all that racial stuff was calculated to upset our southern sponsors in Congress and thus jeopardize all that lovely federal loot they were dealing out to libraries. In the racial climate of today that sounds not only immoral but pretty foolish. But then I remember asking, with youthful naivete, "If you have no principles, what good is the money?" And the question made no sense to some of those of whom I asked it. Political expediency was obviously paying off for libraries. Now which could possibly be more important? Money or morality?

A more recent example of the great interest of ALA's legislative forces in matters fiscal rather than matters moral occurred at the Mid-winter Meeting last January--or, more precisely, began to occur there.

The ALA Council passed a fairly forthright resolution offered by the association's Intellectual Freedom Committee, which commended the Presidential Commission on Obscenity and Pornography for "amassing a significant body of empirical evidence in an area of great social concern...." The resolution also quoted President Nixon's statement: "I have evaluated that report and categorically reject its morally bankrupt conclusions and recommendations," and urged the president and Senate to reconsider this categorical rejection.

The ALA Legislative Committee quickly mounted its opposition. Its chairman (ironically a former chairman of the Intellectual Freedom Committee) tried from the floor to water down the paragraphs which were clearly critical of the president and the Senate because of the effect these might have on the ALA's legislative programs.

Even after the Council passed the resolution, another attempt was made, just two days later, to water it down. Another longtime worker in the ALA legislative fields protested that it wasn't within ALA's field of expertise to take issue with the president's and the Senate's evaluation of the commission report, and that to do so would "detract from our credibility in Congress" and make "legislative work increasingly more difficult."

It was the first time in perhaps many years that anyone had suggested that opinions on intellectual freedom matters were not within ALA's province. To suddenly deny our special interest and involvement in this area, it seemed to me and clearly to many others, might do more to damage our credibility than anything else. Council, at any rate, stood firm, and the executive director was instructed to send the resolution, as an expression of association opinion, to the president and the Senate. The opposition from the legislative group was perhaps not too surprising, but they had been defeated, and that seemed the end of the story.

It wasn't. At the next conference this past summer, we discovered that the resolution hadn't been sent out immediately, as everyone expected it would be, and as it clearly should have been for maximum effectiveness. It had been held up for something like six to eight weeks before being transmitted. The general suspicion, and I believe it was entirely correct, was that the legislative committee and/or the Washington Office had been responsible for these stalling tactics.

Tax and Librarian Exempt

That may be enough to demonstrate, in that one area, the morality gap I referred to earlier. A second area--and another relatively holy one--in which ALA has been under pressure for the past several years is intellectual freedom itself. In the past, the association has made some notably fine and courageous statements--most particularly its freedom to read statement, issued during the dark days of McCarthyism, when many another group was very carefully keeping quiet.

But as the pressures against dissent in the U.S. have mounted these past few years, librarians themselves (not just the books and magazines on their shelves) have fallen victim to repression and attack, and a steady stream of librarians have lost their jobs for supporting the very principles which ALA has long espoused. As the librarian casualty list has grown, the gap between ALA's promise and performance in the intellectual freedom arena has become more apparent. Impatience with the continued parade of noble statements has grown more vocal, and the demands for action, not just words, have grown more insistent.

Once again, however, in this area as in the legislative one, the dollar has been ALA's paramount interest. As each demand for concrete action has been made--notably the demand for a defense fund for librarians--the demand has been met early with the same argument: It cannot be done because it might injure ALA's tax-exempt status. Gone, apparently, is the memory of that final resounding sentence of the freedom to read statement: "Freedom itself is a dangerous way of life, but it is ours."

ALA's master ploy, at once preserving its precious tax-exempt status and at the same time giving the appearance of action, was to set up a separate organization, the Freedom to Read Foundation. The assumption was that the foundation could do what ALA wouldn't because of its fear of being jilted by the Internal Revenue Service. Only a short time after, the foundation told us that it couldn't take some of the actions for which it was set up, because it might lose its tax-exempt status. So the foundation set up another fund under its wing, called the LeRoy Merritt Fund, which was not tax exempt, and which could be used for action purposes. It seemed only logical that if the foundation could set up a separate fund, ALA could have done that too. But, no, the foundation and ALA had different categories of tax-exempt status. It's a sad, funny, surrealist story--but it's clearly written on green paper.

Closely related to intellectual freedom is a third pressure point within ALA. The pressure in this area has come, not just from the radicals, the activists, the young, but also from some of the most conservative in the profession. A few years ago a president of ALA was unwise enough to indicate that ALA was more concerned with the welfare of libraries than with the welfare of librarians (though I couldn't find the actual quotation when I was looking for it). He was speaking the truth, even if it was dangerous. The ALA leaders do think, have thought, institutionally for most of the years of the association's existence. You need only to look at the ALA's statement of purpose to see the emphasis, "The promotion of library service of excellent quality, freely available to all." No one could quarrel with that statement, but it is possible to differ with the emphases in the implementation of that purpose. Listed under that statement are seven ways in which that purpose should be fulfilled; only one of them deals at all with librarians. It reads, "Improvement of professional library standards through better professional education, working conditions, salaries, and certification."

The words, again, read better than the performance record, as the mounting cries for ALA to show its teeth in such matters as status, tenure, salaries, working conditions, and the protection of librarians' rights have testified. ALA has begun to move in this area, and at its last conference it set up a new procedure and a new committee:

the Committee on Mediation, Arbitration and Inquiry, which was given as its domain the broad sweep of "tenure, status, fair employment practices, due process, ethical practices, and the principles of intellectual freedom."

It is obviously too early to expect or to pass any judgment about the prospects of this committee producing the kind of results the membership wants but, pessimist though I am, I believe this is one part of the machinery that may move into action. This is not pure optimism, but is based on the belief that ALA can, in this instance, see its dollar interests at stake. It has seen the steady growth of library unions the past five or more years, and must know that they have grown because the association left them room to grow. If the unions do what librarians want, and ALA doesn't, it obviously won't be long before much of the ALA membership income is translated into union dues. Self-satisfied as it often is, ALA is not stupid, and it has seen, for example, the rapid transformation recently of the National Education Association, which has become much more militant about matters like working conditions and teachers' rights because it was rapidly losing membership and influence to the booming National Federation of Teachers. If the unions can move ALA off the pot in such matters, they will have rendered a real service to the profession, because it will be a long time before the unions themselves can accumulate the prestige and influence that ALA undoubtedly has in certain quarters, even though it may be timid about exercising it.

A fourth area of pressure, and this is certainly one that just about every organization is experiencing, is the swelling demand for (to use a popular contemporary redundancy) "participatory democracy." (If democracy isn't participatory it isn't democracy.) The ALA membership has grown increasingly vociferous about the continued presence of the same select band of people on all the key committees of the association; increasingly frustrated over the continued rejection of membership proposals by the ALA Council and Executive Board; increasingly angry that priorities and programs are not funded while, at the same time, the huge headquarters grows more obese, eating away at larger and larger portions of the ALA budget, and less responsive every year. Indeed, at the last ALA conference, the membership vented its spleen on the ALA budget committee (COPES) for making no attempt in its 1971-72 budget to reflect the priorities of the association which had been voted in by the membership and adopted by the Council, the supposed policy-making body of ALA. COPES was the first committee that most people could recall ever being roundly censured by the membership.

Nevertheless, despite the swelling volume of membership discontent, the ALA, like the other associations, continues to be dominated by administrators. The principal reason is not hard to discern: while the administrators have such a stranglehold on library policy at the local level, while they are so often the only members of the staff who are paid to attend meetings and conventions, they have an access edge that is terribly difficult to overcome. Until there is more participatory democracy at the local (library) level, it will be hard to achieve at the national level. This is one area, incidentally, where staff unions may play a key role.

The Attitude Gap

But a major part of the problem continues to be one of attitude, and this is most clearly illustrated by a little internal document circulated among members of the ALA Nominating Committee for 1972-73. This document spelled out some of the proposed criteria for candidates for the Council, for president-elect and treasurer. The committee wanted "some evidence of having accomplished good for the association," or "evidence of cultural refinement"; the candidate "must have presence"; and worst of all, perhaps, the committee said "age bracket between 45 and 55 desirable." Other tired criteria listed included "experience," "knowledge of the ALA structure," and such vital elements as "physical stamina," or "international dimension," or "articulate." As *Library Journal* commented: "If you added 'strong baritone' and 'good looks' to the list, you might think we are about to elect the U.S. Ambassador to Monaco, or the MC for the Miss America pageant."

Despite this evidence of the intransigence and durability of nineteenth century thinking, the noisy restlessness of the membership has had some effect, and a number of new faces and voices are infiltrating the committee rooms of ALA. The establishment, though, picks carefully and it seems to know its own kind very well, even when they are in the embryo stage. It is interesting, even if not surprising, how like the establishment some of the young malcontents of only a year or two ago look and sound, after just a short period of close contact with the establishment bosom.

Faced with an attitude gap that will clearly take an intolerably long time to counteract, some of those who seek radical change in ALA have begun to learn the uncomfortable lesson that organization and knowledge are necessary weapons to overcome the fear, the inertia, the defensiveness, and so they are learning the machinery--the Bylaws and the Constitution, the election procedures, and how they can be used to advantage. In the past few years they have pressured for the liberalization of the nomination and election machinery, the one weapon that is not locked in the establishment's arsenal. And there is now a steady input of new names on election ballots, either put there by petition or--and this is important, too--put there by those who control the nomination precedure, as a means of quelling some of the protest.

The thing the change-seekers have not yet done, or certainly have not done effectively, is to go out and organize votes for those they have gotten on the ballot. It's a lot of work, but it can be done and it has to be. All current appearances and the Yippies to the contrary, successful revolutions have never been organized or won by people who want to play games, or who see chaos and turbulence as just another kind of fun. They are won by people who have a target and who go after it. If that makes me a structure freak, so be it.

I have saved the biggest and perhaps most important pressure point for last. The most overwhelming protest in ALA (and this again is true of other organizations, indeed of society itself) is on social issues--race, sex, and war, to name only three potent elements.

ALA has been struggling with racial issues, as I indicated at the outset, for about a decade now, but the pressure has accelerated recently, primarily because of the emergence a couple years ago of the Black Caucus. Adding to the pressure has been the Social Responsibilities Round Table, also formed just a couple of years ago. In the past twelve months these two groups have had the Executive Board, the Council and the Intellectual Freedom Committee of ALA in a turmoil over such matters as: (1) the Black Caucus's charges that southern schools have been providing library services, with public funds, to newly formed private schools which were set up to bypass the law of the land on integration of schools; (2) the same group's charges that the

Library of Congress has been discriminating in employment and promotion against blacks; (3) SRRT's donation to the Angela Davis defense fund, without prior consultation with ALA.

Other groups which have been pushing hard are the Women's Liberation and Gay Liberation Task Forces of SRRT. Indeed, at the Dallas meeting this summer, the Gay Lib group stole most of the association's headlines in the press, on radio and television, with their "Hug a Homosexual" booth in the exhibit area, and a variety of other activities. They also got through the Council a resolution calling for the better protection of the rights of homosexuals in libraries and in librarianship.

Beyond these group pressures, however, there is a more pervasive insistence that ALA deal with and express itself on social issues. The most persistent topic, of course, has been the Vietnam War. This summer, a resolution against the war finally passed both the Membership and the Council. One member, afterwards, commented that it had passed this time after several abortive attempts, because the thrust of its argument on this occasion was the "reallocation" of national resources, with greater emphasis on pressing domestic needs (i.e., libraries, for example), rather than the issue of the war and its killing and devastation. Dollars, again, this member was saying, as I have said repeatedly in this paper, are a more persuasive argument around ALA than morality.

Two other points should be made about that Vietnam resolution, and another about the social pressure in general, because they may demonstrate why I thought this paper might be pertinent at the Dalhousie Library School, remote from your lives though the inner machinations of ALA might be.

First, the Vietnam resolution was drafted and presented by two library school students, part of the Students to Dallas group which was composed of delegates from every one of the accredited library schools in the U.S. and Canada. They proved by their handling and presentation, that you don't need to be well into the sere and yellow before you can hope to have an impact, even on a mammoth, cumbersome, labyrinthine organization like ALA.

The second point about the Vietnam resolution was that it came too late to be very meaningful. Had it been made even two or three years ago, ALA might reasonably have been considered an organization working at the forefront of public opinion. Now, opposition to the war is the accepted, majority position. Thus, ALA's statement is, as so many of its others have been, just another motherhood-and-flag parade.

The point I want to make about the social pressure generally is that it really began for ALA, at least on a heavy scale, at the Atlantic City Conference two years ago. The group that opened up the big guns was called the Congress for Change. It, too, was very heavily a student group. Its real successor, the Social Responsibilities Round Table, though not a student-organized or dominated group, has the youngest leadership in the ALA--unless one counts seriously the Junior Members Round Table, which very few people do. SRRT is the most volatile group in the association, and though it loses more often than it wins, it has done much to upset the equilibrium of the upper Establishment and it has, far more than it knows, I think, changed the climate of ALA. There is nervousness, even fear, among those who were merely complacent before, and some of the inertia has been translated into an unwilling receptivity.

I said earlier that I would suggest some of things that ought or need to be done to rescue ALA and the other associations from the chaos in which they find themselves.

A large step in the direction of democratization must be taken. No valid reason exists, for example, except the economic (and I think I've said enough about dollars dictating all our courses of action)--no valid reason why it should be made difficult for anyone who wants to run for any office whatsoever, to get on the ballot. Those who get nervous about this apparently see no difference between nomination and election. Nomination is only democratic if it is easily available. Election is only democratic if it is competitive.

More people must be brought into the key operating committees of the associations whose views differ radically from those of the traditional incumbents. If nothing else, the committee rooms might become less deadly places to pass a few hours if a modicum of dissident opinion were heard there. The club members, who have served endlessly and repeatedly, must be weeded out and replaced.

The associations must hammer out specific program

and policy priorities, and must then proceed to budget them. Policies and programs mean nothing unless they are financed. Priorities which are not reflected in the budget are no more than pieties.

The associations, to mention further pieties, must desist from continually making public policy pronouncements unless they are prepared to follow them up, and particularly to defend their members who carry out those policies on the front lines. In short, we need not more words but more teeth behind the words.

Decisions must be made as to what activities can best be handled centrally, on behalf of the whole association, and which might better be decentralized and left to smaller, perhaps looser and faster-operating groups. On the really big issues, however, which demand the force of unity, of maximum numbers, the associations must vigorously resist the splintering which has been weakening the library profession throughout this century and must stamp heavily on parochialism, particularly type-of-library parochialism.

The associations must begin to regard themselves as a responsible and potentially powerful voice in society, as bodies with a responsibility and a right to speak out (as many other groups do), not just on matters bibliographic but on major social concerns. They have only to remember the biggest, oldest cliché of them all to get the point. How many times have you heard: "I became a librarian because I love books and people"? It isn't as silly as it sounds, but the people interest isn't as clear from our words and actions as the devotion to books. If we don't talk about social ills, social needs, social concerns, do we really expect anyone to know or believe that we're interested or that we care about people? And if we seem not to care, can we be surprised when libraries get into trouble and no one else seems much to care about that?

Finally, the young, the dissident, the radical, the change-seekers must keep up the pressure, and must resist despondency about the temporary losses. The climate can be changed, even by defeats. And the overall war, which is worth winning, for sanity and responsibility, can be won. And must be.

LIBRARIES ARE FOR LIBRARIANS--A VIEW FROM THE EDITOR'S CHAIR*

Gerald R. Shields

Contrary to popular assumptions, the editor's chair at the <u>American Libraries</u> is not a Chippendale. It is more like a camp chair. It folds easily. It is lightweight. It is very comfortable in fair weather, but it does have a tendency, in foul weather, to attract bolts of lightning. When you sit down in the editor's chair, you find that your position is very like one referred to as fetal. In that position, I have often felt a maddening impulse to be constantly inspecting the navel to determine if there might be an umbilical cord attached. You never can find it, but like the microscopic piece of Mother Earth in your eye ... the itch is still there, even if the inspection denies its existence.

It is possible that at this point you will begin to form a picture in your mind of an office that is like a womb. I do not mean to create such a picture. The office of the editor of <u>American Libraries</u> is not so much the womb as it is the abortion table. I must admit there are womb-like occasions at ALA when the darkness is comforting and warm, causing a willingness to accept blind maternalism. After all, ALA has been the big mother of librarianship for nearly a century now.... Such devotion to motherhood has conditioned the kind of stoicism which can take being kicked in the shins by its children (and in-laws) ... still smile and say, "Be nice, so you shouldn't lose our tax exemption." Being an editor in the midst of such filial affection can be an exercise in frustration that can lead to variant forms of <u>Katzenjammery</u>.

But, enough of that. I don't want to bore you with

---

*This was originally a paper delivered at the Virginia Library Association meeting on December 2, 1971, and published in <u>Southeastern Librarian</u>, Spring 1972. Reprinted by permission.

twice-told tales. I am here to take a good solid position in my editor's camp chair, glare balefully out at you while mouthing the kind of wisdom that only mantles the shoulders of what someone else terms "the national library press."

Before we proceed, let me offer a point of clarification. Editors are just as opinionated as you think they are. They have told and untold vices, charms, great strengths and tottering weaknesses, just as do any other people you know and especially the one in your morning mirror. The difference is that they have some place to exhibit these qualities on a regular basis. This exhibitionist quality is given to only a few in our society ... like actors, talk show hosts, comics, newscasters and clowns. As a result, the editor is allowed to make Olympian statements that will, at best, shake the library world or at least send a tremor up its collective spine. That editors fail at this requirement more often than they succeed is often overlooked by those so insecure that they are willing to shoot at anything that flies out of the bush.

Therefore, I am going to share with you my opinions, my personal piques, gripes and aggravations. These are offered you without hours of research, intuitively drawn so as not to be construed as fact and prepared, I can assure you, with considerable malice aforethought. The facts I leave to those few authors in this world that have been able to discover them and slip them past an editor.

What do I see from the editor's chair? I see doubt, misgivings, some panic and many pathetic practices rising to cloud the surface of good library service. For as long as I can remember, librarians have been pouring ashes on their forelocks and rendering their garments in one long funeral procession hell-bent on interring librarianship. In the past few years, the keening has become so loud that I find that I am turning off to those sounds just as I have turned off to the T.V. commercial hell-bent to give me a guilt complex because my underarms get wet.

How many times have you been told that libraries are for people? If that were true, people would be for libraries. Since that is not true and the only ones going around saying such things are librarians, then it might just be the truth to say that libraries are for librarians. I realize that this is a difficult concept for many to accept. Some of our part-time liberals and our pantomimic radicals would not be able to accept such a concept and still be able to grow at least a mustache if not wear belled jeans to work or carry a genuine wool shoulder bag woven by the peasants of Peru and/or Upper Maine.

Since the end of the sixties, we have been dancing around on our everyday sensible shoes because the Women's Lib, the Gay Lib, the sexism cult, the red, white, black-and-blue caucus and the would-be presidents of ALA clubs have been nipping at our heels. All of these factions deal in code words accompanied by raised eyebrows and carefully manufactured spontaneity or ennui. Though they may be entertaining and diverting, the question remains, have they really raised the consciousness-level of librarianship, or have they contributed to a further withdrawal of many people employed in libraries who don't have time to take on the marching to seventy-six different drummers? From where I sit, it seems that they have generated little more than polite applause from the majority of the library profession (applause is the liberals' method of booing). Considerable underground activity has been generated as a counter-reaction on the part of the status-quo militants. And, too many librarians have despaired of ever attaining the status of some kind of sociological Florence Nightingale.

I am going to use some code words to save time and keep this entertaining. Let me speak, first, about the organization freaks. There are two kinds. One is the lighthouse freak who has anchored himself on a good solid rock and stands surveying the scene looking neither up nor down ... just turning around and around unblinking. The other I call the Cervantes freak who was pioneered by our brief and dedicated Don Quixote, Ralph Blasingame. His was a brief chorus of "To Dream the Impossible Dream" in the 1968 Kansas City ALA Conference. He was quickly put out to pasture by the steers that occupied the same china shop when they discovered they had a bull on their hands. Now, we have more tilters than we have windmills.

Our elitist freaks also come in two sizes. There is the giant economy size librarian who is so elite he won't be seen with anyone but himself. But more interesting are the Janus freaks--a group I find that I understand and sympathize with more than is good for me or them. The academic and the school librarians are the more visible factions in this category, although, I will admit there is some good hunting in the special library field as well. Both the academic and

the school librarians are minority groups within their own
communities. The school librarians are never certain if
they are merely teachers who have avoided pushing a book-
truck over their toes, or if they are media buffs with a
lightshow no one can see. The academic librarian has been
looking so fondly at the parade of mortar boards past his
window as he slaves over a hot bibliography that he has only
recently looked up to discover his status is no better than
that of the maintenance man and often he is not as well paid.
However, both groups have been chattering away to themselves for so long that I am afraid they have lost sight of
the common denominator which sets them apart from the
teacher or the maintenance man--librarianship.

There are *mole* freaks, too. They are busy in their
little burrows making random ripples in the landscape, but
really upsetting nothing. The public librarians are the best
example of this type. A few of this group have been seen
wandering around on the surface of late, but, for the most
part, the entire business is only as good as the individual
and the amount of earth that can be moved in the dark with
the nose. This labeling process could continue, but
maybe the point has been made. Each of us is some
kind of freak. Since 1954 we have been wealthier freaks
than we had been led to believe we had a right to be.
I think it has gone to our heads. We went flying off
like sailors on shore leave into a wild series of diver-
sifications and complications that, as I said, have been
diverting and entertaining, but have resulted in little more
than a hangover.

Now, we are faced with a library depression. The
money flow is down to a trickle of its old self. And, to
those who scream doom, I say let them scream. It is
better than some of the words they have been shouting for
the past few years. Real librarians know what is expected
and they are setting out to do it. They are looking over the
goodies that have been packed into their storehouses and are
trying to assess how they can best be used, even shared.
In addition, they have gone back to an acquisition program
instead of a squirrel festival. They are evaluating needs
and resources in terms of their collections. They are looking at staff, too. Many for the first time are beginning to
evaluate staff members in terms of investment returns. And
staff are beginning to take a serious look at the administration, and are making evaluations that can affect library
economy for years to come.

We must all remember that the library is a collection point for an arrangement of materials and a supplier of access to those materials first. Therefore, libraries are for librarians, first. Real librarians who will collect, organize materials, fight for the right of access--and not just spend money. Libraries are for librarians because real librarians are more interested in service to people than they are in anything else in their lives. Think about the librarians you admire the most and see if they do not fit that criterion. Libraries are for librarians and librarians build the unique service called librarianship. The others will become sociologists, late-night T. V. talk-show hosts, maybe even paranoiacs.

THE LITERATE PROFESSION*

D. E. Gerard

> To send a cry of protest or a call for
>   Protection up into all
> Those dazzling miles, to add, however sincerely,
>   One's occasional tear
> To that volume, would be rather silly,
>   Nor is there one small hill
> For the hopeful to climb, one tree for the hopeless
>   To sit under and mope.
>   (W. H. Auden. <u>Pleasure Island</u>).

    Sometimes it seems as if our fate as a profession is analogous to Auden's island beach, which gives back a sense of radiant emptiness under a pitiless blue sky without shade, exposing us uncomfortably to the indifferent gaze of the transient world. The act of reconsidering ideas I once indulged in about the nature of our peculiar stance as librarians in a changing world is perhaps, conducive only to the kind of gay, skeptical melancholy that informs the poem, but it is an act curative of any lingering illusions and the selfrighteousness that crystallises about one's psyche with the growth of middle age. A reassessment ten years afterwards, of some of my convictions, might prove of value as an exercise in the measurement of rate of growth in one professional's life.

    The simplest way to test a mass of vaguely held beliefs is perhaps to condense them all into one objective term, a metaphor even, that embodies the life view simply and concretely. The word which most readily achieves this for me in reflecting on what a librarian should do and be, is the word "literate". It is there present as a continuous refrain throughout all the pieces written in the past. Clearly it was intended to bear a weight of meaning that other

---

*Reprinted by permission from <u>Assistant Librarian</u>, January 1972.

Libraries and Librarians 77

epithets or clinching notions would not answer, and I seemed confident that its meaning and implications, when fully examined and explained, would be manifestly revealed as the main desideratum for us all in the profession which had for so long teased us for a definition. What did I mean by it, and would I mean the same today, are questions that will still bear the asking. When I have recently abandoned the realities of administration for the new complex of relationships known as "teaching" this is surely the ideal moment for further analysis and reappraisal? The process of helping to turn out the new professionals of the 70's must give one pause, for what will be the commonly held picture of the librarian in the future depends critically on what the Schools are producing now.

Socio-Political Awareness

Ten years more of higher education and increased sophistication has meant that there is now less need to labour the point that seemed so outrageous to audiences of librarians in 1960--that every member of this calling needs to develop to a high degree his personal sense of sociopolitical awareness, his place in the national pattern. No need conversely, to whip the Laodiceans, insisting repeatedly that librarians as faceless servants of a faceless clientele were a dead number. Commitment is taken for granted by the generation which reads AL today. So--in two sentences I have already leaped a decade and lost a cause that once was all consuming, a seizure of obsessive proportions. It is orthodoxy in the whole contemporary spectrum of thought, from Oz to the Bow Group (possibly even unto the Daily Telegraph) that social and political and emotional life, personal or professional, involves inner and outer space as one continuum; that we are undivided selves, as Laing and the prophets now assure us with impressive self-effacement and a jargon as demotic as Tin Pan Alley.

All of which makes the redefinition of my keyword in context, literacy, so much easier. Support for its more ample definition--what I am edging towards--seems given. It almost seems superfluous in the present exciting age. I wonder.

To have the feeling of commitment, and to understand the contemporary place of libraries in our society means a developed sense of history, particularly of what happened in

the 19th century, and a consequent understanding of where
you fit into the stream of history. What ways of thinking
about your daily chores, the very routines you discharge,
have you inherited from your predecessors? You will need
to be conscious that you are still, despite the fluidity of
thought and acceptances today, children of the Utilitarian
Age; still guided by a sense of civic service which fatally
cuts you off from your clients, secures you within a bond of
fellowship called the profession, insulates you from the rest
of the public, sets you as in cement, in a fixed relationship
with your users, with your governors and with your colleagues. At all times of the working day you are acting out
all these fixed forms of contact, because of the social shape
and conditioning which have made you and the institution you
serve. Although the service and the building and the relations with others may be strikingly conventional, familiar,
traditional, they are not lifeless, but have a daily renewed
life drawn from the energies, the attitudes, the enactments
of the people within the whole framework which we call a
library system. It cannot actually die, but will continue
vitally, since its being is nourished by continually living
participants within the process, generation by generation.
Methods and terms and means to the technical improvement
through professional education may alter and improve, grow
more sophisticated, demand more time and skill and enterprise of succeeding new entrants into the system, but essentially the action and reaction of all the constituent parts
of the undertaking called "the library" persist as before.
Thus the most important impulse for change must come
from the sensitivity and consciousness of those who are
made by and make the service. In a library it is the degree of literacy that will ensure its nervous tact in its dealings with the transient world which uses us, and its ultimate
influence. This is my belief.

Literacy of Public Service

A sense of tradition and form, the shaping forces
which have bequeathed us whatever libraries we work in,
must be seen with detachment, and not assumed like an old
jacket. The public and every other kind of library in the
UK is part of the figure in the national carpet; that is a
truism. Political and historical perspective is therefore
the beginning of literacy for a librarian, the literacy of
public service, the assumptions that come from that kind of
intercourse; you in relation to the network of needs,

expectations, education, deprivation, social grievance, racial and cultural discordance, age, the resentments of women, the deafness between any two generations. There is a mountain of responsibility to shoulder once it is clear what place currently and traditionally the librarian occupies. Space is not available to examine any one of the categories listed and to consider just what their implications might conceivably be for our work: each could happily justify and accommodate a whole article to itself, and be the basis for a new textbook on librarianship. Perhaps I may be allowed to select just one crucial fact that confronts us daily inside the library, and incarnates one central contradiction that is peculiarly at the heart of our function. I do not recall ever seeing it even mentioned, yet I suspect that it is all unconsciously the reason for the uncertainty of so much of our aims. This is the matter of the dilemma. The dilemma arises out of the interaction of two factors in the lives of all librarians: that they serve two masters, stand at the confluence of two competing forces, commerce and education. On the one hand they assist (with increasing refinement) the education of a people; on the other they serve business. We support publishers, supply them with their revenue without being invited to collaborate in their very private enterprises, although the result of their profitable activities depend so much on their private assumptions about what their customers want. We the professionals are not invited to help increase either the profits by our own expertise, or engage in more than a passive connection with our clients, using the commodities provided by business, without benefit of our co-operation, which is neither sought nor wanted. There is thus a large dichotomy between the means and the ends of communication and the tension of opposition between private gain and public good. One points to books as the supreme example from our world, for obvious reasons, but in the building of a new library the same dilemma holds, because we still divide society into arbitrary sectors. We are a sacred public trust, like health, education, welfare, others are the sacrosanct province of private speculation. The librarian and the architect who jointly plan a new library do not compete for the privilege, but put their most disinterested talents into it. But the actual builders of the library compete as fiercely as possible. Furnishing a children's department, the rebinding of the books, the choice of curtains is equally a part of librarianship as book selection, yet one is strictly separate from the other. This is our own perfect illustration from our own domestic library interiors of the wasteful society which we serve. Our

profession's unease is related to this fact, is it not? I
suggest that it is due simply to the fact that we are in an
environment which is working against our best intentions.

Victorian Standards No Longer Apply

Doesn't social and political literacy seem essential,
as at least an aid in seeing that one major dilemma, if
nothing else? Without it, pioneered and refined as a study
at Library School, not as an option but as a basic discipline,
we will be an illiterate profession, without a grammar or a
language to express ourselves within a community that is
dying to hear us speak. Such literacy can uncover unspoken
prejudice and fears shared by so many on each side of our
counters, and it will begin to replace the goody-goody Victorian idealism with something appropriate to a new age:
this is to be a literate librarian. Culture is society is a
condition of life and our contribution must come through
literacy, our nitrates for the soil. The standards of our
Victorian forebears no longer apply--we must dispose of
them. "Do we not sow for posterity?" crowed Edward
Edwards. God bless him, yes we do, but we must be reminded that his ideals are now out of date, they linger too
long with us. He and his fellows created a public library
with standards of miscellaneity which is a curse to us today.
It was the literacy of its day. But now those ethics, and
the laissez faire which consorts with them, are defunct in
practice, even if they persist as cloudy notions. If they do,
they are a barrier we must break through. Clouds can be
dense.

Two more quotations to conclude this sketch towards
a definition of literacy. The first is halfway nearer our
own time, and is the prevision of a lively mind, offered at
a time and place I leave you to contemplate as incredible.
It is a hint that we have arrived at a period of total commitment. It is Ortega Y Gasset addressing an International
Conference of Librarians in Madrid in--1936 (now whose
side are you on?):

"If our generation accumulates printed materials at
the rate of recent years, the culture which liberated man
from the jungle will thrust him anew into a jungle of books.
Not only are there too many books, but they continue to be
produced in torrential abundance. Provision is without plan,
abandoned almost wholly to chance." He went on to appeal

for the control of book production as a librarian's duty. He
anticipated the shock by adding "Don't be frightened. Collective organisation of book production has no more to do
with liberty than has the regulation of traffic in overcrowded
cities." If literate, you must have an attitude to this, you
must recognize it as an issue. You will know that the library turns in upon itself, serves a minority of "serious"
users and concentrates on book selection and other faded
mystiques to earn small gratifications within its closed cell,
when a completely open society needs it as never before,
and wants to thrust a limitless role upon it. But you must
be willing to want this role, and the social discomfort.

The next brace of quotations put the two ends of the
argument, and tie them up neatly:

"The public library cannot outdistance the intellectual
climate in which it finds itself" (A major conclusion of the
Public Library Inquiry, USA, 1948).

"To me the changes in time change everything. The
applications of the keepers of books in our time are positive
applications because they have no choice but to be positive."
(Archibald MacLeish, Librarian of Congress).

Whose conclusion is valid? Which consequence would
you like to bear? The professionally literate can deal with
them. The professionally illiterate doesn't even know they
are questions.

Chaos of Ideals

So, in sum I still feel, ten years after I first used
the term, that the notion of literacy is larger than the
technical use of the word, that to view our work in society
(it exists nowhere else) with proper detachment means surprising ourselves with what we are really involved in. The
recognition of that dilemma, expressed for us in terms of
buying for private gain what is being turned to public use,
is only the result of our inheritance, but the nature of that
legacy is vital to an understanding of this first point about
socio-political literacy. And it makes a perfect transistion
to the second part of the definition. If public libraries began last century just after the death of Chartism and the unsuccessful socialist revolutions on the Continent in 1848,
just before the legalised organisation of the first trade union,

while Matthew Arnold was formulating his ideas on reading which gave rise to the present critical orthodoxy, and while Ruskin was appealing for a humanised industrial society, then clearly our libraries were born in an atmosphere of cloudy idealism (Edwards and Ewart), mixed with vicious economic and class tyranny (the Statutes of the period). This paradox is our inheritance. Is it any wonder that we are still in need of a defined aim? We are its historical products; our history is that we come from a divided society of divided economic interests and therefore (an important "therefore") a divided culture. While we need a common culture--a sense of mutual identity--because we depend more than most nations on mutual co-operation, we in libraries can't help feeling that those influences which operate silently in a mass society organized for profit must make for the depression of standards. It is the chaos of ideals and the confusion and contradiction in practice which works against us. That is all of my case in pleading for more training in a professional literacy that is pervasive in helping us read the past and so the present.

But there is the more usual sense of the word, and for us as individuals whether at the counter, in the committee room, or at the seminar, there is an obligation to engage with and apply at work some form of personal seeing.

Literacy As Personal Discipline

Looking at libraries as places where ideas are embodied in books, and their significance for the men and women whose career lies within libraries means a more literal attention to what is our stock in trade.

A library is a repository of work done in all fields, and it not only reflects growth but actually creates growth through the uses made of it by minds actively employing its materials to construct more works, more evidence of the expansion of mind and of individual lives expressed and realised on behalf of the society which made it possible. The library thus keeps open access to individual minds and offers unique experience through a seemingly multiplicity of choices. Libraries are the centres from which future ideas emerge. It is not enough to start a career in them with the limp feeling that books are a good thing, but rather--and here is my own precise definition of literacy in the instrumental sense--that the essential collaborative act between humans

beyond our own circle is brought about by the frequenting of
imaginative literature. That in fact an interest in literature
is an interest in man and society. To expose oneself to the
grip of an imaginative work is to feel the impact of ordered
experience organised through language, the most human
idiom of all the methods of communication open to us. This
is not the place to take this very personal assertion to the
proof, an exercise which would need more time and patience
and exposition than readers of this piece would be willing to
afford. Without the attempted proof I am conscious that this
more acutely personal view must rest on an avowal, like a
credo, on a recognition that something has validity and from
which further consequences flow, but cannot be taken as
demonstrated. Here let me say that this kind of literacy,
if supported by and informed with social intelligence, will
help us towards that recovery of belief in the worth of our
profession because it is exclusively and firmly based on the
resulting conviction that libraries supply firstly <u>Experience</u>
(embodied in their book stock) and secondly <u>Evidence</u> (of the
state of the world): the criteria on which to rest judgment.
Only a felt and tested literary experience could furnish the
clue that in the two qualities just underlined lies the peculiar
contribution of the library in a culture. I cannot take this
point any further right now; I hope that the connection between the purely literary approach to (entry into) man and
society, and this concept of the library can be seen to be
intimately related.

Know the Context in Which We Work

Because I see it so, as much as I ever did, I see
the two properties contained within the definition as requisite
for the young librarian: awareness of his condition in the
scheme of things, and a controlling vision that can be
trained in various ways, the literary being most apt because
it is derived from our native language in which we talk,
think, feel, dream. To know the context in which we work
means that we will acquire instinctively those objectives,
goals, opportunities we find apparently so elusive. Together
with the personal values an identity of interest in the profession and with our readers could be created because we
know that our minds exist in fellowship each side of the
counter, despite that atmosphere of competing pressures,
commercial and financial expressed through so many blank,
impersonal agencies. A literate profession of this kind
would have a personality that is missing at present and

would be an antidote to much that collectively we feel we dislike but have no associate voice to condemn.

If we feel that we are unhappy visitors to that Pleasure Island of Auden's, that we are exposed uncomfortably there, that society is indifferent or even hostile to us, and that the real occupiers of that middle ground are the emasculators who are interested in nothing, then I can only repeat that I know of no other attribute which can render the Island properly habitable, by us and our fellows.

[The following articles are relevant to the above, which is based on a paper given at the A. A. L. Joint Weekend School in Aberystwyth on 18. 7. 71:

Who are our enemies? (Library World, 61 (709/711), July and August/September, 1959.)
The library: service or critique? (Library World, 63 (735), September 1961.)
Total commitment. (In Book provision for special needs: London and Home Counties Branch (L. A.) Weekend Conference papers, 1962.)
New styles of architecture. (LAR, 65 (1), January 1963.)
Face to face. (LAR, 68 (11), November 1966.)]

A LIBRARIAN'S FIRST LOYALTY*

W. G. K. Duncan

Many of you will remember the Draft Code of Ethics submitted for discussion to the various branches of our Association a couple of years ago. No one, in the South Australian branch at least, was very enthusiastic about it. The wording was far from satisfactory, and doubts were even expressed whether the Association needed to elaborate and adopt any such code. I shared those doubts, and this seems an appropriate occasion to say why--and to suggest, as an alternative, a statement of policy which the Association might both formulate and publicize.

Most of us agree that the prestige and standing of the profession of librarianship is not yet what it should be in the Australian community, but I, for one, doubt whether the adoption of a formal code of ethics would do much to improve our position--or our own conduct, for that matter. Whatever we do, we should be careful to refrain from pretentiousness--and pious humbug. Here is an example of what I mean. A code of ethics was adopted by the International Advertising Conference held at Wembley in 1924, and the first three resolutions of this code ran as follows: "We pledge ourselves: (1) to dedicate our efforts to the cause of better business and social service; (2) to seek the truth and to live it; (3) to tell the Advertising story simply, and without exaggeration and to avoid even a tendency to mislead." Speaking with the greatest restraint of which I am capable, I should say that this is plain humbug. The purpose of advertising is NOT to "seek the truth." It is to sell something, and the tendency to exaggerate is

---

*Originally the Presidential address, 11th Library Association of Australia conference, 1961; full paper published first in the Australian Library Journal, 10:4 (October 1961), 163-74. An edited version appeared in the July 1972 Australian Library Journal and is here reprinted by permission.

therefore inherent in its very nature and purpose. Perhaps
that is why advertisers claim so much in their code--they
just can't get out of the habit of exaggeration.

But the profession of lofty standards is not confined
to advertisers. Business men have been known to claim
that their concern is not to "make profits" so much as to
"give service." No doubt there is a measure of coincidence
(or overlap) between these two purposes, but to try to cloak
the motive of profit-making strikes me as a denial of the
very inspiration and rationale of a business undertaking in
a market economy such as ours.

In any code of ethics which librarians adopt they
will, I hope, be careful not to claim too much as their professional standards. On the other hand, unless they have
something distinctive to claim and to announce to the world,
they shouldn't bother with a code at all. Pious platitudes
won't impress anybody, and to say--as our draft did--that

> a member of the Association shall be honourable in
> his professional dealings with the public, [and that]
> patience, tact, self-control and courtesy are essential
> qualities in a librarian

is about as helpful as to say that librarians are expected to
be "decent chaps."

If there is to be an explicit code of ethics for a profession, it should derive from, and draw attention to, the
special obligations and responsibilities of the members. Do
librarians have any such special, and distinctive, obligations
and responsibilities? To whom? To the state, or to the
community at large (and there is an important distinction
between the two)? To majority opinion in the community or
to minority groups, or to neither of them as such? To
some special aspect or purpose, then, within community
affairs? And if, as I shall argue, to the last-mentioned,
how is this purpose affected by the type of community in
which they live--in particular, whether it is democratic or
authoritarian? Let us see whether we can discover anything
distinctive about the obligations and responsibilities of a
librarian (especially a public librarian) in a community
which claims to be democratic.

Libraries and Librarians 87

What Makes a Community Democratic?

What does a belief in democracy imply? I take it to mean more than a form of government--with universal franchise, say, and such representative institutions as a parliament, or congress. Communist and Fascist regimes have such forms. And more than "government by majority opinion," or "government by the consent of the people"--for dictators often muster well over ninety per cent of the votes at plebiscites. And more, even, than "government for the good of the people," for the Communists argue, with some plausibility, that our Western form of democracy is a "bourgeois sham,"--that it is more concerned with the rights of the propertied classes than with the interests and needs of the masses.

What makes a community (and derivatively, a government) democratic is, at bottom, the degree of respect it pays to the dignity and worth of the individual citizen, to his right to have a say in fashioning public policy, and to have a choice of political leaders. A genuine choice of leaders implies the right of organized opposition to the government--the right of freedom of speech, of publication, of public meeting. Democracy believes in the free play of minds, the open ventilation of grievances, the legitimacy of dissent. As Milton said, more than 300 years ago: "Give me liberty to know, to utter, and to argue freely according to conscience, above all liberties."

Does this sound to you a mere rhetorical commonplace? A great many people do, in fact, pay lip-service to freedom of speech without realizing what it implies, and treat it as a pious aspiration, fit for a code of ethics but not to be taken too seriously.

If, as Milton thought, the most important of all human rights is "liberty to know" (or freedom of information) and "to utter and argue freely" (freedom of speech and publication) how is it to be secured and protected? Protection it will need, it seems clear, not only from invasions by governments and executive authorities of all kinds (who are always tempted to stifle criticism and brush aside restraints) but from betrayal by the unthinking general public with a very imperfect grasp of political principle. It is for this reason that I propose to argue that a librarian's first loyalty, or prime responsibility, is neither to the state nor to sectional (or even majority) opinion within the community. It is rather, within a genuine democracy, to the principle of freedom to know and to communicate.

Freedom of Communication and the "Mass Media"

In the field of communications the modern world is in a curiously paradoxical situation. In one sense, communication is nowadays supremely easy, and almost instantaneous, from one end of the world to the other; but in a different sense, in the sense of effective ventilation and consideration of issues by all interested parties, communication is becoming increasingly difficult. The reasons for this are obvious enough. On the one hand, radio, TV and continuing improvements in the printing presses make it possible to cater for the enormously widened market, brought about by the spread of literacy, increasing leisure and a rising standard of living (enabling people to buy--or at least to hire-- their receiving sets). On the other hand, it is extremely expensive business these days to run a newspaper or a TV station, and there is a marked tendency towards the concentration of control of these media into fewer and fewer hands.

The economists have an appropriately ugly term for this dominance of a market by a few giants; they call it "oligopoly" (control of a market by a few, as against complete mono-poly, or control by one only). I say "appropriately" ugly, because its implications are ominous--for democrats, at least, who believe in the free play of ideas. Mass production by giant enterprises implies standardization and uniformity. This may be all right with motor cars and refrigerators, but in the realm of ideas uniformity means conformity, the insistence on a prevailing orthodoxy, and therefore the stifling of that clash and challenge which both Milton and J. S. Mill regarded as essential to progress.

The trouble in the modern world, with an oligopolistic control of the means of communication, is that Truth may not be allowed to enter the field, and never given a chance to show her strength in "a free and open encounter." Truth has a habit of being disturbing, to vested interests of all kinds--to habits of mind, and traditional beliefs, as well as to vested economic interests. Why should newspapers (who have to maintain their circulation in the millions, to "hold" their advertisers ... "disturb" their readers? or the advertisers themselves (who have to pay thousands of pounds

Libraries and Librarians 89

for every minute on TV)--why should they run the risk of antagonizing any section of their potential customers? And as for governmental authorities, are they likely--in the midst of a cold war and a world-wide revolution against colonialism--to encourage, or even allow, "all the winds of doctrine ... to play upon the earth?"

We should, of course, be careful not to exaggerate our difficulties. There are still significant differences, in this field of freedom of communication, between democratic and totalitarian regimes. But the trend is against us, if only for technological reasons. It is becoming increasingly difficult to maintain the free give-and-take of public discussion: you can't answer back to your radio or TV set; you may feel vaguely, that you are being manipulated, even seduced, by the "hidden persuaders," but how can you escape them, and think and judge for yourself? How can you get at the facts--when the very sources of your information are controlled, if not poisoned? This access to facts and information is felt by many people to be a basic human right, and efforts have been made in recent years to declare and protect it--with, I'm afraid, rather disappointing results.

Freedom of Information

Freedom of information was included in the Universal Declaration of Human Rights adopted by the General Assembly of the United Nations in 1948. Article 19 speaks of "the right to seek, receive and impart information and ideas through any media and regardless of frontiers."

Everyone agrees on the importance of "freedom of information"; the problem is how to define such a right in enforceable terms. In 1952 a United Kingdom delegate to one of the UN committees declared that "not only was freedom of information and the press a fundamental human right and the touchstone of all the freedoms contained in the United Nations Charter, but also that it was essential to the preservation of peace and the existence of democracy."

The Key Position of the Librarian

Well then, what can be done? Freedom of information may very well be "a fundamental human right," and "the touchstone of all our freedoms" as asserted by the United

Kingdom delegate, but when it comes to defining this right
in such a way as to make it enforceable, it has to be
limited and qualified in many ways. In trying to restrict
the press to "accurate and objective information" we may
run the risk of news being confined to innocuous "hand-outs"
from public relations officers. In trying to stop the mischief caused by a sensational and "irresponsible" press, we
mustn't make it responsible to the government of the day.
We expect the press to be the "watchdog of the public interest," but who is to define this "public" interest? It
certainly is not identical with the interests of those in
office--nor is it identical with the interests of the share-
holders and advertisers who control the press--and the
other mass media. How, under modern conditions, can the
unorganized "public" defend, or even discover, its own
interests? Everything is so BIG nowadays--the size and
sprawl of our cities, the size of our industrial and commercial undertakings, of government departments and of the
political parties themselves, the size of trade unions, of
the press, radio and TV, of commercialized sport and
entertainment--the size of everything tends to overwhelm
the individual, making him feel anonymous, impotent and
lost. How can we preserve in such a world any genuine
respect for the dignity and worth and significance of the
individual? But unless we do, democracy will become a
mere sham.

This--of course--is where the librarian comes in,
especially the public librarian. Public libraries are, I
believe, essential to meet both the needs of modern technology and to counteract some of its less fortunate, and
indeed dangerous consequences. A properly-stocked library
caters for, and fosters, a diversity of interests and tastes
and a genuine independence of mind. With a mind of his
own, and tastes and interests of his own, no individual need
feel lost or insignificant, and no government will remain
safe from his critical scrutiny and control.

But the libraries need to be "properly stocked." It
is the responsibility of the librarian to see that, to the limit
of his resources, his collection caters for a width of interests
and a diversity of opinions. He must foster the circulation
of whatever information is available within his community.
Just because of the oligopoly which now controls the mass
media, it is his supreme duty to keep the channels of communication open, and take his stand as the champion of what
Mr. Justice Holmes of the U.S. Supreme Court called "free
trade in ideas."

Libraries and Librarians

Attacks on Libraries Can Be Expected

Such a stand takes courage, for it means resistance to efforts by governments and all sorts of pressure groups to suppress material they deem worthless or dangerous. A librarian can take it for granted that sooner or later he will be attacked by some section of his community for including on his shelves books it deems treasonable, blasphemous or obscene.

In 1954 Professor Samuel A. Stouffer and his associates at Harvard University published a book called Communism, Conformity and Civil Liberties[1] which summarized the results of some 6,000 interviews with a cross-section of the American people, inquiring into their attitudes towards Communism. Twenty-seven per cent said they would not allow a Communist even to speak in their community if they had their way. When asked "Suppose he wrote a book which is in your public library. Someone in your community suggests it should be removed. Would you favour removing it or not?" Two-thirds said yes, they would, and ninety-one per cent said they would fire him if he were employed as a high school teacher. As you might expect, many of those interviewed made no distinction between Communism and Socialism. They were asked: "If a person wanted to make a speech in your community favouring government ownership of all railroads and big industries, should he be allowed to speak or not?" Only fifty-eight per cent said yes; thirty-five per cent would remove a book by such a man from the library; and the majority said that such a man should not be allowed to teach in a college or a university.

Attacks Made

With such illiberal attitudes widespread in a community, it is only a matter of time before its library gets into hot water. Attacks come in waves, as the community becomes stirred over some particular issue--political, religious or moral. But of one thing you can be certain-- that one wave will be followed by another; and that some selfappointed arbiters of taste will go on trying to limit and control other people's reading. Libraries in the United States, as would be expected, had a torrid time during the heyday of McCarthyism and in one year alone, 1953, the American Library Association reported over a hundred library controversies of greater or less intensity. Studies

are now being published of the effects of these attacks on
library service and book selection, and I should like to refer
to one of them (reviewed in the January 1961 issue of our
Journal)[2] called Book Selection and Censorship: A Study of
School and Public Libraries in California, by Marjorie
Fiske. [3]

Here, in California, pressure groups succeeded in
having all UNESCO publications withdrawn from the state's
school libraries (being accused of "indoctrination") and a
campaign by a housewife (who had drawn up a list of fifteen
"objectionable" books) led to attacks on school and public
libraries. Eventually a bill allowing complete censorship of
library materials was passed by the state legislature, but
was vetoed by the governor. One of the findings of this
study is somewhat reassuring: it shows that librarians who
stick to their principles and fight back, and enlist press
support, can successfully resist outside pressure. But
another of its findings is far from reassuring: it shows
librarians themselves to be weak and muddled on principles,
and that internal censorship is widespread. As Miss Fiske
says: "Librarians avoid the word censoring. They 'screen,'
'select' and 'guide.' As one of them in a large municipal
library put it, 'We haven't been censoring but we have been
conservative. After all, this is a conservative community,
and that is how parents here want it to be'."

Now, what is your reaction to such a statement?
Pity for the naive creature who made it, or 'alarm or
despondency' that such a person should be in charge of a
library? (Perish the thought that you should accept it,
as "in the nature of things"!) I regard it as tantamount to
treason--a clear betrayal of the principle of freedom of
communication, for which I expect a librarian to stand. In
this I believe I have the support of at least one professional
librarian--Mrs. Barbara Buick, who commented as follows
in her review of Miss Fiske's book:

> The results of the survey were revealing and shat-
> tering to the library profession, to our philosophy of
> librarianship and our responsibilities to our profes-
> sion and to readers. Restrictive practices were
> found to be widespread and deliberate. Although
> half the librarians interviewed expressed unequivocal
> 'freedom to read' principles, two-thirds actually
> practised some form of restriction. The most
> popular form of censorship was 'censorship at

source' or non-purchase of controversial material, but once bought 'reserve' or under-the-counter collections were the main means of limitation.

But though I have some support, I know I have formidable opponents within the profession, and now--greatly daring--I propose to cross swords with two of them, both well known to you. First of all, Mr. Ralph Munn, the director of the Carnegie Library at Pittsburgh (and of Munn-Pitt Report fame, here in Australia) and secondly with my own good friend--and the very father of this Association--Mr. John Metcalfe.

Should a Librarian Trim His Sails?

At the First Conference on Intellectual Freedom, sponsored by the American Library Association, held in Chicago, in 1954, Ralph Munn said quite explicitly that a librarian must be prepared to trim his sails to what he called "the prevailing wind of a locality." I must quote him at some length, for I wish to criticize his whole approach.

> As citizens and librarians, we should recognize that propaganda has become a vital weapon of warfare. Its purposes are to instil doubts, cause dissension and strife within a nation, and to undermine purpose and morale. This knowledge places certain positive obligations upon the librarian. Among these is that of trying to identify items of disguised propaganda and eliminating them from the library's general collection. Call it book selection or censorship as you will, I believe it to be our duty to try to discover and eliminate disguised propaganda from the general collection.... Some libraries, of course, may wish to form a special collection of these propaganda items, and study its technique....
> Regard must be paid to 'administrative feasibility--which will vary with the prevailing opinion of the locality.
> Too many discussions concerning the library and subversive literature have proceeded as though the library were a completely free agent, with full independence from its environment, and which owes no obligation to any government or public policy or to public opinion. A more realistic approach is to

recognize the basic fact that practically all public libraries are either an integral part of local government or a quasi-public institution which the lawyers call an instrumentality of government.[4]

In the discussion which followed Mr. Munn's paper, quite a number of pertinent criticisms were voiced, but Mr. Munn remained unshaken. One speaker said that:

> Keeping books which are objectionable in a special place, where the public may obtain them only on request, is a vile practice--for either a book is worth having or it is not suitable at all. We know from experience that to hide a book is to reduce its use; if, therefore, we have carefully selected a book in the first place, we see no reason why we should deliberately reduce its value to the community by restricting its reading in any way.

Mr. Munn was asked whether the propaganda that comes from our side of the Iron Curtain wouldn't have just as bad an effect on human minds. He replied that the library is "a government instrumentality," and that in having books advocating American institutions, in subtle or other fashion, "we are quite all right." He was also asked who was to determine what was "disguised propaganda," and how we were to distinguish between Communist propaganda and legitimate American criticism. And where a librarian is to draw the line between what is "administratively feasible" and what is not. All these points seem to me well taken, but I propose to concentrate on Mr. Munn's basic position that a public library is not "a completely free agent," but as a "government instrumentality" must rather adjust itself to "government or public policy, and to public opinion."

The Librarian's First Loyalty

In what sense is a public librarian a public servant? From a strictly legal point of view his library may well be a "government instrumentality," and his own position be governed directly by a public service act. Even when this is the case, should he accept uncritically the orders of the government of the day? Any orders? Even when they result in purging his shelves of what the government deems "dangerous" books? "Dangerous thoughts" and the "burning of books" are the preoccupation of dictatorial, not

democratic regimes. Our public servants are expected to
serve the best interests of the public as a whole, and on
occasion it is their duty to resist not only the pressure of
sectional groups, but even the policy of a government,
especially when it yields to the demands of a frightened,
or excited, public.

But you will say, how can a country be governed if
public servants are allowed to pick and choose among the
orders they receive? Shouldn't we remember Mr. Munn's
advice and be a little "realistic" in our discussions? Well,
what are some of the realities relevant to this issue? Take
the law courts. Are they not expected to resist the demands
of the community, perhaps an overwhelming majority of
them, for the summary punitive action known as "lynch
law"? This on the one hand, and on the other to resist
the arbitrary acts of government? Judges are expected to
insist on the law, as they understand it, being respected
by executive authorities as well as by ordinary people. To
strengthen their hand in resisting governments we have made
them irremovable (except by resolution of both Houses of
Parliament). With their security guaranteed in this way, a
tradition of integrity has been built up that influences the
mind and strenghtens the will of the bench, as a whole, and
prevents even newly-appointed judges from acting as mere
tools of the government. The independence of the judiciary
is, we feel, one of the basic features of a democracy.

A judge's first duty, then, is to the law, as it stands,
and not to the government of the day. The government's
will can, of course, be made to prevail in the long run, by
amendments to the law. Once this is done, the judges must
fall into line. But the point is that it is "a long run," and
can only be done if the government can retain popular support
over that period.

Take another case, where there is no such solution
available to the government but where resistance to its
policy may be equally legitimate--and indeed necessary for
the well-being of the community. I mean the academic
freedom claimed by the universities. It may seem anomalous
that institutions, supported in the main these days by public
money, should claim the right to be free from outside control,
and should allow their staff to voice opinions which
embarrass, and occasionally infuriate, the very government
that provides the money. Surely this is "biting the hand
that feeds them." It is, and it wouldn't be very difficult

to name one or two politicians who would like to stop it. And yet--remembering, I assure you that it may cost me my own scalp, I believe it would be harmful to the community, as well as ruinous to the universities, to stifle or surrender this academic freedom.

At bottom the problem is the same as with freedom of speech--a principle which, we have seen, is very imperfectly understood even by those who pay lip-service to it. How can people be brought to understand that they should, on this principle, be prepared to defend the right of people to go on saying, and printing, things which anger and distress them? Sidney Hook has made this point, in connection with universities, in these words:

> The university serves a community always 'in the making,' so to speak, and in which natural piety to the values and achievements of previous generations is joined to intelligent anticipation of the needs of generations to come--without in any way neglecting the legitimate concerns of the present. At a certain moment, the opinions and beliefs accepted in a university may be quite different from those entertained by a majority of the community. But this very majority must stand prepared to defend the right of the university to disagree with it, its right to be loyal to the community 'in the making,' provided such disagreement flows from its vocation of inquiry. [5]

Applying this approach to our field, I should say that a librarian is not only entitled, but is in duty bound, to disagree both from the government of the day and from a majority in the community whenever this disagreement "flows from his vocation." His vocation is to promote and foster the free flow of information and ideas throughout his community, and somehow or other he has to educate this community into an awareness that it is in their own best interests that he be given something of the independence and discretion of a judge or a university professor.

It is because I believe this that I am driven to differ from John Metcalfe--my own mentor in library matters. He argues that a librarian has no special duty to resist censorship, no special expertise in such matters, and in practice, "there is little he can do about it, because he is not one of the major forces for or against censorship." His duty is simply to circulate the materials that the prevailing ethic of his community deems "permissible," and if he tries to break through such taboos he may very well be "left out on a limb," because the majority of the people in the community favour censorship. [I gathered these points from his lecture notes which he very kindly lent me. My use of them confirms what I said a moment ago about the academic's habit of "biting the hand that feeds him."] Here is a passage from his presidential address at Adelaide in 1957:

> There have been professional pretentions that he [the librarian] has a right or duty to override prohibitions and censorships, in politics, in religion, in morals, in literature. In a public library in a liberal, free-thinking society he has his widest range ... but even in such a society there are taboos and laws which he must obey, or if he disobeys them, do so in his right and conscience, not as a mere librarian, but as a citizen and a human being. [6]

I am arguing the precise opposite of this--that no matter what a librarian thinks and feels as a private person, he should feel obliged, *qua* librarian, to resist the pressures in his community towards censorship. To be specific, I should regard it as obligatory on a Roman Catholic librarian to acquire and circulate many of the books which his own Church has publicly denounced and placed on the "Index"; even more distressing perhaps, obligatory on a rationalist librarian to circulate books on dogmatic theology, even though in his own opinion they serve merely to stunt and degrade the human intellect; and just as obligatory on a refugee from Hungary, say, who knows from personal experience what it is like to live under a Communist regime, to go on acquiring and circulating books which in Mr. Munn's opinion makes him "part of the Russian propaganda machine." Whatever the librarian feels as a private person, as a parent, or as a member of a Church, he is committed as a librarian within a democracy to an "open go" for ideas, opinions and beliefs. And, as we have seen, this obligation is the greater the more difficult it becomes, under modern conditions, to keep the channels of communication open, to give truth an opportunity to prevail in "a free and open encounter." Oligopoly among the mass media--freedom and independence then, for the public libraries.

Organizing His Defences

This is all very well, you may say--in theory. It is a very different matter when "the heat is on" in practice. Hasn't Mr. Metcalfe a much shrewder sense of reality when he speaks of a librarian being left "out on a limb" if he tries to break through the taboos of a community, known to favour censorship of what it dislikes and fears? Well, let us see what a librarian can do--in this real and imperfect world. Two things are obvious: one, he must not break the law as its stands--otherwise he will be punished and perhaps dismissed, and rightly so. But should he leave it at that, or should he try to get the law changed? Secondly, if the librarian takes a stand as an isolated individual, he is not likely to achieve very much. Should he reconcile himself, then, to Mr. Metcalfe's dictum: "there is little he can do about it, because he is not one of the major forces for or against censorship"? I propose to argue that, properly organized, librarians could become precisely that-- "one of the major forces against censorship" (not that they would always win, of course, but those who beat them would certainly know they'd been in a fight).

Let us first of all look at what has been achieved elsewhere. Under attack, the libraries in the U.S.A. and especially the library profession as a whole, has learnt how to fight back.

An Agenda For Us

I believe our Association should set about doing two things: first, the formulation and adoption, as official policy of the Association, of the basic principles for which the profession stands; and secondly, the welding of closer and closer links between our organization and other groups in the community who can be expected to share our concern for the preservation of these principles. A word about each.

How are these basic principles to be formulated? I started by expressing doubts and uneasiness about a formal code of ethics--in case it rang both false and empty. I doubt also, the wisdom of speaking of a bill of rights for librarians. That is an American idiom and tradition; we are cautious (perhaps too cautious) about defining our rights, and in any case, it is not the "rights" but the "responsibilities" of librarians that we wish to define--and insist on discharging. But I see no reason why we shouldn't draw up an official statement of policy. That's common enough, surely. But is it necessary? Why go to the trouble of elaborating the obvious?

Is it obvious? To whom? To the public who believe in freedom of speech, for certain types of people only? To municipal councils and other library authorities? (I could quote you figures, similar to those relating to the public, showing that even chairmen of library boards are only slightly less intolerant than the surrounding community.) Obvious even to librarians themselves? How clear about, or well grounded in, the principles of her profession is the average library assistant--shortly to be married, probably. Think of the turnover in your profession--how are the newcomers to be initiated? Wouldn't a statement help? Surely we can't count on all librarians, even senior ones, having the courage and intelligence of the librarian at Burwood who recently stood to her guns and carried her Council with her, praise be! And even when a librarian has no intention of yielding to pressure, isn't it handy (to say the very least of it) to be able to point to an official statement showing the complainant that it's not a personal matter--and that he's up against the whole organized profession?

But how frequent are such attacks, here in Australia, and do they add up to very much? My guess is that there is far more discreet evasion of controversy than open resistance to pressure--such as the case I heard of, in a Sydney suburb, where the librarian refrained from putting a copy of Koestler's Darkness at Noon on her shelves because it would upset Mrs. X--"who has been a good friend of this library." And if this is a time of quiescence on the censorship front, now is the time to secure agreement and endorsement of a statement of principles, American librarians have thanked their lucky stars that their Library Bill of Rights was written, discussed and adopted at a time when it was possible to distinguish between principle and expediency--that is, before the voice of reason had been drowned by the hysteria of McCarthyism.

[On the second point], if our Association began looking round for friends in its cause--the cause of free communication--wouldn't it be possible to link up with, and discuss common problems with--authors, publishers, booksellers, university and other teachers, Councils for Civil Liberties, bar councils, and the press--at least enlightened sections of the press. (And Californian experience showed that it is almost essential to have press backing when it comes to a fight). If these links grew at all firm, would it be true to say that the librarian can do little about censorship, but must accept passively, the judgment of noisy minorities within the community, or even the government of the day? My argument is that he could, if he bestirred himself, organize himself into a position of considerable strength--sufficient to daunt even governments; and secondly that he should do so, because it is his supreme obligation to keep open the channels of communication--that free play of ideas that it indispensable to a democracy.

Need I add that I do so fully aware of the danger of ideas. But no one should pretend to be a democrat unless he is prepared to live dangerously. That is the note struck in the closing paragraph of the American Library Association's Statement on "The Freedom to Read":

> We state these propositions neither lightly nor as easy generalizations. We here stake out lofty claim for the value of books. We do so because we believe that they are good, possessed of enormous variety and usefulness, worthy of cherishing and keeping free. We realize that the application of these propositions may mean the dissemination of ideas and manners of expression that are repugnant to many persons. We do not state these propositions in the comfortable belief that what people read is unimportant. We believe rather that what people read is deeply important; that ideas can be dangerous; but that the suppression of ideas is fatal to a democratic society. Freedom itself is a dangerous way of life, but it is ours. [7]

Notes

1. Stouffer, S. A. and others. Communism, Conformity and Civil Liberties. (Doubleday, 1954.)
2. Australian Library Journal 10 (1) : 38-9, January 1961.
3. Fiske, M. Book Selection and Censorship: A Study of School and Public Libraries in California. (University of California Press, 1959).
4. Munn, R. "The Large Public Library." In Freedom of Communication, edited by W. Dix and P. Bixler. (ALA, 1954) : 45-.

5. Hook, S. Heresy, Yes; Conspiracy, No. (Longman's, 1953) : 154-.
6. Metcalfe, J. "The Profession of Librarianship." Australian Library Journal 6 (4) : 160, October 1957.
7. McKeon, R. and others. The Freedom to Read; Perspective and Program. (Bowker, 1957.)

FROM REACTION TO INTERACTION: THE DEVELOPMENT OF THE NORTH-AMERICAN UNIVERSITY LIBRARY*

Samuel Rothstein

Let me begin my account of the inter-relationship between libraries and learning by a magnanimous concession: learning did come first. But I would hasten to add--only just. While there must be some recorded knowledge before there can be any agency for conserving and distributing it, it is difficult to conceive of that body of knowledge gaining any degree of mass or significance in the absence of, 1) a system to organize it and, 2) the willingness to make such knowledge broadly available.

The point may be illustrated by the scant development of libraries in most early civilizations. The ancient Babylonian society, for example, possessed an effective script; its clay tablets were a cheap and technologically satisfactory material for communication; its methodology for organizing records was by no means primitive. The Babylonians, it would appear, even established something like the first principle of librarianship. A recently discovered clay tablet, which goes back to some 3,000 B.C., turned out to be, of all things, a statement of library regulations. The inscription read: "This library is open one hour each fortnight. No book shall leave these premises. We have sworn it with an oath!"

By the way, the author of that inscription and thus perhaps the first librarian in recorded history is presumed to have been the king himself--Ashurbanipal. He may thus have been the only librarian ever to have been able to enforce his regulations--but King Ashurbanipal has also inspired the lugubrious observation by Philip Ennis that, since no succeeding librarian ever reached similar rank, our whole history is a downward spiral of social mobility.

---

*Reprinted by permission of the Canadian Library Association from <u>Canadian Library Journal</u> (March-April 1972).

I really do my profession an injustice in calling such a concept librarianship and such a collection of graphic materials a library. For accessibility and utilization were hardly the ruling principles in the mind of the Babylonian who wrote that inscription, and without them his collection was an archive rather than a library. In much the same way, the Egypt of the Pharaohs, while possessing in papyrus, script and slave labour a perfectly adequate instrument for the communication of knowledge, deliberately limited its accessibility to the priestly class.

The classical world was distinctly more "open," more concerned with spreading knowledge, and it is no coincidence that it produced some notable collections--the storied library at Alexandria with its 700,000 rolls, its great rival at Pergamum from which parchment takes its name, the 28 libraries of Rome which, in Pliny's memorable phrase, "first made men's talents public property."

But "public" in this context requires a good deal of qualification. Roman civilization was essentially aristocratic and authoritarian, and was hardly prepared to encourage free inquiry. By the same token, the basic impulse behind the establishment of the Roman libraries was more ornamental than educational, in much the same way that a latter-day tycoon might amass objets d'art for reasons of prestige. Thorstein Veblen could always have found ample material for his thesis in the history of libraries.

In all fairness, though, I should exempt at least one of the Roman founders of libraries from the charge of vulgar display. Gibbon tells us of the Emperor Gordianus II that "twenty-two acknowledged concubines and a library of sixty-two thousand volumes attested to the variety of his inclinations, and from the productions which he left behind him, it appears that the former as well as the latter were designed for use rather than ostentation."

Mind you, I do not want to seem to cast scorn on either the archival impulse or the wealthy collector's motivations as factors in the establishment of libraries. Together they have worked to retain for us the treasured books of the past. In point of bald fact, the less that these were actually used, in a very real sense the better for us who came to inherit them. Henry Clay Folger, the founder of the unrivalled Shakespeare library in Washington, D.C., did not even open many of the parcels of books which he purchased.

But I must say that the Four Shakespeare Folios, which my university received on permanent loan from the Folger Library, are in marvellous condition.

Still, one must concede that the motive of preservation, whether for reasons of piety, as in the case of the mediaeval monasteries, or for reasons of ego-enhancement, as in the case of the princely collectors during the Renaissance, constitutes a quite inadequate basis for the full development of libraries. Even more surprising--and this is a principal point of my argument--neither does the motive of education per se. Though one tends to suppose a necessary and inevitable correlation between education and libraries, history shows that the connection has actually been tenuous and occasional at even the highest level of instruction. Neither in the cathedral schools of the Middle Ages, nor in the early European universities, nor in Oxford and Cambridge much before the twentieth century, nor in universities outside the western world even now, have libraries flourished.

The point is best made by the example closest to home. In 1850, more than two hundred years after its establishment, the Harvard University Library had only 72,000 volumes. In the same year, Yale University, founded as far back as 1701, had only 21,000. The holdings of the other universities on this continent were negligible. Indeed, one can fairly say that all they had was what had drifted in through the back door--a ragtag and bobtail of gifts, mainly from defunct clergy.

Why such pitiful collections? It was not that books were particularly scarce. The invention of printing had long since made them plentiful and cheap, and some North American libraries were already of considerable size. In 1876, the Boston Public Library, founded only in 1852, easily exceeded in number of volumes the holdings of Brown, California, Cornell, Columbia, Michigan, Pennsylvania, Princeton and Toronto put together!

Nor was it that the university libraries have been worn down, so to speak, by heavy use. On the contrary, the North American university libraries were hardly used at all. In almost every instance, narrowly conceived and rigorously applied regulations made college book collections all but untouchable. Thus at Brown in 1843 no undergraduate could take a book off the shelves without the special permission of the librarian. At Amherst until 1852, the library was open only once a week for the withdrawal of books and provided no facilities at all for reading on the premises. At Columbia right up through the late 1850s, the library was available for the use of students on Mondays, Wednesdays and Fridays from half-past-one until three o'clock.

The classic example of such restrictive regulations is the oft-told story of John Langdon Sibley, librarian at Harvard. Sibley was encountered as he was hurrying across the campus, an expression of mingled determination and joy on his face. On being asked why he seemed so intent and pleased, Sibley replied that he had all but two of the library's books back on the shelves, he knew just who had those and he was about to render the security of his collection complete.

The story sounds too good to be true, but astonishingly enough it has been verified. However, the point of the tale has usually been misplaced. It is not, as it seems, the epitome of overzealous custodianship, of librarians' disregard for readers. The truth is that the Harvard University regulations of the period compelled the librarian annually to muster all books in their places for physical inspection by a Visiting Committee. Any losses or damages would have been cause for severe reprimand. Indeed, until fifty years before, the librarian of Harvard would have been required to make good any losses out of his own pocket.

The Sibley story, it seems then, loses its customary moral. But it gains two others. The first is that ultimately the university librarian does not determine his own function. He is a servant of the university and works within the context of goals and procedures and priorities imposed by the institution. He can persuade but not assert.

The second conclusion is that the North American university for most of its history, indeed nearly to the end of the nineteenth century, had precious little concern or regard for the state of its library, other than its preservation. Meagerly supported, ill-stocked, seldom open, its management relegated to part-time and untrained personnel, the university library was useless, in both senses of that word.

Both aspects may be summed up in a couple of quotations. A professor of the 1850s stated: "I conceive that the chief educational use of a university library is to lend an occasional book to a professor who does not happen to have the book in his own library." And here is a Yale university president of the 1860s in reply to his librarian, who had threatened to resign because he was paying his sole assistant out of his own salary and he himself had to stoke the stove that was the only source of heat for the entire building: "In regard to your leaving your place, my thoughts have shaped themselves thus: the [position of librarian] does not possess the importance which a man of active mind would naturally seek: and the college cannot now or hereafter give it greater prominence."

The librarian in question was Daniel Coit Gilman, who did resign and who went on to become the founding president of Johns Hopkins University. And of course the Yale University Library also eventually went on to somewhat bigger and better things.

What happened at Yale and other North American universities was that the institutions themselves were transformed by two major changes, which in turn transformed their libraries. The first was the idea--then the very novel idea--that students should be actively engaged in learning for themselves. The older curriculum had made do with lectures and textbooks and the library was, in the phrase of a university president, "an ... aside in education, to be almost entirely omitted without making a serious change in the sense." As William Poole recalled of his own undergraduate days, "Books, outside of the textbooks used, had no part in our education. They were never quoted, recommended, nor mentioned by the instructors in the classroom." The newer curriculum emphasized wide-ranging reading and so the library became, in the words of another university president, "the very heart of the institution."

Even more important was the change symbolized by Gilman himself. With Johns Hopkins in the vanguard, North American universities rapidly expanded their curricula to include scientific, technical and professional education, made graduate study a requirement for appointments to the faculty, and, most of all, gave research work a very high priority, higher perhaps than instruction itself. The North American college faculty of the mid-nineteenth century gave room only for teachers; the new university made a place for the scholar and made scholarship itself into a profession.

Now the basic condition of scholarship is that it is cumulative, building on what was known before. Inevitably, then, the scholars' necessity forced the growth, the wholesale growth of libraries. As Librarian Davis of the University of Michigan, perennially hardpressed by the demands of his faculty, put it almost pathetically: "My life is a struggle for books."

Davis' pathos turned out to be misplaced. He and other university librarians won that struggle, as evidenced by the fact that more than fifty North American university libraries now have holdings of over a million volumes. And in building up their collections, the librarians also brought in a brand new factor in scholarly library development--themselves.

Howard Winger has defined a librarian as someone who is self-conscious about his job. That is to say, he thinks of himself as primarily a librarian and of his work as a "self-sufficient career," calling for his first attention. Looked at in this way, librarianship must unfortunately give up its claim to such eighteenth century notables as Goethe, Leibniz and Casanova all of whom held positions in libraries. In fact, apart from such predecessors as Naudé, Dury and Ebert, librarianship can be said to have hardly begun until the nineteenth century expansion of libraries brought a need for purposeful thinking about them.

It was, then, the new element of growth--the problems of mass--that converted library work from an amateur or clerical occupation to one calling for specialized knowledge--a profession, if you will. Almost anyone can arrange a small collection serving only himself or a few readers. An aunt of mine arranges her books by colour and seems very happy with the choice. But a collection of many hundreds of thousands of volumes, serving a large and varied clientele, requires detailed and close classification. Similarly, mass creates the need for rules of entry regarding authors' names, and so cataloguing codes are born. A multiplicity of subjects necessitates subject heading lists and authority files. And so on and so forth--in short, growth calls for the development of a whole range of organizational skills (we now call them "technical services") which transforms an accumulation of books into a library.

Even more important, the professionalization of Librarianship brought a new spirit into library work--the

goal of service and the idea that librarians could make of
their work a significant factor in the educational experience.
And here the university librarians owe a greal debt, too
seldom acknowledged, to the public librarians who pioneered
in the professionalization of librarianship. From their colleagues in the burgeoning public library movement, university librarians imported the heady notions of "open access"
and reader services. Being new, public libraries were not
fettered by the restrictive custodial tradition which had been
imposed on the university library. On the contrary, faced
from the outset with the necessity of justifying the expenditure of city funds, public librarians had an incentive to look
for ways of promoting greater use and developing reader
services. Melvil Dewey, describing the Brooklyn Public
Library in 1885, proudly called it "the modern library idea":

> So came into prominence what we fondly term the
> 'modern library idea.' The old school librarian was
> a jailer who guarded his books, often from being
> read.... The modern librarian is active, not pas-
> sive. He is as glad to welcome a reader as the
> earnest merchant a customer.... He magnifies his
> office, and recognized in his profession an oppor-
> tunity for usefulness to his fellows inferior to none.

And then Dewey, who was at the time librarian of Columbia
University, significantly added: "We are trying to work out
the modern library idea in a university library."

The development of that "modern library idea" has
been a steady expansion in the scope and importance of the
librarian's participation in the university. The functional
design of library buildings, the speedy circulation service,
the multiplication of indexes and bibliographies, the efforts
to teach students bibliographical method and the use of books,
the promotion of reading by means of exhibits and lectures,
the latest of responsibilities--the selection of the libraries'
books and serials themselves; all these represent a substantial contribution by librarians to the educational enterprise. In some respects, indeed, librarians may fairly
claims to have led the way to learning rather than just
smoothed the path. I refer here to the fact that librarians
have actually done what other university people usually just
talk about--co-operate. Inter-library lending, shared cataloguing, even a nation-wide plan of co-operative acquisitons--
in these important respects librarians have made visible
progress toward the elusive goal of eliminating needless

Libraries and Librarians 109

duplication and rationalizing academic effort.

Perhaps the function that best epitomizes the librarian's determination to (I quote Dewey again) "maximize his usefulness to his fellows" is the library's reference service. A North American innovation and still infrequently offered in universities beyond this continent, reference service provides a truly remarkable assistance to student and faculty. Smile politely at one of York's reference staff and she will identify your quotation, verify a footnote a needed book in a library three thousand miles away, perhaps even prepare a bibliography or supply a translation.

I will admit that reference service is not without its hazards as Charles Ferguson once complained. "Never ask a librarian anything you don't really want to know," he advised, "[they] are a breed apart.... Long weeks after you have quite forgotten your casual request, here comes the information inexorably tracking you down."

As a former reference librarian, I apologize to our besieged scholars, but not much. We librarians may carry some of our virtues to excess but I submit that by the large we have done pretty well with the responsibilities that we have acquired. In North America, unlike most parts of the world, universities have come--rather slowly, to be sure-- to be willing to entrust their libraries to librarians. Where librarians once could only react to their universities and were thus part of the problem, they now interact with their universities and may thus be part of the solution. In a two-way flow of stimulus and response, productive energy accumulates on both sides.

Interestingly enough, the most recent and telling testimony comes from right here at York. Reviewing the University's first decade, President Murray Ross stated: "Perhaps the greatest single cause for satisfaction in the development of York has been the growth of our libraries.... I am convinced that the major direction of the library must remain in the hands of the professional librarians."

And so, I should like to close by taking due cognizance of the present occasion. Please remember that in building this fine library, you have completed nothing, but have merely added another wing to the endless mansion of learning. There must be many more to come. A report of the United States Senate once stated that "larger library expenditures can have a multiplying effect on the capacity and quality of higher education generally." Verily, I believe it, and I wish York and its Library many happy multiplications.

FUNCTIONS AND ORGANIZATION OF A RURAL LIBRARY SYSTEM*

F. A. Sharr

Library service of any quality in rural areas is a very new, indeed a revolutionary, concept: as revolutionary in its own way as computers or satellite communication, yet it is a concept which, by and large, has stirred little interest among librarians. This issue of the Unesco Bulletin for Libraries, devoted mostly to rural library service, is therefore very much to be welcomed.

The history of libraries extends over several thousand years and throughout that period they have been characteristically urban institutions, found in palaces, noblemen's houses, religious institutions, universities and major towns but seldom or never in country villages. It is only in the twentieth century, and particularly the second half of that century, that the need has been recognized for effective rural library service, that funds have become available to finance it and techniques have been developed to make it practically possible. Even today, all the most famous libraries of the world are to be found in major cities and the profession in general tends to regard rural library service as a rather unimportant poor relation--an attitude adopted by townspeople to country dwellers in other fields also.

Yet it is in the country that food must be grown, without which the cities would starve, and it is in the country that two-thirds of the world's population lives. Undernourishment is one of the major problems of the world today; the drift to the towns, another. We recognize that effective library and information services are essential for urban industry, for urban education and for the urban public in general, yet, while we lament the drift to the towns, the poverty of the villages and while we discuss at length the

---

*Reprinted by permission of Unesco from Unesco Bulletin for Libraries, 26:1 (January-February 1972).

problems of world food supply, we seem blind to the obvious inference that if library service of quality is important and necessary in the towns for technical information, for education, for cultural development and for social well-being generally it is equally or more important for the same reasons in the country where the great majority of the world's population live and work.

It is time to change these traditional attitudes, to recognize that rural library and information service represents one of the major professional challenges of today--at least as important as the challenge of the computer, and above all to recognize that the citizen who lives in the country is just as important as the one who lives in the city and deserves at least as much of our best professional thought and a fair proportion of our resources. To do less is to perpetuate the social inequalities of the past.

This is the nub of the matter. Throughout history, the wealthy, the powerful and the educated have been centred in the cities and particularly the capital cities. They may have drawn their wealth from country estates and have possessed country houses but the city was the centre of their interests. The country was inhabited by peasants--illeducated classes, or aspiring to be regarded as such, adopted the accepted attitudes towards the country dwellers, and in many cases still do so.

It is only of recent years, with the world-wide revulsion against inequality, that these traditional assumptions have been challenged. Education, health services, agricultural extension services, literacy campaigns, radio and other media have pushed out into the country. More important from the viewpoint of libraries--and largely as a result of these other influences--the expectations of country people, particularly the younger ones, are rising. They want better opportunities than their fathers had. This is the crucial change which makes the provision of rural library service worth while. No one is compelled to use a library. Only if people want to do so can a library function effectively. The ground is now ready for the seed, in many parts of the world.

Just as early European colonists or settlers found that their traditional methods were not the best in a different environment, so traditional methods of librarianship have to be challenged, modified and adapted in the new environment of

Libraries and Librarians

rural service. But essential professional standards should not be compromised, because country people are as important, as people, as city dwellers. This is the challenge of rural library work: to find means of bringing service of acceptable modern standard to areas into which no one has ever attempted to bring it before, where resources of trained personnel, of finance, of premises are lacking initially and, most important of all, where many of those in authority, however well-disposed they may be, have never seen a modern library and have little or no idea either of its potential or its cost.

It follows that there is no golden rule or standard practice for rural library development which may be recommended for general application. Each territory has its own particular problems deriving from its history, cultural tradition, geography and so on.

All that is possible is to suggest a few principles which are probably of a fairly widespread validity but which must be implemented differently in different areas and in a way appropriate to each one.

The purpose of rural library service is the same as that of urban service. It is in brief to improve the community which the library serves by: (a) making available to all who can benefit therefrom books and other sources of information, education and recreation (in that order of priority) which will tend to the personal development of the individual or the social development of the community; (b) providing staff trained (but not necessarily professionally qualified) to exploit its book-stock, to give information to users, and to assist them to make the best use of the library materials and resources; (c) housing the library in premises calculated to encourage its use and to reflect its values to the community.

The two characteristic forms of rural library are the school library and the public library, though there may well be other more specialized libraries as well, such as those of agricultural colleges. The role of the school library is normally to assist and enrich the educational programme of the school. The public library, on the other hand, has more diffuse aims, and therein lies a danger: than in an attempt to provide "all things to all men" it may lack clarity of purpose, of priorities and of policy, and as a result do nothing really effectively. There are plenty of urban libraries that

have fallen into this error, but the danger is greater in
rural areas because the libraries are smaller, the librarians
are likely to be less professionally aware, and because local
pressures are more immediate.

If the rural public library is to fulfil the purpose suggested above it must clearly identify one or more segments of the community upon which to concentrate its service and from which to secure support. Its methods must be geared to the satisfaction of those segments in particular. The appropriate segments may vary in different societies, but in general they should comprise those who want or can benefit from information (even if initially they do not recognize their need). This implies, in particular, the young, the better educated, the more alert and progressive members of the community, those in fact who will derive most benefit from the stimulation to be derived from books, information and new ideas and who will contribute most to the community as a result.

Rural communities are small and have limited finance. Small independent libraries face three difficulties which impede or prevent their giving effective modern service: (1) They lack the bibliographical and personnel resources to do good book selection; (2) Because of the small numbers of readers in a small community, the stock tends to be read out before it is worn out, and thus to remain unread on the shelves for long periods; (3) They cannot meet the needs of the readers whose interests are out of the ordinary, nor provide information on unusual subjects. In addition small independent libraries are wasteful both of money and of staff. They duplicate the cost of technical processes such as acquisition and cataloguing, which could be done better and more cheaply centrally. They absorb staff on these processes who would be more productive in assisting readers directly. Perhaps more significant, in book selection they tend to duplicate a narrow range of material and so restrict the over-all coverage available to readers, even if interlibrary lending arrangements exist.

Finance for adequate library service may in some parts of the world be absolutely lacking. In such cases it is probably better not to attempt to establish libraries until the situation has improved, because their inevitable inadequacy will prejudice future development, and also because in such a society there are unlikely to be sufficient people able and willing to use a library service.

In most parts of the world, on the other hand, the apparent lack of finance is relative not absolute. People who have never had the opportunity to see an efficient modern local library cannot be expected to imagine what it is like, to appreciate its full value, or to understand what it requires in finance, staff organization and accommodation. It is often found, in areas where libraries are not an accepted part of social provision, that public authorities believe that they cannot be afforded. Whether one can afford something or not depends to a great extent on how much one wants it. People who do not know public libraries cannot be expected to want them. One of the first tasks--to be faced uncompromisingly-- by a librarian concerned to establish libraries in rural areas, is to create a desire for them among the people and the authorities. When desire is aroused, funds are likely to follow.

In most countries of the world there is a shortage of librarians; in rural areas it is acute. The widely accepted view that there should be a qualified librarian in every library is impossible of attainment--even if it were a desirable aim. Its result, too often, has been that new libraries, needed by the public, have not been started because there was no librarian available; and because libraries were not started there were no jobs in which librarians could be employed and trained.

For all these reasons, it may be confidently asserted that rural library service, to be effective, must be organized on a network basis, so that each library does not stand alone, dependent on, and limited by, its own resources, but forms part of a system of libraries. In unity is strength.

In most countries the initiative for the development of rural library service has come not from the villages and small towns, but from some higher governmental level. This situation favours the development of networks or systems, because the initiative derives from the centre and it should be the responsibility of the centre to establish the network.

Such a network comprises a number of libraries, linked with each other, and with a strong headquarters organization. This link may be direct or through intermediate regional libraries or headquarters.

The functions of a headquarters might well be: (a) to plan the development of library service over the whole area

and to establish standards; (b) to provide professional
leadership towards the achievement of the plan; (c) to administer the allocation of central funds or resources to
various purposes and to individual libraries; (d) to provide
central services to local libraries; for example, book acquisitions, central cataloguing, interlibrary loan service;
(e) to provide training, know-how and encouragement for
local librarians; (f) to link its own system of libraries with
other systems or other types of library (university libraries,
special libraries, libraries in other countries, etc.) so that
the widest possible resources not only of books but of direct
information may be mobilized when required for the benefit
of a user of any library.

This does not imply that the local libraries would be
wholly financed and administered by the central authority.
They might be, or they might be mainly locally controlled.
What is important is the linkage with other libraries and the
ability to call on wider resources not as a matter of special
favour but as an acknowledged right.

Such a network or system involves, of course, some
abridgement of local freedom, in return for the wider resources offered. If local libraries grow up independently,
they are more likely to guard and cherish their unfettered
freedom--despite the limitation of service potential which it
inevitably involves--than if the central authority takes the
initiative from the outset. In an area where library service
is non-existent or minimal, the first step should be the establishment of the central authority and headquarters organization.

The advantages of such a system are that: (a) it
facilitates planning for effective and economical service and
in consequence is likely to attract greater financial support;
(b) it enriches the service at any one library by mobilizing
larger resources, thus affording greater satisfaction to library users which again tends to greater public support and
finance; (c) it may offer the well-known economics of central purchase, central cataloguing, etc. which, when explained to the financial authorities, are likely to impress
them favourably and thus to incline them to make more funds
available: (d) it can bring pressure to bear on local authorities for the establishment and maintenance of adequate
standards of provision, premises and service; (e) it utilizes
scarce resources of skilled manpower to the best advantage:
the work of a few professional librarians in headquarters

will permeate and benefit the whole area, whereas if they were employed in local libraries their skill would be of only local benefit; on the other hand, the existence of a strong and active headquarters can enable the necessary small rural libraries to give an acceptable level of service by the employment of unqualified local people, particularly if all books for the whole system are centrally processed; and (f) central processing in conjunction with a centrally organized mobile book-stock eliminate the need for both staff and space for these back-room functions in local libraries.

No library will be used if its stock is not relevant and appropriate to the needs and interests of its community, and this is particularly true of rural areas where a habit of reading and library use does not exist. Two matters arise: the segments of the population at which the library should aim and the problem of lack of publication in vernacular language. These are interrelated and both affect public libraries most.

An important function of a public library is to improve the economic level of its community by the provision not only of books, periodicals, etc., but also of commercial and technical information. In rural areas, and particularly those in the Third World, the most urgent economic problem is to improve the productivity of agriculture, yet in many countries the farmers are not yet ready to use books and other printed sources of information. What they need is verbal advice and encouragement. Again, a substantial proportion of the population may be illiterate or at least not sufficiently literate to enjoy and profit by reading normal library material. It is idle for the librarian to disregard these limitations on his service. What he should do is to identify those segments of the community to which the library can make an effective appeal and then aim the service specifically to their satisfaction. For example, when the writer was in Nigeria he formed the conclusion, which was endorsed by the government, that the public library should aim to serve those who had had at least seven years of primary education, leaving to another agency responsibility for meeting the needs of new literates and illiterates. Equally, referring back to the need for verbal advice to the farmer, the library's role would be to assist the advisers, but to recognize that for the time being it could not reach the farmers themselves--though it might reach their sons.

A difficult, indeed intractable, problem is the lack

of material in the languages spoken by villagers. The
languages are so numerous, the purchasing power of the
villagers so limited, and the means of distribution so weak
that commercial publication is almost impossible. The headquarters organization of a library system can help in two
ways. First, its greater resources and influence may enable
it to bring pressure to bear for the subsidized publication of
suitable material, while its distribution system can ensure
that what is published reaches readers. Second, all experience shows that the existence of effective libraries increases the amount of reading and the demand for publications. In theory, at least, these two factors should reinforce
each other. The hard fact must, however, be faced that
there is no point in trying to establish a public library service for village people unless a supply of material is available which they will not only want but also be able to read.

Many educated townspeople, including some librarians,
make the mistake of underrating both the intelligence and the
alertness of country people. In consequence they assume
that rural library service should accept very limited goals
and standards. Even in a country as progressive as the
United Kingdom, a government report in 1927 stated that the
principal aim of rural libraries was "to relieve the tedium
of idle hours quite irrespective of intellectual profit or educational gain." The writer, who has more than thirty years
experience of rural library work, would rebut this attitude
most emphatically. In any nation, the country people are
not very different, level for level, from townspeople. They
need the same standard of library service. Their interests
may be different: they may, for example, be more concerned with practical things than with speculation, and these
differences should be reflected in the stock and service of
their libraries, but this does not mean that they should be
offered an inferior level of service.

The major difference between city and country is that,
in the city, people of like interests are geographically con-
centrated and can easily reach a library. In the country,
on the other hand, they are scattered, one or two in this
area, a few more in another and so on. This offers the
library the dynamic role of finding means of bringing effective service to these isolated and scattered readers or
seekers after information. If they cannot come to the central library, it must find means of taking its service to them.
This is another reason why network development is essential
for effective rural service.

The preceding paragraph may have given the appearance of leading up to the need for mobile libraries. It was not intended to do so. Mobile libraries tend to attract attention because they are different or seem modern. They certainly have a place in librarianship, but they should not be used just as gadgets.

A mobile library may be efficient if three conditions are met: (1) That the population is static and expects its service to come to it; (2) That the vehicle spends more time as a library than it does being mobile; (3) That the roads and climate are such that schedules can be consistently maintained and that the vehicle will have a reasonable life. In many rural areas these conditions cannot be met.

For any given level of service a mobile library is likely to cost more to serve the same number of people than a number of static libraries. It should not be regarded as a less-expensive method of service than a well-organized system of static libraries. If, in fact, it costs less to run, it is probably giving an inferior service.

In most parts of the world, the social nucleus of the rural area is the village or small town, to which people naturally go for numerous purposes. By and large the people who will use a public library are, for other reasons, among the more mobile of the population. As a generalization it is probably true that static libraries in the local villages or towns, open at convenient hours and offering much more space than is practicable in a mobile library, afford better service than mobile libraries provided that they are organized in systems with a strong headquarters backing. In this connexion the practice adopted in small rural centres in Western Australia has much to commend it. Public libraries are not set up in separate buildings, but in a separate room designed for the purpose in the local authority's office building, entrance to which is under observation from the main office. Thus the library can be open throughout office hours, without the necessity for it to be staffed continuously if no one is using it. It is staffed by a trained member of the local authority's staff who has office duties in addition.

A public library should be more than a place where books may be borrowed or questions answered. It should also be, at least, a place to browse, and desirably should be a centre for the intellectual and cultural life of its community. These the mobile library can never be.

Rural librarianship is a new development, as special librarianship was some years ago. It calls for a new approach and new techniques, not merely for the reshuffling of old professional shibboleths. Above all it calls for central planning by librarians with a pioneering spirit and with open and alert minds, and who possess the intellectual skills to assess the needs and opportunities of the particular area concerned and to devise specific methods appropriate to that area. One of the greatest mistakes is to assume that the techniques and assumptions which are accepted in an urban environment elsewhere will be equally successful in a new rural situation. Each is different and each requires its own solution.

LIBRARY LIFE IN MIDDLE AMERICA*

Art Plotnik

Wahoo, we were free again! Free, and in a library, halfway across the country in Wahoo, Nebraska, pop. 3,800, watching Old Glory flap in a warm October breeze across the street, looking out through the Conestoga covered wagon etched on the glass door of the Wahoo Public, with a sweet Czech kolachi in our belly, and feeling good.

Freedom isn't absolute. One is free only <u>from</u> something. For us it was freedom from the East-Coast urban perspective of life so limiting to us New York library journalists. Even if--as almost happened after Wahoo--we had been jailed on the Winnebago Indian Reservation for taking pictures of a library van, we would have still found some solace in our altered perspective on American librarianship.

For it truly is another world, library life in Frontierland, as opposed to the perennial struggles of libraries in the Metropolitan corridors. Perhaps you have to be a city-bred Easterner to marvel at some of the distinctions. For one thing, it <u>looks</u> so different. You step out of the showcase school library of the Omaha area, and you're in a cornfield as endless and eternal as the lapis lazuli sky above. You visit a regional librarian at home, and your gaze travels from a bookcase filled with Bowker and Wilson imprints, out the window, to a 320-acre ranch surrounding the house like an ocean and some chestnut brown, limousine cattle far out in that golden autumn sea. You see the hand of Carnegie still in many little towns, a classical grey temple immutably fixed against the wide open spaces. Inside the libraries, your eyes soon find the ubiquitous stars and stripes--not on seat-patches or socks, belts and motorcycle helmets, but on--of all things!--the American flag. (The Nebraskans are

---

*Reprinted by permission from the May 1972 issue of <u>Wilson Library Bulletin</u>. Copyright 1972 by the H. W. Wilson Company.

not blind patriots by any means; but if you've got it, flaunt it--and they've got a beautiful chunk of America, right in the heart of the continent, with plenty of space for everyone, the way it used to be, the way they like it: lots of churches, clean air, strong families, decent cities, hardworking immigrants, thick steaks, cheap living, God-fearing librarians. Why not fly the colors?)

Something else looks and sounds different. Wherever you go, the spirit of a championship football team haunts you. Go Big Red! That slogan! Nebraskans eat, pray, and even read by it in the library. It refers, of course, to the University of Nebraska Cornhuskers, the Big Red, who, as we were almost getting arrested at Winnebago, were busy winning their 17th game in a row to keep them ranked number one among the nation's collegiate football teams. The State Library Commission has wisely created a bumper sticker in bright red and white that says:

Go Big--READ
a message from your Nebraska Library

But you don't see as many of these as you do the original Big Red slogan, which can always be observed within a book's throw of the libraries, on gas stations, banks, supermarkets, autos, sweatshirts, and marquees. And if you don't see the red slogan, you'll be sure to see another message: "We're Number One!"

Nebraskans and most Middle Americans have a real thing about that number-one business--a neurosis probably induced by years of football rankings and one that has perhaps caused more feelings of insecurity than anything else. There's only one number one at a time, after all. Last year, President Nixon used the term as a rationalization for further American deaths in Vietnam--to keep America number one; but Nebraskans have at least recognized the superficiality of victory on the field and are heard to ask one another questions such as, "What are those two other things we're number one in again?" Also, the slogan is employed to benefit such humanistic ends as library service. "Any time you say 'number one,'" a leading public librarian in Lincoln told us, "the people respond." Thus, when the University of Nebraska's Don L. Love Library ran a special Homecoming Day fund-raising campaign, it used the slogan, "Make Love (Library) Number One!"--and the students responded by giving up their traditional homecoming floats and donating to the library the money they would have spent on them.

Where Past Meets Present

Nebraska had its centennial of Statehood only five years ago, and its colorful past--woolly pioneer days, Indian life, Union Pacific trailblazing--is still prized everywhere. Two rummage sales on Saturday morning in Wahoo-- one in a church, the other in a meeting hall--found scores of townsfolk picking lovingly through the relics of territorial and early Statehood days: through another generation's junk, and this day's treasure.

But down the street, the public library held something just as important to them: the relics of man's intellectual and creative history, as recorded mainly in his books. In pioneer country, where nothing is taken for granted, schools and libraries, learning and learning resources, are cherished and maintained often at considerable sacrifice. For Nebraska has a few millionaires, but the rest of its wealth is spread out pretty thinly over its 77,000 square miles. In our own brief travels in Eastern Nebraska, we came across little red schoolhouses still standing monumentally, and towns with public library service 100 years old.

Nebraskans love their past, all right, but they are neither locked into it nor do they always fear the presence of modern ideas. Their best new libraries--thanks largely to Federal funds carefully spent--are as architecturally au courant as those anywhere; and as a result of those same funds, modern hardware for learning is accessible in most regions, and any book in the country can be requested through TWX centers and interlibrary loan. Most important, however, books representing a broad spectrum of political opinion and social mores were observed on open shelves in the local libraries. It is true that many Nebraska parents would just as soon blockade any East or West Coast imports threatening the status quo. But for the sake of their children, they usually don't. Too many talented and bright young Nebraskans--Karl Shapiro, Willa Cather, Wright Morris, and Dick Cavett, for example--go away or make good elsewhere. Now the idea is to build local pride without stifling freedom of expression. Make it a good place to come back to. One university librarian, known as a conservative to former colleagues in Washington, D. C., is considered a liberal back in his native Nebraska and enjoys the role without persecution. And, although Nebraskans will sometimes draw the line when acts like a gay librarian and his husband play the University lecture hall, book collections have been pretty much left alone. We talked to dozens of librarians from all areas and specialities, and not one felt that library censorship was a particular problem in Nebraska. Several, however, admitted that if ever a book's purchase became a cause célèbre--as had the showing of the skin flick The Stewardesses in Omaha--the latent forces of censorship could be devastating.

What are the major problems of Cornhusker librarians? Aside from the frequent lack of local money to support the kind of programs that the State and Federal agencies have seeded and would like to keep going, it's hard to say. One problem they do not seem to share with librarians of urban America is that of low morale. Into a State without a single library school, graduate librarians have come or returned with the conviction that there is good to be done through libraries and they can do it. The many small-library directors without degrees are equally committed and confident. It wasn't so long ago that Nebraskans, with nothing but windtorn grass around them, raised up trees and houses and farms, whole towns and cities. Why shouldn't a spirit of optimism prevail in all endeavors? As for the relevance of libraries--never does one hear the disparaging and despairing indictment: "Nothing but a lily-white, middle-class institution!" For what else would you have in a white, middle-class, Nebraskan town?

There are some exceptions, which are discussed later. But in general, the main problems have to do with the geographical remoteness and isolation of some libraries, the need to make modern services better known, and a great unevenness of facilities and resources from town to town. But these are wholesome problems. The most gruesome tribulation we heard, of those peculiar to Nebraska librarians, was one told to us by the head of reference for the State Library Commission: as she drove to work through the fields and farms surrounding Lincoln, a pheasant smashed neatly through her windshield and on to the front seat. Otherwise, most Nebraska librarians will tell you that library work is a pretty clean business. And a noble one.

One can imagine what must be an incredible shock

Libraries and Librarians

and confusion when some of these librarians attend their first ALA national conference and hear at the membership meetings the rhetoric of the street, of anarchy, of culpa, and despair. "Libraries are irrelevant to the Gay People! Libraries are fascist, establishment, rip-offs! Librarians are fat cats! Racist pigs! Tools! Off the Libraries! Burn them down!"

Of course, not even Nebraska is invulnerable to changing times, and its librarians had a chance to hear some fairly funky rhetoric right in their own back yard when Ernie Chambers, the only black Nebraska State Legislator, socked it to about seventy-five during the State library association conference (covered more fully below) that we attended in Omaha. Some of the librarians--not used to the zingers of guilt that Easterners have learned to parry lest they be bled dry--were, as they say, visibly shaken. But Mr. Chambers, born and educated in Nebraska, addressed himself to all librarians, not just those of his State or those in the room, who were there because they were forming a new institutional and social responsibilities section. Speaking extemporaneously--and very beautifully and forcefully--the young, angry, T-shirted legislator told all librarians:

> Each man's death diminishes us--but does a mental death diminish us at all, or is it only when the body ceases to live?.... Is it all right that a black student can be graduated from a black high school and not be able to read?.... You librarians, with the repositories of _all_ man's knowledge--why are _you_ not the force that electrifies society? You know the stereotype people have of you!.... I would die and go to hell ten times before I'd let anyone destroy my child.... You are spineless, anemic, too timid ... to be activists.... There hasn't been one ripple out of you....

It seemed an unfair generalization to one who had seen many a library ripple--a preoccupation with activism, East and West. But Chambers' image of librarians, after all, was formed in Nebraska; and the library group he addressed was, after all, the _first_ in the 73-year-old Nebraska LA with any expressed interest in social activism as it is understood today.

But does that mean that Nebraska's librarians are

afraid to get their hands dirty? Are they all square? Apathetic? Out of it? If raw social change has reached the Gateway to the West, who are the librarians that must deal with it? What are they like?

The Beautiful and the Beefy

Of course you can't generalize about people; but being human, we began to perceive Nebraska librarians as either the beautiful--those clear-eyed frontiersmen with their graceful, flared nostrils and farm-hardened limbs--and the "beefy," as one local librarian herself put it. You can go to beef fast in this country--mainly from eating too much of it because it's the best in the world--and a lot of folk do.

Nebraskan hair is kept short--the library women wear what looks like a freeze-dried bouffant--the spectacles are horn-rimmed, the skirts are long, the suits a size too large. Even the college and university librarians--those mavericks--don't break these rules very often. But within the costume, you might find any kind of player from reactionary to avant garde--although rarely a radical. Two grandmotherly librarians sat in the back of our car during one side trip from the conference. From appearances, you could never have told which was the "urban" school librarian and which the small-town public librarian; but when they started talking about library service to youngsters, they could not have been more different. The school librarian's rap was rich with images of discovery, of freedom, of self-determination for her students, of room and encouragement for them to spread their wings; the public librarian spoke of restrictions, of enforced silence, of guarding her books against the mischief of the town's youngsters. She got on the subject of crime and criminals; lock them up for good, she told us.

The public librarian was an "Out-Stater," which means anyone not from Omaha or Lincoln; but one could not attribute her attitudes to this characteristic any more than to her status as a rural public librarian. Reactionary and progressive spirits were found to inhabit every area of library life in Nebraska.

But we did find one characteristic shared by almost all the librarians we met--one that will play an important part in the future of library services in Middle America:

trust. Trust of one another, trust in human nature, trust in authority, and in the future--something long gone in the population centers of the nation.

We talked at length about this quality to someone who deals with thousands of area librarians in the course of his work: a "representative" of a large Midwestern library services firm. That's right--a salesman! No kidding, in Nebraska you talk to them as if they were human, as if they weren't out to get you in one way or another for a lousy buck. As if they were exhibitors of something potentially useful, not exhibitionists of the commercially obscene. Imagine? At the first general session of the conference, the full corps of exhibitors was paraded across the front of the room and praised to the sky, and each representative was introduced to the audience. Is that trust?

"Yes," said the rep we talked to. "Librarians know they're not going to get screwed by regional salesmen because they rarely do. So they trust us. And you can't hard-sell the people here. They'll back right off." Himself a native of a town of a thousand in Iowa, he admitted that it helps if one is from the local area. "But I'm afraid that even a slick operator from the East could make a killing here before they stopped trusting him.

"But you know," he mused, "it's *fun* to work with these people. It's almost a treat for them to get a service visit. They don't think of it as a sales call."

We encountered this trust everywhere in Nebraska life. Nobody locks anything. Cigar boxes with petty cash stand unattended on counters; you make your own change. Librarians were generally shy of our camera and notebook, but not one objected to being photographed or interviewed-- which happens to us elsewhere, to be sure. The only instance of mistrust was at the Winnebago Reservation, discussed later, but then, why should Indians anywhere trust Great White Library Journalist?

Trust is exactly what is necessary if Nebraska libraries are to overcome their remoteness and their isolation from resources for changing times. They need to cooperate. They need to hook into systems. In the metropolitan areas of the country, interlibrary cooperation may be more a game of librarians than a demand of users, which is why untrusting libraries have been able to refuse to cooperate or drop out of systems without a peep from their patrons, who may have more resources than they use already. But in Nebraska, where 229 of the State's 261 public libraries serve communities of less than 5,000, if your local library doesn't have it--where do you go? In the next decade, the State Library Commission hopes to coordinate the development of six multi-regional networks giving local service through union listings, centralized processing, cooperation between all types of libraries and other agencies, professional staffing at the centers, common borrowers' cards, and telephone and TWX requests. You don't bring about these developments without trust. Nebraska librarians have been trusting so far. But will it hold up?

First, they will have to trust their youthful new Nebraska Library Commissioner, Robert E. Kemper, who was brought from his library school teaching post at the University of Oregon to coordinate the new cooperative movement.

Kemper's doctoral work concerned cooperation between people, and, although he seems knowledgeable in human engineering, in behaviorism, he sounds a good deal more humanistic than most of that bunch. At Eugene, for instance, he taught cataloging as the cataloging of people, not documents--as helping one group of people find the people who have written information for them. He looks trustworthy--solid build, innocent Colorado-bred, Kansas-fed smile, an air about him that goes well with the open Nebraska landscape--and he works hard. But even if they accept his leadership, Nebraska librarians are not about to be herded as easily as the cattle some of them raise into anything they don't like.

"You can easily get cooperation involving machines-- TWX, computers, and so on," Kemper told us as we lit into some of that Nebraska beef in Omaha, "but to get people to cooperate with people--that's another story. You can find that suddenly old friends won't even say hello to each other."

We saw evidence of the theory here and there. For instance, one small library was suddenly told by its regional headquarters that no telephone or TWX requests were to be sent later than noon. Since the library didn't even open until that time, it was the end of system borrowing for the people of that community. A representative from the State Commission was looking into it.

Libraries and Librarians   129

But Nebraskans are human, after all, and there are always exceptions, always extremes. At a banquet table during the conference, we observed one native Nebraskan public librarian so untrusting of a State Commission librarian across from her that she would accept no opinion on any subject. "Are you from Nebraska?" she asked the State librarian during a discussion of Lincoln's medical facilities. "No? Well then that's the kind of attitude I'd expect from you." She discounted the importance of health services. "The sooner people realize that we're only on this earth for a short trial, the better off we'll be." It made one reluctant to contemplate her attitude toward library service.

Another extreme is found in those librarians who are so taken with the brightness of the future that they sometimes view the present with rose-colored glasses, a shield against the glare of their own optimism. When we dared to suggest to the librarians of a city system that they might be closing some old Carnegie branches faster than the local clientele wanted to switch to the spiffy new locations--why we were blitzed by a defense that would have challenged the Big Red! "This library is not about to abandon any part of this community!" we were told, so don't you give us any of that Library Journal kind of muckraking.

We didn't have time to check out the neighborhood people, but, whatever their feelings, it would have been very difficult for them to overcome the momentum of the system's rosy "progress."

The first three librarians we ran into during an unannounced visit to the Omaha Public Library displayed an interesting range of attitudes. "Is there any censorship in this library?" we asked. "No," said Number One. "No," said Number Two. But the third: "Yes." He admitted, however, that it wasn't so bad. The library has Do It! and Steal This Book, but not The Sensuous Man. Had the mayor of Omaha ever been in the library, there might have been more problems. But he's never stopped by.

"Are there black ghettos in Omaha?" we asked. "No," said One. "No," said Two. "Yes," said Number Three, who has lived in what he considers a ghetto in North Omaha for four years, first because it was cheap, but now because he has many friends there. Intelligent, idealistic, Bob Flood, the third librarian, represents good young blood for the Omaha Public. That he can work as a Librarian I with only a bachelor's degree is to the library's benefit. (He will need to go out of State for a master's in librarianship, which will make him eligible for promotions.) Like all libraries, Omaha can stand to have a little racial consciousness-raising imposed on them now and then. There are relatively so few blacks in Nebraska that the need for library materials and facilities to serve them is not always visible. But in spite of a 76-year-old main building that looks like something dredged up from a Venetian canal, the Omaha Public Library is moving reasonably well into modern times.

And so the variety of people working in Nebraskan libraries is considerable. Perhaps the best generalization one could make about them, even more than that they are trustful, is that they are in libraries out of love for the work. Because as Rose Zumpfe, librarian of the Crete Public, summed it up: "It is not a job at which one gets rich." And if low pay weren't proof enough of the librarians' enjoyment of the work, then one could consider the long hours of volunteer duty that many library workers throw in. The assistant head of the Lincoln Public Library puts in about fourteen hours daily and hasn't taken a work day off in three years. Half-time employees at the State Commission have a way of looking like full-time workers. Louise B. Shelledy, on a one-quarter-time line as executive secretary of the Nebraska Library Association, when cited for her full-time dedication, remarked: "I seen my duty and I done it." The malady is contagious: Richard Bailey, a partner in a Lincoln public relations firm, has become practically a full-time friend of Nebraska libraries--far in excess of what would be expected for the small jobs his firm does for them. These slim pickings have already been repaid by an estimated quarter-million dollars of free air time promoting libraries that young Bailey secured. But you can tell just from the quality of the work he does for them that he's no false friend--there is love in it.

NLA--The Living, Dead, and Unborn

"Civilization is a partnership between the living, the dead, and the yet to be born," said Frank Wardlaw, editor of the University of Texas Press. "Libraries are essential if this partnership is to exist." He was addressing an awards dinner at the 73rd Annual Nebraska Library

Libraries and Librarians 131

Convention, held Oct. 21-22 in Omaha. Have you ever been to a Nebraska library conference? Well, folks, it's pretty much like any other State conference, about equally divided between living dead, and yet-to-be-born ideas.

There's nothing dead or constrictive about Omaha itself, with its busy, mile-wide streets and mountainous buildings. Why, four-tone men's shoes were in the windows, female impersonators were in the San Moritz, and the Filthy Follies were headlining at the Cheetah Lounge. So a New Yorker felt right at home outside the plastic-posh Hilton. Inside the conference hotel, however, we ran smack into a historical Nebraska display and never, throughout the meetings, lost that Cornhusker's sense of place: Nebraska this, Nebraska that.

We chatted with a school librarian before the meetings began. Eunice Parrish of the Tecumseh Public School is head of the NLA's School, Children's and Young People Section, but that doesn't make her top anything in Nebraska; too many of the school librarians have organizational allegiance elsewhere, such as in the Nebraska Educational Media Association. But Mrs. Parrish chatted wisely about school libraries and her own community of 2,058. About half her school kids are from farms, but they are generally "liberated" from the limitations of agricultural interests. There is one black child--"in a foster situation"--and, reportedly, he's having a ball in the library. So is the librarian, a native Nebraskan, except when budget time rolls around--when funds for items like AV hardware are nowhere to be found. (A little later, we visited the "showplace" Millard School Library outside Omaha. "Where is your media center?" we asked one of the school's thousand teenagers when we arrived at the sleek new building. "I don't know," she said, "but the library's that-a-way." The library facility was posh, but there was neither the kind nor amount of materials on the shelves and tables necessary to create an appealing educational environment. Only two or three students were motivated to browse there after school hours.)

We found a few librarian mavericks strolling about before the conference meetings, but in this case they were only some shy members of the UNO (University of Nebraska at Omaha) community, where the football team is nicknamed the "Mavericks." Next to the Big Red of UNL, the Omaha gridders suffer inescapably from an inferiority complex--and probably more than that: "I've never seen a football player in the library," said one of UNO's shy librarians.

Shyness is another generalization one is tempted to make about Nebraska librarians. At the first general session, a score of them crowded uncomfortably at the door to watch the proceedings rather than occupy seats in nearby rows. But this sort of thing happens at most library conferences. At this session, San Francisco Librarian John Anderson addressed his topic of "Our Libraries, Today and Tomorrow, and Other Platitudes," and then added a few platitudes of his own (albeit, some worthy ones): "Get out on the street as missionaries." "We are lousy communicators." "Our main question is, 'Who is the user?'" He told how San Francisco had just spent $80,000 for market research on the user--and had found out that they needed to find out a lot more.

The Nebraskans blinked. The sum was half the total annual budget of their State Library Commission. No wonder Kemper (Commission director) at the Public Library Section meeting could speak authoritatively on accountability; a lot is expected of him for that sum. He emphasized that results are accomplished only through a whole chain of cooperating individuals, beginning with the patron. "The Congressman wants to know," he said, "what, after $15 million has been spent, are the library patrons doing now that they weren't doing before?" The Commission is now working on a five-year plan that must be completed by June 30 and which will define accountable goals to achieve with Federal and State funds.

The morning of the business meeting we talked to a University of Nebraska at Lincoln librarian whose hair was a little longer than his colleagues'. We called him the Token Radical, but he was simply a gentle and responsible young man with a social consciousness who was a little worried about the ability of Nebraska librarians to overcome complacency, hit-and-run paternalism, and other pitfalls as the library-activist movement seeped in from East and West. Even some young Nebraska librarians, we observed, are so nervous about power-to-the-people politics that the new social responsibilities round table formed at the conference eschewed any such nomenclature or association with ALA's SRRT. The thirty gathered together called themselves the Special and Institutional Libraries Section and talked only about services to the blind and physically handicapped and to prisoners. For these purposes, however, it was a good show of enthusiasm and a hopeful development.

If you grew up at ALA annual business meetings, you generally associate the term business with blistering bombast and even some talk of burning and bombing. There was nothing like that at NLA's business meeting, which was attended by about 200 of the association's record 732 membership. Some solid developments were reported, such as legislation being introduced for the Library Commission to become a depository for State documents and publisher of a checklist; a handbook in the works on intellectual freedom was returned to committee; and some "hot" announcements were made by President Kathlyn King Lundgren, at least one of them, like the Williams & Wilkins/NLM copyright suit, more than three years old.

We go to too many conferences, perhaps. After a while, all business meetings begin to sound to us like whisperings of the dead, a slavering drone of jargon and clichés babbled in self-torment by lost souls in limbo. (Into which circle would Dante place librarians whose monologues are as warmed-over cabbage?) But a refreshing rebirth, a rejuvenating burst of living spirit, came to us in the nick of time from a 90-year-old Nebraskan who was guest of honor at the NLA Awards Banquet: John J. Neihardt, beloved Nebraska Poet Laureate.

Mr. Neihardt was there to receive the association's first Mari Sandoz Award, and both writers instill such incredible pride in the hearts of Nebraskans that their names are usually spoken in a semi-swoon. When Neihardt appeared on the Dick Cavett show, which reaches Nebraska at 10:30 p.m. their time, he drew one of the biggest responses of all time from the national audience. One Nebraskan librarian told us, "It was the only time I ever stayed up late enough to watch Cavett."

The small, white-maned poet, lecturer, and scholar of Indian philosophy and religion recited--sang--some of his poems, and you could hear the sighs when he expressed his hope of dying as "a fiddle string/that hears the master's melody/and snaps."

Neihardt told the happy librarians that he would treasure the Sandoz award and keep it among those he is saving for old age.

And so, the dead revived by the living, we left the conference with a good feeling and headed toward a ceremony of "the yet unborn" downstate in Lincoln.

Dedicated Lincolnites at a Dedication

On Sunday, October 24, we attended the dedication of the beautiful new Victor E. Anderson Branch Library of the Lincoln Public Library; a week earlier, another new branch had been dedicated. Lincolnites had voted a total of $860,000, for the two libraries in a bond issue, and they showed up by the hundreds to see the ceremonial birth of each new child. The whole event was a marvelous symbol of modern Middle America. First of all, the libraries had been designed to replace two classic old Carnegie buildings, symbols of American public librarianship for as long as anyone can remember. All Carnegie buildings were given outright, of course, with the condition that the town provide land and a yearly operational budget equal to the cost of the structure. Lincoln PL Director Charles E. Dalrymple checked with the Carnegie Corporation people before he went ahead with his plans, and Carnegie decreed that, yes, the buildings had served their original function, go ahead and tear them down. And so two little temples of nostalgia will eventually give way to modernization and expansion, which is so very American. Not everyone in Lincoln is crazy about the idea, especially those living near the old branches. But dissent giving way to the will of the majority isn't so strange to Americans, either. The new buildings themselves, constructed with an open space concept with few interior walls and much window space, reflect the openness of the Heartlands very nicely. And at the Anderson branch dedication ceremony, Lincoln's Middle Americans heard the board president give 20 minutes of credits--flag by American Legion, etc.; the mayor came forth in chortling good humor; U.S. Representative Charles Thone grasped constituent arms and shoulders; and the citizens milled about in reverent delight over their newest possession, although not quite sure what to do at a library opening other than flip through dictionaries and atlases.

If there is a slight tone of cynicism here, it is only because the temper of the times makes it impossible to write reverently about USIS-style Americana. But Lincoln was a positive experience, all told. And if there is political power behind the growth of the city's libraries--well, hooray for us! Assistant City Librarian Dick Ostrander, dynamo and former New Jerseyite, wouldn't go back East for a million bucks. "There's just as much pressure here," he told us, "but there's more that you can get done. A lot of young library people are involved. It's less frustrating. You see results faster."

It sounded good, and for Lincoln, which has dough, it is very probably true. But before we returned to New York, we wanted a look around for ourselves, up and down the eastern edge of the State, to get a feeling about how others were getting things done.

A Lightning Library Trek Outstate

Everyone writes about the yellow-green cottonwood trees running along the streams through infinite Nebraska fields of grain. But seeing it, feeling its beauty, is probably the only way for a New Yorker to understand why Nebraska librarians brave the freezing winters, the chilling isolation, the cultural emptiness of Outstate just to enrich a few souls with the offerings of their modest libraries. The message of the cottonwoods is, perhaps, that what is most beautiful is not profusion, but a spare oasis that appears out of virtual emptiness; and intellectually, in some of the places we visited, the library is just that oasis.

In Wahoo, described earlier, the library has been around for 60 years. Its new building is warm, carpeted, inviting; bright new books and other materials, are displayed everywhere. Its collection supplements those of two school libraries and circulates at the rate of 150 to 200 items a day--well above the national per-capita average. New materials have already created a space problem, and yet they add to the oasis-like environment, the richness, available here for the small community.

At Crete, a town of 4,444 in the southeast of the State, the library is in an old brick Carnegie building, packed to the rafters with old and new materials, and again, is one of the oases in a town dominated by the most enormous grain elevators ever to loom over a small main street. Here, in this Czechoslovakian community where an old-country respect for learning has carried over, there are also substantial school library collections for children. But Librarian Rose Zumpfe has practically a free hand in choosing materials for the public library, and she does not hesitate to incorporate those that tell of an America very different from what was going on outside the day we visited: it was Veteran's Day, and there were so many flags flying, so many cub scouts running around, cannons going off, and patriots standing tall, it looked like a scene from Music Man. Protesters would have been decidedly unwelcome.

Mrs. Zumpfe had let us into the library, but it was not open to the public on this holiday.

"I started to open," she said, "but everyone thought it would be unpatriotic."

The skillful and self-taught librarian of Crete came from Czechoslovakia when she was ten, and has an easy and natural charm about her that has probably helped her to maintain control of her collection if not always the library hours.

"One man does come in twice a year to censor," she told us.

"What happens?"

"Nothing," she said modestly. Then she grinned, and allowed herself what is probably a very rare indulgence in pride.

The oases nurtured in the open spaces by the traveling regional librarians are even more dramatic. Last month's Wilson Library Bulletin featured an outreach program on Nebraska's Winnebago Indian Reservation, set up by a librarian responsible for a bi-State regional project and run by Winnebagos. The librarian, Marie Jones of the Sioux City (Iowa) Public Library, arranged with the tribal authorities on the reservation for a WLB visit, but some wires crossed, and we were unable to enter the church in which the library was housed. Even our look at the traveling library van parked outside was cut short. There are intra-tribal hostilities arising from differences between militants call Apples (red outside, white inside), and suspicions of strangers run high. As we were taking a few pictures and talking to the Winnebago library aides, a redneck trooper with two guns approached us and advised us: "Move out or you're goin' to jail." We glanced at a concrete outhouse across the street that was marked JAIL in crude letters, and we moved out smartly. Nothing in library school had prepared us to do otherwise.

But we were there long enough to perceive that the reservation is no Happy Hunting Ground. Outside the spare homes of the Indians and the spiritual institutions that sustain them, the reservation is a cluster of broken-down nothingness rising out of the bleak northeastern area. But now there is a library and library service. It is modest, it has not yet "sold" itself to the people. But for those who have discovered it, seen its Indian-related books and films, found a link to the past and to the world outside that they might never have expected--for these people, it must be something of an oasis. And unlike some other Federally funded services that have come and gone like mirages, the library is there, open some 36 hours a week, reaching out via the book van, and it will be there as long as a dedicated regional librarian like Marie Jones can do anything about it.

[At a later tribal meeting, the Winnebagos censured the party who had reported us to the redneck trooper.]

After we had seen a few more small and proud rural libraries, we visited another regional librarian, this time in her home near the Kansas border in southeast Nebraska.

The home happens to be that 320-acre cattle ranch we mentioned earlier in the story, and it was a perfect setting on which to wind up our interviews, richly symbolic of the open spaces, the hard work, and the good souls that make up library life in Cornhusker country.

You wouldn't find nicer folk than the owners of the Callaway farm if you had the librarian of the Census Bureau to help you start looking. Evelyn, a professional librarian trained in California and with children's work experience in the East, is now a regional librarian for the State Library Commission, helping the small libraries in the southeastern area to train staff, and solve technical problems or any problem that comes along. The library people are thrifty and self-reliant when they need to be, but not afraid to ask for help or to help one another.

Her husband, Cal, is a retired Navy pilot, who, when he decided to take up ranching in his native Nebraska, did it right and picked up a degree in agriculture. "But don't ask me how anyone can make a living at it," he laughed.

He hasn't yet broken even at "breeding grass and turning it into beef," as he calls it, but he is clearly not the sort to despair, any more than is his wife in her own line of work. The Callaways came to this ranch six years ago and put an enormous amount of energy into restoring an old farmhouse. Soon after it was finished, one of Nebraska's famous lightning storms descended upon them like an artillery shelling. A blockwide bolt of lightning reduced the house to ashes. Everything was lost--even their beloved and irreplaceable collection of nature and science books. There would be more such storms; no lightning rod or other device was big enough to protect them against it.

But they stayed. They built again, converting a trailer into a pleasant, permanent cottage, and from the windows of it they can still watch those block-wide bolts ripping up the terrain around them and casting an eerie light on the new book shelves.

But the openness of Middle America holds them. They have created their own oasis, and they have helped others sustain theirs.

Another Big Red

The Big Red from the University of Nebraska whipped their number-one rival a few weeks later and were off to the Orange Bowl. Football mania was likely to become even more maniacal. It will be months before Nebraskans can remember what those other two things were that they are Number One in. We never did find out ourselves, but we know that they are not quite Number One in library services. And yet, by God, you look at those empty spaces and think that they've actually got libraries out there with new books and with controversial titles, and you've got to hand it to them.

Another Big Red, the People's Republic of China, was admitted to the United Nations the evening we ended our visit and soared out of Omaha en route to New York. A lot of Cornhuskers aren't so big on that Commie Big Red; but they'll be able to learn just about anything related to it through their local libraries. And they are very big on that.

Part II

TECHNICAL SERVICES / READERS' SERVICES

WILLIAMS & WILKINS v. THE U. S. *

Ralph R. Shaw

[The case of Williams and Wilkins v. The United States** is of great importance to scholars, libraries and to the advancement of learning and of knowledge in the United States. It ranges far beyond the case as originally brought--involving not only the copyright law (hereinafter referred to as 17 USC Sections 1 et seq.) but introducing erroneous arguments by analogy from the patent law. It also questions the right of scholars to make notes or copies for their own study and private use, regardless of the means used, as well as the right of libraries to act as agent for the scholar in making single copies for his private use and at his specific request. It brings up questions of the alleged parlous state of medical publishing, and repeatedly brings up the alleged danger of government control, and many other topics.

[In citing 17 USC, the <u>Copyright Law of the United States of America</u>, the copy used is Bulletin 14 of the Copyright Office, The Library of Congress, revised to January 1, 1967.

[In citing court cases, will power was exerted to keep from citing all pertinent cases, since that would make this paper book length. Some federal courts have had much more experience than others in copyright cases, with the highest authority, of course, being the United States Supreme Court, followed by the Second Circuit Court of Appeals, The United States District Court for the Southern District of New York, and the Ninth Circuit Court of Appeals, and these were given

---

*Reprinted by permission of the American Library Association from <u>American Libraries</u>, February 1972.
**In the United States Court of Claims. No. 73-68, filed February 16, 1972. <u>The Williams & Wilkins Company v. The United States: Report of the Commissioner of the Court.</u>

Technical/Readers' Services   141

priority in citation when applicable.

[Reference numbers in the text which are enclosed in parentheses and are preceded by R are references to the Commissioner's Report (**see previous page). They are reproduced in the appendix, in the numerical order in which they appear in the Commissioner's Report, with citation of the page and lines of the report to which each one refers. -- Ralph R. Shaw.]

The case originally brought was much simpler and more specific than the Report of the Commissioner indicates, but it does involve both Common Law Literary Property and Statutory Copyright. As originally brought, "Plaintiff alleges that defendants ... National Institutes of Health (NIH) and the National Library of Medicine (NLM) have infringed plaintiff's copyrights in medical journals by making unauthorized photocopies of articles from such journals" (R2). "The four journals in suit are Medicine, Journal of Immunology, Gastroenterology, and Pharmacological Reviews (R4). Medicine is published by plaintiff for profit and for its own benefit. The other three journals are published in conjunction with specialty medical societies which, by contract, share the journal's profits with plaintiff" (R4). "... due to the esoteric nature of the journals' subject matter, the number of annual subscriptions is small ..." (R5). "The journals are published with notice of copyright in plaintiff's name. The notice appears at the front of the journal and sometimes at the beginning of each article. After publication of each journal issue ... and after compliance with the requisite statutory requirements, the Register of Copyrights issues to plaintiff certificates of copyright registration" (R6, R80).

In the words of the Commissioner, "This is a copyright infringement suit" (R1), (R1a), (R74). The plaintiff does not claim that either NIH or NLM has photocopied any whole issues of any of the four journals in suit. The specific alleged infringement (first filed in the Court of Claims on February 27, 1968, and amended on July 23, 1970) simply alleges infringement by reason of unauthorized copying of eight articles from five volumes of the four journals (R75) named above, which are identified in a table on page 33 of the report, and requests compensation therefor.

The case has been broadened in the testimony and in

the Commissioner's Report far beyond these bounds and includes quotations (R2a) from selected articles and textbooks on a wide range of subjects: cited the total copying done by NIH and NLM from many different volumes of thousands of journals (R8, R10), many of which may be in the public domain; argued that since medical journals are alleged to be of low circulation (R5) and little advertisement income is received, photocopying (in general) may cause them to lose subscriptions (with no evidence offered) so that some or all of them may have to go out of business; repeatedly raised the booger man that this would result in government takeover and control (all without evidence). On the other hand, the plaintiff itself asserts that photocopying is essential and that it does not want to interfere with it in any way--they just want to get paid for any photocopying from their journals.

There is much general material about NIH and NLM (R8, R9, R10).

On the basis of citing one part of Section 3 (R11) and Section 1 of 17 USC plus much material that is neither copyright statute nor its interpretation by the courts, the commissioner states, "I hold that defendant has infringed plaintiff's copyrights and that plaintiff is entitled to recover 'reasonable and entire compensation' ..." (R3).

The Seventh Circuit Court of Appeals, in the case of Taylor Instrument Co. v. Fawley Bros. Co. stated, in 1943 (139 F 2d 98, 59 USPQ 384), "Congress has legislated with reference to copyrights (Title 17 USC 1 et seq.) thereby furnishing protection to Inventors in their discoveries ... Thus it appears that Congress has provided two separate and distinct fields of protection, the copyright and the patent ... so it is plain that protection must be sought in one field or the other, it can not be found in both. In other words, there is no overlapping territory ..."

This is a case dealing with Statutory Copyright. As such, it is strictly a creature of the Copyright Law as expressed in Title 17 and as interpreted by the courts. The commissioner should have based his decision on Title 17 and the pertinent court decisions. Instead, he cites patent law cases and argues from these by false analogy (R15, R29, and R64) even though he himself says in R65, "This case, of course, is fundamentally different from patent license cases ..."

Technical/Readers' Services

The commissioner states, "<u>Despite</u> plaintiff's <u>prima facie</u> showing of infringement, the Government and its amici raise a host of arguments why the libraries should not be held liable for infringement" (R12). [Emphasis supplied.]

<u>Prima facie</u> evidence, according to Webster's Dictionary, means "Evidence sufficient in law to raise a presumption of fact or establish the fact in question unless rebutted." And of course <u>prima facie</u> evidence is no evidence at all if rebutted successfully, so despite the commissioner's "Despite ..." above, the defendants have every right to question the <u>prima facie</u> evidence, and to rebut it if they can prove it wrong.

The commissioner says, "Defendant conceded that ... NLM and the NIH library made at least one photocopy of each of eight articles (designated by plaintiff as the Count-I-to-Count VIII articles) from one or more of the four journals in suit. Defendant also concedes that plaintiff is the record owner of copyright registrations on the journals. That would appear to end the matter ..." In support of this, the commissioner cites Section 1 and the last sentence of Section 3 of Title 17 (omitting the first sentence of Section 3) (R11).

In reply to the defendant's claim that plaintiff is not the "proprietor" in the Count I-to-Count VIII articles ... and therefore does not have standing to bring this suit, the commissioner states: "As was noted earlier, defendant concedes that plaintiff is owner of record title of copyright registration on the journals in which the articles appear; and defendant also concedes that plaintiff is entitled to a presumption that it is the owner of the individual articles in the journals published by it" (R12a). And the commissioner cites 17 USC Sections 3 and 209, but must obviously be referring to the last sentence to Section 3.

"However, defendant says the presumption is rebutted by evidence that the authors of the articles did not make written assignment to plaintiff of their proprietary interest in the manuscripts from which the articles stemmed ..." (R13). From this, defendant urges that the authors did not assign to plaintiff ownership of their manuscripts, and at most, granted to plaintiff only a license to publish the articles ... and [cites cases to prove] the proposition that "absent an express assignment, the author (rather than the publisher) of a copyrightable work retains title to the work, even though it is published as part of a composite on which there is blanket copyright in the publisher's name" (R14).

The commissioner goes on to say that the cited cases are not apposite and cites the Dorr-Oliver case decided by the United States Court of Cliams, "which held that the owner of record title of a patent (and by analogy, a copyright registration) is the proper party to bring suit for infringement in this court ... and that equitable rights of ownership of strangers to the suit cannot be raised as defenses against the legal title holder" (R15). And the commissioner goes on to say, "As a matter of law, therefore, it would seem that defendant cannot assert the ownership defense since by doing so it seeks to raise equities of persons not parties to the suit" (R16).

The commissioner is unquestionably in error in arguing his alleged analogy here.

The federal courts, all the way to the Supreme Court, and for at least seventy years, have ruled almost universally that only the author or his assign (who may also be termed the "proprietor") may obtain copyright or may bring suit for copyright infringement. The copyright registration is simply prima facie evidence of what it states, and unless the plaintiff can prove that they are the proprietors of the articles and periodicals in suit, they can not have a legal copyright in the issues, or volumes, or in the articles. They would have invalid copyrights and would have no standing in court in bringing this suit, and the suit should be dismissed.

The commissioner states further (R17), "However, even if that issue can be raised, defendant cannot prevail on the merits. Authors of two of the articles in suit testified at the trial, and neither asserted an interest (legal or equitable) in their respective articles. It is reasonable to infer that testimony of the other authors would be the same." The commissioner does not include the evidence on this matter, on page 58 of the brief of the amicus curiae, of the principal author of Exhibit I (and the footnote on the same page) which says: "see to similar effect, the testimony of Dr. Starr (Transcript 713), co-author of Exhibit No. 8...."

Dr. McKusick testified that his paper, in suit, "was written to disseminate information concerning the particular ... area that I have been working in, and the findings and conclusions that I have arrived at as a result of the work ...." (Tr. 664) "... He agreed that it was correct to

Technical/Readers' Services 145

describe his interest, as an author, as a desire for dissemination of the article 'in whatever form'" (Tr. 670). He testified further that "Research without communication is useless" (Tr. 666), not only in terms of making one's own results available but in terms of "consulting the prior literature" (Tr. 666).

"In response to a question by the commission, Dr. McKusick testified that he had never had any conversation or writings with the plaintiff concerning copyright (Tr. 676). The "Instructions to Authors" in the issue of Medicine in which Dr. McKusick's article appeared made no reference to any 'assignment' of copyright to the publisher."

Unlike patents, there are two kinds of literary property in the United States. There is the Common Law Literary Property, which accrues to the author by the act of creating the "writing," and which continues until the "writing is published with the author's permission...." This is the right of first publication and it is subject to no time limit; it is ended only by a general publication of the "writing" by the author or his assign, who, on assignment, becomes the "proprietor."

Section 2 of 17 USC states, "Nothing in this title shall be construed to annul or limit the right of the author or proprietor of an unpublished work, at common law or in equity, to prevent the copying, publication, or use of such unpublished work without his consent, and to obtain damages therefor."

The author, as owner of the Common Law Literary Property, has several options. He may make limited or restricted publication in a number of ways, while refusing to permit general publication and there is no time limit to that right, or he may grant permission to make a general publication, in which case his Common Law Literary Property comes to an end and he must either meet the requirements for Statutory Copyright under Title 17 USC or his writing goes into the public domain. He may have the writing copyrighted in his own name and then may license others to use it, including his copyright notice on all copies. Or he may assign his total literary property in it upon publication, in which case the assign becomes the proprietor and has the same right as the author to publish without meeting the requirements of Title 17, (in which case it becomes public property) or he may, by meeting all the requirements (not

just the second half of one section) of Title 17 become the
owner of the statutory copyright granted by Title 17. In
Public Ledger v. N. Y. Times (275 F563, 1921) the Court
quotes the Supreme Court decision in the case of American
Tobacco v. Werckmeister (258 U.S. 627) which says, "Not
being an 'author,' the plaintiff concedes that he must be
'proprietor' of the literary property ... in order to secure
a valid copyright in the United States, and so of course the
statute requires"; the decision goes on to say that there
must be a full assignment of the literary property.

Judge Learned Hand, who was widely recognized as
one of our most outstanding authorities on copyright, said
in Société des Films Menchen v. Vitagraph Co. of America
et al (CCA2, April 10, 1918, (251 Fed. Rep. 258), " ...
the registration by Cromelin is, as pleaded, void for under
the act no power exists in an 'agent' to copyright, that
privilege is reserved to 'Authors or proprietors.' " And
in Swift v. Collegian Press (CCA2) 131 F2 902, 1942) the
Second Court of Appeals said, "It cannot be doubted that the
copyright owner who might elect to publish without any copyright notice and thereby forego whatever protection that would
give could also authorize the defendant so to publish."

There are two fundamental points that must be settled
before one can decide whether there has been infringement of
a copyright: (1) Is there a valid copyright in the magazine
as a whole, and is the plaintiff the proprietor of that valid
copyright? and (2) If the plaintiff is owner of a valid copyright in the journal and its issues as a whole, have the individual articles been assigned to him so that he has a valid
copyright in the copyrightable articles based on his copyright
in the journal, volume, or issues as a whole?

In reply to the first of these questions: there is
nothing to rebut the prima facie evidence that the plaintiff is
proprietor of the periodical Medicine which he publishes for
his own account. So far as the plaintiff's agreement with
the American Gastroenterological Society is concerned (R79),
there appears to be a clear and complete assignment to the
plaintiff by the society such as would make him proprietor of
the journal Gastroenterology, and the agreement supports the
prima facie evidence that the plaintiff could copyright this
journal under Title 17 and bring suit thereunder.

However, the agreement relating to copyright between
the American Society of Pharmacology and Experimental

Therapeutics and the plaintiff, dealing with <u>Pharmacological Reviews</u> (R77), clearly states "The Society is sole owner of the periodical, but for the sake of convenience, copyright shall be taken out in the name of the publisher...." It goes on to provide for reversion of the rights to the society under a number of circumstances. This is not a clear and total assignment of the literary property to the plaintiff, and since the society did not copyright the journal, there is no valid copyright. In fact, it is the opposite. The plaintiff, therefore, not being an author or a proprietor could not receive a valid copyright, and it appears that all volumes of <u>Pharmacological Reviews</u>, having been published with permission of the owner of the literary property and without valid copyright, are in the public domain. It has no protection under 17 USC, and all its volumes are free for use by anyone for any purpose, with the possible exception of articles reprinted from other sources, if any, which are validly copyrighted and which bear their own copyright notices.

The same must be said about the <u>Journal of Immunology</u> (R78), in which the agreement relating to copyright (R78) states, "The Association is the owner of the periodical but for the sake of convenience ... copyright shall be procured by and in the name of the Publisher ... The Association reserves the right to have the copyright assigned to the Association if at any time in the future this seems desirable." Thus, there has been no assignment, the plaintiff is not the proprietor, and there is no valid copyright.

Going now to the question of what is copyrightable in a copyrighted issue or volume of a journal, issue or volume, or composite work, it is essential that we bear in mind that in the construing of the Copyright Law (17 USC) all pertinent parts of the <u>title</u> must be applied and not just one section or a part of a section as the commissioner does here. He cites Section 3 (R11), and again is referring to the last sentence only.

Taking Section 10 of 17 USC as an example, in common parlance it is frequently said that all that is required to obtain copyright under Section 10 is "To publish with copyright notice required by this title." However, that is not true. The first sentence of Section 10 says "Any person entitled thereto by this title may secure copyright...." This means that the person must be entitled to copyright by the pertinent provisions in all of Title 17, including Section 16, the manufacturing clause, Section 9, in the case of foreign authors, etc., and not just by Section 10 or the excerpt from Section 10.

The whole of Section 3 of 17 USC reads, "Protection of Component Parts of Work Copyrighted; Composite Works or Periodicals. The copyright provided by this title shall protect all copyrightable component parts of the work copyrighted, and all matter therein in which copyright is already subsisting, but without extending the duration or scope of such copyright. The copyright upon composite works or periodicals shall give to the proprietor thereof all the rights in respect thereto which he would have if each part were individually copyrighted under this title."

Reading this last sentence alone cannot make sense since it does not even express the requirements of Section 3, let alone the other sections of Title 17, which must be met to obtain a valid copyright; for example, see Section 8 (dealing with material in the public domain) which states: "No copyright shall subsist in the original text of any work which is in the public domain, ... or in any publication of the United States Government, or any reprint, in whole or in part, thereof, except that the Postmaster General may secure copyright on behalf of the United States in the publications authorized by section 2506 of title 39." Nor does the commissioner's report supply evidence that the numerous articles by alien authors that appear in the plaintiff's journals meet the requirements set forth in (a), (b), or (c) of Section 9 of Title 17, etc.

There are many pertinent sections of Title 17 USC, rather than just the last sentence of Section 3, and there has been no showing that these have been met or have been set aside by this section. In fact, some have not been met and some notices in journal issues in this suit may represent false claim to copyright.

The Commissioner says (R6), "The Journals are published with notice of copyright in plaintiff's name and sometimes at the beginning of each article."

The "sometimes at the beginning of each article" did not explain when the plaintiff put the notice at the beginning of each article; and while, as pointed out above, Pharmacological Reviews and Immunology, based on the cases cited, are clearly in the public domain--so that the notice, wherever

Technical/Readers' Services   149

placed is erroneous--the volumes containing all of Count I
to Count VII have been examined in detail as to the copyright notice in the volume as a whole, in the individual issues and in the individual articles. Their instructions to
authors have been examined to determine whether anything
in the instructions to authors might be construed as a requirement that he assign the literary property. The volume
of Medicine containing Count VIII, Medicine, v. 38, was not
available and has not been examined, but so far as this case
is concerned, it could not make any material difference in
the clear points that are made by examining the volumes
and issues containing Count I-VII articles. Taking these in
order of the exhibit Count:

Count I appears in v. 44 of Medicine, which was
published in 1965. The copyright notice appears in the
proper form on the verso of the title page. There are no
copyright notices on any of the articles in v. 44, no. 1,
but starting with v. 44, no. 2, for March 1965, there is a
repetition of the publisher's copyright notice at the head of
every article throughout the rest of the volume. The advertisements bear no copyright notice. The only references
to copyright in the "Instructions to Authors" are: "Written
permission to cite someone else's unpublished observations
must be obtained from the observer by the author." Also,
"Permission to use illustrative material published previously
must be obtained from the copyright holder and from the
author." There is no reference to assignment of the manuscript to the publisher.

[Special note: the articles cited as government publications, which are in the public domain, include no articles
done through grants, nor do they include articles where
there is more than one author, one or more of whom are
not government employees. The matter of copyrightability
of grantees' papers is discussed very fully in the commissioner's report and that will be discussed separately.]

Articles by government employees in v. 44 of Medicine are on pp. 187-231, which is from the National Institute
of Arthritis ... of the NIH, and on pp. 233-48, which is
from the National Heart Institute, NIH.

Both of these were obviously done on official time as
part of the official duties of government employees and according to Section 8 of 17 USC, no copyright shall subsist
in any publication of the United States government. Each

of these articles bears the plaintiff's copyright notice despite the fact that they appear noncopyrightable, and thus may subject the plaintiff to the penalties in 17 USC Section 105.

Article Count II appears in v. 15, no. 2 of the Pharmacological Reviews, published in 1963.

The copyright notice appears in the name of the publisher on the verso of the title page and on the verso of the cover page of each issue. None of the articles bears a separate copyright notice. There are no "Instructions to Authors" in the issues of the bound volume examined, and no advertisements. There are no U.S. government articles in v. 15, but v. 16 which is bound with it has two articles from governmental agencies: one on pp. 179-91 from the National Institute of Mental Health, NIH, and the other on pp. 245-300, from the National Institute of Arthritis and Metabolic Diseases, NIH, neither of which is copyrightable (see 17 USC Section 8).

Counts III thru VI are all from the Journal of Immunology, v. 95, July to December 1965. Examination of this volume shows a copyright notice on the verso of the title page, dated 1966, which is the date of publication of the December 1965 issue only, the first five individual issues covering July-November each bears a notice on its front cover giving the date as 1965. Every article has the publisher's copyright notice repeated as a caption. There are no copyright notices on the advertisements. The "Information for Contributors" which appears in the front matter of each issue notes, "Authors will be charged $35 per page for all pages in excess of 6 per article." It makes no mention at all of copyright.

Articles that are governmentally produced, yet bear the publisher's copyright notice, appear as follows: (1) pp. 1-8, from the National Institute of Allergy and Infectious Diseases, NIH, (2) pp. 70-4, from the Division of Biologics Standards, NIH, (3) pp. 282-87, from National Heart Institute, NIH, (4) pp. 300-05, from National Institute of Allergy and Infectious Diseases, NIH, (5) pp. 368-77, from Oak Ridge National Laboratory, (6) pp. 442-45, from National Aeronautics and Space Administration, Ames Research Center, (7) pp. 559-66, from National Cancer Institute, NIH, (8) pp. 743-52, from Division of Biologics Standards, NIH, (9) pp. 781-90, from National Cancer Institute, NIH, (10) pp. 823-33, from National Cancer Institute, NIH, (11) pp. 1041-47, from Immunology Branch, IR, NCI, NIH, (12) pp. 1100-06, from Plum Island Animal Disease Laboratory, USDA, (13) pp. 1142-46, from Aerospace Medical

Division, and (14) pp. 1165-73, from U.S. Army Biological Laboratory, Ft. Dietrich.

Article Count VII appeared in Gastroenterology v. 32, no. 6, 1957. This volume bears no copyright notices on the title page or the verso of the title page of the volume. It does have a copyright notice on page iv of each issue, mixed in with the advertisements, on a page that serves as a title page for an issue, (sometimes in a previous volume). It has a copyright notice on the advertisement by Quaker Oats Co. on the verso of the cover of v. 32, no. 6, in the publisher's name, but the other advertisements carry no copyright notice. There is no copyright notice on any of the articles in the journal. Since the copyright notice does not appear in any of the locations, specified by Section 20 of 17 USC, which says, with regard to the location of the notice: "The notice of copyright shall be applied ... in a periodical either upon the title page or upon the first page of text of each separate number or under the title heading ... One notice of copyright in each number of a newspaper or periodical published shall suffice." The volume notice does not appear on the title page or its verso, but rather is interspersed with the advertising front matter, which is frequently removed in binding periodical volumes and is lacking in no's. 1 and 5. It is doubtful that the notices in the volume or in the issues for January through June 1957 meet the statutory requirements. On page xx of No. 6, at the back of the number and mixed in with advertisements (the general location is the same in the other numbers but varies in page number according to the number of advertising pages), there is a page bearing "Instructions to Authors." It includes a statement, "Exclusive publication--Articles are accepted for publication on condition that they are contributed solely to this Journal."

The sentence does not infer assignment of the copyright, which would be the sole basis of proprietorship. It merely requires that it not be submitted to other journals, which, lacking assignment from the author, simply puts it in the public domain.

Articles in this volume that are produced by the government are: (1) pp. 325-31, from 3700th U.S. Air Force Hospital, (2) pp. 528-33, from V.A. Medical Teaching Group Hospital, (3) pp. 704-07, from 3700th U.S. Air Force Hospital, (4) pp. 708-16, from Walter Reed Institute of Research, Walter Reed Hospital, (5) pp. 861-67, from Walter Reed Hospital, (6) pp. 887-94, from VA Hospital, Coral

Gables, Florida, (7) pp. 937-38, from U.S. Public Health Service Hospital, New Orleans, La., (8) pp. 943-51, from VA Hospital, The Bronx, N.Y., (9) pp. 1058-65, from National Heart Institute, NIH, (10) pp. 1113-21, VA Hospital, Philadelphia, Pa., and (11) pp. 1131-42, from National Institute of Allergy and Infectious Diseases, NIH.

Summarizing the findings based on the contracts of the plaintiff with the societies involved in the three journals which it published under contract with the societies; as well as the facts adduced from examining the volumes as a whole that contained the Count I-VII articles in the case, we find that the journal Medicine, as such, has a valid copyright since the plaintiff is proprietor of the journal, which he publishes for his own account. The copyright notice does not appear on the articles in no. 1 of this volume, but all articles starting with no. 2 of volume 44 (March 1965) bear the publisher's copyright notice, including two articles that were done in their line of duty, by employees of NIH, and which are undoubtedly in the public domain. This is made clear not only by 17 USC Section 8, but also in many court cases, including Eggers v. Sun Sales ((CCA 2) 263 F373, 1920) in which the Second Court of Appeals says, "Copyright in a pamphlet containing an official report does not copyright the official report it contains." Similarly, in Sawyer v. Crowell Publishing Co. (District Court, S.D. New York, April 30, 1942) (54 USPQ225 46 F. Suppl. 471), says "The copyrighted map and Map No. 8 were set up in the form of a government publication ... it is clear that Map No. 8 was a Department of Interior map ... and as such was not subject to copyright." Many more such cases could be cited. Altogether, more than two dozen uncopyrightable government reports were found in the four volumes cited in Counts I-VII of plaintiff's suit claiming violation of their copyrights in these journals, as enumerated above, and about fifteen of these articles carry the publisher's copyright notice. Medicine also carries advertisements which do not have their own copyright notices and are, therefore, in the public domain. (See Official Aviation Guide v. American Aviation, in which the Seventh Circuit Court of Appeals in 1945 (USPQ) 553) held that advertising copy supplied by advertisers is not covered by copyright in a journal). Thus, while the journal is copyrighted as such, it contains much that is not copyrightable, which is not copyrighted by the copyright in the journal or its issues and is in the public domain. The plaintiff has no right to collect a tariff for copying of anything in the public domain, nor would he appear to have any right to put

Technical/Readers' Services   153

his copyright notice on government articles (see 17 USC Section 8).

As noted above, Pharmacological Reviews and the Journal of Immunology are both published under contracts with societies which state specifically that the literary property in the journals is retained by the societies. Since the plaintiff is, thus, not the proprietor of these journals, his copyrights in all issues of these journals published under this contract appear clearly to be void, and since the societies which specifically retained the literary property in these journals did not copyright the journals, the journals, including all their issues and volumes and contents, have been dedicated to the public, and plaintiff has no legal standing in bringing this suit since they were published by authority of the proprietor without legally valid notice. Only an author or a proprietor of the literary property may copyright it or defend the copyright.

There are too many cases supporting the position that only the author or proprietor of the literary property is eligible to obtain copyright for all of them to be cited here, so only a few of the most important ones will be cited.

Two classic cases in the Supreme Court, neither of which has been negated by any change in law and both of which are still cited in related cases are Mifflin v. White (190US263, 47LE1035, 23SC803, 1903), which dealt with Oliver Wendell Holmes's Professor at the Breakfast Table, and Mifflin v. Dutton (190US266, 47LE1035, 23SC803, also in 1903), which dealt with The Minister's Wooing by Harriet Beecher Stowe. In both cases, parts of the books were published serially in Atlantic Monthly which was copyrighted in the name of Ticknor and Fields as proprietors of Atlantic Monthly. Before the serial publication was completed in Atlantic Monthly both Oliver Wendell Holmes and Harriet Beecher Stowe had their books published bearing their own copyright notices. Thereafter, they permitted Atlantic Monthly to print the rest of their books serially in issues bearing the copyright notice of the issue but no notice of the material copyrighted by the author in either case. The court held that the parts published by Atlantic Monthly by permission of the authors were not covered by the copyright in the magazine since the later publication with their own copyrights by both the authors showed that there had been no intent to transfer the literary property to Ticknor and Fields. These parts, thus having been published with

permission of the authors but without their own copyright
notice, went into the public domain. After their books were
published, both authors permitted the magazine to print the
remaining chapters without reproducing the author's copyright
on these chapters which were covered by Holmes's and
Stowe's copyrights, respectively. This subsequent publication, by permission of copyright owners, without reproduction
of the proper copyright notice on the articles, invalidated
the copyrights remaining valid until then on the remainder
of each book, and both of them were ruled to be completely
in the public domain.

In **Arthur Morse v. Sidney Fields and Hearst Corporation** (United States District Court, S.D. New York,
December 16, 1954, 127F Supp. 63, 104 USPQ 54) the
court said, "I shall first dispose of the defendants' contention as to the procedural irregularity of the copyright registration which I believe has merit ... **Collier's Magazine**
obtained a registered copyright in its name on September 25,
1950 for its September 30th issue, ... and assigned all its
right ... in plaintiff's article to the plaintiff on October 17,
1951. The nub of the defendant's claim is that plaintiff
never assigned all of his rights to Collier's before the latter
obtained copyright. The legal theory of this claim is clear
and correct: that only the 'proprietor' of a work may copyright it; that a person to whom the right to copyright is
assigned is a proprietor [cites Supreme Court case of
American Tobacco Co. v. Werckmeister] but a mere licensee
cannot copyright a work. [Cites two additional cases].
Moreover, a general copyright in an issue of a periodical
(a 'blanket copyright') does not protect the rights to a particular contributed article unless such rights have previously
been assigned to the publisher [cites case].

"I find here, however, that the plaintiff did assign
his right to copyright to Collier's before the latter obtained
its copyright ... This is unequivocally confirmed by the
memorandum attached to the check received by plaintiff on
November 28, 1949 ... Ultimately, Collier's formally assigned all rights in the copyright to the plaintiff."

And in the case of **Quinn-Brown Publishing Co. v.
Chilton Co., Inc.** (District Court, S.D. New York, March
1936) (15 Fed. Supp. 213) the court said, "The amended
bill fails to show how proprietorship of the article passed
from the author to the Wire Association and is defective on
this point. The motion to dismiss will be granted."

Technical/Readers' Services   155

In Mail and Express v. Life Pub. Co. ((CCA2) 192F899-900) the Second Circuit Court of Appeals said, "Stated more particularly, the claim seems to be that when a periodical contains articles or pictures made by persons who have not transferred their rights to the publisher the copyright of the periodical does not cover them.

"We have no reason to question the correctness of defendant's contention."

And finally, although many more cases could be cited to the same effect as the above, Judge Learned Hand in the case of Public Ledger v. New York Times et al. (District Court, S. D. New York, August 8, 1921) (275 Fed. Rep. 562; See also (Circuit Court of Appeals, Second Circuit, January 26, 1922) 279 Fed. Rep. 747. (Certiorari denied 258 U.S. 627) said,

"1. Not being an 'author' the plaintiff concedes it must be 'proprietor' of the literary property ... in order to secure a valid copyright in the United States, and so, of course the statute requires. The statute of 1909 does not define proprietor ... the words 'proprietor' and 'assign' were taken as synonymous in Mifflin v. White (190 US 260, 262, 23 Sup. Ct. 7659, 47 L. Ed. 1040.)

"Under American Tobacco Co. v. Werckmeister (207 US 284, 296. Sup. Ct. 72, 52 L. Ed. 208, 12 Am. Cas. 595) it was held that a licensee could not obtain copyright but there must be a full assignment of the literary property" [cites five additional cases].

These cases make it quite clear that:

1. The author does not automatically make assignment of his total literary property when he submits an article to a periodical. His rights in this regard are protected by 17 USC Section 2.

2. Lacking a written or other verifiable understanding about transfer of the total literary property, which would make the proprietor of the magazine a proprietor of the article, the intent of the author is ruling, and as in the Supreme Court cases of Mifflin v. White and Mifflin v. Dutton, it may be some time before the author makes his intent clear. After much of their books had appeared in Atlantic Monthly, these authors published the books as a

whole with their own copyrights. This clearly showed that they had had no intent to assign the literary property, and the net result was that the parts already published, having been published with permission of the authors but without assignment, were in the public domain; then the authors permitted Atlantic Monthly to publish the rest of the books, but since these did not show the author's copyright notice and Atlantic Monthly was not the proprietor, its notice did not protect them and they went into the public domain.

3. Publication of a "work" in a periodical with the author's permission, lacking evidence of assignment of the literary property to the proprietor of the magazine, puts the work in the public domain.

4. The burden of proof of his proprietorship rests on the party claiming assignment to him of the total literary property in the particular article.

Insofar as the journals in suit are concerned, the plaintiff has not received assignment in the literary property in Pharmacological Reviews or in the Journal of Immunology, both of which are not validly copyrighted by Williams and Wilkins, who are not the assigns or proprietors of the literary property and thus are not qualified to obtain copyright. Insofar as the journal Gastroenterology is concerned, while the plaintiff's contract clearly assigns the literary property and thus makes him eligible to copyright it, his copyright appears to be voided insofar as v. 32, including no. 6 of that volume, is concerned by his failure to meet the notice requirements of Section 20 of 17 USC.

In reaching his conclusion that the plaintiff is proprietor of the articles in copyrighted issues of his journals, the commissioner relies on the second sentence of Section 3 of 17 USC, on analogy with the patent case of Dorr-Oliver (R15), which has been discussed above, and on the fact that (R17) "Authors of two of the articles in suit testified at trial and neither asserted an interest (legal or equitable) in their respective articles. It is reasonable to infer that testimony of other authors would be the same, for the evidence supports the conclusion that by custom of long standing and absent any written or oral agreement to the contrary, authors who submit manuscripts to medical journals do so on the implied understanding that the publisher will obtain statutory copyright on the journal (and the individual articles therein) in the journal's name...." (R18).

Technical/Readers' Services   157

In the case of Quinn-Brown v. Chilton (15 FS 213, 1936) the court said, "... in pleading a case of infringement the plaintiff must show title, not merely by broad allegation of proprietorship, but by setting forth facts which indicate how he became proprietor ... a mere licensee has no right to take out copyright." [cites 4 cases].

But the commissioner also states "... that defendant cannot assert the ownership defense since by doing so, it seeks to raise equities of person not parties to the suit" (R16).

With regard to the last statement, the patent case cited does not apply to whether under copyright law and decisions Williams and Wilkins are proprietors and have the right to bring the suit. In copyright law and decisions all the way to the Supreme Court, it has been held overwhelmingly that only authors and proprietors may obtain copyright and bring suit to defend it, and this is, as stated earlier by the commissioner, a case under 17 USC, the copyright law.

So far as the two authors who are cited as having no interest (legal or equitable) in their suits, and the three cited by the Amicus Curaie (though there was probably some overlap in the two groups), that is not surprising and it does not constitute an assignment to any journal to enable the journal to monopolize the article through copyright. As stated in the cases cited above, the owner of the Common Law Literary Property has the right to dedicate it to the public or to authorize his publisher to dedicate it and he may dedicate it to the public simply by not putting the copyright notice on it. The statements of the authors are quite in keeping (and Dr. McKusick's statement, quoted from the brief of the Amici in particular is quite in keeping) with their desire to get maximum dissemination of the article, and they are not at all interested in limiting its distribution in any way. But one cannot infer that they have made an assignment of the literary property simply because they have authorized publication, and so the courts have ruled in the cases cited above, generally putting the burden of proof on the person claiming to be the proprietor.

So far as general practice is concerned, authors in scholarly fields are primarily concerned with dissemination of their findings to the public, which they have every right to do, and these statements are quite in keeping with a desire to dedicate. There is nothing in any of the journals cited that even raises the question of whether or not they are to assign the literary property to anyone. Moreover, this is not universal practice and two of the largest publishers in the medical and related fields--the American Medical Association and the American Chemical Society--have for decades required a written assignment of the literary property as a condition for publication in their journals.

If the plaintiff wanted to claim proprietorship in the literary property, he had an adequate precedent to follow in his own field simply by practicing the same policy as the American Medical Association and the American Chemical Society.

It is interesting to note that the commissioner cites a long-time practice (which was not universal and which was more likely to mean a desire to dedicate than to assign the literary property) in the case of the author's relations with publishers, but takes no notice of the three-score-years-and-ten-plus that libraries have been making single photocopies of articles for the use of individual scholars, as a precedent justifying that practice.

The commissioner's decision is based heavily on just the last sentence of Section 3 of 17 USC; therefore, it might be well to refer the reader back to the whole of Section 3 of 17 USC, which is reproduced earlier in this review on p. 148.

Note that the first part of Section 3 of 17 USC requires that <u>this title shall protect all copyrightable component parts</u> of the work copyrighted ... This means that there may be and frequently are noncopyrightable component parts--such as works in the public domain, government documents, works of foreign authors (of which the journals in this suit have a substantial number)--unless they meet the requirements of Section 9 of 17 USC, and other types of material. The second sentence does not copyright these and other material, such as advertisements supplied by the advertiser, etc.; it merely provides that a valid copyright in an issue or volume of a periodical <u>protects copyrightable component parts</u> as if such <u>part, copyrightable by the proprietor, were separately copyrighted</u>.

The question of whether authors get paid and

Technical/Readers' Services 159

publishers make money is not really germane to a copyright action (R23). 17 USC provides a monopoly for limited periods but it does not guarantee cash profits to authors or publishers. There are many factors that go into the profit-and-loss statement of a publisher, and except for trade publishers, map, sheet music and movie producers, and others who meet mass markets, copyright is probably the least important of them. Certainly so far as authors of articles in scholarly journals are concerned, immediate cash return is a negligible factor, at least in the United States where it is rare for a scholarly journal to pay the author. In fact, it is increasingly the other way, and page charges and excess page charges and other forms of subsidy to scholarly periodicals are increasingly common.

The commissioner's report states, "The record shows that over 95 percent of all published medical research appears in medical journal articles" (R20). This figure is probably reasonably accurate and it does not represent any increase since a study of the publication of research reports (unpublished) made by Dr. Merrill, then Chief of Publications, and the author of this article, at the Department of Agriculture some 25 years ago, showed that about 90 percent of the research reported by the U.S. Department of Agriculture was published in nongovernmental scholarly journals. However, the commissioner switches this statement (R24) to read

> In short, absent private publishers whose efforts provide for dissemination of 95 percent of the current medical literature, most of the findings of medical research would go unpublished and undisseminated; or at least the burdens of publishing and disseminating would fall upon other organizations, one of which would no doubt have to be the government.

This switch in the statement is erroneous and misleading.

No evidence has been presented as to the percentage of the medical literature that appears in private journals as against the amount in membership society journals and the switch in the statement is without foundation, since a very large part of this 95 percent appears in noncommercial journals. Yet the switched statement is used by the commissioner, in a footnote from the UCLA project, to raise fear of government domination of the medical press. Since the plaintiff averaged pretax profits of over $500,000 per year in 1968-1970, there appears to be no danger of this in their case (R99).

Having served a term on the Science Information Council of the National Science Foundation, the author can attest that its Office of Science Information Service has for years made many substantial grants to scholarly societies in its fields, particularly to strengthen and update their journals. Not once did any question of government interference in any of their editorial policies or programs arise.

The commissioner then reviews the defendant's claim that the plaintiff is not the real party in interest--(R25), (R26), (R27) and (R28) (see earlier discussion under R12-R15)--and again cites the Dorr-Oliver case (R29), a patent case tried under patent law and fallaciously argued, by analogy, to this copyright case.

There can be little doubt that only an author or a proprietor can secure a valid copyright or defend it before the courts and the contracts between the parties involved do not control the copyright law 17 USC. Under 17 USC, the plaintiff is undoubtedly not qualified to bring a copyright suit in the case of the two journals of which he is not the proprietor, and there is doubt about the validity of the copyright in the third society journal in suit, because its notice does not meet any of the three placements required in Section 20 of 17 USC. The only one of the journals about which there is no question of the plaintiff's status as proprietor or of the adequacy of the copyright notice is Medicine, which the plaintiff publishes for his own account (R29), but it contains uncopyrightable government articles upon which plaintiff has placed his copyright notice.

In (R30) through (R38), the Commissioner attempts to interpret the words in Section 1 of 17 USC, which define the exclusive rights of copyright proprietor. The words in Section 1, "print, reprint, publish, copy and vend," have, in several court decisions, been held, in sum, to mean "to publish," i.e., to make a general publication. Certainly the work "vend" does not apply to selling the book once legally obtained by the purchaser and is not reserved to the copyright proprietor, and there is nothing in USC 17 that prohibits private uses. In fact, general publication (i.e., offering or exposing it to a general public) is prerequisite to copyright and no cases have been found in which the suit did not involve an alleged general publication; that is what

Technical/Readers' Services

17 USC and statutory copyright is all about!

The method of reproducing the copies for general public use is irrelevant, and the courts have held in several cases that the word "print" encompases mimeographing and even typing of copies.

The commissioner's citation of the Fortnightly Corp. case, in the Supreme Court in 1968, (R31) deals with cable television, which is certainly a general public use or general publication.

The basic difference is public use versus private use for personal study, and the method of reproduction of single copies for this purpose is not significant. In the case of copying a map or sheet music, for a public use, even one copy (and it would generally be the whole publication) if used to violate the author's rights to public uses would undoubtedly be ruled a violation; the method by which it is copied is not determinant of whether or not it is a violation.

Under (R34) the commissioner says, "NLM and the NIH library did not merely 'copy' the articles in suit; they, in effect 'reprinted' and 'published' them. 'Printing' and 'reprinting' connote making a duplicate original, whether by printing press or a more modern method of duplication ... 'Publishing' means dissemination to others, which defendant's libraries clearly did when they distributed photocopies to requesters and users ... The defendant's contention that its libraries make only 'single copies' of journal articles is illusory and unrealistic. Admittedly, the libraries, as a general rule make only one copy per request, for different users ..." and the Commissioner goes on to say (R35) "In short, the libraries operate comprehensive duplication systems which provide every year thousands of photocopies of articles ... and, in essence, the systems are a reprint service which supplants the need for journal subscriptions. The effects of this so-called 'single copy' practice on plaintiff's legitimate interests as copyright owners are obvious." "The Sophar and Heilprin report, at 16, puts it in terms of a colorful analogy (R36): 'Babies are still born one at a time but the world is rapidly being overpopulated'."

As stated in the commissioner's report (R87), "Authors whose articles are published by plaintiff usually purchase from plaintiff reprints of their articles (on the average, about 300) for distribution to interested colleagues."

Examination of the four titles under suit indicates that none of them prints the copyright notice on each article before March 1965, and all of them starting with March, 1965 have the publisher's copyright notice at the heading of the article. Examination of a few reprints available for articles published by the plaintiff in these journals after March 1965 shows that they are reprinted with the notice just as they are in the journal. No reprints of articles published by the plaintiff's journals prior to 1965 were available, but some of these should be examined to determine whether the copyright notice was added. This is rarely the case and if the plaintiff reprinted the articles prior to 1965 without the notice, that, according to 17 USC Section 10, would invalidate the copyright even if there were a valid copyright in the first instance.

Also, it is very difficult to see that the total of (perhaps) fifty photocopies out of all the articles in the five volumes in this suit can have any substantial effect on possible subscriptions in view of the fact that the plaintiff attests that he has on the average, and over the last ten years, supplied 300 copies of every article in the journals for free distribution by the authors.

Now, taking up these arguments in (R30) through (R36) above; there are two kinds of publication, not one. There is limited publication, also termed restricted publication, which does not entitle the author to obtain copyright and does not lose his Common Law Literary Property, and then there is general publication, which involved exposure or sale, with the author's permission, of the "writing" to the general public, i.e., to a public not selected by the author for his own private uses. Copyright cannot be obtained without general publication and the Common Law Literary Property is not lost by any but general publication with the author's permission. The word "publish" so far as copyright cases are concerned has always dealt with the making available of the work to a general public, and it has not in any case dealt with the private use of copyrighted publications legally obtained from the copyright owner or from one who has legally obtained it from him.

The commissioner's statement that NLM and NIH, in effect, printed and published them is nonsense, regardless of the method of reproduction used. In National Institute Inc. for the Improvement of Memory v. Nutt et al (District Court, D. Connecticut, August 13, 1928, 28 Fed (2d) 132)

Technical/Readers' Services   163

(affirmed) 31 Fed 2d 236 by the Second Circuit Court of Appeals), the Court states "Publication of a subject of copyright is effected by its communication or dedication to the public. Such a publication is known as a 'general publication'." And the court goes on to say, "... In the case of Nichols v. Pitman (L. R. Ch. Div. 374) ... even where hearers were allowed to make copies for their own use, such license was limited to such individuals for the purpose of their own information, and they could not publish for profit that which they had not obtained the right of 'selling'." [Emphasis supplied.]

In R35 the commissioner says that the libraries operate comprehensive duplication systems which provide every year thousands of photocopies of articles ... and in essence these systems "are a reprint service which supplants the need of journal subscriptions."

The use of the term "reprint service" applied to editions of one copy is incomprehensible. No one can do reprinting in editions of one and stay solvent. And there are no facts to justify this statement. The commissioner's statement goes far beyond the number of pages of the articles in suit that were photocopied. Using a low estimate of the text pages of volume 38 of Medicine, which has not been examined, but using the actual number of text pages of the other four volumes in suit, and multiplying each by the number of subscriptions for each journal, the plaintiff produced and sold well over 30 million pages of text of the five volumes in suit, as compared with something less than 3 million pages of articles produced by NIH and NLM from the long files of many volumes of thousands of different journals during the year.

But getting back to the items in suit, there is the statement by the commissioner that this "... supplants the need for journal subscriptions" (R35). Every one of the four journals actually in suit has increased in circulation over the last five to ten years, and there is no evidence that they have lost potential subscribers because of the copying of articles cited from these journals that were photocopied by NIH and NLM (R98).

More specifically, and using the figures given in the commissioner's report for the articles in suit and the journals in suit, the table on page 36 of his report shows (R82) a total of 13 copies of articles Count I-VIII made by the two libraries from September 27, 1967, to January 12, 1968, a total of 108 days. Translated to an annual base, this would give 40 photocopies made of these eight articles in a year, and adding 25 percent as a safety factor would make this a maximum of 50 photocopies made by the two libraries of the eight articles over the year. The copies made by NIH were for staff at NIH and those made by NLM were for the country as a whole. However, even if we were to assume that they were all made for the professional personnel of NIH alone, which according to the report is 4,000 people (R7), remembering that there are five volumes involved--and the plaintiff sells volumes not articles--we would have a total of 10 articles per year copied for four thousand people. Dividing the 10 by 4,000 to get the average number of articles copied per scientist per year (of the articles in suit) we come up with a figure of 25/10,000ths of an article from each volume per year per scientist.

This means that, on the average, the scientists at NIH would have to subscribe to each of the journals for about four hundred years in order to get the one article he might find useful in each of the titles in suit, and that would be a good trick if he could do it (though a mighty unlikely one, and most uneconomical).

If this does not fit the definition of <u>De Minimus non Curat Lex</u>, what could? Back as far as 1839, in <u>Bell v. Whitehead</u> (3 Jurist 68, 1839) it was held that damage to a journal by extracting an article is probably so minute as to preclude consideration by the courts. And what evidence does the commissioner have to support his flat statement (R35) (R40) that the copying of the <u>journals and articles at issue in this case</u> "... supplants the need for journal subscriptions?" [Emphasis supplied]

The Sophar and Heilprin quote (R36) about babies being born one at a time has nothing to do with case, even though it is "cute." Scientific findings and other scholarly discoveries are made one at a time and the tremendous increase in research over the last thirty years or so has greatly increased knowledge in many fields. This requires more publishing, and more scientists, and more need for the literature, and more subscriptions to magazines, but that has nothing to do with this particular case.

In (R37) the commissioner says, "Finally, and in any event, there is nothing in the copyright statute or the case

Technical/Readers' Services 165

law to distinguish in principle the making of a single copy of a copyrighted work from the making of multiple copies...."

This is not true, and the commissioner himself says (R52) "... a library, no doubt, ... can supply attorneys or courts with <u>single photocopies</u> for use in litigation ..." [Emphasis supplied].

The statute itself does recognize both single copies and private use. 17 USC Section 107, which deals with importation during copyright of copyrighted books, etc., says: "During the existence of the American copyright in any book, the importation into the United States of any piratical copies thereof or of any copies thereof ... which have not been produced in accordance with the manufacturing provisions specified in Section 16 of this title ... is prohibited; <u>provided, however</u>, that except as regards piratical copies, such prohibition shall not apply: ... d. To any book published abroad with the authorization of the author or copyright proprietor when imported under one of the four subdivisions following, that is to say:

"First, when imported, <u>not more than one copy at a time, for individual use and not for sale</u> ... [Emphasis supplied].

"Second, when imported by the authority or for the use of the United States

"Third, when imported, <u>for use and not for sale, not more than one copy of any such book in any one invoice, in good faith by or for any society or institution incorporated for educational ... purpose ...</u> [Emphasis supplied.]

"Fourth, when such books form parts of libraries ... purchased en block ... <u>and are not intended for sale.</u>" [Emphasis supplied.]

Note that this section recognizes single copies as different from multiple copies and it recognizes private use, and it recognizes the right to use an agent just as the library in photocopying single copies for private use of scholars acts as his agent in doing for him what he has every right to do.

For cases on private use see the <u>American Institute of Architects v. Fenichel</u>, (District Court, S. D. New York, August 11, 1941, 51 USPQ29 41 Fed Supp. 146) which cites the Supreme Court case of <u>Baker v. Seldon</u> (101 US 99) and also states, according to <u>Fitch v. Young</u> (230 F743), "It has been held that the words 'copy, publish, print ... vend' are all clearly intended to be covered by the word 'publish.' Publication means to issue copies to the public ... It is sufficient for the decision in this case to hold as we do that the defendant's use was not the kind of use intended to be forbidden by the statute and does not constitute an infringement." See also West Publishing Co. v. Thompson (169 F854, 861, 865-6, 878, 1909).

Throughout the report the commissioner uses polar terms such as "wholesale copying," and "reasonable royalty" without defining the terms. Certainly, with the total of William and Wilkins journals making up only about two-thirds of one per cent of the total number of medical journals currently published, the total photocopying of NIH and NLM together represents an almost microscopic percentage of the articles appearing in all the volumes of all the different journals from which they photocopied less than 210,000 articles in the whole year, according to the commissioner's report. Considering the number of volumes of all the 6,000 different journals (each containing many articles) from which they photocopied would make the percentage of material copied, on the average, from any one volume of any one journal, a tiny Sub Minimus ... rather than wholesale in any sense of that term.

The "reasonable royalty" referred to repeatedly in the commissioner's report, insofar as NLM is concerned, is two cents per page (R101), and with respect to other licensees is five cents per page. However, a letter from Mr. Alan Latman, attorney of record for the plaintiff, to the assistant attorney general (attention: Mr. Brown), dated February 25, 1972, spells out a proposed licensing agreement for the two libraries with a fee of five cents per page applied (at the option of the libraries) based on: "(a) five cents multiplied by the number of text pages scheduled for production for the particular journal ... or [even if none is ever photocopied]; (b) five cents multiplied by the number of pages in the journal actually photocopied by the libraries, or [which would require a tremendous amount of bookkeeping for the thousands of journals involved]; (c) five cents multiplied by the number of pages which the parties agree represents the approximate number of pages photocopied by the libraries without actual counting of pages [which could mean anything]."

The commissioner gives no basis for repeatedly

Technical/Readers' Services 167

calling the licensing fee "reasonable," whether the two cents in the report or the five cents per page, or vastly more, depending on the option selected, proposed in the letter. This is particularly peculiar considering that there are serious questions as to the validity of the copyrights in several of the journals at issue as well as in many of the articles.

There is a lengthy discussion of fair use, but the question of fair or unfair use is one that so far as we can discover has never been handled by the courts except as part of a case alleging general public use or general publication of the item in contention.

The commissioner then has a lengthy report on the Gentlemen's Agreement, which, while it showed good will on both sides, has nothing to do with the Statute or its interpretation by the courts.

Then we come (R54), (R55), (R56), (R57), (R58) to the "little old lead pencil" argument, which holds that while perhaps scholars have the right to copy out what they need, the introduction of new equipment has changed all that and has greatly increased the copying that is done. There is no evidence given in the commissioner's report as to any increase in photocopying over the last ten or twenty years, and libraries have been making photocopies for some seventy years. In addition, for more than a generation, many scholars carried Leica cameras with stands and attachments and lights, folded up in their briefcases, and did their own photocopying in or out of the library. Furthermore, with the invention of the Contura by Mr. Ludwig of Yale, this small, folding reflex photocopying machine traveled widely in the briefcases of scholars all over the world.

The standard photostat camera fitted with a roll pick-up and a roll developer was capable of producing close to one thousand copies per day on a two-shift basis, more than twenty-five years ago, and the method is still competitive with the "newer machines" where immediate delivery of copy is not required.

The change in technology that has affected photocopying is the vast increase in research funding and staffing that has taken place. This has not increased the use per scholar since there is only so much time that a scientist or other researcher can spend on reading. With this vast increase in research expenditure and staffing has come a great increase in findings and in research staff and in papers to be published, and no one can subscribe to more than a tiny fraction of the journals published in almost any field. As an example of this change, NIH spent over $1.5 billion for medical research in 1970, of which about $100 million went for intramural research (R88) as compared with a total of $160 million in 1950, and there have been vast increases in the research budgets all along the line. But there is no real evidence that the changes in copying technology have changed the amount of copying done per scholar (who might be the potential subscriber to the journal if he could buy all the journals published that are of concern to him in his work, and which he cannot do).

Varmer (R58) says (R59), "Publishers' copies are bought for the private use of the buyer ..." All this statement proves is that Varmer has not read the cases. In Bureau of National Literature v. Sells et al (211 Fed R. 379, 1914) and in Henry Bill Publishing Co. v. Smyth (CC 27 Fed. 914) among many other cases, the court has ruled, "Plaintiff can claim no exclusive right to the sale of 'second-hand sets.' Its exclusive right of sale of a particular copy is gone when it parts with the title to such copy."

Pages 24-28 of the commissioner's report deal with administrative decisions, varied from time to time by Public Health Service and other administrative agencies of the government with regard to their policies on permitting grantees to copyright their reports. This is a confused matter that has nothing to do with 17 USC. The administrative departments have made all sorts of rules about this but they do not affect 17 USC and until they are tested in the courts, they are meaningless. Nevertheless, this does not justify the complete omission from the commissioner's report of all treatment of in-house government research, which produced a large number of papers, a number of which appear in the plaintiff's journals in this case. These studies are done in line of duty by government employees, using government facilities both in the research and writing of the papers and, by statute, are not copyrightable. 17 USC Section 8 expressly puts them in the public domain. A number of such papers, listed above, were published in journals in this case, some of them with plaintiff's notice of copyright at their headings. As indicated above, these are in the public domain by law and court decisions interpreting the copyright law, and if the plaintiff claims copyright in them he may well be violating Section 105 of 17 USC;

Technical/Readers' Services 169

according to the last sentence of that section he could be liable to a fine of $100 each time. And if, as indicated, these are in the public domain, many of them from NIH, the plaintiff, in attempting to collect royalties on these, is really "selling Brooklyn Bridge."

While there are many additional points in the commissioner's report that should be discussed, the major ones have been raised and the others will be indicated in the Appendix with citation of page and line.

As a practical matter, there would be no way of policing copying for private use, and the issue here is copying for private use, not copying for general publication.

Scholars may have access to copyrighted materials in many ways. They generally buy a few and use them in the privacy of their homes or studies; they borrow some from libraries and from colleagues, and they obtain access to them in many lawful ways. Their note-taking, or copying for them, may be done by themselves or their secretaries, and there are few buildings around any campus or research establishment that do not provide ready access to copying machines.

Policing all these sources and methods of making copies for the pennies involved in each case (and with a very large percentage of what they copy probably in the public domain) is too ridiculous to contemplate and even a Big Brother society would find this somewhat of a problem.

Even with the permission of the proprietor of the copyright in the journal, there would still be problems in many scholarly journals, such as advertisements which are copyrighted in the name of the advertiser and which would, if interspersed with the text, inevitably be copied with the text. These are clearly not the property of the proprietor of the copyright in the journal and he would have to get permission from his advertisers for blanket copying before he could license copying of his journal without violation of the copyrights of others.

Furthermore, publishers who have authorized commercial organizations to copy back files of their journals, in which there are copyrighted advertising and syndicated articles, and articles copyrighted by others which they have been permitted to reprint but to which they do not own the copyright (as is true of many scholarly journals), may have been violating copyright for years by these <u>public</u> uses, so they would have to make sure to get licenses for all these. Poetic justice?

The fundamental fact is that the Copyright Act has nothing to do with private uses of copyrighted materials by scholars. In fact, that was the purpose for which the Constitution authorized the Congress to pass a Copyright Act, giving authors and their assigns a monopoly of <u>general public uses</u> for limited periods. So long as the scholar's private use does not impinge upon the author's or his assigns' (proprietors') monopoly of public uses, his copying of validly copyrighted materials has nothing to do with 17 USC, which in itself and its interpretations, and in constitutional intent, deals solely with general public uses.

He has a right (see cases cited above) to make a copy or import a copy, etc., for his private study and use, and what he can do for himself he can do through an agent. The library, making a copy, by any means, at the specific request of a scholar, of an article for his private study and use, is simply acting as his agent to do for him, at his specific request, and for his private use, what the scholar has every right to do for himself. The method of copying has nothing to do with this, and the Copyright Law has nothing to say about this. It is completely outside the scope of 17 USC.

If, later, the scholar makes a <u>general public</u> use of the material, then the statute and its interpretation apply, regardless of whether the source from which he made the use was the original or a copy prepared by any means.

Appendix

R1--p. 1, 1. 19; R1a--p. 1, footnote; R2--p. 1, last line; R2a--p. 2, 1. 8 and footnote; R3--p. 3, 1. 18-20; R4--p. 3, 1. 6-8; R5--p. 3, 1. 15-24; R6--p. 3, 1. 24-30; R7--p. 3, 1. 37-38; R8--p. 4, 1. 7-9, 28-31; R9--p. 5, 1. 10-13; R10--p. 5, 1. 8-42, and p. 6, 1. 1-5; R11--p. 6, 1. 13-29; R12--p. 6, 1. 32-34; R12a--p. 7, 1. 5-14; R13--p. 7, 1. 14-18; R14--p. 7, 1. 19-36; R15--p. 7, 1. 37-41, and p. 8, 1. 1-3; R16--p. 8, 1. 7-10; R17--p. 8, 1. 10-13; R18--p. 8, 1. 13-20; R19--p. 8, 1. 21-34; R20--p. 9, 1. 7-8; R21--p. 9, 1. 13-24; R22--p. 9, 1. 25-29; R23--p. 9, 1. 30-37; R24--p. 10, 1. 20-26 and

Technical/Readers' Services

footnote; R25--p. 10, 1. 21-35, and p. 11, 1. 1-2; R26--p. 11, 1. 2-13; R27--p. 11, 1. 13-17; R28--p. 11, 1. 17-23; R29--p. 11, 1. 24-28; R30--p. 12, 1. 6-11; R31--p. 12, 1. 34-37, and p. 13, 1. 1-6; R32--p. 13, 1. 7-13; R33--p. 13, 1. 26-39; R34--p. 13, 1. 40-44, and p. 14, 1. 1-7; R35--p. 14, 1. 21-27; R36--p. 14, 1. 28-30; R37--p. 14, 1. 31-34; R38--p. 14, 1. 38-43, and p. 15, 1. 1-2; R39--p. 15, 1. 3-10; R40--p. 15, 1. 29-32; R40a--p. 15, 1. 37-39; R40b--p. 16, 1. 26; R40c--p. 16, 1. 27-33; R41--p. 16, 1. 37-42; R42--p. 17, 1. 2-4; R43--p. 17, 1. 5-9; R44--p. 17, 1. 12-17; R45--p. 17, 1. 18-29; R46--p. 30-36; R47--p. 17, 1. 37 and p. 18, 1. 1-7; R48--p. 18, 1. 7-12; R49--p. 18, 1. 12-17; R50--p. 18, 1. 23-28; R51--p. 18, footnote 12; R51a--p. 20, 1. 4-9; R52--p. 20, 1. 48-51, and p. 21, 1. 1-10; R53--p. 21, 1. 9; R54--p. 21, 1. 11-17; R54a--p. 21, 1. 17-23; R54b--p. 21, 1. 23-27; R55--p. 21, 1. 27-30; R56--p. 22, 1. 17-20; R57--p. 22, 1. 40-43; R58--p. 22, 1. 44-45; R59--p. 22, 1. 46-51; R60--p. 23, 1. 20-27; R60a--p. 24, 1. 14; R61--p. 24, 1. 16-19; R62--p. 24, 1. 33-36; R63--pp. 24-28; R64--p. 27, 1. 1-17; R65--p. 27, 1. 18-19; R66--p. 28, 1. 2-4; R67--pp. 28-30; R68--p. 28, 1. 34; R69--p. 29, 1. 6-7; R70--p. 29, 1. 14-34; R71--p. 30, 1. 4-8; R71a--p. 30, 1. 16-24; R72--p. 31, 1. 27-29; R73--p. 31, 1. 37-38, and p. 32, 1. 1-2; R74--p. 32, 1. 16; R75--p. 32, 1. 32-36; R76--p. 34, 1. 1-25; R77--p. 34, 1. 26-43, and p. 35, 1. 1-3; R78--p. 35, 1. 9-28; R79--p. 35, 1. 29-37; R80--p. 36, 1. 1-16; R81--p. 36, 1. 17-23; R82--p. 36, 1. 38 (Table 24); R83--p. 36, 1. 39-42; R84--p. 37, Table; R85--p. 38, 1. 33-41; R86--p. 39, 1. 1-15; R87--p. 39, 1. 16-25; R88--p. 40, 1. 11-13; R89--p. 40, 1. 16-22; R90--p. 40, 1. 37-40; R91--p. 42, 1. 21-23; R92--p. 52, 1. 36-43; R93--p. 53, 1. 1-4; R94--p. 53, 1. 5-17; R95--p. 53, 1. 18-29; R96--p. 53, 1. 30-34; R97--p. 53, 1. 35-39; R98--p. 53, 1. 98-100, and p. 54, 1. 1-16; R99--p. 54, 1. 17-22; R100--p. 54, 1. 37-42, and p. 55, 1. 1-12; R101--p. 55, 1. 32; R102--pp. 55-57; R103--pp. 58-62, NLM policy; R104--pp. 62-63, LC policy; R105--p. 63, HEW policy; and R106--p. 63, last paragraph.

CATALOGING-IN-PUBLICATION: WILL IT SUCCEED?*

Margaret C. Brown

Cataloging-In-Publication is not a new idea; it is a revived idea. An earlier version known as Cataloging-In-Source (CIS) was born in 1958 and died in 1959. CIS and CIP are nearly identical in concept, although they differ significantly in details. Consequently, if CIP is to prove successful, care must be taken to avoid or resolve those problems inherent in the CIS program that presumably contributed to its demise. We are assured that a review of the CIS experience was the first step taken at the Library of Congress when the resurrection of CIS (in the form of CIP) was viewed as a possibility.

In a consumers' survey conducted in April-May 1959, the librarians interviewed expressed themselves as strongly favoring the continuation of CIS. But CIS was not continued. Why? What reasons were given in 1959 for not continuing CIS? One was that the publishers found the whole enterprise very costly. The publishers' schedules, particularly at the time cataloging could be undertaken, were often very tight and delays were undoubtedly inconvenient and costly. The printing of catalog copy in the book was thought by some publishers to detract from the book's design and to be unpleasing aesthetically. Not an insignificant number of publishers objected to the use of an author's name on the back of a title page when a pseudonym appeared on the title page itself.

Other dissatisfactions were expressed by the Library of Congress catalogers: the page proofs were hard to handle and sometimes incomplete--lacking tables and illustrations essential to an understanding of the text. The information submitted by the cataloger regarding such details as collation and bibliography did not always accurately describe the book

---

*Reprinted by permission of the Pennsylvania Library Association from PLA Bulletin, 27:3 (May 1972).

Technical/Readers' Services

as finally published.

But, Cataloging-In-Source did not die because publishers objected to the use of the authors' real names, nor because the collation statement was occasionally in error. These objections could have been met for CIS as they are being met for CIP; the same solutions were offered in 1959 as were adopted in 1971. As for collation, it was evident then, as now, that entries, main and added, and subject analysis in the form of subject headings and classification numbers were the pieces of information most in demand by librarians. The rest could have been omitted then as it is being omitted now.

If proposed solutions to CIS bibliographic problems were similar in substance to the solutions incorporated in the CIP program, it is obvious that these were not the crucial issues in the decision to discontinue CIS.

There were other problems. One, which there seemed to be some hesitancy in discussing at the time, might be called "feasibility-itis," defined here as something which is feasible for a short time but not necessarily for the long pull. It is possible for staff members to work under adverse conditions when they know these conditions, be they poor lighting, unusual pressure, limited space, or what-have-you, will not last for an indefinite period. CIS was seriously disruptive to the work of the Processing Department of the Library of Congress, made especially so since turn-around-time was only one working day. Exceptions to normal procedures had to be made all along the line and material had to be hand carried in its progress through the departments. It was not surprising that the average cost (in 1959 dollars) was $25.00 per publication. Consideration of these factors could have bulked large when making the final decision to discontinue CIS. We know that many of these internal problems were resolved before CIP was undertaken, including the matter of turn-around-time, expanded to ten days by substituting galley proofs for page proofs.

Today we hear from some that CIS was allowed to die because it cost too much. The question of adequate financial support is as important today as in 1959. It is understood that following this initial period July 1, 1971-June 30, 1973, during which the Council on Library Resources and the National Endowment for the Humanities are supporting the program with a $400,000 matching grant, financial support for the program must come from the U.S. Congress. This support can not be guaranteed at this time.

There is still one other circumstance--and this is not unrelated to the fiscal question--that may have been significant in closing down CIS and could conceivably bring about the failure of CIP. Not enough librarians, those who presumably were to make the most use of the product (CIS), wanted it badly enough. This may seem an unwarranted statement in view of the results of the consumer survey referred to earlier. The consumer survey of 1959 had several weaknesses, acknowledged at the time, but one surely was that 1203 books were too few to permit any librarian interviewed to have sufficient experience in the use of CIS to say with authority exactly how the new tool would affect his procedures. Consequently, the enthusiastic endorsement of CIS was based more on theoretical reasoning of what it ought to do than on what it actually had done. At the time of the consumer survey almost no librarian could be found who did not think CIS a "good thing." Maybe it sounded like a progressive step which they did not want to be caught criticizing. Maybe they were intimidated by the high-level librarians constituting the survey team. In any case, they usually considered it a "good thing" in a general sense and almost always for someone else. A public librarian did not think CIS would alter markedly the procedures in her library, but she thought it would be very useful in a school library. On the other hand, the school librarian thought the college library would find it useful, etc., etc. The results of the consumer survey could have been predicted: a ringing endorsement without much concrete evidence.

The CIP program, on the other hand, can be expected to provide, during these first two years, far more evidence on which to base sound judgments for the future. The program has already (February 2) resulted in more titles cataloged (2300) than were cataloged in the entire CIS program (1203) and practical applications may be expected to yield concrete results by 1973. Moreover, CIP is not considered an experiment but a viable program whose initial stage of development has been subsidized.

However, to insure adequate financial support, its usefulness must be demonstrated. CIP will be expensive for everyone, publishers included. Whether or not financial support, including the cooperation of the publishers, is forthcoming may depend ultimately on consumer demands

Technical/Readers' Services 175

and the informed expression of these demands, minus the high-sounding phrases and pious pronouncements voiced to date by some enthusiastic supporters of CIP. Misleading claims could damage the cause and make the whole idea suspect.

We return to the question asked in 1959. How is the "new" service going to change our way of living?

There are three distinct "products" that develop out of CIP: (1) a record on MARC tape of the cataloging data provided by CIP prior to the appearance on MARC tape of final cataloging copy; (2) Library of Congress cards available prior to the book's publication date; and (3) cataloging data printed in the book. It would be possible, presumably, to have 1 and 2 without 3, or 2 and 3 without 1, should a given feature seem less necessary than the others.

Probably no one would question the desirability of being able to purchase LC catalog cards in advance of the book's publication. There is no room for debate here. However, if the final copy in the form of printed card appears three weeks in advance of publication date--and consequently will also be available on MARC tape earlier than at the present time--is there a need to furnish on MARC tape incomplete cataloging data, a kind of preliminary edition, at the time the information is supplied to the publisher?

Some university librarians have maintained that such a record on the MARC tape will serve as a book selection tool or an awareness file. Surely there are better selection tools unless a librarian is buying a title simply because he knows how to catalog it. The availability of LC cataloging sometimes does seem to be one of the chief criteria in book selection. But this argument alone does not seem sufficient justification for including CIP on MARC tape prior to final editing of catalog copy.

What about the cataloging data in the book itself? First of all, what cataloging data are in the book? Information has been trimmed down to the essential elements as it undoubtedly would have been had CIS survived another year. Entry, title proper, series, notes, subjects, added entries, classification numbers (Dewey and LC), ISBN(s), and the LC card number will appear in the book. Sub-title, collation and page citations (in notes) have been omitted, and when the real name is supplied for pseudonymous authors the publisher may delete and may substitute a long dash to indicate omission. It is expected that such a device will rarely be needed since the Anglo-American Rules permit entry under pseudonym.

Catalogers will work with galleys unless a publisher is unable to furnish his material in this form. When a complete galley is not available, catalogers will work from photocopies of the printer's copy for the title page, the verso of the title page and the half title; the photocopies of transcripts of the preface, table of contents, and introduction; and a précis of the book furnished by the publisher. (See Cataloging Service, Processing Department Bulletin 101/Nov. 1971.) The absence of text may prove a handicap to the cataloger in some instances!

With long experience as the devil's advocate I would like to suggest a few things CIP will not do, at least not now. It will give the cataloger no help with his most time-consuming tasks, namely the cataloging of serials and nonbook materials. In addition to serials, other categories of print material of considerably less concern to most catalogers are also omitted from the present phase of CIP: impressions of new printings, books paid for or subsidized by authors, religious education materials, and less expensive editions which are designed for retail outlets such as supermarkets.

At the time CIS was inaugurated the nonbook was nowhere near so important as it is today. At the present time, some libraries, particularly school libraries, are designating between thirty to fifty per cent of their library materials budget for the purchase of nonbook materials, i.e., microforms, filmstrips, recordings, etc. It is promised that CIP will eventually provide cataloging for virtually all forms of recorded information. It is not impossible to catalog any of these forms, but it may be hard to arrange the "in-publication" part of the program.

What else will CIP not do? It will not supply complete catalog copy in a form that can be photographed or otherwise reproduced as a basis for duplicating catalog cards in the library. The actual means for reproducing cards on site may not be affected significantly one way or another by the introduction of CIP.

The chief advantage for CIP is that it will eliminate

the need to match a book with its catalog record. However, those librarians purchasing Library of Congress cards frequently know the Library of Congress card number at the time they order books. The catalog record itself, should they elect to make their own cards, is available in Library Journal, School Library Journal, and Publishers' Weekly, some of the most widely-used book selection aids in small libraries. For those libraries it is more important to have the Library of Congress card number and/or the Library of Congress cataloging copy at the time of ordering the book than at the time of receiving the book. Records prepared in advance of the arrival of the books can be filed by title and matching these with the books can be a simple procedure.

Contrary to some claims made for CIP, it is not reasonable to expect the introduction of CIP to reduce significantly the workload of catalogers unless these catalogers have been performing what have long been recognized as clerical operations. For it is only the time devoted to file maintenance and/or the searching for Library of Congress copy which will be reduced by the appearance of the cataloging information in the book. The cataloger will have no more information available to him--in fact, somewhat less--than at the present time. Also, the cataloger will be responsible, as he is now, for integrating the data emanating from the Library of Congress, however obtained, into the fabric of the local catalog.

CIP will not eliminate the need for someone in the local library who understands the structure of catalogs and knows the difference between a catalog and a file of cards whose only relation to one another is an alphabetical one. Neither CIP nor the Library of Congress card service can guarantee the integrity of a card catalog's contents in any library outside the Library of Congress. Establishing and maintaining authority files and cross references will still be necessary if the semblance of a catalog is to be retained in the local library.

One last word from the devil's advocate. Subject headings supplied in CIS did not always meet with the approval of the publishers and usually for the same reasons that librarians, including catalogers, find a given heading objectionable. The appearance of an outmoded subject heading on the back of a title page, far removed from the catalog whose content dictates the form of the heading, appears especially disconcerting, even incongruous. This can still be a problem. As the years go by, if CIP becomes a permanent part of our environment it will be necessary to remind catalogers and other users of this information that the data were accurate <u>according to the rules of the game at the time</u>. The cataloging will be contemporary with the book and may be out of date before the book itself is outdated.

We mention what CIP cannot be expected to do--at least for the present--to enable us to think more clearly about what it can do. Leaving aside fringe benefits, such as enabling a harried reference librarian to determine quickly the scope and subject matter of a book in hand, we shall assume the chief purposes of CIP are to: reduce to a minimum the time it takes to prepare a book for circulation and use; and reduce the cost and improve the quality of cataloging in individual libraries.

The usefulness of CIP in a given library will depend on many factors unrelated to CIP, such as the size of the library operation, book buying procedures, management policies, administrative efficiency, and staff shortages. Consequently, well-controlled studies of "before" and "after" will be difficult to conduct. But it is important that some effort be made to do so.

By way of illustration, we shall mention two types of library operations and consider how CIP might be used in these instances. A large library that subscribes to proofsheets has as cost items: (1) the subscription to the proofsheets, (2) the cost of sorting and filing, and (3) the cost of retrieving the appropriate record as a basis for preparing cards locally.

If by June 1972 the CIP program is geared to supplying catalog copy for 17,000 titles per year, as presently anticipated, such a library could contemplate eliminating that portion of the three cost items named above that pertains to American imprints. (Availability of non-CIP proofsheets would have to be assured.) Unlike present procedures, a cataloger or an assistant would then be required to type some or all of the cataloging data in the book onto a work sheet from which the typist would prepare a multility master or a catalog card to be reproduced by photographic or electrostatic method. Which process, proofsheets or CIP, costs more? Only by careful study could the answer be known with certainty.

Another library (independent) buys Library of Congress cards. Temporary cards may still be required, if Library of Congress cards (complete cataloging as opposed to CIP cataloging) are not in hand at the time the book is cataloged. Is CIP cataloging less costly than cataloging upon receipt of the Library of Congress card? Probably very little. The advantage, under CIP, lies in the accuracy of the classification number chosen and the main entry selected for the temporary record and most likely the speed with which both are done. There would be no temptation to "hold" a book with CIP and consequently current titles would be cataloged upon receipt.

In these two examples it would appear that the chief advantage of CIP is in improved service.

The library that now has no convenient access to Library of Congress cataloging, either in bibliographies or cards, has the most to gain from CIP. In fact, it has everything to gain. The well-managed library, sizable enough to distinguish between clerical and professional duties in a catalog department but not sufficiently affluent to purchase Library of Congress catalogs or proofsheets, will benefit to a considerable extent, even though Library of Congress cards are customarily purchased. The larger, well-organized catalog department may stand to profit the least, although since this type of library probably catalogs proportionately more noncurrent titles, it could benefit greatly in the years to come. The truth of this last presumption cannot, unfortunately, be established before June 1973.

It seems clear that reports from small or moderate size libraries will be very important when an evaluation of CIP's utility is needed. Representatives of large libraries are often the ones who do the most talking, but in this case they may be the last to know.

CIP could change priorities in other ways. It could be that the most critical administrative decision a catalog librarian will have to make regarding English language monographs of American publishers will relate to the purchase or reproduction of catalog records. The libraries will not be buying cataloging; they will be buying only catalog cards. This might make MARC look like an expensive printing press. And it might make thirty-five cents a package for LC cards look like a bargain. Or it might introduce the multilith machine where it has never been before. These libraries subscribing to proofsheets, as such or on microfiche, might favor an arrangement that would permit them to subscribe only to Non-CIP titles. Centralized processing centers could concentrate on cataloging non-CIP titles and CIP books could be shipped directly to the ordering library. The American cataloging world may be conveniently divided into CIP and non-CIP.

At this point it is difficult to consider changing cataloging procedures when CIP appears only in an occasional book and is viewed by most as a curiosity rather than a reality. But it is important that some solid evidence of its utility be available by June 1973. CIP is not designed for the benefit of the Library of Congress, although LC's books will be ready for public use at an earlier date than previously. CIP benefits the publishers only slightly. The library's readers, who probably stand to gain the most, are not likely to voice their approval. But the librarians who want this program, if they really want it, ought to be prepared to show and tell--the Library of Congress, publishers, and eventually their Congressman. Otherwise we can lose CIP as we lost CIS.

Proof of savings in terms of processing costs will be most welcome, but this is not to play down the importance of evidence of improved service to the reader, either in terms of better quality of our product or in terms of its prompter delivery to the consumer. Other changes in library procedures have taken place when improved service was their only justification. When we introduce book catalogs or eliminate fines for children we are hard put to prove a saving in cost, but, under certain circumstances, these innovations are worthwhile in terms of service. What about CIP? Does its utility justify the cost? Do _you_ want it to succeed? If so, you are being given a second chance to state your case.

OF MICE AND LIONS AND BATTLESHIPS AND INTERLIBRARY THINGS*

R. H. Blackburn

In olden days, before the flood of universities and graduate studies, when all librarians were literary scholars or at least aspired to be considered so, our thinking about the various aspects of our work tended to be colored and guided by familiar texts and analogies. Inter-library cooperation, for instance, was a simple matter of doing unto others; and interlending between a large library and a small one, once the question of postage was settled, was treated as a straightforward reciprocal arrangement analogous to the exchange of vital favors between Aesop's lion and his mouse.

Nowadays, when the voice of the cost-analyst is heard in our land, librarians are frequently obliged to assume the protective coloration of engineers, accountants, and other practitioners whose pursuits run much closer to mathematics and management than to metaphor. When we do so we begin to notice fallacies in the old fables. The similarity between nets and networks is a matter to ponder, and perhaps to measure. The mouse which gnaws through the rope and returns the lion's good turn, life for life, is unlike the small library which borrows and borrows from a big one but lends little or nothing in return; and besides, the proportions are all wrong. It becomes increasingly noticeable that interlibrary services do not drop as the gentle rain from heaven, but have to be paid for by somebody and are an unequal blessing to him that gives and him that receives. Even for those of us with antediluvian recollections, it becomes possible to ask whether an interlibrary loan is worth what it costs,[1] and necessary to begin looking for answers.

Answers are not easy, but a few have been found. Gordon Williams has sampled the dollar cost of borrowing journals, assuming that someone has them to lend and that

*Reprinted by permission from IPLO Quarterly (Institute of Professional Librarians of Ontario).

delays cost nothing, and has developed a formula which defines the point at which it is cheaper to own than to borrow.[2] The New York State Library, on the basis of a cost study, reimburses the cost of lending in certain resource libraries to the tune of $2.50 per request searched plus $2.00 per item supplied.[3] The characteristics of borrowing done by Ontario universities are being analysed by the Office of Library Coordination of the Council of Ontario Universities, and a more comprehensive study of interloan content and costs and traffic is being done by consultants for the Association of Research Libraries. The problem was not very worrisome as long as the traffic was only a trickle and budgets were fairly adequate, but has become painful now that the flow is heavy and growing fast; and many a large library must choose whether to cut out its external lending or to cut out some of the activities which serve its own institution.

In Canada there is so little information about the current state of affairs that I found it necessary last spring, in connection with some committee work for the National Research Council's Advisory Board on Scientific and Technological Information, to do a quick survey. Replies from three-quarters of the libraries in the institutions which are members of the Association of Universities and Colleges of Canada indicated that academic libraries sent out about 190,000 items on interloan in 1969-70, at a median out-of-pocket cost of $4.58 per item lent, and that the traffic was increasing at the rate of about 25 per cent annually. Toronto, McGill, and the University of British Columbia accounted for more than one-third of the total. Public libraries lent something like 50,000 volumes, the National Science Library about 48,000, the National Library about 15,000.[4] Other libraries in the country probably lent between 50,000 and 100,000, making a national total of between 350,000 and 400,000 interloans in 1969-70.[5] The National Union Catalogue handled about 90,000 location-requests, and the rest of the traffic was apparently routed by union-lists or other means.

It is evident that interlending is already a million-dollar business in Canada, that it is growing rapidly, and that the heavy end of the load is being carried by a few large libraries. In my own library we borrow less than 5,000 items a year altogether, or only about one-sixth as much as we lend, and about half our borrowing is from large foreign libraries. In 1969-70 for instance our loans to Canadian libraries amounted to 24,443 items at a direct cost to us of around $122,000, and from Canadian libraries we borrowed 2,127 items at a direct cost to them of perhaps $10,600. In struggling to understand this imbalance of trade and the forces which bring it about, I have come upon a fascinating new application of what Lanchester called his "n-square law."[6]

Frederick William Lanchester (1868-1946) was a crusty genius who may be thought of as a latter-day Leonardo, an English version of Henry Ford, Thomas Edison, the Wright brothers and Igor Sikorsky. He was "a great scientist, a great engineer, a mathematician, an inventor and a true artist in mechanical design."[7] He was also one of the fathers of operations research. His law of squares was first propounded in 1916, and "ever since, the use of differential equations to study the attrition of the forces of two sides engaged in military combat has been known as Lanchester's theory of combat."[8] The theory is simply this: "the fighting strength of a force may be broadly defined as proportional to the square of its numerical strength multiplied by the fighting value of its individual units."[9] To illustrate it we need only to imagine one blue battleship in an engagement with two green ships. If we assume all three ships to be of equal size and speed and firepower, each able to fire one broadside per minute, then the blue ship will be shot at twice a minute but each green ship only once in two minutes: the advantage of the green ships, and the relative hazard sustained by the blue, is therefore four to one. In the same way, three ships against one would have an advantage of nine to one. If instead of "broadsides" we say "interloan requests" then the relevance of Lanchester's law for our peaceful purpose springs to light.

Before pursuing the gleam, it is worth pausing to note that the law applied only when concentration of fire is made possible by long-distance weapons (long-distance requests!) and not when forces are in hand-to-hand contact.[10] Lanchester quotes Macaulay's <u>Horatius</u>, "In yon straight path a thousand may well be stopped by three" to illustrate the strategic limitations of broadswords as compared to rifles.[11] He shows the power of his theory by describing Horatio Nelson's apparently instinctive use of the law of squares in his strategy at Trafalgar in October 1805, and more clearly in his memorandum twelve days before the battle, to overpower the French and Spanish fleet.[12] Some of the literature which continues to grow up around this law is full of refinements and fancy equations, and is hard going for one who carries only faint thirty-year-old scars from his last hand-to-hand encounters with differential calculus, but I have not seen any writing which contradicts Lanchester's own assessment of the advantage inherent in his law of squares: it "is not negligible or trifling, it is overwhelming, and of such a character as to entirely outweigh any objections which can be raised from a gunnery standpoint."[13]

With this assurance, and with little but blind instinct to guide me, I have attempted to apply this law in what may be called a theorem of interloan advantage. In so doing I have encountered a dearth of bibliothecal terms to cover all the ideas involved, and have resorted to some of Lanchester's military terminology, not because it is appropriate to my subject but because it is easy to understand. The "action" I have studied is not Trafalgar, but one which is much closer to home, the firing of interloans between the University of Toronto Library and the thirteen other provincially-assisted universities in Ontario. I have used the latest figures at hand, those for 1969-70. During the year, Toronto suffered more than thirteen hits to every one she inflicted (7,537 to 577) and may be excused for becoming curious about the forces which create this disadvantage. Hence I have tried to identify and define these forces, and to put the "dry ingredients together"[14] to form an explanation. If we can increase our understanding of the problem, and trace its roots to particular parts of university programs, we may increase our ability to cope with it.

Let us see what happens if we begin by assuming that the Ontario libraries, with equal access to the National Union Catalogue and the national union lists, all have equal range and accuracy in their firing of requests. Let us assume also that the number of inter-loan "hits" any library makes is dependent on its own "numerical strength" and the area of "target" at which it fires.

The target I have defined simply as the total book collection of each university library as reported for 1969-70 by the Dominion Bureau of Statistics[15] minus 50,000 volumes as a rough allowance for a basic undergraduate collection which is not subject to interloan. The consequent size of target presented by each of the 14 universities is shown in the fifth line of Table 1 (pp. 186-7).

The "numerical strength" of an institution, in terms of its ability to generate requests for interloans, is more difficult to define. Obviously its basic ingredient is the number of faculty members and graduate students, since these are the people for whom interloans are obtained. In Table 1 the first three lines show the concentration of such "manpower," in full-time equivalents, at each of the universities.[16]

The significance of this manpower as a source of interloan requests is partly dependent on the volume of needs which cannot be satisfied by the collection which is at hand locally. I have called the size of this unsatisfied demand the "interloan need" and have derived it (Table 1, line 6) by dividing the local manpower (line 3) by the size of the local target collection (line 5) divided by 1,000. That is, I have imagined an "interloan need" which is the total number of graduate students and faculty members per thousand volumes in the local target collection.

I have supposed, further, that the effectiveness of this interloan need varies directly with the amount of time each faculty member has to consult individual students and conduct his own research. The heavier the workload, the less time a professor has to engage in wide-ranging research or to give his individual graduate students guidance and encouragement in that direction. Here we encounter something akin to what Lanchester calls "moral concentration, the narrowing and fixity of purpose"[17] as distinct from concentration of material strength. To find an index to the workload of staff members at each university I have passed over the ordinary "staff-student ratio" and have used instead the number of "basic income units" (BIU's) per staff member. Since Ontario supports its fourteen universities on the basis of a weighted formula in which a junior Arts student counts as one basic income unit, for instance, and a Ph.D. student as six units,[18] it is easy and perhaps useful to define the workload of professors according to these weights. The raw workloads per faculty member (line 7) are seen to vary from 13.5 (Laurentian) to 27.5 (Waterloo) with an average of 21.4 which happens to be the same as the figure for Toronto.[19] I have assumed that the average workload is a norm which would neither augment or diminish the "interloan need," and have divided each of the other figures into 21.4 in order to derive a "workload adjustment" in line 8, since there is an inverse relationship between the workload and the adjustment it causes. At Brock, for example, where the weighted workload is only 16.3, the workload adjustment

TABLE 1 -- 1969-70*

	Brock	Carleton	Guelph	Lakehead	Laurentian	McMaster	Ottawa
1. Teaching staff FTE	142.2	521.3	550.5	197.4	193	676.7	813.5
2. Grad. Students FTE	18	765	553	53	5	1,215	1,217
3. Manpower (Lines 1+2)	160.2	1,286.3	1,103.5	250.4	198	1,891.7	2,030.5
4. Total holdings, vols.	143,378	424,149	350,000	125,163	148,733	551,898	468,082
5. Target area presented (Line 4 - 50,000)	93,378	374,149	300,000	75,163	98,773	501,892	418,082
6. Interloan need (Lines 3 ÷ 5) x 1,000	1.72	3.44	3.68	3.33	2.00	3.77	4.86
7. Weighted workload (BIUs per professor)	16.3	22.9	22.5	18	13.5	21.1	18.1
8. Workload adjustment (21.4 ÷ line 7)	1.31	0.934	0.95	1.19	1.59	1.01	1.18
9. Numerical strength (lines 6x8)	2.25	3.21	3.5	3.96	3.18	3.81	5.73
10. Relative firepower (Line 9 ÷ 2.55)	0.882	1.26	1.37	1.55	1.25	1.49	2.25
11. Firepower advantage (Line 10 squared)	0.778	1.59	1.88	2.40	1.54	2.22	5.06
12. Target advantage (2,607,402 ÷ line 5)	27.9	6.97	8.69	34.7	26.4	5.20	6.24
13. Interloan advantage (Lines 11x12)	21.7	11.1	16.3	83.3	41.2	11.5	31.6
14. Toronto received	5	30	18	2	5	125	60
15. Toronto could therefore expect to supply (13x14)	109	333	293	167	211	1,438	1,896
16. Toronto actually supplied	137	384	843	472	335	1,616	363
17. Difference of more than 50%			high	high	high		low
18. Line 15 multiplied again by workload adjustment.	143	311	278	199	335	1,452	2,237
19. Doctoral degrees granted, Humanities & Soc. Sci.	-	-	1	-	-	7	23
20. Doctoral degrees, Phys. & Biol. Sci.	-	8	17	-	-	46	29
21. Undergrad students FTE	1,957.7	7,755.9	5,235.6	2,322.6	2,539.5	6,710.5	6,823

TABLE 1 -- 1969-70* (continued)

	Queen's	Toronto	Trent	Waterloo	Western	Windsor	York
1. Teaching staff FTE	735.8	2,209.7	105.3	681.3	798.3	458.6	638.8
2. Grad. Students FTE	1,006	4,435	5.3	1,343	1,534	416	770
3. Manpower (Lines 1+2)	1,741.8	6,644.7	110.6	2,024.3	2,332.3	874.6	1,408.8
4. Total holdings, vols.	703,503	2,657,402	141,387	360,469	848,853	442,632	491,292
5. Target area presented (Line 4 − 50,000)	653,503	2,607,402	91,387	310,469	798,853	392,632	441,292
6. Interloan need (Lines 3 ÷ 5) x 1,000	2.67	2.55	1.21	6.52	2.92	2.23	3.19
7. Weighted workload (BIUs per professor)	21	21.4	16.7	27.5	26	19.9	21.3
8. Workload adjustment (21.4÷line 7)	1.02	1	1.28	0.78	0.82	1.08	1
9. Numerical strength (lines 6x8)	2.72	2.55	1.55	5.09	2.39	2.41	3.19
10. Relative firepower (Line 9÷2.55)	1.07	1	0.608	2.00	0.937	0.945	1.25
11. Firepower advantage (Line 10 squared)	1.14	1	0.37	4.00	0.878	0.893	1.56
12. Target advantage (2,607,402÷line 5)	3.99	1	28.5	8.40	3.26	6.64	5.91
13. Interloan advantage (Lines 11x12)	4.55	1	10.5	33.6	2.86	5.93	9.22
14. Toronto received	67	-	7	34	119	27	78
15. Toronto could therefore expect to supply (13x14)	305	-	74	1,142	340	160	719
16. Toronto actually supplied	996	-	181	688	827	177	518
17. Difference of more than 50%	high	-	high	low	high		
18. Line 15 multiplied again by workload adjustment.	311	-	95	891	279	173	719
19. Doctoral degrees granted, Humanities & Soc. Sci.	17	89	-	11	12	1	3
20. Doctoral degrees, Phys. & Biol. Sci.	34	105	-	43	38	10	3
21. Undergrad students FTE	7,047.7	20,697.7	1,425.6	8,117.6	11,082.6	5,922.1	8,887.8

*Data in lines 1, 2, 7, 19, 20, 21 are from the Report of the Minister of University Affairs of Ontario, 1969-70. Data in line 4 was supplied by Mr. E. Wicks, Dominion Bureau of Statistics. Data in lines 14 and 16 are from the Annual Report of the Chief Librarian, University of Toronto, 1969-70.

is 1.31 (i.e. 21.4 ÷ 16.3) and when multiplied by the interloan need (1.72) produces a "numerical strength" of 2.25 (line 9).

The numerical strength of Toronto appears as 2.55, and when this figure is divided into each of the other thirteen columns (line 10) we see that the "relative firepower" of each, compared to Toronto, varies from 0.608 at Trent to 2.25 at Ottawa. When we square these relative firepowers (because Lanchester said so) we find that the firepower advantage over Toronto varies from 5.06 (Ottawa) down to 0.37 (Trent).

Having calculated the firepower advantage of each of the other libraries as compared with Toronto, we can also calculate the "target advantage" by dividing each target area into 2,607,402, which is the size of the target presented by Toronto. We find in line 12 that the target advantage varies from 34.7 (Lakehead) down to 3.26 (Western). Multiplying firepower advantage by target advantage, we can calculate the total interloan advantage of each of the thirteen libraries (line 13). It varies from 2.86 (Western) to 83.3 (Lakehead).

My theorem, then, is that the interloan advantage of an academic library, in its dealings with a larger one, is:

$$\left(\frac{\frac{M_s \times 1000}{T_s} \quad W_s}{\frac{M_b \times 1000}{T_b} \quad W_b} \right)^2 \times \frac{T_b}{T_s}$$

or more simply

$$\frac{M_s^2 \times W_s^2 \times T_b^3}{M_b^2 \times W_b^2 \times T_s^3}$$

where sub-s and sub-b indicate the smaller and bigger library, respectively, and where

    M is manpower (teaching staff plus graduate students, FTE)
    T is the area of the target presented (collection less 50,000 vols.)
    W is the standardized work load adjustment (the number of basic income units per faculty member in an institution, divided into the norm).

Now to test the theorem against real life. We know how many loans or photocopies Toronto received during the year (line 14) and by multiplying this figure by the interloan advantage of each other library we can calculate the number of loans Toronto could have expected to send out to satisfy the theorem. Our total number of loans according to the formula (line 15) would, therefore, have been 7,187. The actual number of loans we made to these libraries in 1969-70 (line 16) was 7,537, only 5.16 per cent more than we could have expected by formula. Eureka, perhaps!

The theorem seems to provide a remarkably accurate reflection of the total interloan traffic between Toronto and the other thirteen libraries in 1969-70. It is apparent however from lines 15 and 16 that there are some wide discrepancies between the expected and actual traffic relating Toronto to particular libraries in the list. Of course we have to expect various kinds of accidental annual variations to occur in particular cases, especially in lines in which the numbers are rather small; but such variations should be expected to average out in the longer run.

Some of the discrepancies can be explained by local conditions which are not accounted for in the formula. For instance Guelph actually borrowed about three times more (or lent us three times less) than the formula would have predicted, but Guelph happens to be the one library in the list which is not yet represented in the National Union Catalogue, and it therefore does not present a visible target for requests. Closer inspection of the record shows that while Guelph's theoretical advantage is 16.5:1 her actual advantage in our balance of trade was 100:1 in loans (which are mostly books) and 27.6:1 in photocopied items (which are mostly journals). Guelph's journals were partially represented in the national union list of serials, and so it appears that her very large overall advantage (46.7:1) was at least partly the result of her books being invisible to other libraries such as ours. And of course Toronto offers no courses in Agriculture which is a highly developed specialty at Guelph.

The four libraries from which we borrowed fewer than ten items (Trent, Laurentian, Lakehead, and Brock) are all small new institutions, and the figures are so small that they have little statistical significance. The fact that the first three actually showed a high interloan advantage, compared to the formula, means very little, though it may suggest that there is something special about their manpower, or their collections, or the position of their location symbols in the National Union Catalogue.

The largest discrepancy in the list is for the University of Ottawa, which borrowed only 363 items as against 1,896 which the formula would have predicted. The Chief Librarian at Ottawa suggests three reasons, and there may be others. First, Ottawa professors and their graduate students seem to require fewer interloans than those at other universities; for instance, Ottawa borrows roughly the same amount as does Carleton from the universities in Quebec, in spite of Ottawa's bilingual programs and in spite of the fact that her firepower advantage as represented in Table 1 (line 11) is three times that of Carleton. Second, Ottawa's rate of borrowing may be affected by the direct use her readers can make of the National Science Library and National Library nearby. Third, in a welcome gesture of charity, the Chief Librarian has directed his staff not to send requests to Toronto when there is an alternative source in Ontario.[20]

Another large discrepancy appears in the column for Waterloo, which borrowed only a little more than half as much as we might have expected. Again the Chief Librarian has suggested reasonable explanations. First, Waterloo's budget for serials in 1969-70 was the highest of any academic library in Canada, and so Waterloo may have an unusually low need to borrow serials. Second, Waterloo readers frequently drive to Toronto and check their references on the spot. Third, the Waterloo library staff does not send requests to Toronto if there is an alternative location. Finally, Waterloo's enrolment and staff are unusually heavy on the scientific side, and the weighted workload at Waterloo is very heavy. These things may reduce the need for interloans.[21]

The only two sizeable discrepancies for which I have found no ready explanation appear in the columns for Queen's and Western, which both borrowed roughly three times as much as the formula would have predicted. These differences seem too large to be accidental and must arise from factors we have not considered, factors such as the age and content of collections, the level and emphasis of academic programs, and so on. It is probably significant that the two libraries which show large unexplained discrepancies are old institutions nad have large collections; but I have not been able to establish what the significance is. Still, when all the discrepancies are added together, they seem to cancel each other out fairly well in the total.

My theorem of course leaves many questions unanswered. Its variables are rather closely related, and perhaps are not the best ones, or in the best proportion. What light can be shed by applying the theorem to the lending patterns of other libraries in our list, or of other regional groups of libraries? Should graduate students really be given the same weight in the formula as professors? In 1969-70 our reference librarians received 2,167 interloan requests from our 2,209.7 faculty members and only 1,955 request from our 4,435 graduate students; if this pattern is typical then perhaps staff members should be counted at double-weight in the tally of manpower. Should professors all be given the same weight regardless of age and subject field and citizenship? How is the pattern affected by the fact that all fourteen libraries in the list depend heavily on the National Science Library for loans and photocopies in Science? How is the traffic affected by the relative age and depth of collections, by the amount of duplication within and among universities, and by the promptness and accuracy of inclusion in national union catalogues? How is it affected by the vigor of local acquisition programs, the speed of local cataloguing, the readiness of reference librarians to search inside and outside the local collection, or by the route of the daily van service among twelve of our fourteen libraries? What patterns emerge from the quality and age and nature and interdependence of graduate programs within each of the institutions? What is the relationship of requests made to requests filled, and what systematic factors if any are at work in the routing of a request when alternative sources are possible? What happens to the calculation if, instead of making a rough allowance of 50,000 volumes for a basic undergraduate collection in establishing the interloan target, we make a different allowance on some other basis such as the Clapp-Jordan formula?[22] What happens if the target is defined in terms of titles instead of volumes? How is the pattern affected by the ratio between graduate students and undergraduates? How accurate and comparable are the relevant figures which are available for the different institutions?

This last question leads into another which may have important implications far beyond our libraries. Why is it that the calculated volume of lending (line 15), when each item in it is multiplied again by the appropriate workload adjustment (line 8) predicts a new total (7,423) which comes within 1.5 per cent of the total number of loans we actually made in 1969-70? This result may be too good to be true, but it is interesting to see that the theorem works better if the workload adjustment, already squared in the formula, is cubed instead. Perhaps it indicates that the weighting of basic income units for various levels of students should really vary from 1 to 14.7 (i.e. 1 to $6\sqrt{6}$) and not from 1 to 6 as at present.

I hope that my theorem will be interesting enough to tempt others to work on some of the questions which it raises. For them I have included in Table 1 some information for which I myself have not found a use. Perhaps together we can gnaw through the rope before the hunters return.

Notes

1. Arthur McAnally, in a book review in Library Quarterly vol. 40, no. 3, July 1970, p. 356.
2. Gordon Williams, et al. Library Cost Models: Owning Versus Borrowing Serial Publications. Bethesda, Maryland, Westat Research Incorporated, 1968. Publication PB182304 for the Office of Scientific Information, National Science Foundation.
3. Private communication dated March 22, 1971 from E. J. Josey, Chief, Bureau of Academic and Research Libraries, The University of the State of New York.
4. Report of the National Librarian, 1970. (Ottawa, Queen's Printer, 1970) p. 8.
5. This estimate is my own and a poor thing, full of extrapolations and guesses. I shall be glad when more accurate figures are available.
6. This law of squares was first brought to my attention in casual conversation by Dr. K. F. Tupper, then Vice-President (Administration) of the National Research Council of Canada.
7. H. R. Ricardo, "Frederick William Lanchester" in Royal Society Obituary Notices vol. 5 (1945-48) pp. 757-65.
8. P. R. Wallis, "Recent Developments in Lanchester Theory" in Operational Research Quarterly vol. 19, no. 2, 1968, pp. 191-95. This paper reports the Operational Research Conference on Recent Developments in Lanchester Theory held in Munich in July 1967 under the auspices of the NATO Science Committee.

Technical/Readers' Services 193

9. Frederick William Lanchester, <u>Aircraft in Warfare: The Dawn of the Fourth Arm.</u> (London, Constable, 1916) p. 48.
10. <u>idem</u> p. 58.
11. <u>idem</u> p. 57.
12. <u>idem</u> p. 63.
13. <u>idem</u> p. 181.
14. This phrase is from an anonymous inscription found on the English end of a 15-ounce box of <u>Kellogg's Special K</u>, Canadian Patent No. 559,326, Kellogg Company of Canada, Ltd., London, Ontario. It illustrates the persistence of a literary tradition in industry as well as in other sectors of the environment. My Baker Street Irregular colleague Donald Redmond has pointed out that the Kellogg phrase is a verbatim echo from paragraph 1871 entitled "A Nice Useful Cake" in Mrs. Isabella Mary Beeton's <u>Book of Household Management</u>, New Edition (Three Hundred and Seventy-Third Thousand) with a publishers' note dated 1880 [London] Ward, Lock & Co. p. 891.
15. Figures were provided June 20/71 by Mr. E. Wicks of D.B.S., since the preliminary printed release for 1969-70 was officially recalled before it ever reached me.
16. Figures in the first two lines, and in lines 7, 20, 21 and 22 are derived from tables in the <u>Report of the Minister of University Affairs of Ontario, 1969-70.</u>
17. Lanchester, <u>op. cit.</u> p. 39.
18. <u>Report of the Minister of University Affairs of Ontario,</u> 1967, pp. 100-102.
19. <u>Report of the Minister of University Affairs of Ontario,</u> 1969-70.
20. Private communication from the Reverend Paul Drouin, O.M.I., on July 20 and 27, 1971.
21. Private communication July 14, 1971, from William Watson.
22. Verner W. Clapp and Robert T. Jordan, "Quantitative Criteria for Adequacy of Academic Library Collections," <u>College and Research Libraries</u> vol. 26, no. 5, Sept. 1965, p. 374.

THE SERIALS LIBRARIAN
AND THE JOURNALS PUBLISHER*

Huibert Paul

I am a serials librarian. That is to say, my chief concern is with continuing publications, as opposed to monographs. In the narrow sense, a serial is a continuing publication which is issued less frequently than twice a year; but in a braoder sense the term includes journals and it is in this way I shall for the most part be using it. I am also in a small way a publisher; that is to say, I am assistant editor of the PNLA Quarterly, official publication of the Pacific Northwest Library Association, and from that vantage point can see some of the difficulties of dealing as a publisher with serials librarians. In my opinion it is high time that both parties started paying more attention to the practical, common-sense aspects of serials publishing and the administration that goes with it. My approach in what follows is strictly nuts and bolts.

A medium-sized academic library today may well subscribe to some 15,000 periodicals and serials which altogether produce about 55,000 issues per year. One can easily imagine how inefficiency on the part of the publisher and librarian alike can take a frightful toll in dollars and cents. And many publishers are hampered by inefficiency--including commercial publishers, university presses, learned societies, professional associations, institutions, or individuals, all of whom may issue serials. So too are librarians. The cumulative effect may be seen in the high cost of handling serials. Now that money for education is becoming tighter, and taxpayers increasingly impatient with the expenses that have built up in the post-Sputnik education boom, librarians are caught in a financial squeeze. So are publishers, who must face higher operating costs and mailing rates, possibly with less financial support than in the past.

---

*Reprinted by permission from Scholarly Publishing, January 1972. Copyright 1972 by the University of Toronto Press.

Therefore it is high time that publishers and librarians put aside their whims and fancies and haphazardness. We must become more efficient.

As librarian vs publisher I would like to make a number of observations from which both publishers and librarians may benefit. (Later I will speak as publisher vs librarian.) These first observations, which are addressed to publishers, fall into three broad categories: obligations, administration, standardization.

Let's first explore some of the publisher's obligations. When you--whether you are an organization or an individual--start a periodical or serial, there is of course no obligation to continue publishing it until time shall be no more. The world does not expect another Journal des Savants, which was first published in 1665 in France, was suspended briefly during the Reign of Terror, the early revolutionary wars, and Napoleonic wars, but is still going today--possibly the oldest journal in existence. But the world--and it's a big one--does expect the title to last a reasonable number of years. Libraries spend a considerable amount of time getting a subscription started. They spend time on temporary records, on cataloguing and classifying after the first issue has arrived, and on permanent records. Subscription agents spend time listing any new title. It will also appear in the library literature, and libraries will report it to the Library of Congress, whereupon it will probably appear in that serials librarians' tool of tools called New Serial Titles. (This publication from the Library of Congress lists serials from all over the world that began publication on or after 1 January 1950. It is kept up to date by accumulations and a rough guess would indicate it contains 60,000 titles. Its predecessor, the Union List of Serials, boasts 156,449 entries.) Furthermore, prospective authors may start drafting articles for your new journal, and advertisers may start wondering if they should not write you about buying space. To make a long story short, when you start a new journal the world is full of expectation. Publishers should be fully aware of the seriousness and magnitude of the undertaking. They should not waste the world's time on a publishing venture that has not been adequately thought out and fizzles out after the fourth or fifth issue. Yet this sort of thing does continue to happen. Nor is it just the publishers of "little magazines" that waste the world's time and money: scholarly and academic publications also crash shortly after take-off. Ask any serials librarian. In the case of academic journals, librarians often find themselves in the miserable position of having just built up a respectable number of exchange relationships when the crash occurs.

No one except an occasional fool will attempt to cross an ocean without adequate supplies, without compass, or without a grasp of the rudiments of navigation. Yet when it comes to journal publishing this kind of light-hearted behaviour does not infrequently take place. New Serial Titles, 1966-1969 lists about 900 titles that have ceased publication or were superseded by other titles before the publications were five years old. I am well aware of the many adversities that may beset publishers, but I am sure not all publishers of these titles were well equipped when they started their journeys. The costs for libraries are very high. It takes anywhere from $53 to $72 to acquire initially and catalogue a serial [see note]. So it took from $47,700 to $64,800 ($53 to $72 times 900) for one library to acquire these 900 serials, not to speak of the cost of removing them from active serials files after their demise.

It can happen, of course, that publishers run into unexpected difficulties. Temporary suspension of publication can be endured, but the world has a right to know about it. There are many publishers, however, that conveniently forget to notify their subscribers. Or perhaps not so conveniently: an avalanche of claims from librarians and subscription agents from coast to coast may soon bury the publisher. Again, this kind of thing does not happen only to the ordinary common or garden-variety publisher, but also to respectable higher-education publishers. It may cost a publisher $100 or more to notify several thousand subscribers, but he should set some money aside for that rainy day. Librarians are sometimes on the verge of nervous breakdowns when they are left guessing as to whether a publication has faded away temporarily or forever. New Serial Titles is of no help in such cases either, because it depends largely on reporting libraries for its information and libraries that are left guessing have nothing definite to report.

When a publisher decides to bow out altogether, he should do so gracefully. For heaven's sake, notify your subscribers. This is all the more important when the subscriber is a university library, which may spend $200,000 per year on subscription costs alone and not be a notably large institution. Hardly a day goes by that academic librarians do not encounter the problem of a publisher who simply has vanished or does not reply to inquiries. And here we come to the topic of payment in advance. It's nice for the publisher. It's not nice for the librarian. Payment in advance means that the librarian bears all the risk and the publisher, as far as I can see, none. There are still publishers, even those of journals of considerable scholarly value, who cash in on a subscription for a year or two and then cease publication after one of the first issues of the new term. The library is not going to spend $100 on time and effort trying to recover the $10 it is owed.

It would be well to say a few words at this point about ethics--and the ever-increasing tendency, especially of publishers of scholarly journals, to charge libraries two or three times as much as individuals. It's true that libraries have more money than individuals have, but aren't such publishers using public (library) funds to promote private interests? Every academic library, and every larger public library as well, is now involuntarily subsidizing private publishing ventures to the tune of hundreds or even thousands of dollars per year. One might even say that one part of an academic library's budget is used to make knowledge available to patrons and that another part is used, via the higher subscription rates for libraries, to make knowledge available worldwide. My indignation was somewhat diminished when I read the publishers' argument that libraries make serials available to many people who otherwise would be subscribing individually, thereby drastically reducing the number of possible subscribers. On the other hand, if the number of subscriptions stays relatively small because of libraries and because of photocopying, publishers only too obviously know how to make up for this. At our library we used to subscribe to two copies of a very expensive but indispensable publication. In order to stretch our budget we dropped the second subscription. Alas, we now pay as much for one subscription as we did for two only four years ago. The whole affair of higher rates for libraries should be further explored.

I should now like to bring up a few aspects concerning administration. First, terms of subscription should be stated clearly. If this sounds silly, ask any serials librarian how often he has to guess about foggy terms when attempting to order or renew. Publishers of "little magazines" are the undisputed champs, of course, but in the academic world the

fog often kills efficiency too. I see very often that we really
don't know what we are ordering or under what terms we are
renewing. Statements such as "subscription $12" or "$8 for
3 issues" are of little help without a period of time or frequency of publication. Publishers then become the victim of
their own carelessness: hazy statements about terms produce
hazy orders, which in turn produce volumes and issues the
librarian did not aim for and invoices which he returns to
the publisher with questions. The more confused the records
at both the publisher's end and the librarian's become, the
less likely it is that the publisher's invoice will be paid
promptly, if indeed paid at all. The librarian will not be
able to renew on time, whereupon the publisher can spend
time and money on renewal notices. If he cuts the library
off, it will only produce claim forms, letters, and telephone
calls. Time and space do not allow me to tell the hair-raising stories all librarians know. In short, clear and precise subscription terms prevent confusion and correspondence;
they save time and money for the librarian, for the publisher,
and for the subscription agent.

When stating subscription terms publishers can cut
down considerably on administrative costs by encouraging
two- or three-year subscriptions, either at the same yearly
rate or at a small discount. Serials librarians like such
multiple-year subscriptions even without discounts for the
simple reason that payment records need updating less frequently. The same is true for the publisher, who needs
send fewer statements or renewal notices. (In many cases,
however, stifling state regulations, at least in the USA, forbid payment for more than one year in advance when there
is no discount. This kind of rule goes against the better
judgement of the librarian but he must put up with things
that are largely beyond his control.) While there is less
work for both librarian and publisher, they also assume
some risk. The librarian runs the risk of losing money
which he has paid for a three-year subscription and then
sees, to his chagrin, the publisher close shop before the
time runs out. On the other hand, the publisher may find
it necessary to charge more for subscriptions because of
unexpected costs, only to come to the unhappy realization
that he is stuck with numerous three-year subscriptions at
the old rate that may still have two years left to run. This
is what happened with the PNLA Quarterly, which had to go
from a very low $2 per year to a more realistic $5 per
year. A number of subscribers had paid $6 for three years
over which they otherwise would have paid $2 + $5 + $5 =

$12. There are publishers who would send an invoice for an additional charge to libraries in such cases. In my opinion this is a breach of contract, but librarians usually do not protest for fear of interrupted subscriptions.

Another device that possibly saves labour is for the publisher to insist that subscribers pay in advance without an invoice or renewal notice. This "cash in advance" approach is for the publisher similar to the use of a subscription agent, inasmuch as he receives his payment without having to send out invoices, but by this technique he does not have to spend a cent on agents' discounts. Attractive as the arrangement is, however, very few publishers insist on it. There are many libraries in the United States, and likely elsewhere, that are apparently unable to pay, because of regulations, without having received an invoice. There is thus a danger of losing subscribers who insist on invoices. Perhaps the "cash in advance" rule can be enforced only for indispensable publications when librarians are willing to put up with almost anything in order to acquire issues. Even then, the correspondence that will inevitably result may cancel out any advantage the publisher may have gained.

The fact is that whenever a publisher makes things difficult for librarians he merely invites trouble and expense. This is especially true in the case of academic libraries. Conversely, both publisher and librarian can expect reasonably smooth sailing when neither one sows seeds for potential trouble. I think, for instance, about memberships and package deals. Whatever advantage publishers see in them, large libraries often find themselves in a situation where they must become a member of such-and-such an organization in order to acquire a certain serial. Organizations would do well to realize that librarians are interested only in certain publications. They are not interested in occasional newsletters, invitations to meetings, ballots, brochures, flyers, and other paraphernalia that memberships tend to bring. There is often also the question of what does and what does not come with membership. Again, it leads to correspondence. And to delayed invoices and materials returned because the library could not find orders for them. Later, often much later, the library finds out these materials came free with membership. Package deals provide the same problems. There often is confusion about what is and what is not included. Again, correspondence and delayed invoices that could have been avoided. From the librarian's point of view it would be much better if publishers would allow for separate subscriptions for separate periodicals and serials, especially where organizations with memberships are concerned. Dear publisher, your particular title is only one of 15,000 titles that your university library subscriber is trying to keep track of.

Still under administration, here are two more bits of business advice for publishers from the librarian's viewpoint. They concern payment records and sample copies. Enter payment data correctly and completely and be especially careful when your volumes are not on a calendar-year basis. That in itself is a seed from which sprout erroneous claims, fuzzy renewal orders, and foggy invoices. One small example: a library starts a subscription with calendar year 1971. If the publisher honours this order and sends the library volume 13, numbers 2 to 4, and volume 14, number 1 (supposing the journal is a quarterly with issue number 2 in, say, January, number 3 in April, number 4 in July and the first issue of the next volume in October), chances are the library will later erroneously claim volume 13, number 1, not realizing it never paid for that issue, or the library will try to purchase it separately in order to make the volume complete--librarians are obsessed by the idea of completeness and they instinctively abhor gaps. So you as a publisher will have extra work. The alternatives are to switch the volume year to the calendar year, or to accept subscriptions only for full volumes. And then there are those sample copies. Larger libraries receive several every day. Curiously enough, many samples come without explanation. Whereupon they are sidetracked because clerks can find no entry for the titles in their records. At best the publisher harvests a new subscription from his undesignated sample only after considerable delay, and at worst the unexplained sample copy disappears forever, resulting in a total loss to the publisher. University publications are often among unexplained samples. Things become even more interesting when the mystery issue does not reveal how one might go about subscribing.

So far we have talked about some of the obligations a publisher has towards his subscribers and about a few aspects of administration. Now a few words about standardization.

Because I am a serials librarian with 15,000 titles to take care of, standardization is my favourite subject. I have dealt with it extensively in an article in <u>Library</u>

Resources and Technical Services, volume 14, number 1, winter 1970. There I pointed to U.S. standard Z39.1-1967, also known as the U.S. Standard for Periodicals: Format and Arrangement, approved 7 June 1967 by the American National Standards Institute. Believe it or not, most publishers and even most librarians apparently have never heard of it. I stumbled on it myself more or less by accident. This standard goes into considerable detail; two important parts deal with identifying dates and numbers, and width of margins. It is the librarian's dream that on some blessed day in the future all publishers will put volume and issue numbers and dates on the front cover of issues. Academic libraries record the receipt of about 1,500 periodical or serial issues per week, and it is impossible to process these quickly if clerks must hunt for identifying numbers and dates for each of the 1,500. I realize that publishers are very picky about the appearance of their covers, but surely a clearly printed title and exact identifying numbers and dates need not detract from attractiveness.

Standardization of width or margins is the other big unfulfilled dream of the storekeepers of knowledge. For adequate binding, margins should be from 3/4 to 1 inch wide. Otherwise, it can be quite a struggle to read the words at the inner margins after binding, and when the reader tries to bend back or flatten out the volume the consequences to the spine are disastrous. Serials with narrow margins also cannot be bound in thick volumes, so that the library's physical volume holds fewer issues than would be the case if margins were wider. This adds to the binding costs. The importance of adequate margins is easy to see when one realizes that the average medium-sized academic library spends about $40,000 per year on binding nowadays.

Until now I have talked mostly about my experience as librarian vs publisher. Now a few words, in my role as assistant editor of the PNLA Quarterly, about publisher vs librarian. Space does not permit me to dwell very long on the publisher's end of subscriptions and my work as assistant editor is only a sideline. Since I do it largely on my own time, I avoid extra work and correspondence like the plague. I think I have been quite successful. During four years in the job, the Quarterly has not misnumbered volumes or issues or dropped an issue number; it has come out reasonably on time; and subscribers have received invoices that stated exactly what they were going to get and at what price. These are important factors preventing correspondence.

In this context I appreciate subscription agents. It is very pleasant to see subscription monies roll in <u>via</u> agents without having to bother about sending invoices or renewal notices. The <u>PLNA Quarterly</u> gives agents a discount of 10 per cent and it is well worth it. As a publisher I especially long for the services of subscription agents whenever I deal with libraries that either will not or cannot use them. Such is not infrequently the case with school, college, or university libraries. After waiting in vain for money to come in, I find myself forced to write tedious invoices. As a reward for my labours I then do not receive money but rather a form, to be filled out in triplicate or quadruplicate. These forms do not differ a whole lot from state to state, but they differ just enough to make the publisher's life miserable. And there are, after all, no fewer than fifty states as well as ten provinces in Canada, plus states, provinces, counties, and departments all over the world. The publisher is also requested to wade through longwinded instructions and warnings, and sometimes gets the impression he has practically to sign his life away to get his meagre five dollars or so. In extreme cases the publisher once even had to get the form notarized, but for the sake of mercy this requirement seems to have been dropped. Whatever reasons governmental agencies may have for these procedures, they require a scandalous amount of work by publisher and librarians alike, not to speak of mailing costs. Even when it is crystal clear that a subscription is due for renewal, many schools and academic libraries are unable to honour a publisher's invoice without a purchase order number, a vendor number, or whatever the blessed number is called. It's bureaucracy at its best or worst.

Librarians often criticize and sometimes even ridicule publishers, but as a publisher I find libraries do some funny things, too. Like drifting from agent A to agent B to agent C and then back to A again. Or subscribing via an agent, then "direct" (without an agent), then back through an agent again, etc. Sometimes, in the United States, state regulations require bidding, with all the disastrous results in costs, but there seem to be other mysterious reasons involved also. Such librarians manage to waste the time of themselves, of the publishers, and last but not least, of subscription agents.

There are also libraries that never make up their minds what their exact address is going to be. Sometimes they call themselves the John Q. Broadside Library and sometimes the "library," the "general library," or whatever.

The danger is that the publisher no longer knows whether he is dealing with one or with two libraries. If someone gives a lot of money to a library, fine, but librarians should not burden publishers, agents, and the world at large by saying that the University of So-and-So Library henceforth will be called the John Q. Broadside Library. Nor am I, as a publisher, thrilled when as a result of a brainstorm a library starts calling itself a "learning resources centre." Should several hundred, or perhaps several thousand, payment records and mailing lists around the world be changed? I don't think so.

Finally, a few words about missing issues. As a librarian I have always complained about publishers failing to send all issues due, but as a publisher I have developed second thoughts. The publisher is not always to blame, nor is the mailman. While it is probably true that the majority of claims from libraries are genuine and the issues indeed never were received, there must also be many cases where issues arrived but simply got lost in the library itself. I do not know how otherwise to explain some of the complaints that a library has claimed nonreceipt of the last four or so issues while we could find nothing wrong with our mailing list. We almost always honour such claims and as a publisher I feel obliged to answer all of them.

The above are but a few ways to save time and money for publishers, librarians, and, incidentally, subscription agents. There is much room for improvement in publishing house and library alike. Inefficiency results in higher costs. Instead of forever passing on such higher costs to subscribers and taxpayers, we had better do something about them. Budgets have become tighter and tighter during the past two or three years and I am afraid the worst is still to come. If ever there was a time to search for more efficient operations, it is now.

Note

The figures are from "Library Cost Models: Owning versus Borrowing Serial Publications," by Gordon Williams, Director of The Center for Research Libraries, Chicago, Ill., and by Edward C. Bryant, etc., of Westat Research, Inc., Bethesda, Md. The study was done for the Office of Science Information Service, National Science Foundation. Published in November 1968, it contains most interesting and revealing cost figures, especially in the tables on pages 75-84.

THE CATALOGER'S WHITE KNIGHT? MARC*

Hillis L. Griffin

Sometime, on a nice, quiet day in your library, when all of the problems have been solved, and the phone is not ringing off the hook, give a thought to the part of your library where problems are eternal and where, if they are ever solved, it is at great expense and redundant effort. This activity is called cataloging, and holds forth day and (sometimes) night, depending upon the balance of the input of books to be cataloged. It is influenced to some extent by requests from users for books, obviously received by the library, to be cataloged. Output will rise or fall depending upon the weekly arrival of proof slips from the Library of Congress, or the receipt of an occasional printed card from the Library of Congress for a book received months earlier. As a last resort, you may decide to give original cataloging to a book which has been on hand for some time and for which, as surely as night follows day, cataloging will issue forth from the Library of Congress within two weeks of the time you catalog it. Worse yet, they will not agree with you. Indeed, if we were to convene an international symposium (federally supported, of course) with the attendance of the 473 catalogers who have already cataloged this book, we would probably fail to find substantial agreement among them on almost any contentious point. What should really cause us dismay, however, is that 472 of these people had to spend any time at all cataloging that book. Given a certain level of professional cataloging, I would imagine that most of the 472 would have been able to apply appropriate modifications (the name of this game is called proof-sheet cataloging, in case you do not recognize it) to the catalog record received from the Library of Congress in rather short order, which would have given more time to demonstrate against the 17th edition of Dewey, or to demonstrate for the 18th. At any rate, I submit that one of the real problems in librarianship

---

*Reprinted by permission from Special Libraries, May/June 1972.

today is not whether rugs have a place in all libraries, or whether the computer will replace the book. As things are going now, we will still have some 1970 imprints awaiting cataloging if and when the computer is ever ready to replace them. And while you are at it, you might shed a tear for the user who could have profited from having the use of that book. Poor fellow! Our real problem is getting those books cataloged.

If there is still a dry eye among you at this point, consider the number of publications which were not listed in Publishers' Weekly last week, or the week before that, and so on. These were the publications of societies, institutes, symposia, and other bodies both noted and obscure. We each have our secret methods for finding them and acquiring them, so that we can "not-catalog" them because they are so difficult that even the Library of Congress will not touch them, except under extreme duress.

I sometimes think that we rate rather poor marks as information merchants to ourselves. Not only do we have problems identifying the world's literature, and cataloging it, but we also have problems in making known to ourselves the availability of catalog information. And once it is available we spend time and effort in typing cards, in typing call numbers, tracings and the like on the card sets which must then be broken up, alphabetized, and ultimately filed in the right place in our catalogs. In all of this the real problem is the amount of time we spend--clerk and cataloger--looking for information, identifying items to acquire so that we can try to locate catalog information for them.

Cataloging in Publication

Cataloging in source would be a marvelous answer to this dilemma. Some of you may remember when, for a time, some books arrived with a catalog card printed on the back of the title page, or at the end of the book. Things were certainly easy then. Unfortunately, this scheme apparently made life so easy for the librarians that it was abandoned. Some attempts are now being made to resuscitate this ghost under the guise of Cataloging in Publication. I hope that it will succeed, for we very desperately need every program of this kind that we can nurture to assist in getting the cataloging done. I wish that I could view this as the answer to the problem, but reflect for a moment.

Consider which publishers will never put the standard book number on their publications, because they do not know what the standard book number is, much less what their standard book number is. This same tribe of bibliographic gypsies will not be champing at the bit to catalog their books in publication either. Indeed, I would gather that some of the pleasure they derive from publication is thinking about librarians around the world trying to establish reasonable subject headings for their last offering before the next one comes along.

Before you decide to throw in the towel and line up at the local unemployment office, I do want to say that help is on the way. The good guys in the white hats at the Library of Congress have not been idle. We have been watching the emergence of a solution for several years now, and it seems more viable with each passing year. Not many librarians have seen it, although many have heard of it. Some who have heard of it have wondered what it will do for them, and others have wondered what it will do to them. Others have written it off as just another half-baked antic of the computer crowd, doomed to be too expensive and too limited to be of much use to any library, except the largest, for whom it will surely be too expensive simply because of its sheer bulk. And anyhow, computers are too expensive for libraries. And if they are not too expensive, then they will not do "it" right. And besides, we do not understand about computers, and we do not want to understand about them either.

An Answer?

The name of the white knight is MARC, which stands for MAchine Readable Cataloging. I have never ceased to marvel at the genius who was able to connect cataloging with an acronym of any sort. Its genesis came from a meeting in 1963 at which the computer-related future of the Library of Congress was discussed by librarians and computer-related non-librarians. Very little was settled, but it seemed rather basic to some that the basis for any substantive computer applications at the Library of Congress was the development of some way to represent and manipulate bibliographic information. Not just 80 columns of bibliographic information in a punched card, but an even more comprehensive representation than was then found with the Library of Congress printed cards. Henriette Avram and her group persevered, and from this work came the MARC Pilot Project in 1966, distributing comprehensive bibliographic information for over 55,000 English language monographs to the 16 participating libraries in 2-1/2 years. These libraries did things with the information--produced catalog cards, book catalogs, acquisitions lists, cataloger work sheets, book selection lists, and more. They evaluated MARC for the jobs that they had in mind in their libraries. They found its weak points--and its strengths too. Most of all they determined that it was an answer, and that it has to be refined, expanded, made to work, and continued. The Library of Congress, for its part, had not only to evaluate MARC in relation to its own bibliographic activities, but had to explore efficient and accurate methods to put this information into machine-readable form, and to do it rapidly.

Both of these groups saw the fruition of their efforts in MARC II, which seems to have two meanings. First, we have the MARC II format which is really a scheme for fully representing bibliographic information in machine-readable form (Let us say "on computer tape" for convenience) in a standard arrangement that will be generally usable and can easily accommodate such changes and modifications as are later found to be desirable. The main problem arises with the identification of the elements of information within the bibliographic record. The computer, because of its gross stupidity, finds it very difficult to distinguish a geographic subdivision from a form subdivision in a subject heading, for example. It can do it, but at considerable expense. Better that this information be formally identified as such if we are to minimize expense to the user. So MARC II is, for one thing, a standard, and is so recognized by the American National Standards Institute, and by the professional library organizations. It is a format for the transfer of information from one library to another, but it is certainly not the ideal format for the storage of this information. It is not even used by the Library of Congress to store MARC data. But it is an elegant and sophisticated format for the transfer of information among and between a large group of information receivers.

Second, then, is the meaning of MARC II as a distribution service of the Library of Congress. The Library distributes weekly, on magnetic computer tape, the accumulation of new data records for the cataloging of English language monographs which have been accepted into the system during the past week. This information is distributed to over 65 users in the United States, Canada, Great Britain, Europe, and the Far East. An average week's output will be about 1,200 records--over 60,000 records each year--representing all the English language monographic cataloging output of the Library of Congress. The service costs subscribers $800/year--about a penny per record. It is now in its third year of operation.

What to Do with It

What can you do with these records that come to you each week? One thing you can do is to use this information to prepare catalog cards. That is what the Library of Congress is doing with it--photocomposing catalog cards instead of producing them on the old brass press. It has sometimes been rumored that Capitol Hill is nothing more than a great dome built over the filing cabinets that contain all of the in-print LC printed cards produced since Man was created. If this is true, then this new method of card production means that the Pentagon is safe from requisitioning as a depository for further card storage, since cards will now be photocomposed and printed "on-demand" as they are ordered.

Library and library-related users have followed suit, albeit less elegantly, printing their cards on computer printers--some in upper and lower case character sets with a full complement of diacritical marks, and some in upper case only without diacriticals. Some libraries use MARC as input to their production of book catalogs. One library is providing a current awareness service in several subject areas (library science among them) to many libraries about the country. The important thing to note is that MARC is being effectively used by a number of libraries (many not even subscribers) in this country, probably nearly 100. I could go on at some length about how MARC can be used to provide these products, but this is an ongoing activity, and more applications are developed each month.

I hope that I will not provoke a rush of tears to your eyes by harking back to the agonies of cataloging to which I referred earlier. You remember--everybody cataloging the same book. The reason that they were all cataloging it, of course, was that none of them knew that the other was. Given their druthers, some of them would not have cared if somebody else were cataloging it--they would have gone on and done it "right," anyway. The problem which we face in our library, and which I wish all libraries faced, is that the books arrive at our library the same time as they arrive at the Library of Congress. So we are tempted to play the waiting game, seeing whether we can outlast them, before we finally yield and do original cataloging for these books. Some libraries wait forever for the Library of Congress, and some have even been known to purchase a microfilm copy of a book which crumbled to dust waiting on a shelf in the catalog room to be cataloged.

MARC should be able to get the cataloging information to libraries sooner, especially since the regular catalog cards will be photocomposed from the MARC information. Libraries should no longer have to file proof slips, but should, instead, be able to rely on locally generated indexes to a MARC data base, or to interrogate this file via remote consoles. I emphasize that such a system can work very nicely in a non-interactive environment. A major difficulty in finding catalog information is that most files are arranged by main entry, and main entries are rather difficult to predict. It would appear that indexes arranged by title offer some advantage is searching for catalog information. With the computer, and with machine-readable catalog information, you can arrange the indexes in any form, for any time span, and even reject certain materials automatically.

Another important use of MARC information is as a selection tool for ordering. Although the MARC record can be used to generate purchase orders, it can also be used very nicely to generate a selection list, arranged by class. The best material to order is the material you can catalog as soon as it arrives at your library, and, if you use the MARC data base as a source for ordering, you guarantee that you will move these books out into circulation very rapidly.

Toward a National System

All of this activity still places each library in a rather passive role relative to generating catalog information. We are still in the same situation--waiting for the Library of Congress to get around to cataloging our book. We have defined a method of communicating information from one library to another, and we have defined the rules for the bibliographic elements which must be included and identified. But it is still a one-way street. Now we need to consider sharing. We need an interactive catalog information system which will enable us to secure cataloging information if it is available. If it is not available, we need to be able either to leave a message that we want to receive it when it is available, or that we will volunteer to catalog it and make it available. Such a system would be much like a reservation system for airline seats.

If we have to catalog all of our books without outside assistance, we pay a terrible price, and without giving--or receiving--charity. Or we may refuse to pay the price, letting the users pay instead, by not providing them with the information they need. If there was ever a method devised for giving a library a reputation for poor service, and for creating a large group of ex-users, then this is surely it.

We talk very glibly about cooperation, but you have probably noticed that libraries have great difficulty cooperating among themselves, especially after the euphoria of conferences and discussions has worn off. Costs are rising, and budgets are decreasing. There are more books and journals to acquire, and fewer dollars with which to process each one. Surely no area of librarianship is in such tragic condition, or suffers so much active neglect, as this business of getting the materials processed and out on the shelves. And things will continue to go this way until we all realize that it is in the best interest of all of us to do something about this problem. The methods and equipment are at hand. We lack only concerted and responsible support for such an undertaking. I am amazed that so many people wax eloquent about conserving our human resources and yet condone our technical processing systems.

I am looking toward this needed, and logical, next extension of MARC. You must remember that the Library of Congress is simply that--the congressional library. It is not our national library, built to serve the national community of libraries. What we are really looking for is an interactive National Union Catalog to make available to libraries everywhere our current bibliographic resources, and to give them active support in building these resources together, not in splendid isolation. MARC is the vehicle through which this can occur, and which makes it possible. The MARC system which we see today must be the forerunner of a more comprehensive, interactive system of shared bibliographic information. We simply cannot afford to re-invent the wheel thousands of times each day. Nobody is going to offer you this system ready-made. You are going to have to invest _your_ time and sweat and money in it, and others are going to have to do the same. The ultimate worth of such a system is beyond measure, and the time for its appearance on the library scene is long overdue.

FROM INFORMATION SCIENCE TO INFORMATICS:
A TERMINOLOGICAL INVESTIGATION*

Hans Wellisch

> Science begins when the meaning of the words is strictly delimited. Words may be selected from the existing vocabulary or new words may be coined, but they all are given a new definition, which prevents misunderstandings and ambiguities within the chapter of science where they are used. [--L. Brillouin (D, p. ix)**]

The famous French physicist's statement holds true for any science, although it was probably not a coincidence that it was made in the preface to a work on statistical information theory. It was originally written in 1956, a few years before people began to talk and write about a new discipline, also concerned with the phenomenon of information, which came to be called Information Science (IS).

Both the newness of the discipline and its claim to be a science have been challenged. Some practitioners of the discipline as well as people working in related fields have repeatedly asked: is there an information science? and is it indeed a science? In the following investigation, I shall try to arrive at an answer by applying Brillouin's criteria to IS. It is not my intention to find out whether IS has all or some of the attributes of a true science, or whether it is a meta-science, a supra-science or maybe a pseudo-science. At least one such attempt has already been made (33)† and others may yet follow. I shall only try to investigate the basic component which is the touchstone of any field that aims to be recognized as a science: its central topic of investigation, as implied in the name of the science and

---

*Reprinted by permission from Journal of Librarianship, 4:3 (July 1972).
**Letter references are to Bibliography (end of article).
†Number references are to Appendix (end of article).

defined by its terminology as it is used by people who are active in the discipline and who publish the results of their research.

In other words, I shall look at the statements made by information scientists themselves, to see whether the scope and aims of IS have been described so that "misunderstandings and ambiguities" are avoided, and whether old or newly-coined words have been given new and unique definitions.

It seems to me that this is necessary for three reasons:

(a) IS (under that specific name) has been with us for more than a decade, and much has been written about its status as a new science, its scope, methods and applications;

(b) Many writers on information, its generation, communication, storage, reception and use, have claimed scientific merit for their work on the grounds that it pertains to the new IS;

(c) IS is primarily concerned with words and the way in which they are used to record and communicate knowledge, so that the concepts and ideas that are basic to this science itself should be expressed and defined in the most rigorous manner--more so, maybe, than in any other science.

But before we set out to investigate the central topic of IS and its terminology, we must look briefly at the evolution of concepts and ideas that led to the proclamation of a new science. IS did not spring forth full-fledged like Pallas Athene from Zeus' head, but had its origins in developments that can be traced back for about a century.

From Library Economy to Information Retrieval

Almost 100 years ago, in the annus mirabilis of 1876 that saw the foundation of the American Library Association, the first edition of Dewey's Decimal Classification and the first issue of Cutter's Rules for a Dictionary Catalog, the all-embracing term for the study of recorded knowledge, its collection, storage, display and dissemination (mostly, though not exclusively, in the form of books) was "Library economy."

The term "economy" had then still its original connotation and was used in a sense largely synonymous with present-day "management." There is no doubt, however, that Library economy meant primarily the physical handling of books and other documents in places where these were stored for preservation and possible future use. Even the analysis of a book's subject content and the use of classification for this purpose was seen primarily in terms of physical arrangement of books on shelves, a trend that continues to this very day in practically all American libraries.

Towards the end of the 19th century the field of Library economy became gradually known as "Library science," following a popular trend to call almost any human activity that could be studied and about which a certain body of literature had accumulated a "science," although this had but little to do with the narrower sense in which this term is used in the English-speaking world--the observation and study of naturally occurring phenomena and the endeavour to discover universally applicable laws underlying these phenomena by performing experiments, formulating hypotheses and theories, and employing the tools of mathematics and formal logic. This happened because of the vastly enhanced prestige enjoyed by any activity that could claim the name of "science" (whether rightly or wrongly) and maybe also to a certain degree as a consequence of the German, French and Russian use of the word "science" which, in these languages, means a scholarly activity in any of the fields of human knowledge, whether concerned with natural phenomena, human relations or the products of the human mind. Yovits (33) has put this very succinctly:

> No real thought is generally given to the significance of calling a field of study or research a science.... The term science is appended without any real understanding of the implication, meaning, or significance of using this term.

Thus, merely changing Library economy to Library science did not, of course, mean that any kind of truly scientific method was applied to the study of libraries, their functions and operation--it merely seemed to librarians that it might do a lot to enhance their status among the professions (not, however, daring to go so far as to call themselves "Library scientists" instead of librarians...). We need not be concerned with this stage in the development of nomenclature in the field of the study of recorded knowledge, because

"Library science" does not qualify for the epithet "science" any more than "sanitation science" which is concerned with problems of garbage collection and disposal--a very necessary and even complicated field of study, but not really a science. Conversely, however, Librarianship (to call it by its proper and less pretentious name) is certainly one of the primary fields of application of IS, much as chemistry is a science that must be applied to effective waste disposal.

The first significant development in the field after Dewey and Cutter was made, both conceptually and terminologically, by Otlet and La Fontaine who founded the <u>Institut International de Bibliographie</u> in 1895, to encompass recorded human knowledge not only as preserved in books but in any kind of document such as in articles, theses and reports and even in largely or entirely non-verbal records such as maps, diagrams and pictures. They stressed particularly the aspect of subject content as being independent of form of presentation, thus breaking away from the unfortunate preoccupation of librarians with physical (and therefore linear) arrangement of documents on shelves. Soon, they began to use the term "documentation" in their writings, and defined it as "a process by which are brought together, classified and distributed all the documents of all kinds of all the areas of human activity." From the late 20s onwards and until the eve of World War II, the study of conceptual as well as physical aspects of recorded knowledge and its utilization (particularly in science and technology) was increasingly referred to as "documentation." The <u>Institut de Bibliographie</u> was renamed <u>Institut Internationale de Documentation</u> in 1931, and became the <u>Fédération Internationale de Documentation</u> (FID) in 1938. After World War II, the term "documentation" became fully established with the publication of Bradford's book bearing that title, in which he said that "documentation is the art of collecting, classifying and making readily accessible the records of all kinds of intellectual activity ... " (C).

Despite Bradford's succinct definition, however, the term very soon underwent the metamorphosis that at about the same time began to affect the term "Information": it became ambiguous, amorphous and was used for the most divergent notions, sometimes by people who had only a very dim idea of what they were talking about but were happy to have a vogue word which could be bandied around freely. In central and western Europe, Documentation is still the official designation for the whole field, i.e., the study of recorded knowledge as well as its physical carriers (documents), while in the US (and much later also in the USSR) different developments took place which gave rise to significant changes in terminology.

The American Documentation Institute, although displaying the term "documentation" prominently in its name, concerned itself in the early 50s very much with microfilm and punched cards as carriers of recorded knowledge, i. e., it stressed the same physical and technical aspects of documents that were the main concern of the much older "library science," but contrary to the developments that took place in Europe (especially in England and later in Germany and France), almost no research efforts were devoted to the subject content of recorded knowledge, or even worse, it was assumed that the words in which it was expressed were equivalent to concepts and ideas (an unfortunate error that persists in the minds of many people to this very day). Thus, documentation in the US came to mean only part of what it meant in Europe--the technology or the hardware, but scarcely ever the conceptual content or the software.

This was probably the reason why a new term "Information retrieval" (IR), first coined by Mooers in 1950, was considered to be necessary and also why it was so eagerly adopted. Although originally meant to signify only the operations necessary to gain access to recorded knowledge irrespective of the form of documentary carriers and aimed at making a distinction between the physical and mental activities that have to be carried out to this effect, the term IR became an "in"-word, and again everybody who wanted to be "with-it" talked and wrote about IR, so that the term supplanted "Documentation" almost entirely, and became virtually equivalent to the European idea of "Documentation." Somewhat later, it was realized that, to "retrieve" information from a place, it obviously had to be stored prior to the retrieval, so the term was augmented to "Information storage and retrieval" (ISR).

Since the advent of ISR roughly coincided with the first commercial applications of computers and it was then thought that very rapid handling of coded data was all that was needed to cope with the "information explosion" (another of the terms coined approximately at the same time), two entirely erroneous notions were compounded and somehow implied whenever the term ISR was used. One was that ISR could be performed only with the help of sophisticated machinery, primarily computers, and that anything done manually in conventional storage places of recorded information, i.e., in libraries, was not to be dignified with the new name; this misconception had its roots partly in complete ignorance on the part of "information retrievers" about what libraries were actually doing, but partly also in the prevailing preoccupation of librarians with the problems of arrangement of physical volumes on shelves, relegating the much more important issue of subject retrieval to outmoded schemes that had been conceived by librarians for librarians and which, in any case, had not been overhauled for more than a century. In other words, both "information retrievers" and conventional librarians were to blame for this unfortunate misunderstanding that did much harm and generated many needless and sterile discussions. The other misconception was that ISR was concerned only, or at least primarily, with the literature of science and technology, so that the term "Scientific information" was sometimes used glibly and indiscriminately as a synonym for ISR. Neither of these assumptions can stand up to critical examination, and this was repeatedly pointed out, especially by British workers in the field. Information retrieval takes place whenever a document is found in a store in response to a person's query and when that person reads or otherwise perceives its contents; it does not matter in the least whether the person (or a helpful librarian) has taken a book off a shelf in a library or whether a computer-controlled screen flashes digits and letters, or a teletype console prints out a message. Nor is ISR concerned only with a certain segment of recorded knowledge, such as scientific or technological topics (even though these contribute most to the so-called "information explosion"); fairy tales, novels and poems are as vital to the information needs of persons interested in these forms of literature and the topics dealt with in them as are the latest findings on RNA to a microbiologist or data on the strength of materials to an engineer.

The decade of the 50s saw the beginnings of serious and scientifically sound study of the processes underlying the generation, recording and transfer of human knowledge and of the technical operations necessary to make such transfer physically possible. Although much more than mere "storage and retrieval" was involved, the term ISR (or simply IR) reigned supreme as a catch-all designation for all these activities, with the main emphasis on mechanical problems, more particularly the application of computers to IR. Almost all American books, reports, articles and papers presented to conferences during the decade of the 50s and up to about 1962 that were devoted wholly or partially to the study of recorded knowledge displayed the words "Information retrieval" or "scientific information" and sometimes also "documentation" either in their titles or in chapter and paragraph headings. The last major contributions from the "IR era" were:

  i) the International Conference on Scientific Information (I) held in Washington, D.C. in 1958 (which, if held today, would almost certainly have been called "Conference on Information Science";
  ii) C. N. Mooers' exhaustive survey The Next Twenty Years in Information Retrieval (O) written in 1960, where, despite the perspective towards the future, the term IS is not yet mentioned even tentatively;
  iii) F. S. Wagner's A Dictionary of Documentation Terms (V) also published in 1960, which does not yet contain the term IS; and
  iv) a "State of the art symposium" (T) held in 1961 and published in early 1962, in which practically all aspects of what is now called IS were discussed, yet the participants still talked about IR.

The Era of "Information Science"

As far as can be ascertained by a fairly exhaustive search of the published literature, the term "Information Science" (IS) was first used in 1959 as a designation for the study of recorded knowledge and its transfer in the widest sense (1). An important contribution was made in 1960 by Heilprin (2) who, to be sure, did not yet use the term IS but pointed out quite clearly that the problems of the nature, properties and uses of information were such that they had to be studied in a truly scientific manner, making use of the tools of mathematics and applying methods developed in other sciences. He, in other words, all but used the term IS which was already "in the air" but had not yet become current or fashionable.

Although the term IS was no doubt used more or less frequently in oral discussions and meetings in the following year or so, it did not appear again in print until 1961, when for the first time the scope and aims of IS were defined at a conference (3), stating explicitly that the term "documentation" had been rejected "because of the wide variation in ... use and in the numerous interpretations of meaning." Little did the conferees know that the very same fate would soon befall the newly-coined term IS.

From 1962 onwards the term IS became firmly established in the US and gained rapid acceptance, even though, as we shall see later, no one was quite sure what it was or whether it was a science at all. This trend, incidentally, can only be discovered by actually scanning titles, abstracts of texts of articles published in American Documentation (then, as now, the principal American publication in the field), because the index to this journal does not begin to show the term IS before 1965! [footnote 1]. Information Science thus superseded Information Retrieval as a generic term for the whole field, while the latter term is now mostly reserved for discussion of the actual operations of retrieval systems (often still more restricted to mechanized retrieval).

The Definitions of Information Science

In order to find out what people who call themselves information scientists consider to be the basic concepts of their discipline, 39 different definitions of IS, published between 1959 and 1971, were investigated. There exist certainly more definitions of IS, some of which may be hidden in papers that give no clue to this fact in their titles or which have not been adequately indexed, but I hope that the papers and books selected for this investigation represent a fair picture of what some of the leading minds in IS consider its essence to be. The term "Information Science," when first publicly used (1) was not exactly defined but only rather broadly outlined by naming some of the topics covered by it, and it was explicitly linked to "computer sciences" in a study program under the auspices of a School of Electrical Engineering. This circumstance, as well as an examination of the topics of IS in this program, make it clear that the information to be studied scientifically was primarily the kind treated in Shannon and Weaver's Mathematical Theory of Communication [footnote 2], i.e., signals transmitted through a channel, and not semantic or meaningful information generated by and intended for human beings. Although the statistical theory of communication as developed by Shannon and Weaver is a topic that may usefully be studied in relation to IS, it is by no means equivalent to it, so that the importance of this earliest definition lies mostly in the introduction of the term IS itself.

One of the first attempts at scientifically derived definition of IS was made by Heilprin (5): "Information science concerns stored information: i.e., the modulation-stimuli for sensing the information are characteristically converted from short to long duration." Before Heilprin arrives at this highly condensed and apparently circular definition, he introduces the concept of transmission of meaning through systematic or intentional production of direct "sense-impressions" and it can be inferred that it is such transmitted meaning which constitutes "information" in his definition. This definition has stood the test of time remarkably well, and little of real value has been contributed by the many and variegated definitions which have been proposed over the last decade by various authors who generated more confusion than precision, as we shall presently see.

Table 1 (p. 234) is an alphabetical list of all terms used in the 39 definitions, excluding only the (redundant because circular) terms "information" and "knowledge" and terms such as application, description, technique(s), theory, etc. which have almost no definitional value in this context. Altogether, the 39 definitions use 109 terms, including the term "other fields" which is not a catch-all for miscellaneous terms encountered in this investigation, but is actually employed in three definitions without any further specification, leaving it to the reader of the definition to substitute his own particular field of application or derivation (not a very scientific way, of course, to construct a definition for a science ...).

Table 2 (p. 235) lists the 109 terms ranked by frequency. The most striking feature of this ranking is the long "tail" of terms that have been used only once or twice (64.2% of all terms). However, such a ranking would not give a true picture because of synonyms and near-synonyms for concepts that have been used by different authors. Even though the combination of these terms inevitably introduces an element of subjectivity (because not everybody might agree to my conception of synonymity and near-synonymity), this is justified, because it was my aim to find the <u>concepts</u> considered to be essential to IS, not the different words by which these concepts are named.

Table 3 (p. 236) shows the combinations of terms that were made and the resulting combined frequency. Each term stands for a (more or less) unique concept. Table 4 (p. 236-7) lists the resulting 81 terms, again ranked by frequency. The long "tail" is quite obvious also here--terms that have been used only once or twice now constituting 56.8% of the total. This confirms the great diversity of terms used and an amazing lack of commonality among information scientists as far as the definition of their own discipline is concerned. Only two terms, "dissemination" and "linguistics", are common to about 20% of the definitions, another 16% share the term "flow," and the two terms "processing" and "communication" are shared by 13%, but there are only 3 definitions (3, 22 and 26), or less than 4%, that share all 5 top terms (where ref. 22 and 26 repeat the terms listed in ref. 3 explicitly or implicitly, adding or reformulating only a few terms of their own). The picture that emerges is one of utter diversity and lack of agreement on even a single basic concept underlying the discipline of IS, except, of course, the concept of "information" itself which, however, is also highly ambiguous and mostly ill-defined. I shall revert to this particular aspect later on.

There is also great diversity in the number of terms employed in different definitions of IS. As shown in table 5 (p. 237), three definitions are extremely terse, using only two terms that are essential to the definition. One would assume that when definitions are pared down to such a bare minimum, at least some if not all of the terms used would be common to the three definitions which, in addition, were all proposed within a short time period (1970/71); moreover, these definitions were formulated after a decade had elapsed since IS was first defined, so that some consensus should by then have been reached. Alas, these three definitions of IS do not share a single term! The picture that emerges is:

Definition (36): Human beings, Information systems
(37): Informemes, Processes of information
(38): Behavioral sciences, Communication

There is, of course, more overlap between the terms used in other definitions as more terms are being used successively, but no picture of consensus emerges.

Also in this ranking, there is a "tail" of definitions which use a unique (and very large) number of terms.

These definitions include one that seems to be the most-cited, namely (3). They arrive at such a large number of terms (including the term "other fields" as a catch-all for anything the author could not think of) by going beyond a mere definition of what IS is supposed to be or to concern itself with, and naming a whole range of other sciences, disciplines, and possible applications to which IS is said to be related or from which it draws some or all of its topics, or for which it is or will become the super- (or supra-) science. In doing so, the authors of these "expanded" definitions venture outside the proper bounds of defining not only IS but any science. Fairthorne's words are worth quoting here:

> Any discipline must define its scope. That is, it must define what matters it will study explicitly. These matters must then be studied and talked about in their own terms, not in terms of their possible applications. The principles of the applications lie outside the scope of the discipline, and therefore of its own principles and its terminology. [F]

It is, of course, mainly due to the misguided efforts of those who draw in all possible (and some impossible) disciplines and applications in order to clarify what they mean by IS, or to bolster their claim that it is indeed a science, that such a large number of terms is used only once or twice in the definitions and that such a diversity of terminology exists.

One definition in particular goes beyond anything produced by the other pretenders to the crown of super-scientists (assuming that whoever is an active practitioner of a super-science must, ipso facto, become a super-scientist). Kitagawa (22) lists more than 40 terms of sciences, disciplines, activities, elements and devices which he considers to be "basic to the structure of IS." For the purposes of the tabulation in Table 5 (p. 237), only 30 of them have been taken into consideration, because they could somehow be considered to fall within the range of IS as defined by the other 38 authors (presuming that these generated, despite the divergences of opinion between them, a sort of general consensus on the limits of the field). Terms such as "cryogenic elements," "metals," "magnetic elements" and the like seemed to me to fall outside the scope of what can reasonably be termed IS. The author, moreover, apparently has only a vague idea about the meaning and form of words

and terms, inventing the plural "apparata" which he appends
to terms such as language, thinking, adaptation and education.
Clearly, something is wrong with his own "thinking
apparatus" and the attempt to define IS as a super-science
involving practically every other science and discipline can
only be likened to the story in Jerome K. Jerome's classic
Three Men in a Boat, where a young man, upon reading a
medical encyclopedia from cover to cover, finds that he is
afflicted with every disease described in the book--except
childbed fever....

Information Science--A Science or Sciences?

The definers of IS are also split in their opinion on
whether there is an Information science (in the singular) or
Information sciences (in the plural). The difference is important.
A majority of 29 definitions see IS as a single
discipline and tend to emphasize in their explanations that
IS is not only a new or emerging science, but also that it
is a science in its own right. Ten others speak about Information
sciences, and tend to see them as a cluster of
related disciplines and sciences, some of which are of long
standing, others that emerged only during the last decades,
but all having the generation, transmission and use of information
in common to some degree. The term "integrative
discipline" is used by Harmon (28) who elaborates this trend
of thought further in (38) where he speaks of IS as a catalyst
in the formation of a "suprasystem," linking the behavioral
and communication sciences and "integrating the humanities,
sciences and professions." Somewhat similarly, Otten and
Debons (35) see IS as a "metascience" and compare it with
metamathematics or formal mathematics which provide the
unified basis for all mathematical disciplines. They also
propose the name "Informatology" for a discipline which
would concern itself with aspects of information common to
a whole range of other scientific disciplines (probably without
being aware that this term had first been used in Sweden
by B. Tell in 1962 [footnote 3]).

The inter-disciplinary character of IS is, however,
asserted not only by those who use the term IS in the plural.
No less than 17 or almost exactly half of the 39 definitions
do so, but only 6 of them belong to the Sciences (plural)
school; 11 of those who use IS in the singular also think
that it is inter-disciplinary. Conversely, among the 18
definitions which view IS as a science sui generis, 3 use

the plural form, which is somewhat astonishing. By now, however, nothing should come as a surprise any longer to the student of definitions of IS.

Is Information Science a Science?

Several authors expressed their doubts about the true nature of IS, or tell us outright that it is impossible or at least very difficult to define it. Among them are Townley (U) who flatly states "It isn't a science" and asks "Why do we practice an art and not a science?"; Mooers (6) who says that "IS is more an expression of hope or a slogan to rally around than it is the name of a profession"; Taylor (7) who answers with St. Augustine, "I know so long as you do not ask me"; Cuadra (8) who admits, "we are far from common agreement on the conceptual, methodological, or practical contributions to the IS field"; Borko (22) who tells us that "those of us who have tried to make such explanations [of IS] know that it is a difficult task"; and Hoshovsky (23) who, in an answer and sequel to Borko's paper, admits that "our definition of IS is not a true definition"; Hoshovsky continues with the somewhat cryptic statement, "A definition of the field in terms of inputs must of necessity become progressively more inadequate as the advance of science and technology changes the content of what information scientists should properly do to produce the results IS should produce," whereupon he proceeds to give an "output-oriented" definition of this inputless, protean black box as which IS has been portrayed. I cannot think of any other science that could be defined in such terms, nor would there by many people who would care to be scientists in such a field. But information scientists, to whom this last definition was presented at an annual meeting, were apparently quite pleased with it-- at least, no protest was recorded in the proceedings of that meeting.

In a lighter vein, Shera (P) deplores the passing of "documentation" and is sceptical about IS:

> 'What does the North Pole look like?' Christopher Robin asked Rabbit, observing that he had known 'once,' but had 'sort of forgotten.' Rabbit replied that he'd 'sort of forgotten, too,' though he 'did know once.' Christopher Robin conjectured that 'it's just a pole stuck in the ground,' and Rabbit responded 'Sure to be a pole, and if it's a pole, well, I should

think it would be sticking in the ground, shouldn't you, because there'd be nowhere else to stick it.... The only thing is, where is it sticking?' So documentation, with all its history, richness, and connotative subtletly is now passé, and in its place we have a synthetic hybrid called information science, which, as Rabbit would say, is sure to be a science because of calling it a science. Moreover, it must be sticking in somebody's discipline, because there'd be nowhere else to stick it. The only thing is, where is it sticking?

Information Science vs. Science Information

Semantic difficulties of yet another kind are generated by the familiar phenomenon that the same words in the English language may mean different things on either side of the Atlantic. While the American protagonists of IS generally say that people involved in this science should be called information scientists, the British reserve this term for scientists who are engaged in providing scientific information to other scientists. The underlying assumption is that information of a scientific nature can only be collected, interpreted and disseminated in a meaningful way by people who are themselves scientists and knowledgeable in the subject field concerned, and who can serve as professionally accepted interpreters of information in a scientific environment. The Institute of Information Scientists, founded in 1958 by scientists with a thorough interest in information handling and retrieval, has as its aim "to act as a professional qualifying body for those engaged in scientific, technical and economic information work, and to promote and maintain high standards in such work." Here, then, we encounter a completely different view: there are information scientists, yet what they do is not to find out what information is or does but to handle scientific information as such. The discrepancy of views about what constitutes IS and what, on the other hand, is Science Information has contributed still further to the ambiguities of definition which plague the field.

Computer Science vs. Information Science

We have already noted that when the term IS was first used (1), it was clearly implied that it was the same as, or even subordinated to, Computer science. This assertion has led to much confusion and misunderstandings, and even to regrettable terminological difficulties on the international plane, as we shall see later. From the erroneous notion that computers are able to handle or even to produce (!) information (when all they can ever do is to manipulate data which, when interpreted by human beings may or may not result in information), it was only a small step to the arrogant and supercilious assertion that only computers could process "information" in a truly scientific manner, and that therefore computer science and IS were practically identical, or that there could be no IS without linking it to computers and the way these machines handle "information." After the initial euphoria about computers and what they could do with non-numerical data had subsided, this was found to be sheer nonsense, and few of the definitions investigated here imply such a notion any longer, although as late as 1970 we find in a paper by Borko (B) the definition:

> An information system is that combination of human and computer-based capital resources which results in the collection, storage, retrieval, communication and use of data ... [and that] the tools and techniques of IS [are applied] to the operational problems of information systems.

In other words, an information system without a computer is not a system at all, and IS cannot or need not be applied to it! Fortunately, there are better (because less biased) definitions, such as the one by Artandi (21) who states explicitly that "it should be emphasized that the term IS does not imply mechanization. The application of machines is only one aspect of the field; unfortunately, it is often equalled with the field itself." And Hayes (29) who, as the co-author of the Handbook of Data Processing for Libraries, can hardly be considered as a foe of computers, has this to say:

> In some circles, the term 'computer sciences' is considered synonymous with information science. However, ... such an identification is invalid. Although mechanization has provided the catalyst and has made IS of immediate value and importance, the problems are present in any system, whether mechanized or not. And it is the problems with which IS is concerned, not the specific use of machinery as the method of solving them.

The computer, in short, is a tool (and a very important one) in IS but this fact alone does not elevate IS to the status of a true science any more than astronomy or physics became true sciences only when they began to use computers as tools. The proper realm of computer science is computers, as the realm of soil science is soils, and that of crystallography is crystals, all of which can be uniquely defined. The realm of IS, then, should be information--provided it can be defined uniquely and unambiguously. This is what we must investigate next.

The Definitions of "Information"

Patrick Wilson, in his profound study Two Kinds of Power (W), says in the chapter on Relevance (p. 41-42):

> Perhaps there are notions, with which we might be made acquainted by means of a novel definition of the word 'relevance,' which would turn out to be more suitable than those we have used. But if so, then the question is not one of the suitability or centrality of the concept of relevance, but of some other concept to which, for some reason, the word 'relevance' is attached. If one claims that the concept of relevance is central to a study, then we are entitled to assume that what is being claimed to be central is a concept with which we are already familiar, namely the concept conventionally associated with the word 'relevance,' and not some other concept.
>
> Now it is the frequent complaint of writers on information storage and retrieval that the notion of relevance, which they take to be central to their study, is a fuzzy and obscure one which requires clearing up, making precise explication, if it is to play its central role well.

If we substitute the word "information" for "relevance" in this quotation [footnote 4], the central problem of definition in IS is stated in a precise form.

The most amazing result of this comparative study of 39 definitions of IS is the fact that only eight of them find it necessary to define what they mean by "information." All the rest unashamedly in circular definitions, which would be thrown out in an introductory course on logic at the undergraduate level, follow the pattern "information science investigates information" set by (3). This would not be permissible even if the word "information" were entirely unambiguous and could only be understood in a unique sense. Since it is well known that such is not the case and most definers are eager to point out this fact, it is a sad reflection on the status of IS and does not make its claim to be a true science any more reputable.

Yet even the eight valiant definers of "information" as the central concept with which IS is concerned do not succeed to arrive at an agreed-upon definition, nor do their definitions have any common elements, as will become clear from the following summary and comment on their findings.

Not until 1965 is it possible to find a definition of "information" as the central concept of IS. The participants of a working group at the <u>Symposium on Education for Information Science</u> (13) came to the not unexpected conclusion that "information is a category word, for there are many kinds of information" but then went on to define information for the purposes of IS simply as "recorded marks." Although "intellectual processing" by the user of information is mentioned in the same sentence, the definition seems to imply that information is somehow thought to be "imbedded" in recorded marks from which it can be extracted by suitable "processes." This runs counter to the ideas expressed in the same symposium by Fairthorne (12) who ridiculed the fact that information was thought of by some people as "some universal essence, that can be squeezed out of texts like water from a sponge," a mode of thinking which "blurs fundamental differences." The fallacy of such ideas had already been exposed much earlier by Ashby, who said "The information conveyed is not an intrinsic property of the individual message," illustrating this statement with a very simple conclusive example. (A, p. 124).

Mikhailov et al. first defined "information" for the purposes of what they called "informatics" (a new name for the discipline of IS, to which we shall revert later) in a paper (18) published in 1966. They cite Brillouin's definition, "Information is the raw material and consists of a mere collection of data" (D. p. x), which, however, they declare to be too general for their purposes (because it is not valid for semantic information, as stressed by Brillouin himself) and then say: "... [information] could be defined as the objective content of the link between interacting material objects, which reveals itself <u>in the transformed status</u>

Technical/Readers' Services 229

of these objects." [My emphasis.] The context makes it
clear that by "material objects" are meant living persons
(a terminology peculiar to the Soviet Union). Due to a certain critique, Mikhailov et al. elaborated in later works
(25,32) on the nature of information, stating that it is:
"... obtained in the process of cognition and adequately reflects the laws of the material world and of spiritual activities of human beings, and is utilized in the socio-historical
practice." The last words of the sentence reflect the necessity for every Soviet writer and scientist to relate his findings somehow to Marxist-Leninist teachings and the authors
also dutifully support their statement with citations from
Marx and Lenin. We need not be concerned with this ideological embellishment which is irrelevant to the definition
itself. What matters is that this definition is the first one
which expressly includes a reference to the change in the
mind of people that takes place when information is com-
municated, perceived and assimilated.

Hoshovsky (23) quotes McDonough (L) who states that
"information is the measure of the net value obtained from
the process of matching the elements of a present problem
with appropriate elements of data," and elaborates on this
by saying, "... information ... is a process which occurs
within a human mind when a problem and data useful for its
solution are brought into productive union." This kind of
reasoning seems to suppose that the minds of human beings
are constantly occupied with solving problems and that only
such messages constitute information which, when "brought
into productive union" with a problem, result in the birth
of a solution to it. One is left to wonder what problems
are solved in the mind of a person who reads Hamlet (although the text itself is indeed concerned with serious problems: "To be or not to be ..."); or, at a completely different level, when that person reads the text of a roadside
billboard saying "Coca Cola--it's the real thing!" (except,
of course, when the person happens to be thirsty at that
moment and the slogan helps to solve the problem what to
do about it). Such simplistic views, derived solely from
managerial decision-making situations, clearly cannot serve
as valid definitions of "information" in the context of IS.

Hayes (29) reaffirms that "information is a slippery
concept, amorphous, loaded with connotations and implications" and that it "has had a variety of meanings" yet that
"we must have a suitable definition, even if it is at the
most elementary level"--a statement with which everyone

should agree. After having defined "data" as "that which is recorded as symbols from which other symbols may be produced," he goes on to define "information" as "the result of processing of data, usually formalized processing." This definition, although operational on a certain level, again seems to leave out what goes on in the mind of a person informed, and stresses the mechanistic aspect of processing, although information is here no longer considered as a kind of physical substance.

Koblitz (30) distinguishes between three kinds of information, viz. :

> 'Semantic information (as a message)' which is 'a unit composed of meaning and carrier for the purpose of transmission of knowledge and experience from one subject to another'; 'Semantic information (as a process)' which is 'purposeful actions for the creation (including handling), storage, searching and dissemination of information, and coupled with sensory perception (unilateral), logical perception (inner reflexion) or exchange of information between humans (bilateral)'; and finally 'Documental information' which is 'information containing new facts or statements (factographic information) of analytical or synthetic character.

Koblitz, who is German, obviously followed Goethe's maxim in the prelude to Faust: "Wer vieles bringt, wird manchem etwas bringen," but his multiple choices cannot hide the fact that the definitions are circular or ambiguous or both.

Next we have Yovits (33) who first exposed the unfounded claims of IS to the status of a true science by confronting it with some of the basic requirements of genuine scientific disciplines, and then stated: "... if the definition of information is nebulous, varied, and non-rigorous, then the definition of information science is even more nebulous, varied and non-rigorous"--a conclusion at which I also arrived in the course of this investigation simply by looking at the way in which people active in IS use words and define concepts. Yovits then goes on to define "information" for the purposes of a generalized information system model as "data of value in decision-making." Within the limits of his model this might be sufficient, but it is not acceptable as a general definition of what IS is concerned with, because human beings do not always make decisions upon having

Technical/Readers' Services 231

received information (although they may do so later on as the result of many different informations that have been weighed and evaluated, such as deciding to see a performance of Hamlet or to buy a bottle of Coca Cola, after having read books or signs on these topics).

Shortly thereafter, Otten and Debons (35) assert that "information" is a "fundamental phenomenon" like energy, on which operations can be performed. Moreover, in their view "all information processing operations can be performed by digital computers." How such opinions could still be held in the year 1970, long after their futility had been exposed on logical grounds by Bar-Hillel, Fairthorne, and others, is difficult to understand. Moreover, the bald statement that something is a "fundamental phenomenon" does not qualify as a definition, unless one is prepared to accept the paternalistic "because I say so" as the equivalent of a sound definition.

Wersig (36) defines "information" as "reduction of uncertainty," no doubt following the theory of Shannon, although the context of his definition makes it clear that he is concerned with meaningful or semantic information. Here again, information is seen as a mechanistic process or as the result of such a process (the formulation leaves room for both interpretations).

Diemer (37) distinguishes between four different meanings of "information," two of which he sees as fundamental for IS, viz. the change in the state of the informand (intended or achieved) and the "item" of information or the content of the transmitted message, for which he proposes the new term "informeme." The "informeme" is then defined as an absolutely non-material entity which represents a fact (real or imagined) and which ideally is made available to anybody, anywhere and at any time. The informeme is normally expressed in words (as sounds or signs) but need not be restricted to verbal expression. This definition, which sounds at first rather metaphysical, has much in common with one given earlier by Shera (S):

> Information, both in the sense in which it is used by the biologist and in the sense in which we as librarians use it, is 'fact.' It is the stimulus which we perceive through our senses. This information may be a single isolated fact or it may be a whole cluster of facts; but it is still a unit; it is a unit of

thought. It can have any dimension. <u>It is that intellectual entity which we receive, the building block of knowledge.</u> [My emphasis.]

These definitions also happen to be in agreement with the "operational definition" by MacKay (N) who states that "we have received information, when we know something now that we did not know before" and goes on to say that: "it is always information <u>about</u> something ... We may define information in general as that which <u>justifies representational activity</u>" (all emphasized words so in the original). Representational activity, in McKay's definition, means anything a person might say, write, draw, or otherwise signal to other persons. This also coincides very nearly with the definition of "information" given in <u>Webster's Third New International Dictionary</u>: "The process by which the form of an object of knowledge is impressed upon the apprehending mind so as to bring about the state of knowing" [footnote 5].

I have left Fairthorne's definition (12), though contemporary with (13), for the end of this survey. He proposed to treat "information" as a kind of null term which should not be used at all, because "... it is no more than a linguistic convenience that saves you the trouble of thinking what you are talking about." In a later paper (F), Fairthorne elaborates on this statement, saying that " 'information' is a metaphorical designation 'for an amorphous mass of ill-defined different activities and phenomena'," which may or may not be related to each other, yet are all based on only six variables: messages, codes, channels, sources, destinations and designations.

When examining most of the definitions of "information" proposed after Fairthorne's statement, one must either reluctantly agree with him, and abandon any attempt at a scientifically sound statement on the nature of information (which would mean, ipso facto, that there cannot be any information science) or, if one still has hope that such a true science might evolve, then all those who call themselves information scientists must necessarily agree on an <u>operational definition</u> of information. To quote Brillouin again:

> ... As a rule it has been found advisable to introduce into the scientific language only those qualities which can be defined operationally. Words not susceptible of an operational definition have, usually, eventually been found untrustworthy, and have been eliminated from the scientific vocabulary. [D, p. x]

Brillouin's compatriot, the eminent writer and researcher on information, E. de Grolier (H), stated the case very aptly when he said:

> Almost every author [on IS] has his own terminology, and to reconcile these terminologies and to say what is hidden behind the various terms which have been adopted is not an easy thing. So in this respect, we have no science: we are in the situation of chemistry before Lavoisier or physics before Newton.

An operational definition of information in the context of IS can, however, not be the one given by Brillouin, "Information is the raw material and consists of a mere collection of data" (D, p. x) because he stresses repeatedly that this definition refers to information which is entirely devoid of meaning and does not contain "any element involving the human value of information" (ibid.). But it might well be based on the definition given by MacKay, the one found in Webster's dictionary, and on the more elaborate definitions proposed by Shera and Diemer. Such an operational definition of information as the central topic of IS should be formulated and promulgated by international bodies concerned with information activities, such as Unesco, FID or UNISIST.

Towards Informatics

During the last five years, several attempts have been made by various writers to propose or suggest alternative names for IS, partly because they had doubts whether the field really merited the name of a "science," but mostly because they thought that if IS indeed was a science, then it should also have a distinctive name of its own, as in the case of the established branches of science. Among the suggestions put forward are:

Documentistics	(Wersig) (36)
Documentology	(Wersig) (36)
Epistemo-dynamics	(Kochen) (K)
Informantics	(Wersig) (36)
Informatistics	(Wersig) (36)
Informatology	(Otten) (35)
Information and documentation science	(Koblitz) (34)
Informology	(Wersig) (36)
Social epistemology	(Shera) (Q, R, S)

[continued on page 238]

Table 1. TERMS USED IN 39 DEFINITIONS OF IS

(i. = information)

Accessibility of i.	Identification of i.	Operations research
Adaptation	Information circuits	Optimization of i.
Analysis of i.	Information networks	Organization of i.
Automata	Information systems	Origination of i.
Behavior of i.	Information theory	Other fields
Behavioral sciences	Informemes	Pattern recognition
Bionics	Intelligent automata	People
Brain research	Intention	Philosophy
Classification of i.	Interpretation of i.	Physics
Codes	Language	Processes of i.
Cognitive processes	Learning theory	Processing of i.
Collection of i.	Lexical processing	Producing of i.
Communication	Librarianship	Propagation of i.
Computer organization	Library science	Properties of i.
Computer programming	Linguistics	Psychology
Computer technology	List processing	Reception of i.
Computers	Logic	Recognition
Control of i.	Machine manipulation	Recording of i.
Creation of i.	of data	Representation of i.
Cybernetics	Machine translation	Retrieval of i.
Decision making	Machines	Self-organization
Discourse	Man (men)	Semantics
Dissemination of i.	Man-machine systems	Sensory information
Documentation	Management	Society
Duration	Marks	Statistics
Education	Mass communications	Storage of i.
Encoding of i.	Mathematical models	Structure of i.
Engineering	Mathematics	Systems analysis
Environmental aspects	Meaning	Systems engineering
of i.	Means	Thinking
Epistemology	Mentioning	Transfer of i.
Flow of i.	Messages	Transformation of i.
General systems theory	Nature	Transmission of i.
Genetics	Need for i.	Understanding
Graph theory	Nervous system	Usability of i.
Graphic arts	Neurophysiology	Use of i.
Human beings	Not computers	Utilization of i.

Table 2. FREQUENCY OF ALL TERMS USED

Term	Freq	Term	Freq	Term	Freq
Linguistics	12	Usability	3	Graph theory	1
Communication	11	Utilization	3	Identification	1
Mathematics	9	Other fields	3	Information circuits	1
Processing	9	Computers	2	Information networks	1
Storage	9	Duration	2	Information theory	1
Library science	8	Encoding	2	Informemes	1
Origination	8	General systems th.	2	Intention	1
Dissemination	7	Graphic arts	2	Learning theory	1
Flow	7	Man	2	Lexical processing	1
Logic	7	Management	2	Librarianship	1
Retrieval	7	Pattern recognition	2	List processing	1
Messages	6	People	2	Machine mani-	
Organization	6	Philosophy	2	pulation	1
Transfer	5	Recognition	2	Machine translation	1
Documentation	5	Society	2	Machines	1
Information systems	5	Statistics	2	Man-machine sys.	1
Properties	5	Systems engineering	2	Marks	1
Psychology	5	Transmission	2	Mass comm.	1
Recording	5	Use	2	Mathematical mdls.	1
Analysis	4	Adaptation	1	Meaning	1
Collection	4	Automata	1	Means	1
Language	4	Bionics	1	Mentioning	1
Self-organization	4	Brain research	1	Nature	1
Transformation	4	Classification	1	Need for inform.	1
Accessibility	3	Codes	1	Nervous system	1
Behavior	3	Cognitive processes	1	Neurophysiology	1
Behavioral sciences	3	Computer organizat.	1	Not computers	1
Computer pro-		Computer technol.	1	Optimization	1
gramming	3	Control	1	Physics	1
Cybernetics	3	Creation	1	Producing	1
Human beings	3	Decision making	1	Propagation	1
Intelligent automata	3	Discourse	1	Reception	1
Interpretation	3	Education	1	Representation	1
Operations research	3	Engineering	1	Sensory inform.	1
Processes	3	Environmental asp.	1	Systems analysis	1
Semantics	3	Epistemology	1	Thinking	1
Structure	3	Genetics	1	Understanding	1

Rank	Number of terms
1	1
2	1
3	3
4	2
5	4
6	3
7	5
8	5
9	15
10	16
11	54
	109

Table 3
FREQUENCY OF COMBINATION OF SYNONYMS AND NEAR-SYNONYMS
(Terms are combined in order of their frequency).

Term Combination	Frequency
Dissemination/Transfer/Transmission/Propagation	16
Linguistics/Language	16
Flow of information/Messages	13
Processing/Lexical processing/List processing	11
Mathematics/Mathematical models	10
Origination/Creation/Producing	10
Human beings/Man/People/Society	9
Library science/Librarianship	9
Analysis/Interpretation/Classification	8
Recording/Encoding/Codes	8
Usability/Utilization/Use	8
Computer programming/Computers/Computer organization/ Computer technology	7
Semantics/Meaning	4
Brain research/Nervous system/Neurophysiology	3
Machine manipulation of data/Machines	2

Table 4. FREQUENCY OF ALL TERMS
WHEN SYNONYMS AND NEAR-SYNONYMS ARE COMBINED
(Only the first term of each combination in Table 3 is listed).

Term	Fr.	Term	Fr.	Term	Fr.
Dissemination	16	Behavioral sciences	3	Epistemology	1
Linguistics	16	Brain research	3	Genetics	1
Flow	13	Cybernetics	3	Graph theory	1
Processing	11	Intelligent automata	3	Identification	1
Communication	11	Operations research	3	Information circuits	1
Mathematics	10	Processes	3	Information networks	1
Origination	10	Structure	3	Information theory	1
Human beings	9	Other fields	3	Informemes	1
Library science	9	Duration	2	Intention	1
Storage	9	General systems	2	Learning theory	1
Analysis	8	Graphic arts	2	Machine translation	1
Recording	8	Machine manipulat.	2	Man-machine sys.	1
Usability	8	Management	2	Marks	1
Computer progrmm.	7	Pattern recognition	2	Mass comm.	1
Retrieval	7	Philosophy	2	Means	1
Logic	7	Recognition	2	Mentioning	1
Organization	6	Statistics	2	Nature	1
Documentation	5	Systems engineering	2	Need for inform.	1
Information systems	5	Adaptation	1	Not computers	1
Properties	5	Bionics	1	Optimization	1
Psychology	5	Cognitive processes	1	Physics	1
Self-organization	5	Control	1	Reception	1
Collection	4	Decision making	1	Representation	1
Semantics	4	Discourse	1	Sensory inform.	1
Transformation	4	Education	1	Systems analysis	1
Accessibility	3	Engineering	1	Thinking	1
Behavior	3	Environmental	1	Understanding	1

Table 4 (Continued)

Rank	Number of terms	Rank	Number of terms
1	2	8	1
2	1	9	5
3	2	10	3
4	2	11	10
5	3	12	10
6	3	13	36
7	3		
			81

Table 5

NUMBER OF TERMS USED IN DEFINITIONS OF IS

Number of terms	Used in number of papers	Listed in Appendix I
2	3	36, 37, 38
3	6	9, 12, 21, 27, 29, 33
4	5	1, 2, 6, 28, 30
5	8	5, 11, 17, 18, 23, 32, 34, 39
6	4	4, 13, 20, 25
7	2	10, 31
8	1	8
9	4	14, 15, 16, 19
13	2	7, 26
14	1	35
25	1	3
28	1	22
30*	1	24
	39	

*Actually more than 40 (see discussion in text).

and maybe other combinations of the stems inform- and
document- with various scientifically-sounding suffixes.
None of these suggested terms, however, has gained acceptance.

The only successful attempt at new terminology was
made by the Russian information specialists Mikhailov,
Chernyi and Gilyarevskii who jointly proposed the term
"Informatics" in a paper (18) published in Russian in 1966
and translated into English and German in 1967. In this
paper and in subsequent articles and books (25, 32) they
defined the scope of Informatics as:

> ... the processes, methods and laws related to the
> recording, analytical-synthetical processing, storage,
> removal and dissemination of scientific information
> but not the scientific information as such which is
> the attribute of a respective science or discipline.

It should be noted that the term "scientific," as used by
Mikhailov et al. here, is the translation of the Russian
"nauchnoi" which encompasses the results of all scholarly
activity, not only those related to the natural sciences.
They also were careful to point out that:

> ... informatics [is not] concerned with the logical
> processing of existing information with the purpose
> of obtaining new information not contained, in an
> apparent form, in the initial information ... If we
> considered these tasks as lying within the scope of
> informatics we would have of necessity been compelled to declare informatics a science of the
> sciences, which is of course absurd. [32]

In view of the excesses to which at least a few of the definers of IS have gone, this is a very healthy limitation,
and one which should be borne in mind by anybody concerned
with IS, by whichever name he may call his chosen discipline.

The name Informatics is now firmly established in
the Soviet Union, in East Germany and in many East European countries. In the UK, its adoption was urged as early
as 1967 by J. Davies (E), apparently without much success,
but recently the term was again used in a review paper by
Foskett (G) who took it as the title for a survey of the field
of information activities and also considers its possible

adoption as a name for the discipline in the English-speaking world. (Unfortunately, the names Informatique and Informatik have already been claimed in France and West Germany for the discipline known in English as Computer science--a fact that is now somewhat regretted in both countires; this, however, would not militate against the use of Informatics as a more suitable substitute for IS in English-speaking countries, since Computer science already has a name and is not likely to change it.)

The adoption of the name Informatics for the study of information in all its aspects would be beneficial for several reasons:

a) since it can be shown that IS has at present neither a well-defined central topic nor several other attributes of a true science, a neutral name would arouse much less controversy about the scientific nature of the field. The development of Informatics into a true science, to be ranked on a par with other branches of science, will depend on the unique definition of its central topic and on the formulation of its own hypotheses, theories and laws--not on the fact that the word "science" appears in its name. Indeed, most old-established sciences as well as some new ones (such as Cybernetics, Bionics, and others) do not have to call themselves sciences to be considered as such;

b) The name Informatics satisfies several criteria for the designation of a new discipline:

  (i) it consists of one word only
  (ii) it implies the central topic of the discipline
  (iii) it cannot be confused with any other name
  (iv) it will be readily understood, because the stem is familiar to everybody
  (v) other terms can be derived from it, such as Informatician for a person who is engaged in activities in this field (equivalent to mathematician, statistician, etc.) and the adjective informatical, to describe the attributes of the field.

c) It has already been used in several English-language publications (see 27, 30, 31, 32 and J) and will probably be used increasingly in international practice, as indicated by the publication of a textbook by Unesco in 1970, entitled Guide for an Introductory Course on Informatics/Documentation. The fact that this book was also written by Mikhailov and Gilyarevskii explains, of course, the usage of the word Informatics, but the decisive aspect is the official adoption of the term by the world's foremost international scientific organization which clearly did not consider the term any longer as the private invention of the authors.

It is maybe too much to expect that the American Society for Information Science should change its name to American Society for Informatics only a few years after having adopted a new name, nor is it likely that the British Institute of Information Scientists will become the Institute of Informaticians in the near future. But it would certainly be a sign of intellectual integrity and humility if writers in the field would henceforth refer to it simply as Informatics, thereby refraining from claiming a status that is not yet theirs. They might also do well to remember the words of the great social scientist, John Maynard Keynes, who urged his fellow economists to regard themselves as "humble, competent people, on a level with dentists." Informaticians will earn the respect of scientists and other users of information alike only if they will do a better job in providing them with information "timely, efficiently and in suitable forms" to quote Mikhailov (32), by methods based on hypotheses, theories and laws. Whether these will emerge in years to come, and justify the status of a science for Informatics, remains to be resolved in the future [footnote 6].

The task will not be easy, both because the discipline has already been declared to be a science, yet has had, so far, little to show for this claim, and also because of the unusual and somewhat irrational expectations about what "information science" can or should achieve. As I am writing these lines, I can see from my window how the leaves on the trees are changing colour. This beautiful pageant is caused by certain biochemical processes, most of which are now fairly well understood. When the leaves fall to the ground, the laws of physics tell us how gravity affects the mass of the leaf, how air currents may delay its descent to the ground and what kind of impact the fallen leaf will make on the surface. Yet all this theoretical and scientifically sound reasoning will be unable to predict precisely what kind of colour changes will take place in an individual leaf, nor will anybody be able to trace the exact trajectory of the falling leaf, to compute what a sudden gust of wind will do to it, and how and when it will hit the ground and what will happen to it afterwards. Nor is all this ever necessary for a botanical study of a certain phase in the life cycle of deciduous trees. Science, here as in other spheres of nature, is seeking unity in diversity, so we may understand the essence of the phenomena by which we are surrounded.

But when it comes to the leaves of the tree of knowledge, as represented by individual documents in which authors have embodied their view of facts (real or imagined), most people seem to be interested in the way a certain single leaf originated (i.e., who is the author), its form (i.e., is it a book or an article, etc.) and most of all in the impact it will make (the message it has to deliver). Somehow, it is therefore expected that there is a "scientific" way to do just that: to devise infallible methods which will enable us to find among millions of multi-coloured and widely scattered leaves the single one that will best answer our more or less well-formulated urge or need to know.
But if the study of information is to become a science in the real sense, it cannot do anything like that. It cannot concern itself with individual leaves. It can only try to discover and formulate the laws, if any, that govern the creation, transmission and reception of meaningful and therefore potentially informative messages. These theories and laws may then enable us to devise methods for the retrieval of clusters of leaves or even individual leaves, yet it must be realized that these methods will always fall short of the ideal (except in artificially contrived laboratory situations). On the other hand, the methods devised in accordance with truly scientific theories and laws, imperfect as they may be, will be far superior to those that were devised by hit-and-miss producures or which were based on personal whims or prejudices.

This is exactly what happened in other sciences: in physics, the laws of mechanics as formulated by Newton tell us how an ideal planet would revolve around its central star; the real planet approaches this ideal, although not entirely, because it is not a perfectly shaped body; yet the theory superseded earlier notions based on ideas of philosophers about what such planetary motion ought to be so as to satisfy a preconceived notion of harmony. In chemistry, the laws governing the forces acting on atoms and molecules allow us to predict the reactions that will take place when sulphur and oxygen are brought into contact because both sulphur and oxygen will contain impurities; but the theory of oxidation is based on sound scientific principles and superseded the preconceived notion of phlogiston.

Fairthorne (12) has remarked that, as far as IS is concerned, we are still in the age of phlogiston. A unified and logically sound terminology, though not the only prerequisite, will be indispensible on the long road towards the emergence of a true science of information.

Appendix

WORKS CONTAINING DEFINITIONS OF INFORMATION SCIENCE
(compared in this study)

1959
1. Moore School of Electrical Engineering. Computer and Information Sciences Program. Philadelphia, University of Pennsylvania.

1960
2. Heilprin, L. B. On the information problem ahead. Am. Docum., 12 (1), January 1961, 6-14.

1962
3. Conference on training science information specialists. Atlanta, Georgia Institute of Technology, 1961-62.
4. Wooster, H. Implications of basic research in information sciences to machine documentation. Washington, D. C., Air Force Office of Scientific Research, 1962. (AFOSR-492).

1963
5. Heilprin, L. B. Toward a definition of information science. In: Automation and scientific communication. 26th annual meeting of the American Documentation Institute, 1963: 239-242.
6. Mooers, C. N. The educational challenge of information science. In: Automation and scientific communication. 26th annual meeting of the American Documentation Institute, 1963: 127.
7. Taylor, R. S. The information sciences, Libr. J., 88 (19) 1963, 4161-4163.

1964

8. Cuadra, C. A. Identifying key contributions to information science. Am. Docum., 15 (4) October 1964, 289-295.
9. Heilprin, L. B. American Documentation Institute Committee on Organization of Information. Report for 1962-63. Am. Docum., 15 (4) October 1964, 274-288.
10. Welt, I. D. Information science--science information. Am. Docum., 15 (4) October 1964, 249.
11. Wooster, H. Information technology and the information sciences: with fork and hopes. Washington, D. C., Air Force Office of Scientific Research, 1964. (AFOSR-9769).

1965

12. Fairthorne, R. A. "Use" and "mention" in the information sciences. In: Symposium on education for information science. Warrenton, Va., 1965. Washington, D. C., Spartan Books, 1965: 9-12.
13. Symposium on education for information science. Warrenton, Va., 1965. Washington, D. C., Spartan Books, 1965: 171.
14. Kochen, M. Some problems in information science. New York, Scarecrow Press, 1965.
15. University of Chicago. Committee on the Information Sciences. Description of the Committee's program ... Chicago, 1965. (Unpublished. Cited in Annual Review of Information Science and Technology, v. 1, p. 25.)

1966

16. Cuadra, C. A. Introduction. In: Annual Review of Information Science and Technology, v. 1, 1966: 1-14.
17. Donohue, J. C. Librarianship and the science of information. Am. Docum., 17 (3) July 1966, 120-23.
18. Mikhailov, A. I., A. I. Chernyi, and R. S. Gilyarevskii. [Informatics--new name for the theory of scientific communication.] Nauko-tekhnicheskaya informatsiya, No. 12, 1966: 35-39. (Engl. trans. in FID News Bull., v. 17, 1967: 70-74.

1967

19. Gorn, S. The computer and information sciences and the community of disciplines. Behavioral science, v. 12, no. 6, 1967: 433-452.

20. Information sciences: 1967. Washington, D. C., Air Force Office of Scientific Research, 1967. (AFOSR 68-0006.)

1968
21. Artandi, S. Computers in information science. Metuchen, Scarecrow Press, 1968.
22. Borko, H. Information science: what is it? Am. Docum., 19 (1) January 1968, 3-5.
23. Hoshovsky, A. G. and R. J. Massey. Information science; its ends, means and opportunities. In: Information transfer. Proc. American Society for Information Science, v. 5, 1968: 47-55.
24. Kitagawa, T. Information science and its connections with statistics. Fukuoka, Kyushu University, 1968.
25. Mikhailov, A. L., A. I. Chernyi and R. S. Gilyarevskii. Osnovy informatiki. Moskva, VINITI, 1968. (Foundations of informatics. 2nd ed. of Osnovi nauknoi informatsii, 1965. German translation: Informatik; Grundlagen. Berlin, Staatsverlag der DDR, 1970.)
26. Schlueter, R. A. Information science: some questions and answers. J. Educ. Librarianship, 9 (2) 1968, 152-58. (Reprinted in Am. Docum., 20 (4) October 1969, 366-368.)

1969
27. Fairthorne, R. A. The scope and aims of the information sciences and technologies. In: On theoretical problems of information. Moscow, All-Union Institute for Scientific and Technical Information, 1969: 25-31.
28. Harmon, G. Information science as an integrative discipline. In: Co-operating information societies. Proc. American Society for Information Science, v. 6, 1969: 459-462.
29. Hayes, R. M. Information science in librarianship. Libri, v. 19, no. 3, 1969: 216-36. (Reprinted in Hayes, R. M. and J. Becker. Handbook of data processing for libraries. New York, Wiley, 1970. Chapter 20.)
30. Koblitz, J. Librarianship and documentation/information: distinctive features and common aspects. In: On theoretical problems in informatics. Moscow, All-Union Institute for Scientific and Technical Information, 1969: 120-142.
31. Merta, A. Informatics as a branch of science. In: On theoretical problems in informatics. Moscow, All-Union Institute for Scientific and Technical

Information, 1969: 32-40.
32. Mikhailov, A. I., A. I. Chernyi and R. S. Gilyarevskii. Informatics: its scope and methods. In: On theoretical problems of informatics. Moscow, All-Union Institute for Scientific and Technical Information, 1969: 7-24.
33. Yovits, M. C. Information science: toward the development of a true scientific discipline. Am. Docum., 20 (4) October 1969, 369-376.

1970
34. Koblitz, J. Der Gegenstand der Informations- und Dokumentationswissenschaft, Informationswissenschaft and Informatik. Informatik, v. 17, no. 2, 1970: 12-21; no. 3, 1970: 23-26.
35. Otten, K. and A. Debons. Towards a metascience of information: informatology. J. American Society for Information Science, v. 21, no. 1, Jan.-Feb. 1970: 89-94.
36. Wersig, G. und K. H. Meyer-Uhlenried. Versuche zur Terminologie in der Dokumentation III: Dokumentation. Nachr. Dokum., 22 (1) 1970, 14-19.

1971
37. Diemer, A. Informationswissenschaft. Nachr. Dokum., 22 (3) 1971, 105-113.
38. Harmon, G. On the evolution of information science. J. American Society for Information Science, v. 22, no. 4, July-Aug. 1971: 235-241.
39. Grolier, Eric de. Formation et recherche on science de l'information. Tours, 1971. (Prospectus for a symposium held at Instituts Universitaires de Technologie, Tours.)

Bibliography

Note: the following items were not available to the author in their original form, and the definitions of IS were taken from quotations in Harmon (38): 4, 11, 20, 24.

A. Ashby, W. R. An Introduction to Cybernetics. Chapman & Hall, 1956.
B. Borko, H. Systems analysis within the field of information sciences. In: Systems Analysis; An Approach to Information. FID/TM tutorial report. Stockholm, Royal Institute of Technology, 1970.

C. Bradford, S. C. Documentation. 2nd ed., edited by J. H. Shera. Crosby Lockwood, 1953. p. 49.
D. Brillouin, L. Science and Information Theory. 2nd ed. New York, Academic Press, 1962.
E. Davies, J. Letter to the Editor. Inf. Scientist, 1 (2) September 1967, 84.
F. Fairthorne, R. A. Morphology of information flow. J. Ass. f. Computing Machinery, v. 14, 1967: 710-719.
G. Foskett, D. J. "Informatics." J. Docum., 26 (4) December 1970, 340-369.
H. Grolier, E. De. Recent research trends in the field of information retrieval languages. In: Subject Retrieval in the Seventies. Westport, Conn., Greenwood Press, 1972.
I. International Conference on Scientific Information. Washington, D. C., 1958. Washington, D. C., National Academy of Sciences, 1959.
J. International Forum on Informatics. Moscow, All-Union Institute for Scientific and Technical Information, 1969, 2 v.
K. Kochen, M. Stability in the growth of knowledge. Am. Docum., 20 (3) 1969, 186-197.
L. McDonough, A. M. Information Economics and Management Systems. New York, McGraw-Hill, 1963.
M. Mack, J. D. A national policy for the information sciences. Am. Docum., 14 (4) 1963, 275.
N. MacKay, D. M. Information, Mechanism and Meaning. Cambridge, Mass., MIT Press, 1969.
O. Mooers, C. N. The next twenty years in information retrieval. Am. Docum., 11 (3) 1960, 229-236.
P. Shera, J. H. The compleat librarian. Cleveland, Press of Case Western Reserve Univerity, 1971. p. 137-138.
Q. Shera, J. H. Documentation and the organization of knowledge. Lockwood, 1965.
R. Shera, J. H. Libraries and the Organization of Knowledge. Lockwood, 1965.
S. Shera, J. H. Sociological Foundations of Librarianship. New York, Asia Publishing House, 1970.
T. State of the Art Symposium, Am. Docum., 13 (1) 1962.
U. Townley, H. M. "It isn't a science." Inf. Scientist, 1 (2) September 1967, 49-50.
V. Wagner, F. S. A dictionary of documentation terms. Am. Docum., 11 (2) 1960, 102-119.
W. Wilson, P. Two Kinds of Power; An Essay on Bibliographical Control. Berkeley, Univ. of California Press, 1968.

Footnotes

1. The cumulative index to <u>American Documentation</u> 1961-64 does not include the term IS, although at least the 1963 issue has an editorial by Mack (M) on the topic and the 1964 issues contain several articles and editorials on IS, and the term appears frequently in titles and headings. This particular index, however, was compiled by a peculiar method apparently conceived by an "information retriever" who had probably never seen a good index before and knew less about what an index is supposed to do. It did not contain even a single reference to "information retrieval" either, although this term occurred dozens of times in contributions to the journal in the four years covered by the index. Before the appearance of this so-called "index," there were no subject indexes to <u>Am. Doc.</u> at all! Thus, the very same people who for more than ten years had tried to devise all manner of sophisticated gadgets for "information retrieval," and who looked down on lowly old-fashioned librarians and indexers, did not find it necessary to provide even the simplest retrieval tool to their own ideas, and when they finally got around to do so, they botched up the job miserably. All of which does not make their frequent claims to superior knowledge and scientific methods in information retrieval more credible. The old adage about the cobbler's children apparently applies also to latter-day "information retrievers" and "information scientists." It is interesting to note that <u>Special Libraries</u> (a journal only partly devoted to IS, but which always had had reasonably good indexes) listed the term IS as a main heading already in 1963.
2. It is worth noting that Shannon never referred to his theory as an "Information theory." This misnomer is entirely due to his followers and interpreters.
3. Reported by P. Atherton in a letter to the editor, <u>Am. Docum.</u>, v. 16, no. 2, 1965, p. 126.
4. The concept of "information" itself is treated at length in Wilson's work (pp. 16-19) but he does not set out to define it. However, he shows very clearly that a text is not always valued for its informativeness, nor are the informative statements made in a text all it conveys to a reader: "What a text says is not necessarily what it reveals or what it allows us to conclude."

5. There are, of course, more definitions of "information" in Webster's, but all others refer to popular or narrowly professional usage (such as in law or computer science).
6. Shortly after this paper had been submitted for publication, there appeared Louis Vagianos' article "Information Science: A House Built on Sand," <u>Libr. J.</u>, 97 (2) 15 January 1972, 153-157, which expresses almost exactly the same evaluation of IS and also explores the implications of teaching this non-existing "Science."

BIBLIOGRAPHY OLD AND NEW*

Herman W. Liebert

When I received the invitation to deliver the Feldman Lecture† in Bibliography, I knew at once that I owed this honor to the good offices of two very old friends (or rather, two friends for a long time). One is Professor William B. Todd, whose zeal as a bibliographer is exceeded only by his skill. The other is the donor of this lectureship, Lew D. Feldman, the antiquarian bookdealer, who maintains as fully in his stock of books and manuscripts as in his relations with collectors and librarians the standard of his chosen business motto: Quality.

I had intended to entitle this lecture "Bourbon Old-Fashioned Bibliography." That reflected my opinion that the Bourbon royal family is insufficiently appreciated. It is said that they learned nothing and forgot nothing. Now, not to learn is surely a defect; but not to forget is a quality sadly needed in our time, when the fashion is to "trash" the past as if there were nothing to be gained from man's recorded history.

I was told, however, that ambiguity between royalty and alcohol made that title unsuitable at an institution where alcohol does not officially exist. It was with surprise and regret that I realized those glasses of dark brown liquid often seen in the hands of the late great John Nance Garner and of more recent Texan national figures really contained only coca-cola.

What I sought to capture in the abandoned title

---

*Reprinted from the University of Texas Library Chronicle, February 1972, by courtesy of the Humanities Research Center, University of Texas at Austin.
†This was commissioned and written as a lecture. I have not turned it into a "paper" by altering its oral tone or adding references. --Author.

nevertheless remains. I wish to enter a plea for the redirection of the course of bibliography away from its prevailing tendencies and back toward an older kind that I think is in danger of being forgotten.

Let us admit at the outset that bibliography ranks well behind blondes, drunks, and mothers-in-law as a source of belly laughs, or even of restrained chuckles. Some of my darkest hours have been spent enduring papers in bibliography that were all very well, later on, in print, but whose oral recitation of press numbers, signatures, and patterns of imposition would, compressed into tablets, drive phenobarbitol off the market. I will try not to put you to sleep. But I must presume that such of you as have not been driven into this hall by cattle prods have some knowledge of and interest in bibliography.

Public oratory usually issues stirring calls to the future, in the direction chosen by the speaker. Since I am issuing a call back to the past, I should tell you where I think we are before I ask you to turn back: a compass is indispensable to the navigator, but it is very much more useful to him if he knows where he is.

To tell you where I think we are now in bibliography is made much harder because we have come so far so fast. It is only forty years since R. W. Chapman published his book, a bibliographical incunabulum, telling bibliographers what cancels were and why they were important. Since then, we have had press-numbers, paper analysis, studies of imposition, machine collation, and even gutter measurements. From the colonial period of Chapman we have passed through the federal age of W. W. Greg, and, with only a few skirmishes of civil war among bibliographers, past the reconstruction era of F. T. Bowers, and into the present reign of their disciples. The gospels have been written, and we are now in a neo-Byzantine period of their glossing and exegesis.

That has always been a dry kind of work that tends to become more and more involuted and attenuated, and farther away from the simple original message. Elaboration begins to be practiced for its own sake, as an independent mystique, with less and less concern for the mundane problems about which the congregation needs guidance. Even the vocabulary becomes symbolic, meaningful only to the initiated. The Greek letter π, which enjoyed a long and happy life as the ratio of the circumference to the diameter of a circle, now stands also for preliminary unsigned gatherings, and the dollar-sign, as if it had not suffered enough inflation, stands for the number of leaves signed in every gathering.

The arguments for shorthand of this sort are that it saves time and space and avoids ambiguity. I think, however, that there are other motives. I remember the delight with which I first learned, aged perhaps ten, that writing in lemon juice was invisible, but reappeared when heated. The appeal of the cabala to innocent minds is unfailing. And then there is the other motive, which we see in many places more sophisticated than bibliography: the barbarously pronounced Latin of the lawyers, the abbreviated Latin of the physician's prescriptions (C. M. S. A. C. --Cras mane sumendus ante cibum--all of which reduces to--take tomorrow morning before breakfast.) The purpose of all this is to assume the cloak of the wizard and to support esoteric professional standing, including the fee, or, to put it more bluntly, to keep out the slobs. I think it is always a good rule to suspect mystification, and I have never found any means of communication more efficient and less capable of misunderstanding than carefully chosen, simple language. The phrase "two unsigned leaves" at the beginning of a collation has only the disadvantage of a little extra space as compared with the symbol π^2; it does not, however, supply anything arcane to make the bibliographer feel like a professional.

It is just here, it seems to me, that bibliography, in the direction that it is now moving, has lost sight of its fundamental purpose. Most users of a bibliography (I would estimate them at ninety per cent) have a book in one hand and want to know from a book in the other hand what it is that they have--usually, rather grossly, what edition it is that they have. They are not editing the definitive edition of the works of the author of their book; they are not concerned with the significance of their book as an example in the history of the printer that printed it or of the history of printing in general; they are not concerned with the delicate problems of whether a single letter slipped a little in the course of printing a number of copies or was moved infinitesimally sideways by different pressure on the type when it was locked or re-locked into the chase. What the majority of users of a bibliography want to know is whether the copy of a book they have in hand is part of the first printing as the author received it from the press or whether it is part of some later printing in which the differences from the first printing represent a genuine auctorial decision and not merely an accident in the printing house.

Let me cite an example from my own field. For longer than I care to remember, copies of the first edition of Boswell's <u>Life of Johnson</u> have been catalogued as having the word "give" printed on page 135 of volume I as either "give" or "gve." "First issue," the descriptions have read for years, "before the error was corrected." The difference between "gve" and "give" is the result of a trivial correction while the sheets of the book were passing through the press. Anyone who bought a copy on 16 May 1791 might have gotten a copy with the "gve" reading or with the "give" reading. They were, to be sure, different impressions, that is, printing had been halted after some copies had been printed, the missing "i" in "give" supplied, and the rest of the sheets printed off. It is, in short, an event in the printing house which, in my opinion, has no significance. He who prides himself on having a copy with the "gve" reading is living in a world of dreams. What is really important in any copy of the first edition of Boswell's <u>Life of Johnson</u> is the presence or absence of six cancels, which do not correct mere accidents in the printing house, and three of which make alterations deleting matter of very real consequence: Johnson's authorship of the dedication to Percy's <u>Reliques</u>; a long passage about Johnson, Percy, and Joseph Grainger; and Johnson's uncensored remarks on conjugal fidelity. This is material evidence, compared to which the presence or absence of the "i" in "give" cannot be made to seem important even by the most comma-catching bibliographer.

If you do not believe that there are mature bibliographical scholars who catch at commas, let me cite a recent bibliography. The author not only describes in the text but also reproduces in an illustration the fact that in some copies of an edition a comma has slipped one millimeter to the right and that in another book, also illustrated, a colon between two words has moved one millimeter also to the right. Nothing else, you understand, discriminates these two states of the book; the only conclusion this evidence supports is that some time during the run, probably when the printers knocked off for the night, the printing was stopped and that, by the tightening or loosening of the type before printing was resumed, these infinitesimal alterations occurred.

One who is not fully aware of the most recent trends in bibliography may well wonder how such very fine distinctions are detected. They are revealed, as many of you will know, by painstaking (and timetaking) comparison of two apparently identical copies of a book on a machine that superimposes the visual image of a page of one copy of the book on the image of the same page in another copy, so that the slightest difference, even the location of a comma, can be identified.

The author of the bibliography I have mentioned explains that he has thus machine-collated an average of six copies of each of the eighteen first editions of his author. Some difference was discovered, he says, in every one of the volumes examined. But with one single exception, in which an auctorial change was revealed, the differences are mere accidents in the printing house and have nothing to do with the author or his text. These mountains of labor have produced the proverbial progeny.

Some bibliographers use another test: the "gutter margin" which is the interval between the end of the line of type and the inner edge of the page. One recent bibliographer records that, for one title, these measurements, taken at three places in the book, are 4.5 centimeters, 4.5 centimeters, 4.5 centimeters. The measurements are recited to us, then, in order to tell us that there is no difference. If I speak of this as the gutter school of bibliography, do not blame me for any ambiguity.

Effort of this sort could be dismissed as an innocent occupation for anyone who chose to abandon his mind to it, if it were not for several things that may result from it. The first is that such picking of nits will almost certainly affect book-collecting by private collectors, by libraries, and in the long run by the book-dealers on whom collectors and libraries depend, in the same way it always has: by driving them out of the market. For example, the collecting of nineteenth-century books published in parts was at one time very active; but when the list of points required for an ideal copy (such as perhaps never existed) of <u>Pickwick Papers</u> in parts came to eighty-eight pages of a bibliography, then all the fun was squeezed out of the enterprise, and this field of collecting has been pretty nearly dead for thirty years. Of one two-volume nineteenth-century work it has been recorded that copies can exist in eight variant bindings, within which volume 1 may exist in 258 varieties and volume 2 in 9 varieties, and that no two identical copies have been seen. There are thus in theory 18,576 different states. That number is considerably reduced by the fact that only 1,500 copies were printed, and of these 10 are in institutional collections. Is there a collector or a librarian hardy enough to try for the other 1,490, all probably different? And if so, to what end? I am reminded of Johnson's comment, in his edition of Shakespeare, on a long and diffuse note by an earlier editor, to which he merely appended: "All this coil is to little purpose."

Another thing this new bibliography is likely to do is to drive private and institutional collectors away from collecting printed books toward collecting manuscripts, the uniqueness of which does not have to be established by a collating machine. Since the assembling of printed books serves general educational and research needs even more widely (though not more significantly) than the collecting of manuscripts, such a trend would be culturally deplorable.

Still more unfortunate is the competition the new bibliography poses to the huge body of bibliographical work that cries to be done. There is only so much time, there are only so many capable people; above all, there is only so much money for research and publication to carry out vitally needed bibliographical tasks. Just in the area I know better than others--the bibliography of eighteenth-century English writers--satisfactory bibliographies are needed of Addison, Beckford, Cowper, Gay, Goldsmith, Gray, Steele, Sterne, Sheridan.

It seems to me vastly more important, within the available resources of time, money, and people, to get adequate bibliographies of these authors (and of many writers equally neglected in other periods) than it is to record the movements of commas sideways by one millimeter.

It is often illuminating to compare trends in one area of scholarship with those in another area where the problems are similar but the data diverse. This can be done with bibliography, classifying books, and the science of taxonomy, in which natural scientists, from examples at hand, similarly classify animals and plants. These scholars have encountered the same dichotomy that I think bibliography now faces, but the taxonomists have been at it longer and have come clearly to recognize the difficulty. They have learned that taxonomical investigators are of two different kinds, and the terms for these are in common use among them: "splitters" and "groupers." This means that some taxonomists spend their time multiplying categories on the basis of more and more detailed evidence from an increasing number of specimens and that others reduce the numbers of categories when they think the splitters have needlessly multiplied the entities. An example relates to the Atlantic flying fish, Cypselurus cyanopterus. These fishes were divided by one investigator some years ago into eight species, discriminated by the length of the barbels, or slender tactile processes hanging under the lower jaw. That taxonomist was a splitter. Along came another investigator, who observed that the barbels were short in very young flying fish, grew markedly as the fish developed, and then began to shorten until, at the fish's full maturity, the barbels were wholly absorbed and left no trace whatever. He reduced the species from eight to one. He was a grouper. The evidence by which the splitter created many categories was in fact simply not relevant. There were specimens with barbels of varying lengths, but this was just not a datum that was of any use in differentiating species.

That, I submit, is what is happening to bibliography. The splitters have noticed, by laborious examination of a few specimens, differences in what seemed to be one edition of a book and have used those differences to establish categories (that is, variants, impressions, issues) when the differences are in fact not really significant as a standard for any meaningful classification.

Occam's Razor, the law of parsimony propounded by William of Occam, provides that entities must not be multiplied needlessly. The rule should operate to reduce the number of questions just as sharply as the number of answers. If no sensible good is to be supplied by the answer, it is needless to ask the question--or, perhaps more accurately, the question may be asked, but there is no need to report raw answers unless it is clear that they provide useful data.

But we are not yet at the end to which the new bibliography proposes such studies should be carried. A considerable controversy recently raged over Professor William Todd's bibliography of Edmund Burke, a book about which I shall speak more fully a little later. The reviewer of it in The Times Literary Supplement criticized the book because it did not, by its author's design, give exhaustive bibliographical descriptions of many late editions but merely listed them more briefly. This, the reviewer objected, failed to provide information about the history of book-production in that period which might have been available if all editions had been exhaustively described. Indeed, the reviewer took the position that the main purpose of descriptive bibliography is to illuminate the history of printing.

Now I cannot imagine a person better qualified to write a history of eighteenth-century English printing than Professor Todd, and he has in fact recently been engaged in some non-auctorial studies which will be of great interest in appreciating the literary significance of printing practice. But that was not his chosen task in his bibliography of Burke, and he cannot justly be faulted if he kept his work within manageable bounds by leaving the whole history of the printing of that period to another person or another time.

It is as if one who set about to write the history of, say, Bourbon County, Kentucky, was blamed for not taking into account that it borders on 6 other counties and that these and all the successively adjacent 113 counties are part of the state of Kentucky, which in turn borders on 7 other states, and these seriatim on all of the continental United States.

World histories such as the Speculum historiale of Vincent of Beauvais were fashionable in the Middle Ages; they began with the creation of the world and came down to the near present, but their very extensiveness makes them rudimentary records, and true history has become that which focuses on particular times or places and from a mass of detail weighs and extracts that which the writer, according to his idiosyncrasy, judges to be significant. He need not trace it back to the creation or forward until yesterday.

If bibliographers took the history of printing in the time of their authors as part of their tasks, bibliographies, as John Carter wisely observes, would become as fat as Debrett; and even fat Debrett does not trace the customs, habits, manners, and dress of the generations it records.

What is in fact likely to result from the increasing bibliographical use of machines--computers, collating machines, and the like--is atrophy of the judgment. A computer is fit to produce a good concordance, recording all the words and not just the significant ones (provided, of course, that the data have been intelligently assembled and correctly put into the machine) and the virtue of the concordance is its very lack of selectivity. A machine collator will record all of the differences among copies examined, but a bibliography that records all the differences as if they were of equal significance, without the exercise of judgment by the bibliographer, is in my opinion an undigested abomination.

In short, to answer the question I posed at the beginning, "Where is bibliography, as I see it, today?" I think the fad for machines has pushed it past the point where judgment of the significance of data is more important than the accumulation of them and to the point where the bibliographer is expected to attend to the over-particularity of the slipped comma on the one hand and the over-generality of the history of printing on the other.

There is an interesting circularity in the progression from the very small to the very large. The picture of a virus through an electron microscope can hardly be distinguished from an aerial photograph taken at a distance of many thousands of miles. The greater the difference in perspective, the greater the similarity of the results.

This is hardly the receptive moment in our culture to call attention to the virtues of the mediocritas aurea, the golden mean between extremes. And yet I cannot but wonder whether the simple scholar (armed only with spectacles to provide 20-20 vision) who examines books without benefit of machines but with knowledge and judgment is not the best bibliographer after all. To be honest, I really don't wonder at all; I'm sure he is.

But the most important requisite of this best of bibliographers is not his knowledge or his judgment or his vision. It is his interest in, his love of the books he is describing, of their author or their subject or their period, whichever has drawn him into his work. If the books are for him merely so many examples of the production of printing houses of the decade or quinquagenarium of which he treats, then he might as well be collecting stamps.

The book as physical object is consequential to the

humanist for what it contains. To the extent that bibliography can reveal something about its substance (its author's development of his text, its place within its subject, its reflection of the author's ideas or life) it can provide information that cannot be otherwise ascertained. And to the extent that the study of books as physical objects (including their examination by machine) can increase that information, it is a valuable adjunct to literary and historical research. But the book is only a physical container, and the recitation of the facts of its production, when they reveal nothing about its contents, belongs to the history of technology.

It is clear that I am coming to the point where, having said a great deal about what I think a bibliography should not be, I must say what I think a good bibliography should be. This is easiest to do by example, and the best is one that is now nearly forty years old, an age that justifies the term "old-fashioned" in my title. The book is The Literary Career of James Boswell by Frederick A. Pottle, published in 1929 but written chiefly before 1925, without McKerrow or Greg, and before press numbers, collating machines, and gutter measurements. It shows what a zealous scholar can do with a mind and two eyes. And how much more it does! It seems to me to have all the characteristics that Geoffrey Keynes praised in an ideal bibliography: it deals with the physical constitution of the author's works; it gives an idea of the purpose of each book and of its relative importance; the significant part of the printing history of the books is recorded; and the author's character is portrayed. Another great bibliography of ripe age is Allen Hazen's Johnson's Prefaces and Dedications (1937), to which, after nearly forty years of the closest use, I have been able to add two new data of infinitesimal importance, and no corrections whatever. I cite these, not because the work was done at Yale (though I am proud of that) but because they have proved their excellence to me by long and intensive employment. They have told me everything I have needed to know about the books of which they treat, and nothing that I did not want to know, in addition to which they are infused with interest in the books and their authors. Compared with them, some recent bibliographies are more like tables of logarithms or tides. Very much more up-to-date in use of modern investigative techniques but still within the grasp of an ordinarily intelligent reader is William B. Todd's recent bibliography of Burke, which seems to me a model for any but the most unreasonable user. So are Allan Wade's bibliography of

Yeats, Donald Gallup's Pound, and Warren Roberts's D. H. Lawrence, in the same series.

To approach the matter a different way, what I want is what Professor Fredson Bowers prescribes: "The printed description of a book in a bibliography is like the visible tip of an iceberg, the submerged four-fifths corresponding to the unseen investigation which underlies and supports the description." Except for the inaccuracy of the iceberg ratio (eight-ninths being, I believe, the amount of the submerged mass), Mr. Bowers perfectly expresses my ideal. The more investigative work bibliographers do, with all the resources at their command, the better. Let them try casting horoscopes of their authors if they have any reason to think it will be bibliographically revealing, BUT, and I have purposely written that word in capital letters, let them apply sensible judgment so as first to abandon a line of inquiry when it does not seem to produce meaningful results and secondly to digest their data and give us only the significant one-ninth and not the whole mass of raw statistics just to convince us that they are really scientists. Here, as so often, Geoffrey Keynes has put his finger on it. He speaks of "the tendency [of] ... academic bibliographers to exaggerate the claims of their craft. Finding themselves in the company of scholars, who need to be convinced that bibliography really has serious claims on their attention, they instinctively react by behaving as a small persecuted minority. They are forced to push their technical speciality in order to be taken seriously...."

I cannot imagine why anyone, in the presence of an academic, should feel uneasily that he must look up. I am reminded of the response of the rather acid late secretary of Yale University to a letter from a younger college asking us to send, as speaker at its commencement, our President or, if he could not come, another officer, but nothing lower than a dean. To which our secretary replied that the President was otherwise engaged and, as for the second part of the request, there was nothing lower than a dean.

Bibliographers do not need to hide behind an assumed cloak of scientific professionalism by the use of numbers and tables and symbols. Let them go honestly about their work, and if it is any good, their place in the pecking order will take care of itself. My colleague Donald Wing has been plugging quietly away for years on English books from 1641 to 1700. His first edition listed over 80,000 titles. His second edition, just on the way to the press, will list over 90,000. Like the compilers of the STC for the earlier period and of the bibliographies in the Cambridge Bibliography of English Literature, Wing has labored without machines and without concern for his status as a scholar. But I am willing to bet that more inquirers among English books have been set right by these three bibliographies than by all the English single-author bibliographies put together.

Let me say right here, and say it as plainly as I can, that nothing I have said is intended or should be interpreted as an attack on Professor Bowers. His framing of the principles of bibliographical description, his own work within them, and his seminal expressions of the philosophy of bibliography are far beyond any detraction by me even if I would, and I would not. In a recent article, "Bibliography Revisited," he has presented a reasonable and well-reasoned statement of principles with which, while it is possible to differ, it is impossible to quarrel. As usual, the evangelist is infinitely less intransigent than some, at least, of his converts.

One of the latter published last year a very large book of more than 450 foot-high pages with a long introduction which, in the course of setting forth his method, offers the most recent extended discussion of bibliographical principles. The author is Rolf E. Du Rietz of Uppsala and his work is Bibliotheca Polynesia, a catalogue of a remarkable Norwegian collection of books about the South Sea islands. The book is a quite extraordinary production. The table of abbreviations explains to us that "ib." means "ibidem," that "e.g." means "exempli gratia," that "i.e." means "id est," that "vol." means "volume," and even that "Jan." means "January." "O.C.," not the generally accepted but mispronounced "op. cit.," means "opere citato." Capital "F" variously, "first," "folding," or "front." But it is not on these eccentricities that I want to focus here; rather on the conception of bibliography put forward by this Bowers convert who is, I suspect, a source of embarrassment to his priest. Only bibliography, he says, has any legitimate business with rare books, since photocopies will do for other studies. Without bibliographical scholarship, he declares, there would be no textual criticism. And, in a more recent book-review, the same author writes, "To a true bibliographer, working with the ultimate needs of the textual critic in mind, there is, of course, no essential difference between 'first editions' of books, on the one hand,

and later editions, articles in periodicals, offprints, pamphlets, etc., on the other." There is nothing in that sentence with which I can agree, especially the "of course." A true bibliographer does not work for the textual critic alone, or even first; he works for the people (librarians, collectors, book-dealers) who seek to assemble the materials for scholars of many sorts, including, incidentally, the textual critic. First editions of books are almost always much more important to all areas of study than later editions, including the Ten Commandments, of which the unique first edition was destroyed soon after composition. Nor can I agree that bibliographers are the only ones concerned with original rare books and that photocopies will do for all the rest. I do not know the author, but his assurance that he knows what the truth is suggests he is very young.

There would be no excuse for tarrying with him if he were not an example, admittedly extreme, of the opponents of what is called degressive, as against analytical bibliography. And this is a division so deep that it must be considered in any discussion of where bibliography should go. To put it briefly (risking the dangers of that act) degressive bibliography is so called because it degresses from a full-dress description of items such as later editions, reprints, and the like, which are, in the opinion of the bibliographer, of lesser importance, and deals with these by abbreviated descriptions. This is (I almost said, "of course," but let me say, "it seems to me") the only rational method. The bibliographer can and perhaps should investigate items likely to prove peripheral, but to require him to report them as fully as items he knows to be significant is to reduce the bibliographer to a mere clerk. If he whose investigations should make him the best qualified to judge relative importance abdicates the exercise of his informed judgment, then he had better work as a bank teller and deal with indistinguishable dollar bills.

All of the bibliographers whose work I have cited above as examples of "old-fashioned" and what I believe to be *good* bibliography are degressive bibliographers. They are willing to assume the responsibility earned by their research and imposed on them as scholars to judge what is and what is not important and to stand or fall on the results. That will quickly separate the men from the boys.

Or, to put it another way, it will separate those willing to try to distinguish the trivial from the significant, the groupers, from those who take refuge in the security of treating all items alike, as if they were but slightly different but equally important numbers in a series. The strength that is to be had in numbers like that is a strength not worth having.

Bibliography, it seems to me, is suffering from the great, grey disease with which our whole time is sickled over: the loss of idiosyncrasy and even of identity, the surrender of judgment, in a tidal wave of ordinal numbers whose only distinction is that each comes before one and after another. This is the way radio and television and comic books and the flavor of frozen food operate, the way the cultural level of any enterprise is determined when it must be conducted in a purely egalitarian manner, according to the least common multiple.

"What a piece of work is a man," says Hamlet. "How noble in reason! How infinite in faculty! The paragon of animals!" Let us, in bibliography as in all aspects of life, exercise that nobility of reason, that infinity of faculty, that quality of judgment which raises us above the herd of animals.

It will, believe me, be a fight. An advertisement for computers currently on billboards in the northeast reads, "Printing ink, your days are numbered." To which my reply is, "Fold, spindle, and mutilate. You have nothing to lose but your numbers."

You have not come to hear a sermon, nor was I invited to deliver one. Specifically for bibliography, then, when I call for a return to old-fashioned bibliography, what I mean is this:

1. Let us not seek to establish the worth of our studies or our own professional status by resort to a scientific apparatus of symbols, mensuration, and statistics;

2. Let us affirm that the true business of bibliography is to identify and thus encourage the collection, by private collectors, libraries, and book-dealers, of books for the use of other scholars across the whole range of scholarship, including, importantly but not exclusively or even in first place, textual or typographical investigations;

3. Let us affirm the active responsibility of the

bibliographer to exercise his own judgment about the importance of books in various forms and, accordingly, of the degree of complexity with which they are to be described; and

4. Above all, let us not dry up, by a multiplicity of detail, interest in the creation of books by their authors, in the ways books have been changed by their authors (and not merely by their printers), in the contents of books and their significance, in the lives of their authors, and in the role the books played in the history of their times.

Bibliophily is the parent of bibliography. Richard de Bury completed Philobiblon in 1345, and English-speaking peoples have been collecting books ever since. Writing about books and discriminating among them came later, and its vitality still depends on love of the book. Books are not so many machine-produced items of merchandise nor sterile, inert entities that can be fully contained in a collational formula, but parts of men, and usually the only surviving parts of those men. Or, to put it more briefly and less elegantly, one may say to those who, like bibliographers, propose to deal with books: "Love 'em, or leave 'em alone."

GEORGE SMITH AND THE DNB*

George Smith was barely of age when, in 1845, he found himself in sole charge of his father's firm. Smith, Elder & Co., of Cornhill in the City of London, were commercial bankers, export merchants, and agents to the East India Company. They were also, in a smaller way, booksellers and stationers and, almost incidentally, publishers. The fortunes of the firm, and Smith's personal fortune, were founded on general merchandizing from the Ivory Coast to the Java Sea. Had it not been so, there had been no tablet in St. Paul's Cathedral, a stone's throw from Cornhill, commemorating "George M. Smith ... to whom English Literature owes The Dictionary of National Biography and whose warmth of heart endeared him to men of letters of his time."

He became, indeed, the friend as well as the publisher of authors from the Brontës to Mrs. Humphry Ward, of Thackeray and Browning and Matthew Arnold. Yet if he had not, among many other enterprises, imported mineral waters on a large scale from the Rhineland, and supplied munitions of war to the Indian Government at the time of the Mutiny; if, a member of Lloyd's as well as of the Stationers' Company, he had not been both shipowner and newspaper proprietor, he would hardly in his fifties have been in a position to risk £ 150,000 (about £1m in modern terms), and cheerfully to lose half of it, on the DNB.

Smith embarked upon the project with his eyes open--opened, that is, by advisers who dispelled his mirage of a dictionary of universal biography. Even so, history was against him. Had not the second edition of Biographia Britannica (1778-93), which Doctor Johnson had sagely declined to edit, petered out after five folio volumes had

---

*Reprinted by permission from The Times Literary Supplement, no. 3643, 24 December 1971. Articles in TLS are not signed.

barely reached the letter "F"? In the 1830s John Murray II and in the 1850s John Murray III withdrew in time from burning their fingers in this arena. The 1840s, meanwhile, had seen two disasters: The Biographical Dictionary of the Society for Diffusion of Useful Knowledge (1842-44) devoted seven half-volumes to the letter "A" before packing up, and in 1848 Rose's New General Biographical Dictionary, after ten years of hard labour, followed up six volumes of "A" to "C" with a mere six more encapsulating the world's worthies from "D" to "Z."

No, the prospects when Smith first dreamt up his scheme about 1880 were not bright. How in any case should he decide whom to include? How wide a field should be cover? Indeed, what was the purpose of such a work? Biographies of true worthies, of leading lights, were not hard to come by. It was the lesser men, often casually mentioned in such biographies and in works of history, whom the general reader (students as we know them today were hardly a public in 1880) might wish to learn about. But were they worth the trouble and the expense? Had not Cowper just a century earlier composed lines "On observing some names of little note recorded in the Biographia Britannica"?

> Oh, fond attempt to give a deathless lot
> To names ignoble, born to be forgot!
> In vain, recorded in historic page,
> They court the notice of a future age:
> Those twinkling tiny lustres of the land
> Drop one by one from Fame's neglecting hand:
> Lethaean gulphs receive them as they fall,
> And dark oblivion soon absorbs them all....

The solution of these problems was entrusted to a man whose connexion with Messrs. Smith, Elder had not so far been wholly to the firm's advantage. For ten years Leslie Stephen had edited Smith's monthly magazine, the Cornhill. A circulation claimed to be 100,000 in its heyday under Thackeray had dwindled under Stephen to a mere 12,000. But Smith trusted Stephen as a scholar and saw, as a friend, that he needed a change of occupation. Towards the end of 1882 the change was made. As prospective editor, Stephen worked out the rationale of a biographical dictionary. It should be a confidential friend constantly at the elbow of all who were engaged in any historical inquiry, "giving them a summary of the knowledge of antiquaries, genealogists, bibliographers, as well as historians, upon every collateral point which may happen for the moment to be relevant." That Christmas he published a manifesto. The dictionary must give the greatest possible amount of information in a thoroughly businesslike form, with abundant and precise dates and clear references to primary authorities. The biographies must be neither too diffuse nor too meagre--a matter in which it was not easy to draw the line (the drawing of lines was to be one of his hardest tasks).

> Finally I have one remark to add. The editor of such a work must, by the necessity of the case, be autocratic. He will do his best to be a considerate autocrat.

In January, 1883, Stephen issued his first list of names (the letter "A") to be included in the first volumes of DNB. In March he was joined by an assistant, Solomon Lazarus (later Sidney) Lee, a young historian six months down from Oxford. George Smith provided the cash: Leslie Stephen got the machine off the ground; it was Sidney Lee, tiresome, tactless, and touchy though he could be, whose pertinacity saved the project from the fate of its precursors.

There was a little delay in getting off the ground. The first volume was scheduled to appear in October, 1884, but an unscrupulous doctor of divinity seems to have let the publishers in for a threat of an injunction for breach of copyright, and publication was delayed until the following January (not January, 1886, as stated in DNB's obituary of Stephen). Thereafter, perhaps the most notable feature in the history of the original DNB was the regularity of its schedules. Regularly every spring and autumn a list of the next alphabetical batch of worthies was published in the Athenaeum. Scholars were invited to propose other names, and/or to propose themselves as contributors. Approved contributors were allowed six months in which to submit their copy. And every three months a volume was published, as punctual as clockwork, for the fifteen-and-a-half years to midsummer 1900--sixty-three volumes in all.

But if publication was punctual, not everything ran smoothly behind the scenes. It was perhaps rash to have invited readers of the Athenaeum to play a part. One need not take au pied de la lettre Stephen's "inevitable clergyman" who provided a list of 1,400 hymn-writers deserving of inclusion; but there were others who criticized the published lists. There were applicants for the honour of contributing

Technical/Readers' Services

who cut up rough when not given the commissions to which they felt their eminence or special knowledge entitled them. There were specialists who declined the invitation to contribute ("entre amis, you know, neither the pay nor the publicity makes the DNB a great catch"), and there were those who resented their manuscripts being vetted by rival scholars even more than they disliked editorial tinkering with their prose. (History does not relate when split infinitives were eliminated from DNB, or at whose instance, but deliberately eliminated they were. Lee himself had no distaste for them. "It is the art of the biographer," he once avowed, "to sternly subordinate his scenery to his actors.")

Stephen had to rely on specialists to advise him not only in the choice of contributors but also in the adoption of a "house style" for such matters as the spelling of names-- Cassivellaunus or Caswallawn, Boadicea or Boudicca, the familiar of the pedantic. If DNB had been the property of the Oxford University Press in the 1880s, as it is now, the influence of Dr. Furnivall and Dr. Murray would no doubt have led to the adoption of "Shakspere" in DNB as well as in OED. Only in this century have OED's lesser progeny moved over to "Shakespeare," the greater work remaining committed to the less familiar form, DNB meanwhile remains committed to other equally unfamiliar pedantries. Alfred the Great, for instance, must be sought under AElfred, and Elfrida, mother of Ethelred the Unready, under AElfthryth. This Stephen owed to his dependence at the outset on the opinionated historian E. A. Freeman. Freeman soon had a tiff with the editor ("his temper was impatient"--DNB), and after having written the notice of AElfred in Volume I he contributed nothing more.

From the start, more inevitably even than Stephen's clergyman with his massed choir of hymn-writers, there were critics of the published DNB. A month after the appearance of the first volume, Notes and Queries printed the first of a long and valuable series of contributions by "W. C. B." listing errors and supposed errors. "W. C. B." was Walter Consitt Boulter, solicitor, parson and antiquary. Besides matters of fact, he had general axes to grind. The paper on which DNB was printed would not take ink, so that he had to make his marginal notes in pencil. Familiar placenames were given out-of-date spellings. English churchmen were being obituarized by others than English churchmen. Of the very first volume he made a criticism which is of interest in the light of DNB's later policy: "For my part I would gladly have seen much of the space taken up by such lives as Queen Anne and one or two more devoted to smaller folk." Besides scholars reporting factual errors there were surviving relatives of departed worthies. Except where a son or a widow has exposed a man's failings to the world--as sometimes happens in our present age--the editor of a biographical dictionary must observe the rule De nuper mortuis.... How had Halliwell-Phillips, the Shakespeare scholar, come by manuscripts that rightfully belonged to Trinity College, Cambridge? Had or had not his name been cleared of suspicion? And here was DNB raking up the old charge with every implication that it still stood. His widow was indignant. Grudgingly, Lee rephrased his comment in the next edition.

No wonder Stephen, who had a tendency at the best of times to overstretch himself with other work and who, as Lee generously put it, "never quite reconciled himself to office routine" ("that damned thing goes on like a diabolical piece of machinery," wrote Stephen, "always gaping for more copy, and I fancy at times that I shall be dragged into it and crushed out into slips")--no wonder Stephen's "steady application soon developed a nervous depression" which in turn "rendered periodic rests necessary." He holidayed each winter in his beloved Swiss Alps. For the fifth year of his editorship, after a serious breakdown, he absented himself from the dictionary, and in 1890 he resigned his post. He was able nevertheless to go on writing for DNB. Lee, always a great one for statistics, tells us that in the original sixty-three volumes Stephen contributed no fewer than 378 articles covering 1,000 pages. This was out of a total of 29,000 articles in 29,000 pages from 650 contributors.

Among the enduring problems that Lee inherited with the editorship was the prolixity of contributors. It had long been apparent that the fifty volumes originally planned would not be nearly enough. Lee addressed to his contributors what is in effect an argumentum ad misericordiam:

> Every effort is made in the editor's office to remove superfluous detail before the articles are published, but greater condensation might possibly be secured if some writers cooperated rather more actively in the work of abridgement.... The practice of introducing the last scrap of information that patient research can reveal is not to be condemned lightly, but....

But ... as Lee's obituarist in DNB remarks, he himself was too much inclined to the very fault he condemned--that of hunting out scraps and including them whether they were of importance or not--to be an effective preacher. Neither Stephen nor Lee was perhaps enough of an autocrat to keep in control a heterogeneous collection of often prickly contributors.

Not that it was always the contributors' fault if their prickles were stirred. Lee could be tactless, or worse, in his treatment of the young men he recruited. There were two such on the staff of the British Museum, both scholars and each destined in time to become Keeper of Prints and Drawings. Their names were Campbell Dodgson and Laurence Binyon. So offensive were Lee's letters to them that Sidney Colvin, the head of their department, was constrained to remonstrate: "They have done nothing to deserve being written to--to put it mildly--like worms."

Lee had, as we have said, been largely responsible for keeping DNB going in its early years. It was he who saw to it that the volumes appeared on time. As sole editor he became a public personality, free to speak his mind. Most of what he said was platitudinous, and some of the statistics with which he regaled the Royal Institution read a little curiously today. He reckoned that, of all the persons in the British Isles who passed the age of twenty-four in the nine centuries 1000-1900, one in 5,000 was eligible for inclusion in DNB; and since 50 per cent of the population did not pass the age of twenty-four, "an infant's chance of attaining distinction is one in 10,000." With lower infant mortality in the philoprogenitive twentieth century one can only wonder....

In the lecture in which he delivered himself of these figures in 1896, Lee had a word to say about women. There were, he said, some 600 persons living in London who might qualify for inclusion in DNB, of whom "about twenty should be women."

> In this last calculation I perhaps have made inadequate allowance for the recently developed energy among women which seems likely to generate unlooked-for exploits of more or less distinction.
> ... Women will not, I regret to reflect, have much claim on the attention of the national biographer for a very long time to come.

(Women's Liberation, please note.)

One innovation introduced early in Lee's period of editorship was an informal tie-up between DNB and The Times. The initiative came from The Times, whose manager, Moberly Bell, saw the advantage of combining forces in preparing obituary notices of distinguished persons before their deaths. This may account for a tendency of some contributors to adopt a tone more suitable to a newspaper than to a dictionary, but the connexion has proved fruitful over many years.

DNB has always concerned itself only with the dead. "No man's memory can be accounted great," in Lee's words, "until it has outlived his life." In nearly sixteen years and in sixty-three volumes, the dictionary ran its course from Jacques ABADIE (1654-1727), a Frenchman by birth, to William Henry ZUYLESTEIN, Earl of Rochford (1717-1781), whose father was Dutch. (Common Market advocates and opponents, please note.) In those sixteen years many worthies had died, and well before the last volume was out plans were laid, and contributors alerted, for a three-volume Supplement which would do justice to 800 of them, as well as to some 200 other worthies of earlier times whom the editor dubbed "accidental omissions" from the main work.

The Supplement was to end with the end of 1900, but the death of Queen Victoria in the first month of the new century tempted publisher and editor to overrun their terminus ad quem. Hence a regrettable anomaly. Users of The Twentieth Century DNB who know when the Queen died will not find her in the appropriate volume. (Nor, for the same reason, will they find George Smith, who died later in the same year.) In an inappropriate volume, however, they will find a biographical notice of the Queen running to between 90,000 and 100,000 words, contributed by Lee himself, and also issued as a separate monograph. The earlier notice of Queen Anne, though not on the same scale, was a precedent for recounting the events of a reign through the medium of the monarch; and monarchs since Victoria, though again not on quite the same scale, have been similarly treated. The Supplement appeared expeditiously in the autumn of 1901. DNB was now complete. George Smith's dream had come true.

Some years before his death in 1901 George Smith ceded the management of the family firm to his son-in-law, Reginald Smith. DNB he bequeathed to his widow. Under

Technical/Readers' Services   271

their joint aegis Lee edited the first Index and Epitome,
later versions of which valuable compendium have been
named The Concise DNB. This appeared in 1903, and was
followed in the next year by a volume of Errata. In a work
which now comprised some 30,500 pages in sixty-six volumes it is not surprising that errors to a total approximating
to 10,000 should have been detected, and even less surprising
if we accept Lee's assurance that DNB by then contained
"more than two million facts and dates." Copies of this
volume were presented gratis to subscribers to the main
work. Many corrections had in fact been incorporated in
various volumes as they were reprinted earlier than 1904,
and this practice has been continued ever since, in so far
as stereotype plates will stand up to multiple correction.
Much important work in the way of amendment and addition
was undertaken many years later under the auspices of the
Institute of Historical Research. Many a librarian would
cut out contributions to the Institute's Bulletin between 1923
and 1961 to paste into his set of DNB, until in 1966 an
enterprising American firm assembled them in a handy
volume, published not in Britain but in Boston, Massachusetts.

With the Epitome and the Errata out of the way it
looked like a farewell to DNB, Lee's occupation gone. Little
of his time was needed in the compression of the sixty-three
volumes into twenty-two on thinner paper, the form familiar
today. Publication of this was serial, running from March,
1908, to December, 1909. But it was unthinkable to Lee
that DNB, "a living organism," should be allowed to die.
There was still money in the Smith coffers, and Mrs. Smith
was happy to prolong her husband's dream. There should
be a further Supplement, and perhaps yet further decennial
Supplements. ("Decennial" did not prove in the event precisely accurate: the first of the series covered the eleven
years 1901-11; the third restored the balance with nine
years, 1922-30.) Lee allowed himself and his contributors
a greater scope, if not prolixity, than previously, so that
he needed three volumes totaling more than 2,000 pages.
They appeared at quarterly intervals in 1912, and the editor,
though by now busy with Shakespearian and other studies,
looked forward to returning in due course to editing a second
decennial Supplement.

With the death of Reginald Smith in 1916 the fortunes
of the dictionary took a new turn. The publishing business
of Smith, Elder was acquired by John Murray: DNB was

offered as a gift by the Smith family to Oxford University. Needless to say the university was delighted: not so Sir Sidney (he had been knighted in 1911). We shall not, at this late date, complain that in a polemical pamphlet Lee accused the TLS of "rather imperfectly recounting" the history of DNB when reporting the gift (July 19, 1917): any journalistic account of that complex history, even today, is liable to imperfection. But the whole tenor of Lee's pamphlet is to suggest that the university--his own university, to which he accorded the meed of some faint praise--was incompetent to carry on, in the spirit of its founder, a work to which he had himself devoted the best years of his life. All that in fact had happened was that, in the middle of a war, the Delegacy of the University Press had not, within a couple of months of welcoming a very generous offer, made any firm promise for the detailed future conduct of the enterprise--something they could hardly do before their acceptance was ratified by the university after the long vacation. It was a sad day for Lee, and a tactical error if he wished to continue his association with the dictionary.

When the Oxford University Press took over DNB the stock of most volumes was low, and indeed was soon exhausted. Immediately after the war the price of paper was high and there was some delay before the original work and the Supplements and the Epitomes (now Concise) could be reprinted. All were available again in the early 1920s, and in 1923 the Press proudly announced an india paper edition reducing sixty-six volumes to eleven and filling less than three feet of shelving. Meanwhile work was going ahead on the living organism, a single-volume Supplement to cover the years 1912-21. The new editors, H. W. C. Davis and J. R. H. Weaver, were faced with the problem that if they continued on Lee's lavish scale the twentieth century would eventually fill some 20,000 pages of print, or two-thirds of the space allotted to the previous nine centuries. They cut back perhaps rather more than was necessary, and the later decennial volumes have gone some way towards redressing the balance, as the following round figures show: 1901-11 (Lee), 1,600 obituaries in 2,050 pages; 1912-21 (Davis and Weaver), 450 in 600 pages; 1922-30 (Weaver), 590 in 930 pages; 1931-40 (L. G. Wickham Legg), 730 in 930 pages-- after which the figures begin to creep up again: 1941-50 (Wickham Legg and E. T. Williams), 725 obituaries in 1,000 pages, and 1951-60 (Williams and the first woman editor, Miss Helen M. Palmer), 760 in 1,100 pages.

Two signs of the times are worth noticing. The
period between the terminal date of each volume and its
date of publication has progressively lengthened. The three
volumes of the Supplement to 1911 were published within
twelve months; for the volume to 1921 the gap was six
years, for that to 1930 seven years, and for those to 1940
and 1950 nine years each; the latest volume has been
eleven years in the hatching. Prices have not stood still.
The three volumes issued since the Second World War were
priced when first published at £2 10s (now £6), five
guineas (now £7.50), and £9.50.

Readers must often have wondered how DNB editors
allotted--and allot--space to the different worthies. Is the
criterion the degree of worthiness, of public importance?
Or is it the variety of the subject's activities or of the incidents in his or her life? We may never know. But an
analysis of the vocations of worthies made by the statisti-
cally-minded editors of the latest volume suggests a grading
like that of honours degrees: "Within each Subject Group
the lives are divided into three classes by length: I. Two
pages and over. II. Under two pages but over one.
III. One page or less." On this basis, to take only a
few categories, Authors, Scholars, Poets, "Etc." are
awarded nineteen firsts, seventy-one seconds, and seventeen thirds; Public Life (Home) do better with twenty-three
firsts out of ninety-one graduands. Scientists less well with
only five firsts out of ninety-six; no firsts are awarded to
Sculptors, Designers and Engravers, or to Diplomatists or
Sportsmen or Business Men. Queen Mary, though not a
monarch, gets more space than anyone except Ernest Bevin
and Lord Halifax, beating her sovereign son, George VI, by
a page and a half. The proportion of women to men, if
our mathematics are correct, is 1:13, as against Lee's
calculation of 1:30, most of them getting good seconds.
(Another talking point for Women's Liberation?)

The benevolent autocracy of the editors of the new
volume has been effective. In the past there has been a
tendency for what should be biographical notices to fall into
the pattern of the newspaper obituary--"He will be" being
altered to "He was ... much missed by his friends." Contributors have been almost wholly cured of this complaint.
The volume moreover is easier to read for the removal of
horizontal rules under the headlines and vertical rules between the columns. It says much for the designer of the
original DNB of 1885 that otherwise the page has remained

virtually unaltered for eighty-five years.

"I venture," said George Smith seventy-five years ago, "to express a doubt whether a work involving so many years of unremitting labour, so much research, so much anxious care, will be produced for many a long year to come. At all events there will not be another <u>Dictionary of National Biography</u>. We have covered the ground." A proud, and at the time a justifiable, boast. <u>DNB</u> has weaknesses, most of them inherent in the circumstances in which it was compiled. Inaccuracies since discovered apart, shifts of historical interpretation apart, Stephen and Lee had not in the nineteenth century the opportunities the twentieth century could provide to recruit specialist contributors and technical equipment. They could call upon neither the university faculties nor the typewriters of today--how Lee would have valued a computer for his statistics!--though they had a marked advantage in the speed of printing. Never another <u>DNB</u>? It is a pessimistic thought. If some future George Smith, or a courageous Delegacy at Oxford, had a mind to risk £1m (with a chance of cheerfully losing half of it), a new <u>DNB</u> on a different scale and a different plan would be a boon to scholars. For a different plan, perhaps volumes by chronological periods. The institutional library and the moneyed polyhistor could buy all the volumes, but the student of Boudicca and Caswallawn need not pay for a set containing lives of Shakspere and all who came after. "Accidental omissions" like G. M. Hopkins and Wilfred Owen could be honoured. The modern volumes need not be revised until history had shaken itself down a bit, or until widows and widowers and paramours had joined that majority from whom <u>DNB</u> so authoritatively chooses its minority of worthies.

Part III

COMMUNICATION AND EDUCATION

THE MAKING OF THE NEW YORK TIMES BOOK REVIEW*

Thomas Weyr

In January, 1971, John Leonard, then a 31-year-old novelist who had swiftly hacked out a reputation as one of the ablest writers ever to appear in the New York Times' daily book columns, was named editor of the Times Book Review to succeed the retiring Francis Brown. Leonard, as both Time and Newsweek pointed out, thus became the single most powerful arbiter of the American book world.

TBR, as it is known in the trade, is exposed to 1.6-million readers every week. It is the most influential book medium in the United States, a status attested to by the fact that many publishers put as much as 60% to 80% of their advertising budget in its pages, and keep it there the longest, even in times of recession and economic downturn. TBR is something of a Bible for the bulk of American librarians, the largest single institutional book buying market. Sunday Times readers in the Boston-Washington megalopolis, where 1.4-million of them live, still bustle down to their local bookstores--especially in tonier suburbs like Cambridge, Georgetown, Rye, Larchmont and New Canaan--with copies of TBR or with reviews and ads neatly clipped for reference.

Leonard's advent was generally applauded in publishing. He was young, creative, his work as a daily Times book reviewer, critic for Life, and novelist gave him a breadth of book experience few of his peers could match. It was widely believed that he would bring a fresh viewpoint to the TBR, which many in the industry had begun to consider drab and gray. At the same time he was Brown's personal choice as successor. Indeed, Brown had brought Leonard and several other young editors to TBR in the mid-60s in order to infuse new blood into its editorial pages. The close connection between Brown and his heir apparent

---

*Reprinted by permission from Publishers Weekly. Copyright (c) 1972 by the Xerox Corporation.

Communication and Education

seemed to assure a sense of continuity.

Yet the flak began to burst more than a year ago and hasn't stopped flying since. Some undoubtedly is due to the innovations Leonard and his staff have brought to TBR. The new broom swept fairly clean. Regular features and contributors were dropped, new reviewers brought in, the scope of book coverage both widened and contracted. Material considered esoteric by many trade book publishers was given greater space, run-of-the-house books were squeezed into shorter reviews, many books were not reviewed at all. The impression grew that fewer books were being given attention. TBR reviewers took a more definite political stance and it was clearly a more liberal, if not radical, one. Neil Sheehan's omnibus review of Vietnam war crime books (March 28, 1971) stirred the dormant debate over the war into new life. Leonard's penchant for long, probing, essay-style examinations of one writer's world, rather than of one book, pumped new controversy into literary conversation with publishers criticizing the "waste" of space, which, they felt, swallowed their own books unreviewed.

Still, not all of the flak, and certainly not the intensity of feeling Leonard's editorship has aroused, can be traced solely to the changes he has introduced. What emerged clearly from a series of in-depth interviews conducted by PW with leading publishers and editors is the fact that much of the criticism of TBR is rooted in the changes that have seeped through the book industry in the last decade and over which TBR and its editors have little control. The entry of electronics and conglomerate ownership of publishing houses has had its impact. Corporate controllers marched lockstep with show business tinsel-merchants and books began to go Hollywood in a big way. Million-dollar deals for books rated modest headlines; paperback and book club sales in the six-figure range became common even for "warm" rather than "hot" properties. And with the big money came a sense of anxiety and insecurity common to an industry in the throes of major change.

Some of the frustrations these new pressures have engendered are undoubtedly reflected in the critical fire directed at TBR. For years it was an anchor of stability for the whole industry. Its coverage of major books could be relied upon. A front-page review could catapult a doubtful book into a fair seller and push a good one onto the best seller list. A TBR ad was the best showcase for a new book. Publishers complacently assumed that their books would have to be reviewed, that they could count on a certain number and a certain type of review. There was grousing, of course, but it had become comfortable grumbling. Then, suddenly, the comfort was gone. TBR did not make a changing business easier to live with. It was frankly contemptuous of much of the new razzle-dazzle. Its editors were pulling readers in many different directions at once. Whatever common touch many publishers thought "Brownie" had given TBR seemed lost. Editors could no longer point to reviews in the TBR, as they had in the past, to justify publication of books with perhaps dubious sales potential. Inflation took its toll, as did the recession. If anybody bothered to remember, as Doubleday publisher Samuel Vaughan did in a recent interview, that "we used to bitch as much about Brownie as we now bitch about Leonard," it was hard to discern. Again and again publishers and editors complained of long essays while new books were not reviewed, and expressed the conviction that TBR had a duty to its readers at least to inform them of what was being published.

In the process of making that case there was an equally unmistakable tenor of "if I were John Leonard I'd sure as hell do it differently."

The Complex Process of Making an Issue

How does Leonard do it? How does he select books for review, pick reviewers, decide which review goes where, and when and in what form? The process is complex and moves at several levels at once, since TBR editors work on more than one issue simultanously. But any Wednesday morning is as good a time as any to follow "The Making of the New York Times Book Review."

At eleven o'clock four staffers pull away from their book-heaped desks in the bullpen TBR occupies in one corner of the eighth floor of the Times Sunday Department and troop into John Leonard's equally book-cluttered corner office for the weekly scheduling conference. Besides Leonard, participants include assistant editors Roger Jellinek and Raymond J. Walters, Jr. (a TBR veteran who had served as Francis Brown's right-hand man), assistant to the editor Charles Simmons and one of the half-dozen or so staff previewers selected to take part on a rotating basis. The editors have an average of 50 reviews in house, or firmly promised to choose from, for the issue that will bear the date of the Sunday three-and-a-half weeks hence. They will lay out the first eight pages, which do not carry any advertising, then the so-called "second front," the first righthand page after the centerfold--usually a major review that for one reason or another does not rate the flagship space of page one--the "Last Word" editorial column, and a choice of back-of-the-book reviews. The latter cannot be laid out until the advertising department tells Leonard on Friday of the following week how much editorial space is available for a particular issue. The advertising-editorial relationship depends on advertising volume. In a 48-page issue, a recent average, Leonard is given roughly a third for editorial use. Exact percentages vary according to a complex formula based on three advertising "seasons" that approximate publishing cycles: June to Labor Day, Labor Day to Christmas, Christmas to June. But editorial space increases in direct proportion to any decrease in the total number of pages. In a 24-page issue, review material takes up half.

The following Tuesday the TBR staff meets over a wine and cheese lunch in Leonard's office for an informal bull session on general problems affecting the Review. "We talk about what we've been doing and what we're going to do," Jelinek says, "look over the mail, find out the kind of response we've been getting and what we should do about it, check the current new book lists, discuss ideas for columns or features. The discussion is wide open, it's not a hierarchical situation at all. Our format is loose enough so that there's no point scoring, there are no little battles going on...."

On Thursday, eight days after the initial scheduling conference, Leonard meets with art director Robert Melson to consider the art work--another target of publishing ire because pictures take up space, publishers argue, that could be devoted to words reviewing books. Leonard's mild response: "I've asked for fewer illustrations, but they're considered essential for modern magazines."

The following day ad manager Thomas Denny tells Leonard how much back-of-the-book editorial space he has left. Then the fitting begins: shoe-horning reviews into the available columns and their layout.

"It's a question of fiddling," Jellinek says, "if we

have, say, five two-column spaces and our pick at the
scheduling conference was four three-column reviews, then
there's no way anything would work. We generally end up
holding the reviews we had planned upon. The only way we
could run them would be through atrocious cutting or jump-
ing. And cutting on Friday afternoon is bad business. Reviewers are notoriously hard to reach as the weekend approaches. It's simply easier to wait."

The back of the book is laid out initially on Friday
afternoon--ten days before those who subscribe to TBR independently at a cost of $13 a year get their copies, 16 days
before it is folded into the Sunday Times--and is then
worked over until the following Wednesday when it goes to
the printer. The typeface is smaller than up front, the
makeup looser. Some reviews that have waited weeks for
an up-front placement are shoved into the back for topical
reasons--otherwise their timeliness would expire. Longer
reviews that haven't run are often scrapped and the book in
question may be dumped into the shorter review column.

Agreement on a front page candidate is fairly easy--
there aren't many around that fit Leonard's strict standards
for the most coveted review slot in the American book industry:

What Makes a Page One Significant Review?

"It must be a distinguished book whose argument is,
in our judgment, new and convincing and one that is important to the understanding of the past, present and future,"
Leonard says. "Our test is simply: do we think that literate men and women should read this book." Excellence of
style in the book and the review are also page one criteria
though Leonard will on occasion "take a book that is significantly wrong," especially, "if I've got a marvelous review."

André Malraux's recent book, Felled Oaks, Conversations with de Gaulle (Holt), is a case in point. "It wasn't
a distinguished book, but its publication was a literary event
and Murray Kempton just wrote a great review."

Leonard disliked B. F. Skinner's Beyond Freedom
and Dignity [Knopf] and at first was tempted not to review
it. But the enormous exposure Skinner received in the media, including a cover on Time magazine, convinced him

Communication and Education 281

that the Skinner phenomenon had to be covered. He found the review fascinating ("I hadn't thought of Skinner that way"--as longing for a return to the virtues of 19th century America) and "up it went" onto page one.

Leonard tries for front page balance, but does not insist on it. "We won't have three front pages in a row with novels on them. But we don't try to structure page one and we don't worry about having three complex books up front. Still, the number one choice would have to be guided by what has been there in the past few weeks. Take Moravia and Harrington--Alberto Moravia's novel Two [Farrar, Straus & Giroux] and Michael Harrington's Socialism [Saturday Review Press]. If we'd been heavy on politics we'd have to take Moravia." [In point of fact Leonard chose Harrington, perhaps because Leslie Fiedler's review roasted the Moravia book.] "The delightful Houseman book" [Run-Through, theater director John Houseman's reminiscences, published by Simon and Schuster] won front-page coverage "because you can't always be heavy."

Front page impact varies enormously as TBR's editor admits readily. "Some page one books are best sellers, whereas nothing happens to others. Ten years ago the kind of book that can become a best seller appeared regularly on page one. But that changed when Brown hired younger men. Remember that Brown himself initiated these changes."

As a result many difficult or unusual books have received front page treatment with sharply differing impact. Erving Goffman's Relations in Public [Basic] was ignored for months after publication until Leonard ran a page one review on February 27, 1972. The result: a $45,000 paperback offer, unhappily too late because the rights already had been sold for $7,000. "You can help specialized books by calling attention to them," Leonard contends.

But how much? Don de Lillo's second novel, End Zone [Houghton Mifflin] was given a front page Valentine on April 9. In the nine days that elapsed between the closing of the TBR issue and its distribution with the Sunday Times, wholesale jobbers ordered 3,500 copies on top of 3,000 already sold. Houghton Mifflin promptly increased the printing to 15,000. By mid-May sales were still only 6,500 copies. And publishing sources don't credit TBR alone for that one large order, since the daily Times had praised the book during the same week.

Sol Stein, president of Stein & Day, figures a front page review is worth 2,500 copies today. But it is probably impossible to average out page one sales. Front page plaudits for Russian novelist Vasily Grossman's <u>Forever Flowing</u> [Harper's Magazine Press] failed to move the book. Yet Yale University Press's 1,800-page collection of Civil War era letters, <u>Children of Pride</u>, sold briskly after its page one appearance.

TBR editors find the slack publishing periods--January-February and July-August--the hardest to handle up front. Leonard feels that few outstanding books are published then and prefers to push his most controversial and certainly his most noticeable innovation--the long, probing, essay-style appraisal of a neglected author.

TBR's handling of John Updike's <u>Rabbit Redux</u> [Knopf], in the issue of November 14, 1971, was perhaps the most hotly debated example of the retrospective technique. Staffer Richard Locke wrote a long (some critics say overlong), enthusiastic review, more given to proving that Updike had at last made it as a major U.S. writer, than to a discussion of the novel itself. A "Last Word" column made a similar point. And Bech (the writer who figured in earlier Updike fiction) interviewing Updike rounded out the coverage.

Leonard acknowledges that this may have been a bit much but argues that "I felt Updike never got the attention he deserved, and Bech interviewing Updike was just so funny I couldn't bear nor running it." He concedes, however, that he may have overdone retrospectives. "I did too many in 1971 and I'm determined to reduce them. Sometimes an 800- to 1,000-word review is enough."

Nor is the TBR editor altogether happy with how page one has worked out: "I feel ashamed that Don de Lillo's book was the first by an 'unknown' writer to make page one. But I was hooked on intellectual razzle-dazzle. Styron or Steven Marcus on the front page of TBR--that's going to interest people. I was looking for writers who would automatically command respect. The trouble is that they are cultural 'givens,' no one could object to them, and that approach didn't help some very good second or third novels. I thought I was being adventurous, yet Sally Kempton's review of Germaine Greer's <u>The Female Eunuch</u> [McGraw-Hill] didn't make page one. She was not as tough on the book as she should have been, it wasn't that good a book, but as a book it was more interesting than Chester Bowles' memoirs. But in the future I'm going to use page one to discover something. Not just Updike and Mailer. My own taste will be reflected more. I will have the courage of my eccentricity, some odd things will turn up."

The "second front" is another controversial innovation. In conceiving it Leonard and his staff hoped "to eat into the psychology that only one book is important in any one week. We want people to stop skimming TBR, to stop the reader's psychological attitude that there is nothing good to read in the back of the book."

In a lengthy analysis of TBR and its operations, prepared by the Review staff last April as part of a wider study devoted to the exploration of how the Times can improve its coverage and catch up with readers who have quit the city for the suburbs, the rationale for the second front and its impact on the back-of-the-book problem was examined in some detail. That part of the study, written by Roger Jellinek, argued that the back of the book "suffers a special psychological disadvantage ... [it] ... is visually discouraging ... printed in narrow measure ... in part committed to jumps from up-front reviews, and in part to special literary ghettos, such as crime, popular minor fiction, letters, etc. Because of the jumpy 1-2-3 column spaces these are shoehorned into, the whole effect is scrappy ..."

The second front was given a visual face-life, decorated with stylized art and printed in the wider measure of the first eight pages. "The reviews ... generally attempt to revise easy conventions or long received opinions.... (on it) ... are often found books the editor and staff consider important, but perhaps too complex to inflict on the general reader glancing first at page one. Or the review may be extraordinary and original, but quite demanding ..."

"We tend to put reviews there which we liked more for the writing in the review than for the book itself," Leonard elaborates, "reviews that approached our standard ideals. Sometimes we like a book but it simply isn't front page material, such as Amy Vanderbilt's Etiquette [Doubleday], subject of a recent second front dissection, or Mailer's collected stuff--that's not major--or Animals in Art [Gale]. We weren't putting the second most important book of the week on the second front, rather it tended to be a set piece, a reviewer's page, a surprise page. We looked for good writing; a way, really, to make people realize that it's not all garbage back there."

A third major change was "The Last Word," introduced under Leonard. It replaced the Queries and Answers column on the inside back cover and was designed to give TBR a more direct editorial voice than it had before. In a memo Leonard wrote as part of the in-house study on TBR he explains the function of "The Last Word" this way:

"We wanted ... to establish an editorial identity for the Book Review, spelling out our own literary preoccupations, commenting on literary/cultural events, reappraising books unfairly or too briefly dealt with in the reviewing media, keeping an eye open on publishing malpractice, indicating our own criteria for excellence." Leonard also hoped to bring "some playfulness" to TBR, "a parody every once in a while ... some controversy and humor--elements mostly (and properly) missing from formal book reviews and yet necessary to relieve the solemn gloom of serious criticism." Finally, he hoped "The Last Word" would serve the same function as the Second Front--to halt reader skimming. "We sought to interrupt the skimming in the middle ... to improve the quality of the reviews that followed that second front; and to end each issue with a strong editorial feature--to give a sense of motion and design to the way each issue was presented."

Originally Leonard had hoped to utilize the staff's considerable writing talent for "The Last Word." But Walter Clemons left for Newsweek and was not replaced. Other staffers had to sub on the daily Times book page. In order to circumvent these difficulties Leonard instituted "The Guest Word" in which such diverse writers as Jorge Luis Borges and Larry King could follow the drum of their particular fancy. He is moderately pleased with the results, especially with the breadth of topics covered--from the troubles of the New York Public library to Borges on food and King parodying the Clifford Irving-Howard Hughes affair. " 'The Last Word' is looked at and read ... it excites much mail; it has helped stop skimming," his memo said, "but ... it has insufficiently satisfied the desire for a regular literary editorial." And he cites Times art editor Hilton Kramer, a member of the task force studying the newspaper's operations, as saying that the column "serves a good editorial function when someone feels very strongly about an issue, but otherwise has become another space that needs to be filled."

Leonard plans to meet that argument with regular commitments by staff members to write for "The Last Word" at least once a month. "The form these articles will take will sometimes be formal criticism of criticism (Renata Adler's 'Guest Word' column on July 9, 1972, 'A Review Reviewed,' is one example albeit not by a staff member); reviews themselves plus reappraisals; a 'Letter from New York' speaking to the preoccupations of the 'literary culture' as they seem to have expressed themselves recently; (and) comment on controversial reviews we have recently published."

Reviewers Are Always Treated with Gentleness

Despite strong insistence on quality--or perhaps because of it--TBR editors treat reviewers with enormous gentleness. There is sharp copy editing if necessary but usually as a last resort. Wherever possible editing is done by mail with subtle suggestions for changes, cuttings, rewording or restructuring. Permission is always sought before changing copy. Only rarely are reviews dropped or assigned to someone else.

"You do run reviews you don't like," Leonard says, "and you'd be a real totalitarian if you didn't."

To some extent TBR's selection process is autocratic, however, considering the number of books that pour into the "bullpen." A visitor to Leonard's office has to be a broken-field runner to get past the stacks that block his way. Official estimates put the annual flood at 20,000 books (Jellinek thinks "we get only 15,000 books") and TBR is rarely able to review more than 2,200 of them. "That is not sufficient," the in-house analysis states, "but it has been true for 15 years and will continue to be true unless (1) a sudden great leap forward in advertising allows us to double the size of TBR or (2) the editorial to advertising space relationship is reversed ... Neither possibility seems likely."

Roger Jellinek is first on the firing line, doing what he calls pre-previewing to weed out obviously unacceptable books, a category that generally includes scholarly monographs, most (though not all) textbooks, pulp westerns, and books in the how-to and handicraft fields.

Books that survive Jellinek's initial scrutiny are carded by author and title and cross-checked on charts set up months before. Staffer Arlene Youngman maintains the extensive in-depth file in which Jellinek tries to list all the books he might be interested in reviewing months before their publication. He collects fall and spring lists, scouts around for information on why editors and publishers gambled on a book, snatches an editor's fact sheet when he can get hold of one ("some publishers and publicity directors don't like this but they're getting used to it"), lunches constantly with publicity people and editors, scans PW, the London **Times Literary Supplement** and the Kirkus service, collates data from other TBR editors, and enters all this diverse information on the charts or makes sure that forthcoming books of interest are on them. Once books have survived the Jellinek obstacle they are trolleyed into Leonard's office for distribution to the previewers.

"I meditate and look at them," Leonard says, "and at the publishers' letters that accompany them" before dividing the possibles into piles that will go to the staff. "Each editor has a bundle of specialties, competences and skills" and books are assigned on that basis.

Richard Locke, a former editor at Simon and Schuster, specializes in experimental fiction, movies, psychology and general culture. Roger Jellinek's fields are foreign policy, philosophy, science, urban affairs and the social sciences; Raymond Walters does history and paperbacks; Charles Simmons' specialty is belles lettres and he does the editing on Wilfrid Sheed's column as well as on the essay reviews; Richard Lingeman is concerned with politics, urban affairs, Americana and human interest; Mel Watkins handles race, civil rights, jazz and rock, some politics, cultural criticism and sports; William Dubois does commercial fiction--most of the novels that eventually end up in Martin Levin's column, crime and science fiction. Nona Balakian does belles lettres.

There is deliberate overlap in previewers' areas. Jellinek will do some history, coordinating his work with Walters. Fiction is spread around. The idea is to get as much fresh input as possible. About 105 books a week are previewed, with each editor expected to report on 15 books. Reports are written on pink slips wrapped around a book. They are terse and to the point, and inform Leonard whether the book is good, bad or indifferent, why it should or shouldn't be reviewed, who should review the book and why that particular person is competent in the field.

"Then it's up to me to decide if the book is marginal," Leonard explains. "If it isn't I either send it out to the suggested reviewer or decide if it can be combined with two or more books for a longer piece or if I have a better idea for a reviewer. Generally, I go along with the previewer's suggestion. When the review comes in my work comes in with it. Is it a dazzling work of genius, does it merit the front page? If it does, I've read it. In fact, I've read all the books reviewed in the front eight pages and the second front review. If we really need a review in a hurry we call up someone we know who is fast. [V. S. Pritchett's Midnight Oil (Random House) is a case in point. There was a foulup and Leonard recruited TBR columnist Wilfrid Sheed.] Some books I schedule automatically, like the Alvarez on suicide [The Savage God (Random House)]. I made up lists of reviewers and went after them to be sure it went right out. On Mailer's Existential Errands [Little, Brown] it was a question of who could we get to say something fresh." Leonard settled on Cynthia Buchanan, author of Maiden [Morrow].

TBR plans to add some outside help for its screening process by hiring consultant poetry editors for three-month stints. They would recommend reviewers, and write a minimum of three pieces themselves. The poetry editors' names won't be divulged, Jellinek says, because "poetry reviewing is very capricious and arbitrary, perhaps it's the most political of all reviewing fields, with more jealousy per square inch than anywhere else."

The Guessing Game: Who is Newgate Callendar?

(Poetry is not the only area where TBR clams up on reviewer identity. One of the hottest guessing games is the identity of Newgate Callendar, the mystery reviewer. Harper mystery editor Joan Kahn thinks the pseudonym may hide several people because styles appear to differ from week to week. Others guess Callendar is a woman, a homosexual or even Times music critic Harold Schoenberg. Leonard says the first three guesses are wrong, while Schoenberg says about himself, "that's a lot of nonsense.")

Leonard is interested in building a stable of about 20 regular reviewers for fiction but admits to problems in determining the right mix. Many young novelists don't want to review fiction they dislike. Others are unhappy with the space limitations Leonard is beginning to impose. He wants to run tighter fiction reviews, as well as more of them, and is giving several novels to one critic to handle in column length reviews.

"You can say something in 400 words," Leonard insists. "Keith Mano does. There is a quality of craftsmanship in that length you can admire."

Leonard is increasingly critical of his own reviewers, and he appears less ready to accept a sloppy review only in order to get the name that goes with it than he was a year ago. "If you can get a reviewer to bear down you can get a review that's well worth talking about and do it in 700 words. But it doesn't happen very often. The fact is most people don't work hard enough. They will give you a plot synopsis, a few catchy phrases and a couple of sentences of judgment and then bail out."

Many observers feel that Leonard is proving a flexible editor. He is not wedded to the editing approach that emerged in his first year and a half. He is ready to change and innovate, to pull back where he feels he has been wrong, to respond to criticism, often to agree with it. His effort to improve both the quality and quantity of his fiction reviews bears testimony to this. But he does feel that he has been working inside a tight corset dictated by business conditions and that the bald economics of the publishing business have forced him to make tough choices. Advertising revenues have been shrinking steadily since the peak year of 1969 when 80-page issues were common. Now Leonard has much less editorial space to play with--and at the same time a lot of new ideas he wants to test and incorporate. Fiction has suffered because TBR is reviewing more poetry than it ever did, and is also paying more attention to science, literary criticism and literary scholarship as well as to paperback originals. University press books have been getting greater attention, as have esoteric books reviewed only rarely in the past. Politics has moved front and center as have social issues like Vietnam, women, blacks and other minorities, the cities, and so forth. In short, Leonard's editorship has begun to reflect what William Jovanovich, chairman of Harcourt Brace Jovanovich, calls the temper and mood of the times in America.

Leonard and his editors are convinced there is a growing audience for such an approach to books and that it

Communication and Education

is not limited to the subscribers of the Sunday Times. Circulation beyond the East Coast is only about 100,000 which includes 16,000 in California and about 13,000 in Chicago and Detroit. But sales in Kansas City are an anemic 214, Louisville 495, Portland 931, the entire state of Nevada 191, Wyoming 225 and Utah 403.

With California book sales rising steeply over the last five years, Leonard's hunger for the Pacific is understandable. He is mounting a mail order* drive, therefore, to boost independent TBR circulation to 50,000 by fall. The rationale for lagging Sunday Times sales in the West is time and weight. The paper doesn't get there till mid-week and its excessive bulk makes air freight difficult and expensive. But TBR subscribers get it five or six days ahead of its inclusion in the Sunday Times. Presumably those in the West would get it that weekend. Coincidentally, of course, increased independent sales would mean more money for the Times and make TBR more attractive to advertisers.

The Decline in Ads from a Peak in 1969

Advertising has gone down for three straight years, most precipitously after the 1969 peak when total TBR pages hit a record 2,744. The 1970 totals were 2,552, representing a loss of between 100,000 and 150,000 lines of advertising. The 1971 drop was smaller but still substantial: TBR lost 80 pages and 35,000 lines of advertising, down from 1,210,307 to 1,175,069. However, TBR was able to boost gross dollar revenue slightly despite decreasing lineage because prices were raised twice in the last year and a half. Gross 1970 TBR revenues amounted to $4,852,781 while the 1971 figures totalled $4,933,829. A full-page ad now costs $3,715 but BOMC and the Literary Guild get a cut rate for agreeing to run a fixed number of lines a year. BOMC, for example, pays $7,200 for a double-page spread. Major advertisers who buy anywhere from 50,000 to 100,000 lines a year include Random House, Knopf, Pantheon, Harper & Row, Doubleday and its clubs, and Simon & Schuster.

There are premium spots in TBR for advertisers, generally the back cover or near the index and, best of all, near the best seller list. They cost about $50 or $100 more to fill and if advertising manager Denny would allow it, big TBR users would monopolize them. "But we don't do that," Denny says.

Despite ad slippage, Leonard and Jellinek both insist they are free of management pressure to trim their editorial sails. "I've been here six years and I've met Denny once," Jellinek says. Leonard feels he's been treated nicely. Even a letter from George Brockway, president of W. W. Norton, to leading literary agents explaining why he was reducing TBR's share of his advertising dollar--he dislikes TBR's editorial tone--did not rattle cages. "The letter upset them," Leonard concedes, "but when I said, 'Look, here's what I want to do,' there was no further discussion."

Denny is philosophical about the controversy swirling around TBR: "The flak was just as bad on Brownie. They wanted Brownie to run an NYR-TLS combo and Brownie didn't do much of that. John has been here a relatively short time and he's having to cut off sharp corners, not changing principles and goals, but I've noticed he's softening the things there's been outside flak about. I'd say within another year he'll be 95% acceptable everywhere, but there is always a fringe shooting at you."

Right now, however, it is more of an army than a fringe shooting at Leonard. Emotions run deep in the publishing community and few of its members are indifferent to TBR and its young editor. They are loved and hated, often simultaneously, frequently alternately from week to week, sometimes one or the other exclusively. The range of feeling can perhaps best be illustrated by comments from two leading New York publishers:

"John Leonard deserves the Congressional Medal of Honor for transforming the TBR into a major educational vehicle," says Arthur Rosenthal, chairman of Basic Books. "I think that under him it is better, has never been more influential, more in touch with new readers and has never provided more of what it should provide--service. Today's busy people are issue-oriented and they need a lot of help in distinguishing between meaningless fads and books which may affect the style and set of their thinking. They don't get it from news magazines, scholarly journals or TV."

A Sharp Criticism from Putnam's William Targ

"I don't consider the TBR as the world's eighth wonder--as it seems to consider itself," says William Targ, editor-in-chief of Putnam. "The TBR has been seriously remiss for a number of years, on a number of counts, and is guilty of disservice to the cause of authorship, publishing and book-sellers, not to mention the general reader. The TBR has become tribal, with strong in-group concerns and a strong elitism complex.... The TBR suffers from an identity crisis. It is no longer an identifiable creature.... It's a zoological hybrid, an oddity, yet to be named and classified.... So many reviews are written out of personal pique. Depending on the particular neurosis of the reviewer, so goes the review. And heaven help everyone concerned."

Targ is a rarity--an outspoken editor willing to put his name to a critique of TBR and its operations (though he emphasizes that his remarks are personal and do not necessarily represent the views of his firm). Most of Targ's colleagues are not as blunt. Or when they are, their views are much toned down from those expressed at the publishing cocktail circuit. Off the record Leonard is often boiled in oil. On the record he is merely accused of literary opportunism, cronyism, lack of identity, intellectual arrogance and elitism, snide and smartass treatment of books and glaring factual inaccuracies. ("But call me back to check the quotes; I don't want to end up sounding stupid or inarticulate.")

"I got used to it as a daily reviewer," Leonard himself says of the critical barrage. "I wrote three novels before joining the Times. I wrote for small magazines. Then you write for the Times and you become somebody. The violence of the reaction threw me into a tailspin at first. I'm a typical American. I wanted everybody to like me. I wasn't unprepared, you understand--Brownie warned me. But I did expect the honeymoon to last longer. You never do develop a thick enough skin. You feel personally injured. The attacks are so promiscuous and savage, so remote from any decision taken about a book, that you do spend time, hopefully not too much time, thinking of duels at dawn. But your better self says 'what else can you expect?' If there were more competition in town, criticism would be less desperate."

Therein may be the problem--and the explanation for the amount of emotion that is expended on a single publication and its editor. "TBR is the only game in the country," says Doubleday's Kenneth McCormick, and Samuel Vaughan adds, "it is hard to be No. 1 where there is no No. 2." TBR has little real competition nationwide (it remains to be seen if Eliot Fremont-Smith, former daily Times reviewer, can build the new Saturday Review's book pages into real competition) and none at all in the New York metropolitan area where most publishers and agents as well as many U.S. writers are located. For a great number of them a book has no life at all until and unless it is reviewed and/or advertised in TBR.

"The worst of a very bad situation is that we have nowhere else to go," says Holt editorial director Aaron Asher. "There ought to be three or four equally powerful media. I'm not happy that TBR has a near-monopoly and that I spend most of my money in the Times." Dutton president John Macrae attributes TBR's bite to the fact that "it is the recognized standard, the medium of record, and authors and their agents are frequently unaware of anything else." Atheneum president Simon Michael Bessie says that "the most serious problem the TBR has does not derive from its editorial staff but from its solitary position as a virtual monopoly."

And Eugene Rachlis of Bobbs-Merrill feels TBR "is so dominant in book reviewing that a lot of people tend to say let's see what the Times thinks."

Even paperback publishers with their much wider distribution possibilities and greater independence feel TBR's sting. NAL's editor-in-chief Edward Chase believes TBR is the lynchpin for the whole book industry. "The business is so parochial, so bound to Manhattan that people reach for the Times in a kind of cultural reflex, and complacently accept the TBR as the only organ they have."

"We're in a monopoly position," Roger Jellinek admits, "and we don't like it. We feel as if we're working in a vacuum." Leonard agrees, and believes that "Dorothy Schiff, publisher of the New York Post, is one of the enemies of culture" for not giving Book World an outlet in her newspaper. If she had, Leonard is convinced, publishers would have put enough advertising into the supplement to assure its survival.

But she didn't, and TBR retains its commanding position in the literary market place. Reviews and ads seem to count equally, both in terms of prestige and sales (though TBR's ad/review impact on sales is strongly debated). TBR has built up a mystique over the years that is hard to dispel.

Leonard felt it himself as a young novelist long before he came to the Times: "Just give me an ad in the Book Review so I will feel respectable to myself." It is a plea many authors make to their publishers, irrespective of the commercial rationale of placing such ads. And their agents can add the tough-minded muscle to make a publisher bend. Agent Julian Bach says: "Most authors, especially those who live or operate in the general New York area, feel personal embarrassment if their publisher doesn't run one noticeable ad in TBR so that his family and friends can see it."

Ads in TBR Salve the Sorrows of Authors

Roger W. Straus, III, of Farrar, Straus & Giroux, remembers arguing with writers against spending his limited ad budget for their books in TBR because their readership base was in other parts of the country, and being told they didn't care, and if there was money for only one ad, then, please, put it in TBR. Or, after explaining the ad budget to an author and where he planned to place his ad, the writer would ask plaintively, "But how much would that buy in the New York Times?" Perhaps Rosenthal of Basic Books gave the most reasonable explanation--and certainly the most compassionate one--when he said that "you advertise in the Times to salve the sorrow of authors."

But that's expensive salve--even if it is bought to keep authors tied to a house, especially in hard times when corporate pressure is on to make money. Many writers do quit publishers who they feel aren't advertising enough. And it is never a simple matter to justify TBR ads in terms of additional sales volume.

Sol Stein says flatly that "from a commercial point of view it (advertising in TBR) is a waste of time and money, a way of showing the flag, telling agents and authors their book is being advertised. I'd rather send authors and agents the money directly. The best evidence for the declining pulling power of the TBR is that it used to be the best medium for single book coupon ads and no longer is. I would estimate that today only sex books and trashy exposés can make their way on ads alone. I would guess that an ad in the TBR is exposed to at the most a couple of hundred thousand readers. It's easier to waste money in other parts of the country, you don't see it happen. The cost of space is going up, the results are down. But that has nothing to do with John Leonard. The fact is that very few people who buy the Times pay attention to the TBR. It is a small magazine inserted in the New York Times. It affects librarians. Literary books can be made by the Times, not sales."

Few publishers or booksellers are quite as assertive as Stein but most agree that TBR's value as a sales tool has diminished. No one is quite sure of the reason, however. Some blame TBR's new editorial slant with its strong emphasis on "specialty" books and long reviews, others doubt advertising's ability to sell books as well as it once did. "TBR is less effective as a sales tool today because of changes in marketing and merchandising," John Macrae says. "TBR doesn't have a commanding position, it isn't the voice of the book-buying public. There are so many publics in this society, and many separate subcultures, that it would be hard to expect a single medium to speak to all of them. Take the California market: it's equivalent to that served by TBR, which wasn't true five years ago. Advertising on the Coast means several different periodicals and radio and TV. The Los Angeles Times doesn't have the ad clout by itself. You need the regional edition of the Wall Street Journal, the underground press. It requires more thought and work. One reason publishers rely on the Times and give it so much advertising is simply that it is easier to advertise there. You can identify the readers you want, there's less need for market analysis, in short: inertia."

"Ads for specialized books in TBR sell more than for general ones," Thomas Lipscomb, of Dodd, Mead, believes. "Say an ad for (former Chief Justice) Earl Warren's book. You don't see as many ads for supercommercial books as you once did. It's become an advertising showcase for prestigious books. Ads reflect the kind of market the publisher is trying to reach. You've got to share Norton's judgment (see above). It is a more limited market than it used to be with a lot of advertising directed at the subsidiary rights people."

Simon Michael Bessie is much more positive about advertising in TBR but not all that sure of the point of advertising in general. "By any test that I'm aware of, TBR per dollar draws ahead of anybody else. Just compare the ad's pulling power. If you have a budget on a book that allows you ads in just one place what other place

Communication and Education

would you choose?" But in discussing what really pushes book sales Bessie conceded that "I'm not really sure I know what ads do--reinforce something that's moving, a kind of reminder, oh yes, I wanted that book. I saw the fellow on TV." Bessie's view is shared by George Brockway, who says candidly. "I have no answers about advertising books; an ad is hard to think through."

Warren Lynch, executive vice-president of BOMC, has no such doubts. "It's the best sales medium we have," he says of TBR, "that's why we advertise the Club so heavily in it."

Even Bad Reviews Are Better than Nothing

If there is disagreement about the selling efficacy of TBR advertising, there is a battle royal over the power of reviews to move books. Everybody in the industry is desperate to have books reviewed. A bad review is better than no review at all, many publishers and editors believe, and a good review is best of all. But nobody seems certain just what a good TBR review can do for a book. Leonard's critics contend a page one rave can be a kiss of death. And few would quarrel with the assessment of Peter Ritner of World that TBR's negative power "is greater than its positive impact. It can unmake a book faster than it can make it."

Many in the book trade believe that TBR reviews used to sell more books than they do now, just as others feel ads pulled better ten or twenty years ago. It is probably true, as some metropolitan booksellers claim, that potential book buyers rarely running into the stores on Monday morning clutching the front page of TBR and declaring, "I want that." Although many agree that the TBR was a more influential sales tool for the retail book trade in the past than now, it is debatable if this decline in sales power is really due to the fact that "a lot of English teachers are writing to other English teachers" in TBR's pages. Bookstore location may be more important. The manager of a mass-merchandising store in New York or Chicago catering to down- and midtown workers may be right in claiming that "most of our customers aren't intellectuals. We long ago stopped stocking books reviewed in TBR" or that "TBR is too highbrow for me as a retailer to pull in customers to sell my books. It's just not a selling tool."

On the other hand customers of large stores like the Savile Book Shop in the Georgetown section of Washington, D. C., Lauriat's in Boston, or Huntington's book store in Hartford, Conn., still troop down with clippings of ads or reviews from TBR to ask for specific books.

Claire Howell of the Savile Book Shop finds TBR "very helpful to us for buying books they review in the week before the Review comes out in the paper." But she does admit that some of the more esoteric books reviewed have left her scrambling for copies to meet an unexpected demand. She cites <u>The Insect Society</u> (Harvard University Press) as one such experience. "We had a horrible time then. We carry more books of that kind than other stores in Washington and that review caused a lot of reaction. And nobody had it."

Goddard Light of the Lighthouse Bookstore in Rye, New York, says flatly that TBR is the nation's most important book review medium but notes that he sold just one copy of Yale University Press's "Children of Pride," a book that did very well at the Savile shop and at Barnes and Noble in New York. "I think the editors sometimes get carried away with the importance of a book that is not a salable item for me."

Trumbull Huntington says, "TBR remains the most important sales tool we have. Our orders to the jobber are very much influenced by the reviews. It's just as strong as it ever was." And at Lauriat's a number of booksellers claim they haven't even noticed any change in reviewing policy.

And certainly TBR appears to have retained its clout with librarians. In New York the public library's buying habits are heavily influenced by its reviews, according to Bea McDonald, coordinator of adult services for all branches. "Every Monday people line up to reserve books reviewed in TBR," she says, "especially in branches where the big readers are." And she adds that "anything on page one we'll have reserve requests for on Monday, just because it appeared on page one."

<u>Does Anybody Know What Sells Books Today?</u>

All these comments are inconclusive, of course.

There is no exact measure of TBR's sales effectiveness. But then there isn't much agreement on just what sells books nowadays--except perhaps for that incandescent spark that can trigger public attention.

"Word of mouth sells books more than any other medium," Peter Ritner believes. "Sometimes that can happen rapidly, sometimes it takes months." Simon Michael Bessie thinks it's "the intrinsic appeal of the object, the news and comment about it so people get the word. Publicity, TV, column gossip, reviews, anything to make the word get around." Sol Stein feels aggressive promotion through TV and newspaper interviews is one key.

But not every book strikes sparks and not many lend themselves to flamboyant promotion and this obviously leaves a publisher staring morosely at his advertising budget and at the reviews his books have been getting or not getting-- mostly not getting, he feels--while his anger at TBR rises.

The question of space in TBR--the number of reviews, their length and the kind of books reviewed--is perhaps the mostly warmly debated issue within the publishing community, with the long essay review (of what many consider esoteric or special books) drawing the heaviest fire.

"The TBR hires boring essayists to deal at interminable length with tempest-in-the-teapot issues; it runs unbelievably long letters sometimes occupying the space equivalent to at least four or five reviews," William Targ says. "It often throws books of high quality into its now infamous mini-review columns, and at the same time wastes full pages on trivia and self-indulgence. By and large the TBR is boring. I wish they used more work by Elizabeth Hardwick and Alfred Kazin."

The space is too valuable--this complaint is heard again and again. TBR isn't reviewing enough books, the coverage isn't broad enough, books that deserve exposure aren't getting them--these are other strong opinions.

"Trendy stuff is being given too much space," Thomas Lipscomb complains. "The solid political book or biography is being ignored. A roundup piece on a writer who doesn't have a new book out just then is a waste of space, space that's desperately needed for other writers who need introduction."

"They should keep longer reviews under greater control so they could run less often," Sol Stein says, and complains of TBR's failure to review many major non-commercial and commercial books.

"TBR could be improved if it covered more books," John Macrae believes. "I do favor more short reviews."

"A lot of the stuff could be cut," Eugene Rachlis says. "Those lengthy essay pieces aren't always warranted and cuts would allow reviewing worthy books that don't always get their day in court. A lot of books just sink without anybody being aware of them. They dismiss what seem to me to be important books in a couple of paragraphs."

"TBR's coverage isn't broad enough," Vaughan says (though he prefaced a discussion of the magazine by stressing his belief that TBR owed nothing to publishers and authors, and should be edited for readers only). "Books are livelier, better, worse, shallower, deeper, you name it, than you realize as a TBR reader. Sometimes I have the feeling that the editors are telling us what we ought to read instead of what is available. But that isn't its major function. TBR should tell readers what books are worth reading, what's being published this year or this week. Instead, their attitude is prescriptive rather than descriptive: here's what's good for you, not what's good.... A respectable précis for Taylor Caldwell and Arthur Hailey type books is needed. They can always hack it to pieces afterwards. We don't need TBR for the commercial novel ... but Leonard owes his readers TBR's view on commercial novels."

From Targ, whose editorial credits include such non-commercial authors as Simone de Beauvoir and Brigid Brophy, that view comes across clearly:

"TBR is guilty of gross snobbery, contemptuous in the worst way of commercial books--as though only masterpieces were worthy of their attention ..."

What to Do with a Lousy Book

Jellinek says it doesn't much matter what TBR does with commercial fiction. "We could help it, sure, but we don't see why we should and what's the point of destructive reviews. Richard Locke did a model review on Irving

Stone's novel on Freud, why it was bad and the rest, the ideal technical editor's report. So do you give that a lot of space and have fun with it or do you stick it in the back? Just how do you perform well with a lousy book?"

There is no universal reply among publishers to that question. But many feel that TBR carries an elitist cast to reviews of all books its editors dislike--not just commercial novels--or, worse still, only reviews a certain kind of novelist ("Bill Sheed and his friends," Brockway says) heaping scorn and sarcasm on the others. Brockway says, "I don't like the kind of reviewing being done. It's esoteric, smart-ass, but not terribly impressive. I object to the stand-up comic review. Very funny what they did to Desmond Morris ("The Naked Ape"). Maybe it was a lousy book but I don't think that should have been done to it. Either say it's lousy or pass it by." And Sol Stein charges that TBR editors often deal from personal motives. "They are quite capable of doing a hatchet job when they want to, I mean a personally motivated hatchet job, or glorifying someone for the same reason. We've had both, so this isn't sour grapes on my part."

"TBR has some obligation to the author," Vaughan believes. "It doesn't take any but a literary book on its own terms. Why aren't books judged in terms of what the author is trying to do? I wonder how Neil Simon would have fared if he had started out as a novelist writing the kind of comedy he did for Broadway. I wonder if he would have gotten a fair notice in TBR?"

Bessie feels that "if there is important news in the world of books it should find its place in TBR. "The subject may be dead tomorrow but today it is news. Take a popular novel which you know will be successful but will be gone and have no literary significance--if the book is big enough it is news, like 'Valley of the Dolls.' "

Peter Ritner, on the other hand, has little sympathy with the demand for more book news. "Brownie's attitude was that this is a newspaper, I'm a newspaperman who accidentally got into the Review. We're reporting on what's new in books. But Leonard has made it different. His running a review of The Insect Society is what I consider creative management of a book review. Brownie wouldn't have given it that kind of treatment. Then there's 'The Last Word,' the think pieces. It is a little more of a magazine even if progress is slow and tentative. But if I were editor of TBR I'd make it into a literary magazine too. Any influence must come from one person and his taste has to be put across. John Leonard has published a piece that insulted Gay Talese and a few other writers. He's not neutral any more. He's taking part in literary controversy. That's fine, that's a good way of running it."

For Ritner that includes the controversial essay-style and essay-length reviews of often esoteric or special books. "I'm passionately for the big review, unequivocally more than book news. If you need four to six pages to say it right, take it. I'd go further than Leonard. The notion of TBR as a précis of books is utterly ridiculous. Little reviews wouldn't help the book business. It's much more important to have a medium that takes books seriously, to have things said about a new and deep book and to express enthusiasm about it. That can provide the proper setting for books, make them influential, important and respected. We need a strong, serious forum where you can make big statements about big books. Yes, I'd make the sacrifice of my books not being reviewed to get that...."

Page Eight Is Now Devoted to Juveniles

The *Times* is not oblivious to the controversy its reviewing practices have caused and it has gone to some lengths to justify them and to rebut the critics. The in-house study points out that TBR reviewed 1,967 titles in 1971, Leonard's first year as editor, compared to 2,024 in 1970, but notes that TBR had 2,552 pages that year compared to 2,472 in '71, a net loss of 80 pages and 57 titles. "The proportion of titles reviewed to available editorial space, therefore, went up in 1971, very slightly." The number of juveniles reviewed declined sharply, the result of a conscious decision to give more space to fewer books and to upgrade review quality.

"Even in fiction, about which everybody worries and about which nobody does anything, we have improved coverage," the memo states. It admits the number of fiction reviews dropped slightly last year due to fewer pages but that TBR reviewed 169 fiction titles in the first four months of 1972 compared to 144 in the comparable 1970 period.

There are those who agree with Vaughan's contention

that TBR is playing a "numbers game" by weighting the number of short reviews, particularly of fiction, as heavily as long ones. The memo concedes that 325 books were handled in the short review columns in 1971 compared to 143 in 1970. Leonard's own drive for the medium-length fiction review is an indirect acknowledgment of the same conclusion.

Charges that TBR is too highbrow and specialized in many reviews are also dealt with in the memo: "We have, admittedly, made certain assumptions about the function of the Book Review and the kinds of people who read it. While we should ... review books ... destined for the best seller list or the Book-of-the-Month Club subscribers--in fact, we always review such books--our obligation as the literary supplement of the New York Times means that we should also review distinguished and often demanding books that will never reach the best seller list but are considered by the editors to be of lasting value. We have a quasi-pedagogic function: this is why you should read such and such a book.... Our feeling is that the 'general' reader is composed of many 'special' readers, and it is up to us to serve as many readers as we can within the limitations of our space. To that end, we have even instituted a regular science-fiction column, although nobody on the Book Review much cares for science fiction.

"The point is to reflect in the Book Review the variety of books being published, to comment in a way that a non-expert can get an idea of whether the particular book is worth his while or not, to try to make some sense of what the variety means in terms of a cultural mood.... 'Literate Americans' is how we conceive of the general reader. Whether or not he has the time or money to buy the special books we review, he wants--we feel--to know about what is in those books. He even needs to be prodded into thinking about them and possibly purchasing them. Certainly his contemplation of the issues they raise--and our reviewers raise about them--contribute to a cultural conversation of immense importance.... Our responsibility is to heighten the awareness of the reading public as to what is available and what is being said and how it is being said and whether or not it seems to approximate the truth and whether or not it might also be--miraculously--beautiful, too.

"It is true ... that a few trade publishers are complaining that we do not review enough books because of the space we devote to such 'special' books and writers.... Of course, more of those titles during the past year have been university press books, books from out-of-town presses, and paperback originals, which is what really annoys the New York trade publishers. The 'special' book is always published by somebody else. It is also true that our reviews of books like the new Irving Wallace novel tend to appear in the back of the section, with less editorial display, which is precisely what they deserve. We seek not only to reflect the flow of the 'dollar volume' spent on books in this country, but to influence the direction of that flow. If we didn't seek to influence it in the direction of books we knew to be excellent, we would be about as useful to our readers ... as a weekly bottle of non-caloric soda pop."

The memo is equally firm in its defense of the essay technique and the length required to use it properly: "Only long reviews and articles can deal responsibly with the contemporary social and literary situation.... Readers today are far more educated and varied in their interests. They have extensive and sophisticated knowledge of many formerly 'specialized' areas.... The education explosion ... has produced diverse and much more aggressive readers who won't be condescended to and won't be told by a self-appointed elite that this or that is good for them. The confusion of contemporary culture--high and low, right and left--has made it necessary for our reviews to go further into a big book and at the same time to give much more complex background to a review. It's necessary to dig in and dig down to the basic issues. And that takes space...."

Inevitably, Leonard's editorial style has invited comparison with the New York Review of Books and the strong political stands it has taken. In fact, George Brockway argued in his letter to agents that TBR "is now committed to a policy that can scarcely be distinguished from that of NYR." Not many publishers will go that far but most believe the comparison is worth making. Few, however, prefer NYR over TBR since the former is, in their judgment, even more guilty of the sins they feel the Times commits. Nor do they feel that the charge of a NYR-style leftist bias, sometimes made against TBR, is justified.

"TBR is not heavily ideological in its bias," Arthur Rosenthal says, "NYR is," while Washington Post book editor William McPherson comments that "I haven't noticed any strong leftist trend. I'd say in some ways it's quite

Communication and Education

conservative." Lipscomb feels that "Leonard is not an apologist for any ideology. He is left of center but that's standard for the industry."

Leonard himself believes charges of left-wing bias are hard to document. "The stuff we run is against the war, that's not left: most of the country is against the war. And it doesn't explain using William F. Buckley and Russell Kirk or flaying <u>The Limits to Growth</u> [Universe]. We're not part of the counter-culture or anti-technology."

Nevertheless, politics is more important in the pages of the TBR than it used to be. But for publishers like William Jovanovich this is more a reflection of changed American thinking patterns than any left-right split. Revisionist historians in the sixties, Jovanovich believes, began to reinterpret the American experience and no longer saw it in terms of compromise and conciliation but of confrontation and interdiction. This new approach, he believes, has cut across political lines to exacerbate the differences dividing society rather than to find areas of agreements. "TBR reflects a desire to point out where we disagree" rather than to urge any political ideology. The NYR, on the other hand, follows a political line, "even if it is a very tortured one. TBR doesn't have such a point of view but rather an editorial direction. It is obviously interested in young people, blacks, women,--something like the Democratic Convention. Leonard relates American culture to American politics, that's part of the temper of the times. For example, do writers have a civic or civil role and should they--that sort of thing. Leonard strikes me as someone interested, bemused and dismayed. He has attitudes more than partisanships. But then we've all become spectators of current history."

<u>Can Anything be Done with the Best Seller List?</u>

Finally, there is the best seller list, perhaps the most controversial of all TBR departments--and one for which Leonard can disclaim all responsibility. No critic claims it is completely accurate or that it cannot be manipulated or improved. It costs $26,000 a year to run and Leonard is trying to police the book stores that report on sales more closely than was done in the past--principally by having <u>Times</u> stringers in various cities check on sales. But he feels there isn't much he or anyone else can do if a store decides to report on a book the owner feels should

have sold but didn't--a common criticism. Nor can the
Times stop movie companies from buying copies heavily in
key stores to weight the list. And the fact that paperback
and movie contracts have escalator clauses hooked to a
book's position on the Times list is also outside the province of TBR.

"The best seller list bothers me," Jellinek admits.
"It can be manipulated up to a point and it's not as accurate
as it might be. But we'd welcome anyone with a suggestion
of how to do it better."

Still, as Joan Kahn of Harper's points out, a lot of
books with huge sales don't make the list, or make it late.
She cites I'm O.K., You're O.K., which sold 400,000 copies
before it climbed on the Times list, two years after publication. It's also true that a book need sell fewer copies in
the slack season than in the busy one to win a niche on the
coveted ladder--and that some reporting stores get more
attention than others.

Thus the litany of gripes against TBR flows on--not
surprisingly, considering its pre-eminent position as the
book review medium--while its defenders speak in voices
that are submerged by the opposition. Because of what it
is, and what its editor firmly stands for, TBR seems to be
put under a microscope each week, and inevitably blemishes
are found--there is no more critical audience in America
than trade publishing, even when it shrinks from speaking
for the record. Photographs of John Leonard's back, scattered through a recent TBR, brought the kind of attack that
the staff is obviously getting accustomed to. An enthusiastic
review of An Old-Fashioned Darling (Coward, McCann &
Geoghegan), a novel by Charles Simmons, a TBR editor
(November 21), appeared to some irate readers as a flagrant
example of cronyism, especially when the novel spent weeks
on the TBR recommended list as well, although it was
scarcely reviewed anywhere else. (Leonard shrugs off the
criticism. "I sent it to some guy in the South, as far away
from New York scene as I could, and he wrote a very favorable review. Was I supposed to keep sending it out until
somebody panned it?")

Advice and suggestions from the publishing world are
never in short supply at TBR. Why doesn't Norman Mailer
write a column? How about more gossip? A list of newly
published books every week? When will you give up the

long review? The reviews of marginal books? Why don't you run shorter reviews and many more of them? Why do you keep using neurotic, frustrated writers and academicians as reviewers? From his office on West 43rd Street, John Leonard would seem to be taking the stings in good stride. He acknowledges that on some counts TBR is vulnerable, and he confesses to a sense of schizophrenia in parceling out the reviewing space that is available to him. "We'll never stop being consumer guide for books, but it's not my duty to please people who advertise. I look out for what I think is most important--and then tend to feel guilty," he comments.

"In the end, I wind up publishing a magazine which I would like to read."

CONCERNED CRITICISM OR CASUAL COP-OUTS?*

Patricia Glass Schuman

Consider the plight of parents and adult relatives or friends who wish to buy books for their favorite children. Let us assume that they are neither teachers nor librarians themselves, that they know little about their communities' library information services and that they do not have a fully-stocked general book store at hand. What do they face in their children's book buying? Over 35,000 books for children are in print. Over 2000 new books for children were published in 1971.

An adult's most visible sources of information are probably the newspapers and general magazines that pay review attention to children's books in special issues each Spring and Fall. If they read these before buying what do they find out about current children's books? To answer this first question, I compared the Fall children's book issues of the following periodicals:

New York Times "Children's Book" section
    (November 8, 48p.)
New York Review of Books (Dec. 2, 2-1/2p.)
Book World (November 6, 15p.)
Christian Science Monitor (November 11, 6p.)
Saturday Review (November 13, 5p.)
Commonweal (November 19, 12p.)
Scientific American (December, 10p.)

My perusal of these revealed a few prevalent patterns, but provoked many more questions.

---

*Reprinted by permission from School Library Journal, February 1972, published by R. R. Bowker Company (a Xerox Company); copyright 1972 by the Xerox Corporation.

Communication and Education

General Observations

A combined total of only 350 titles out of the possible 1000+ published this Fall were reviewed and another 150 received brief mention. The longer articles and full reviews tended to discuss the latest books by established authors and well-known illustrators. Reviews of fiction and picture books outnumbered nonfiction by better than 2:1. Picture books alone accounted for over one-third of all the titles reviewed. Books written especially for teenagers got nodding attention in the least amount of space. Of the books covered, only 13 percent of the titles were reviewed by more than one of the periodicals.

The unabridged Random House Dictionary of the English Language states that the words review and criticism imply "carefully examining something, making a judgment, and putting the judgment into (usually) written form."

Unfortunately, there is little to indicate careful examination and judgment in the reviews offered to the general public by the popular reviewing media. Over 90 percent of all books mentioned received favorable reviews or, more frequently, short descriptive annotations. No doubt titles were probably pre-selected by the review editors because of limited space, but isn't it just as important to forewarn adults about shoddy--or even "fair" titles, as well as to point out the good ones--and to offer them some clue as to the judgmental and/or weeding process involved?

The uninitiated adult might also wonder about the expertise of the reviewers published. Are they really experts in the field, or just dabbling? Sometimes it's hard to tell. The Christian Science Monitor did not even bother to identify its reviewers beyond giving their names, though it did so for adult reviewers in the same issue, and in several cases Children's Book World neglected to provide any reviewer identification. The majority of reviewers identified were children's book authors, a smattering of adult authors, and a few editors and teachers. Only a few reviewers had any connection at all with children's library service.

The sparse negative criticism went from almost non-existent in the Saturday Review, to a literary essay in the New York Review of Books, and some outright panning in the New York Times "Children's Books."

Round-ups--Advice or Summaries?

Commonweal, Saturday Review, Scientific American, and the New York Review of Books all employed the "round-up" technique in their fall obeisance to the children's book field, with a few variations. The Saturday Review's Zena Sutherland offered ten to 20-line annotations with zingy last sentences--"Deft little drawings enrich a sweet little story." The only critical comment to be found among the 24 titles listed is the one for Edward Connally's Deer Run (Scribners): "It isn't a great first novel, but it's a good one, despite Connally's tendency to paint the commune white and the community black." For the most part Sutherland covers familiar authors, but the age spread is fairly representative, and there is an obvious, if only partially successful, attempt to cover a wide range of topics.

"Turning on Parent Power," the short introductory essay to SR's section by Sophie Silberberg, director of advertising and promotion for children's books at Thomas Y. Crowell, is of particular interest to adults. She offers some advice to parents and other interested adults who are frustrated both because they can't find what they want in local bookstores and because they want to learn more about current children's books, suggesting Books for Children groups along the line of the English model.

"The root of the problem," she says, "is probably that too many bookstores rely today on self-service supermarket techniques, and, especially in the case of children's books, the average customer lacks the necessary confidence to make the right choice. Because it's so easy to pick the familiar classic, many bookstores have learned to concentrate on the tried and true."

Commonweal's children's section was up two pages this year for a total of twelve and included two longer articles in addition to its standard "Selected List." Elizabeth Minot Graves (children's book editor, Garrard Publishing Company) offered a glowing roundup review of 20 titles on the occult in "Year of the Witch." "The authors of this season's books about magical happenings seemed to have gained magic from their very subject matter itself," says she, "and have written with great skill, sensitivity and distinction. These books are more than just entertainment: They will set Children to thinking." (At least in the case of occult books, reviewers in other publications did take issue with Graves.)

Michael J. Ballard follows with an essay highly favorable to the paperback trend in juvenile publishing, offering an overview of who is doing what, for how much, and why, and a "Paperback Sampler" listing 40 "popular" children's books. Ballard is identified in Commonweal's blurb as covering "cultural developments for the United States Information Agency."

The 123-title "Selected List," selected by Elizabeth Minot Graves, does not list any paperback titles. They are arranged under 18 categories, e.g., Christmas, religion, teenage novel, and storybooks for ages nine to 12. Most books have two or three-line annotations, though some don't have any at all. This year she added two additional categories to her list: "drugs" (two titles) and "for adults-- books about children's literature" (three titles).

Minot provides an almost equal balance of fiction and nonfiction, though picture and elementary age titles predominate. There is a smattering of "relevant books"--ecology, the black experience, women's liberation, but this list, as are most others, is still culturally biased. (A fact which may be either a fault of the selector or of the publishing industry.) The closest one can come to nonwestern thought in her religion section in this list is an African version of the story of David and Goliath. The six titles under world history include one each on monsters of the middle ages, Russia, the Sahara, Taiwan, anarchism, and the dynamics of dress.

The New York Review of Books came through this year with a limited roundup of children's books. It is an essay review of 16 titles written by Janet A. Smith, identified as the editor of The Looking Glass Book of Verse and an edition of Robert Louis Stevenson poems. She concentrates heavily on fiction and picture books and includes one title about children's literature. Age levels for the titles were not specified. Smith's tone is generally favorable, but she does include some unfavorable critical comments on a few titles and a fair amount of background detail, though less than usually found in NYRB adult book reviews. "I wouldn't buy the book for a child," says Smith, commenting on Anne Sexton's Transformations (Houghton, 1971) (which may or may not be considered a "children's book," depending on how one classifies a modern verse version of fairy tales--with a dash of Freud thrown in), "but I would much rather a child came across it than many a cute, crude, and gaudy horror of a fairy book." Just what does that comment tell parents about children's reading?

In balance, Scientific American's ten-page "Books About Science for the Younger Reader: An Annual Christmas Survey" is the best of the roundups, albeit more specialized. Written by Philip and Phylis Morrison (unidentified at least on the advance proof pages) it covers 45 books in detailed reviews, varying in length from 20 lines to several columns. Though titles were obviously pre-selected for quality, the reviews point up both assets and faults. The Morrisons say that many of this year's books, "judging by their length, visual design, and presentation, were marketed for readers between eight and ten years old," but make a particular effort to note when titles are appropriate for their age groups. They cover eight subject areas: general, biology, specific forms of life, field guides, man, perception, physics, earth and skies, and mathematics, and have included such "adult" titles as The Whole Earth Catalog.

Newspaper Reviews

The six pages allocated to children's books by the Christian Science Monitor are whittled down to three and one-half by advertisements. As previously mentioned, reviewers of children's and young adult titles are not identified, though reviewers of adult books in the same issue are. About 95 titles are covered, with a three to one fiction to nonfiction ratio, the usual heavy emphasis on picture and elementary age books, some at the junior high level, and a few young adult titles.

Carolyn Klingston's lead article, "It's Hard to Fly a Kite," is probably one of the most valuable of the essay reviews published in the special children's books supplements and sections, with its emphasis on reality in books for children. She asks: "Should children have rats and garbage as well as pleasant scenes in books? If squalor and grime are the furniture of one's life, the question is unnecessary."

"What is more important is to ask what the authors of children's books have to say and if the picture is honest."

Klingston discusses 13 titles for children she considers realistic, and offers the parent some pointed insights:

"Interesting customs are no longer the central themes of books about Spanish-speaking Americans"; and "the picture story, a medium familiar in young children's books, is being used for their older brothers and sisters." She includes a fair range of age levels and a few paperbacks.

Unfortunately, Klingston fails to confront any of the current questions raised about the fact that many of the books she cites about minority groups were written by white, middle-class, Anglo-Saxon adult authors.

CSM covers over 75 other titles in 16 additional shorter essay reviews, following freely much the same categorical and age spread of the other children's supplements. These range from Neil Millar's syrupy "Leapin' Buffalizards: Verse and Worse" ("The whole book squirms with humor. Perhaps Miss Watson has mixed her colors with giggle-juice, which accounts for some rather blotchy washes. But the washes are never wishy, the blotches never bitchy.") to June Goodwin's more lucid and critical "Sitting Lightly on the Whimsy Scale." Unfortunately, Goodwin, as did several other reviewers of children's books in this and other children's sections, found it necessary to rely on a deus ex machina, in this case the "next best thing" to a child--a pregnant sister-in-law--as a literary reviewing device.

Then there are Melvin Maddocks' discussion of "... a few of the season's books for young jocks that came close to winning the Big Game of literature," and Nancy Garden's "Romance and Realism" look at books for eight to 12. Unfortunately, she asks, "Why must books for eight to 12-year-old's fall clearly into 'boy' and 'girl' categories," then proceeds to recommend them, though she does commend one title for "girls with more on their minds than future housekeeping and maternity."

The moralizing in Patience M. Canham's "Left Alone in the Wilderness," a review of A Wild Thing by Jean Renvoize (Little, Brown, 1971), and John Donovan's Wild in the Woods (Harper, 1971) becomes a bit much. "Do I recommend these books for teenagers? Yes, with reservations. Essentially honest as I think they are, these books tell only part of the whole human condition." Janet Farley Smith offers a look at what she considers the good black biographies (seven) in "Some Who Overcame," and in "Make My Trouble Go Away" she points out to parents why their children should read books about drug addicts. Guernsey Le Pelley's "For the Screamy Younger Set" offers a slightly more critical view than Graves of books for younger children.

Children's Book World's 15-page section is about half the size of last fall's section, and is down about six pages from last spring. Eight-and-one half pages are advertisements. A lead article by CBW editor Polly Goodwin concentrates on "Answer to Inflation: Children's Paperbacks," covering much the same ground as Ballard, though she mentions some 30 titles in her text and two bibliographies of paperbacks for children, and says: "The next important step is to see that bookstores and libraries stock and display children's paperbacks so they can easily be found, bought, and enjoyed."

Parents can then turn to some 12 other conglomerate reviews of another 70-odd titles, including "Tried and True," a review of 11 picture books by Michael Ballard, this time identified as "a freelance critic whose five-year old son serves as an unpaid consultant."

"If you find a 'Welcome Home' sign in your favorite bookstore draped above the juvenile picture books, don't be surprised," Ballard tells us. "It merely signifies the return this year of such popular authors and illustrators as Martha Alexander, Ezra Jack Keats, Tomi Ungerer, Charlotte Zolotow, William Steig, and the ubiquitous Dr. Seuss." Two other articles, "A Magical Tour," six "new stories by recognized craftsmen in the field," reviewed by Virginia Haviland, head of the children's section, Library of Congress, and "Favorite Characters Return," a review of six titles by Polly Goodwin, take a similar established author approach.

On the whole, the quality of CBW's reviews vary. Some are completely favorable, some critical, others are gratuitous. (Jane Yolen on Jeanne Hardendorff's Witches, Wit, and a Werewolf: "... it seems silly to waste her professional story-telling art on these trifles." Coverage leans very heavily on the fiction side and includes only a few young adult titles. Authors of reviews are often scantily identified, and in some cases, not identified at all. Some reviews include age levels, others do not. The topics covered include nature, ecology, horror and suspense, art, books for beginning readers, and fiction for ten to 14-year-olds.

Last, but not least, is the New York Times "Children's Book Section," down eight pages from last year, but still the season's largest at 48 pages, even subtracting 27 pages for advertisements. There were only two roundup-reviews--as compared to six last November, and essay reviews were also missing. Joan Bodger Mercer, consultant to publishers and libraries, and supervisor of seven day care centers in Toronto, reviews eight picture books, good and bad, in her roundup. "A Ghoulash of Ghouls," by Richard Elman, "raised by witches in Brooklyn, and ... the author of An Education in Blood," supposedly covers 13 titles, but he liked one so much he devotes half his space to describing it, then discusses two he doesn't like briefly-- without mentioning their titles--pans a few others, and recommends a few. The other titles are never mentioned. His essay does offer fascinating facts and observations about witchcraft and trends in publishing, but it might have been helpful to offer criticism on each, rather than panning jointly--without reference to specific titles--a majority of the titles reviewed.

Some 12 other titles received detailed treatment in reviews; six fell between the elementary and junior high range, three were picture books, and three were young adult; two were nonfiction.

Three young adult titles were reviewed by Benjamin De Mott, author of Surviving the '70s, who really didn't like any of them particularly and gives his detailed reasons why. (Though the books were by Nat Hentoff, Maia Wojciechowska, and John Neufeld, the Times was the only review to mention them.) Selma G. Lanes, author of Down the Rabbit Hole, discusses thoroughly the good and bad points of picture books by adult authors Ionesco, Barthelme, and Delessert--"One hit, one miss, and one near disaster." Toni Cade Bambara, editor of Tales and Stories for Black Folks, devotes a page-worth of favorable review--with plenty of logical backup--to a collection on the third world and a book on being young and black in Africa. Other reviewers include Sarah Webster Fabio, a specialist in black literature, John Hersey (Hiroshima, etc.), Susan Sheehan, a staff writer on the New Yorker, and Ingeborg Boudreau, a faculty member of the Pratt School of Library Information Science, all of whom provide detailed, in-depth reviews.

Among other regular features of the Times are "Best Illustrated Books," with a sample illustration from each of the ten; "Outstanding Books of the Year," 33 titles arranged by age level, with quotes from previously published Times reviews; and "You've Read the Paperback--Will You Buy the Hardcovers?" by Douglas Mount, a former editor of Publisher's Weekly. The latter is more detailed than both the Ballard and Goodwin paperback pieces, and though favorable towards the trend, criticizes the industry for proceeding with the sort of boneheaded caution that characterizes the rest of publishing; i.e., "among the current crop there is a disturbing number of very dated titles from the '30s and '40s of questionable value to the child of the '70s." Mount briefly, but critically, reviews about 15 paperback titles for children and teenagers.

" 'So You Are Another Alice' " and "Lad as a WASP in Dog's Clothing" are two other features the Times chose to publish in its children's section. The first, written by Morton N. Cohen, who is preparing an edition of Lewis Carroll's letters, is an interesting historical piece, but has little new to say. The second piece on the Albert Payson Terhune "Lad" stories by Gaddis Smith, a professor of history at Yale, is long and rambling, but may possibly score a point with "now nostalgic grandparents who fail to see the racial intolerance and other prejudices implicit in the stories," and "supply the demand to keep his books in print." Frankly, though, some of the features cut out from last year, such as the roundup of teen-age novels, or a roundup of books on drugs, might have served the parent better.

General Conclusions

The Times best seller list, leading off with Roald Dahl's Charlie and the Chocolate Factory (Knopf, 1964) and following with Richard Scarry's Best Word Book Ever (Golden Pr., 1963); The Trumpet of the Swan, E. B. White (Harper, 1970); Charlotte's Web, E. B. White (Harper, 1952); The Velveteen Rabbit, Margery Williams (Doubleday, 1958); The Little Prince, Antoine de Saint-Exupéry (Harcourt, 1943); The First Four Years, Laura Ingalls Wilder (Harper, 1971); Winnie-the-Pooh, A. A. Milne (Dutton, 1926); The Giving Tree, Shel Silverstein (Harper, 1964); and The Tale of Peter Rabbit, Beatrix Potter (Warne, 1902) confirms our worst fears. The only ones even published in this decade are Trumpet of the Swan and The First Four Years, both by extremely well established children's authors.

If these books are indeed the bestsellers, current children's books are not something most parents know anything about. There may be a plethora of quality "classics," but children of the '70s desperately need to be more aware of relevant, contemporary literature. Most of the children's supplements are guilty of the "highly recommended" syndrome, but librarians, in their booklists, are too. We, as well as the editors of children's book sections, might take a cue from the general consumer movement, which is calling for advice and warnings, as well as recommendations. Parents need to know which books they probably shouldn't buy, too. They might also find helpful reviews of books about children's literature and information as to good bibliographies available. At present, the message that comes through loud and clear, to quote from John Hersey's review in the *Times*, is of a "spate of flat, safe, bland, commercially prudent books for children...."

As far as balance is concerned, perhaps in this "media-age" children get their facts from other sources than books, but in this age of burgeoning information and misinformation, the lack of attention paid to current nonfiction titles is a glaring gap. Also, as the war and postwar babies reach adulthood, isn't it about time the general review media started paying attention to young adult literature and adult literature for young adults? It seems to be a well-kept library secret. What about subject coverage? Very few books on drugs, sex, alternative life styles, or even science fiction were even considered worthy of mention.

And then there is the question of the final consumer-- the child. "Children's Liberation" is something we haven't heard much about yet, but groups like the Summerhill Collective and others concerned with alternative education are beginning to talk and write about it. Though the notion may seem ludicrous at first, the fact is that children and young people are the single, largest segment of modern society subject to stringent controls by others--legally, educationally, physically, and morally. Whole industries and institutions, including children's publishing, reviewing, and library service, have been built on this premise. The general review media might do well to encourage capable children to review--or at least to solicit their input, rather than rely on one or two reviewers' use of their own children as "unpaid, unofficial" consultants.

Librarians also have a role to play. We are the

market for over 80 percent of the new children's books published. One of our self-assumed professional goals is to inform our clientele about books for children. Why, then, aren't librarians who are children's book specialists sought out as a source of informed reviewers for the general press? Will their letters extending or protesting review coverage in these periodicals be published? Will the letters even be written?

CRISIS INFORMATION SERVICES TO YOUTH:
A LESSON FOR LIBRARIES?*

Carolyn Forsman

Young adult services in public libraries are being threatened with extinction. The elimination of separate departments and of their specially trained librarians in Chicago, Montgomery County, Maryland, and other library systems may signal the beginning of a national trend. The New York State plan to give the school library sole responsibility for services to youth is another step in this direction.

At the same time a new phenomenon, the Crisis Intervention Center, which provides counseling as well as information and referral services to troubled youth, has emerged within the last four years in hundreds of urban, rural, and suburban areas: Anchorage, Atlanta, Denver, Des Moines, Long Island, and Long Beach. Your community probably has one or soon will. Crisis Centers explain themselves by such evoking names at Hotline, Switchboard, Free Clinic, Rapline, Help Line, No Heat Line, Y. E. L. L., Rescue, H. I. P. (Help Is Possible), Somebody Cares, We Care, Inc., Listening Post, Night Line, Drug Aid, Y. E. S. (Youth Emergency Service), Community Youth Line, Your Information Unlimited. Crisis Centers are there to serve the needs of youth ten to 25, not only as students, but as whole persons.

The history and development of young adult services has yet to be written,[1] but young adult librarians have always taken pride in their ability to change with the times, to be sensitive to their clientele's needs and to be innovative in services and programs. Perhaps we can learn from the Crisis Intervention Center new ways to serve the young adult in his complete range of information needs.

---

*Reprinted by permission from School Library Journal, March 1972, published by R. R. Bowker Co. (a Xerox company); copyright 1972 by the Xerox Corporation.

Crisis centers, in philosophy, organization, services, training methods, publicity, and insight into youth's problems, contrast sharply with the whole concept of library service to young adults. They suggest possible new roles and directions for libraries and librarians.

The Crisis Center developed as an alternative to traditional community mental health and medical services. And because information and referral are an integral part of its concept, Hotlines, Switchboards, and Free Clinics can also be looked at as an alternative to traditional library service to young adults. As with any new phenomenon, the definition of terms used to describe it are often not clear, concise, nor consistent with each other. However, agreement seems to be growing that the term "Crisis Intervention" includes three fairly distinct types of crisis services: Hotlines, Switchboards, and Free Clinics.

A <u>Hotline</u> is an emergency anonymous telephone service for young people in crisis providing a listening ear, with referral to agencies and professional backup when necessary. A <u>Switchboard</u> is primarily a telephone information and referral service as well as a message center. Unlike a Hotline, it may also have a walk-in or drop-in facility for visitors. A <u>Free Clinic</u> is basically a walk-in center that provides direct medical services. It also has facilities for individual or group counseling in both medical and nonmedical problems, such as birth control and the draft.

An example might better explain the relationships and differences between these facilities in a community. A teenager thinks she is pregnant. If she calls the Switchboard she will be referred to the local Free Clinic for a pregnancy test. At the clinic, in addition to the free test, if she chooses, she will be counseled on birth control methods as well as possible solutions to her immediate situation. She might also be counseled on her relationship with the father. If she calls the Hotline instead of Switchboard, a nonjudgemental anonymous voice will direct a few questions to determine if she might indeed be pregnant, and also refer her to the Free Clinic for a test. The listener will not advise her to have an abortion, nor to marry the suspected father, nor otherwise tell her what to do. He will instead, in a series of questions and replies, let the caller discover the options for herself. The Hotline will more likely be used for this type of problem since Hotlines emphasize and specialize in interpersonal and individual psychological needs. Switchboards tend to satisfy more concrete needs, such as food, housing, transportation, and information on political and leisure activities. If a call to the Hotline requests a place to crash for the night and the caller is over 18, he more than likely will be referred to Switchboard. If he is a minor who's run away, the listener will encourage the youth to question his action in terms of himself and his family.

Hotlines, Free Clinics, and Switchboards do not advocate or encourage illegal behavior, including the harboring of runaways without the parent's permission, or the use of drugs. In certain crises, the person is not in any state to be referred to another agency, no matter how logical it may seem. Persons experiencing a "bad trip" on drugs or contemplating suicide or who are in other life-threatening situations, and who call in a state of panic, are handled by whichever of the three services he or she happens to call.

Switchboards

Switchboards and Free Clinics arose out of the counter-culture of white alienated youth: The first Switchboard began in the summer of 1967 in San Francisco to serve the Haight-Ashbury community as a message and referral service. Its prototype was the old "Central" switchboard in American communities which not only connected telephones, but was also a source of solutions to human problems. Its initial use was primarily as a crisis and problem center (what the Hotline now serves), but it soon expanded into a "community resource center." The Switchboard, with the help of its community, created a "human resource file," a list of people willing to teach and to share their skills and knowledge with others. The philosophy is to help people control their own lives by providing them information to make their own decisions. Other files developed to further this goal show the extent of Switchboard services: Jobs, Housing, Transportation, Buy and Sell, Music, Theater, Education, Messages.

A Switchboard is usually reached by telephone (San Francisco had 150,000 calls in their first two-and-a-half years). Its number will be found in a local alternative newspaper listing of frequent phone numbers. Some have a walk-in service, where visitors can read bulletin boards for notices on survival, politics, the youth culture pleasures, or leave and pick up messages. The message service is also used by parents of runaways as a possible point of contact.

In all cases dealing with youth, his or her privacy and confidentiality are respected. Switchboard workers are volunteers from the community who try to make decisions in a democratic manner. When there is a coordinator, he or she has no more rights than the volunteers. Often the staff lives together as a collective. Switchboards are funded by donations from the community, including local ministries. The manuals of the Berkeley and San Francisco Switchboards detail the philosophy, services, and policies of two of the oldest and most stable information services to the youth community.

Free Clinics

The first Free Clinic opened in Los Angeles in November 1967 as a drug treatment center for the free community. The philosophy of the Free Clinic movement is to treat the whole person; and so, it was natural that it would extend its services to include counseling on birth control, abortions, diet and nutrition, and drugs, as well as such nonmedical areas as the draft and law. Counseling is performed by community volunteers, professional and nonprofessional.

A client who enters the clinic is assigned a "facilitator" or "advocate" who is responsible for seeing that his or her needs are met by doctor and/or counselor. The facilitator is there to determine the person's needs, to put him at ease, to refer him to the right services(s) and to post-treatment follow-up.

Free Clinics are supported by donations, foundations, and federal dollars. The latter are sought reluctantly because of the restrictions often attached. Like Switchboards, decision-making is communal or by a board of directors composed of volunteers, the few full-time staff on subsistence salaries, and members from the community. Free Clinics are loosely organized into a National Free Clinic Council, which facilitates communication via national meetings and a journal.

Communication and Education

Hotlines

The use of community volunteers, the nonbureaucratic organization, the sensitivity to community needs and the ability to adapt and expand services in response to these needs, are significant features of Hotlines, as well as of Switchboards and Free Clinics.

While the Free Clinics originated in response to the drug problem, Hotlines evolved from suicide prevention centers and the community mental health movement. In 1958 the Los Angeles Suicide Prevention Center opened its telephones and doors to answer the "Cry for Help," described by E. S. Schneidman, its founder, in the book by the same name. Experience and research indicated that most of the persons responding were not contemplating suicide but were nevertheless in a "crisis" situation, i.e. a point of extreme stress in which a decision must be made, but the person feels immobilized and unable to cope and is liable to behave in a self-destructive manner.

Adolescence is a "crisis of status discontinuity," socially, psychologically, and physiologically,[2] and in April 1968 the Los Angeles Children's Hospital began its Hotline for Youth. Hotline, the "port of call for angry, frightened, and frustrated young people."[3] Hotline, a personal, anonymous, emergency telephone service for young people in crisis.

Interdisciplinary Approach

Crisis intervention is a human problem and is therefore the responsibility of no particular profession or discipline. Though it arose out of the medical community, it soon aroused the interest and cooperation of professionals from the fields of psychology, psychiatry, therapy, health education, social work, pastoral counseling, nursing, and even law, anthropology, biostatistics and logic, but not librarianship. Its multidisciplinary approach is paralleled by the multi-service functions of Switchboards, Free Clinics, and Hotlines.

Confidentiality

Implicit in the provision of crisis intervention

services is an atmosphere of Trust, as one hotline is aptly called. To engender this, a potential source of financial support will be refused if it threatens the center's credibility. There can also be no trust without confidentiality.

The relationship between caller and listener on the Hotline, between patient and counselor at the Free Clinic, and between person and staff at the Switchboard is confidential, whether adult or minor. Respect for the confidential nature of the client-Crisis Center relationship when the client is a minor is a unique feature of Crisis Centers. "We are responsible to the youths who come in, not to their parents." Hotlines, in particular, can guarantee confidentiality to both the caller and the listener by means of the anonymity of the telephone. In fact, the location of a hotline is often kept a secret to protect both parties. Should a parent inquire as to whether and why his or her child has used the Hotline, the listener can honestly reply that he doesn't know and can explain the Hotline's purpose.

Can public and school librarians honestly make the same claim with respect to their circulation records? How often are they guilty of telephoning a parent even prior to a teenager's or child's use of materials on, say, sex or drugs?

Alternatives

Hotlines do not advocate drugs, but neither do they preach their evils. Free Clinics are not pro-abortion, but neither will they moralize to an unwed parent. Switchboards do not encourage runaways, but neither do they turn them in. A nonjudgmental approach toward the client characterizes the variety of crisis services to youth. They do not judge the person, nor do they recommend one solution, but for each of the range of alternative solutions, crisis centers do try to evaluate and recommend the best resource, whether it be a person, agency, book, or pamphlet.

For example, an unwed pregnant teenager, during a telephone encounter might discover that abortion or adoption are among her alternatives. The listener would not judge her predicament, nor ask her how she could have been so cruel to her parents, etc. If the caller should consider adoption, she would be given a list of recommended adoption agencies and homes for unwed mothers. In contrast, if the same young woman had asked a librarian, she might very well have received a short sermon or even an unintentional casual remark about the badness of her condition. Then the librarian might have handed her an outdated health and welfare directory for her to evaluate by herself!

Or if a young man were contemplating shooting heroin or smoking marijuana and let the librarian know this, it would not be surprising if he were told about the evils of drugs in general. But the librarian would not feel responsible for misinformation in any book or pamphlet the person might find by himself and would probably not feel confident to recommend one title over another. A Hotline or Free Clinic worker would discuss with him the possible consequences of drug use and would be prepared to recommend a particular book that had been evaluated to contain accurate information in a nonsensational way.

Hotlines do not advise, but they do more than listen. The aim of a crisis line is to provide constructive alternatives to a problem, to help the caller examine it from all angles, making use of his own resources to the fullest extent possible. If it is necessary to go beyond this, the volunteer listener will "patch-in" to the telephone line, from his file of human resources in fields relevant to youth, a lawyer, doctor, psychiatrist, or minister, who has volunteered to be on call as a professional back-up. Alternatives might also be sought from the community resources file for the caller to contact later himself. Crisis centers hope to alleviate the immediate crisis, but also, just as important, to prepare the caller to deal with future crises, to become a better problem-solver. The repeat caller to a Hotline is a problem and is not encouraged.

Contrast this to the dependency relationship implicit in library services, e.g. "hooked on books," "book bait"; not only is one encouraged to frequent the library, but once inside, he is expected to have to "ask the librarian" to utilize its resources to the fullest. The reader's adviser hopes that a satisfied reader will return to him for additional advice.

Volunteers

Hotlines are operated primarily by volunteer youth. In the mental health services community, aides were used initially because of the shortage of professional manpower. Experience proved them to be more than an inexpensive second-best substitute. Their knowledge of the community and similarity to the clientele were qualities that the professional could not substitute with skill, and they became recognized members of the mental health team. It was only natural that youth would have a similar role in helping troubled peers who did not use and were not reached by traditional facilities.

Though the structure and organization of Hotlines is more varied than that of Switchboards and Free Clinics, even the most traditional, those organized by mental health and religious associations, have a youth advisory board and utilize teenagers and college students as volunteers.

Other Hotlines are sometimes part of a City Youth Agency, a University Counseling Center, or are nonprofit corporations. Support comes from their parent organization, if there is one, as well as from civic groups, personal donations, benefits, and foundations and federal grants. In any case, their budget is miniscule compared to that of health or information services in their community.

Problems

An analysis of the problems that are brought to these centers is possible because of the detailed records kept of each contact, whether by telephone or in person. A data log sheet will include age, sex, marital status, and first name; the degree of crisis, the attitude and approach the listener took; whether the problem was resolved by referral, professional back-up, or went unresolved; and where the caller heard about the service.

Though no systematic analysis exists at this time comparing one center to another, a general picture does emerge from inspection of the records of several crisis centers. Most calls involve interpersonal relationships: mainly boy/girl, peer, or family conflicts. Problems arising from an internal mental state, especially loneliness and depression, are the second largest category. Suicidal calls are listed separately and are relatively few in number, though they are the most serious and have the greatest impact on volunteers. Medical problems, including drug information, drug overdose, tripping, pregnancy, venereal disease, and other sex problems rank third. Only about ten percent of the calls are drug related. Questions about the legal status, rights, and obligations of youth, including the draft, runaways, parental support, and marriage, make up the next significant block. School-oriented problems occur less frequently, but enough to be a category. Only a small percentage of problems involve employment or housing.

Crisis Centers do not give advice, including medical or legal advice. Volunteers are not engaged in the practice of medicine or law without a license, but they are nonetheless able to serve youth in many sensitive areas with legal and medical implication, especially runaway, sex, and drug information. The possibility of legal suits has been raised both by Kahn[4] and Leviton[5] on hypothetical and empirical grounds and dismissed by both. It's these very sensitive areas that public and school libraries have feared to tread.

Crank calls, including put-ons and obscene calls, are generally treated seriously. The rationale is that the caller has a problem but is afraid to reveal it, perhaps even to himself. Compare this attitude to the library's response to the "troublemaker," which not infrequently is to ban him from the building.

In every Hotline, female callers predominate over males, between two to one to as much as five to one. But boys, when they call, have more specific problems than girls, who comprise almost all of the "lonely" calls. The average caller is about 16, though older at college crisis centers. In one county, 16 percent of the callers were 12 or under. If this is not an unusual number of preteen callers, what implications are there for the present boundary in libraries between children and young adult services at 13 or 14 years, or the programs and materials in the children's room? Should the territorial boundaries in both libraries and library associations be re-drawn to include 11- and 12-year-olds in Young Adult services? Should junior novels be written, reviewed, and selected with the ten to 14 rather than the 12-to-16-year-old in mind?

Many Hotlines receive over 2000 calls a month. In the Washington, D.C. area alone, over 50 Hotlines, Switchboards, and Free Clinics were identified as providing a configuration of listening, counseling, and information or referral services to young adults. This is not an unusually large number for a metropolitan area. The combination of

many centers, each with a potential large volume, indicates
the possible, if not actual, impact of these services upon
other information and referral services.

Referral Files

A referral system of community agencies and professionals is an essential element of any crisis center:
Hotline, Switchboard, or Free Clinic. The degree the problem can be matched to referrals is one measure of the effectiveness of the center. Before an agency is used, as
much information as possible is collected about it, including
the identification of a particular contact person, so that a
client is told who to see and not just where to go. Sometimes, an agency is checked out by means of a fake call.

Crisis Centers rely on users to improve their files.
Volunteers are guided to ask the person for feedback on how
helpful the referral was. If the center is unable to provide
the information needed, he might be asked to call back and
make the files more complete should he discover other
sources. This mutual learning process also takes place
between the center and the agencies themselves. The crisis
center influences and educates professionals and agencies in
more effective ways of handling the problems of young people, while the professionals and agencies provide training
and expertise. Both user and agency feedback to the Center
provide a mechanism for the continual up-dating of the files'
"vital" information. The data sheets also encourage the
search for and development of new referral resources.

Advocacy

Crisis centers not only intervene in individual immediate crises, the "band aid" function, but work to prevent future crises in a community. With the data collected
on user problems and the follow-up and feedback provided
on referrals, they function as a social indicator of the needs
and gaps in community service. Perhaps the hours or regulations of an agency inhibit or prohibit its use by potential
clientele, or there may be no agency at all that is concerned,
or maybe a local ordinance on minors' rights needs changing.
With data in hand and a constituency of community groups
and professionals behind them, the crisis center is a powerful persuader to appropriate bodies to alter services or

Communication and Education

regulations. Alfred Kahn[6] names this "Program and Policy Advocacy" in describing the range of services a neighborhood information center could provide.

The library could assume the function of group advocacy. Even if it is not an advocate for individuals, it could use its accumulation of "unanswered questions" to be used by appropriate groups or organizations to substantiate and justify changes in services.

Access

Since crises can occur at any time and by their nature require rapid intervention, Hotlines and other crisis centers try to be open 24 hours, seven days a week. When this is not feasible, it is the daytime hours during the week that are closed, those nine-to-five Monday-to-Friday hours when public and especially school libraries are open, since emotional emergencies tend to occur most often at night. Crisis centers seem to have no problem recruiting staff for these hours, yet libraries base their limited hours as much on the unwillingness of paid employees to work at other times as on budgetary constraints.

It is not enough to be open; a service must be made known to its target audience by any media necessary: calling cards distributed at schools, stickers in phone booths and on cars, public service announcements on TV and local radio rock stations, stories in the local paper, listing in the alternative press, posters in neighborhood stores. These are the imaginative ways crisis centers try to reach troubled youth, while parents are informed by a Center's Speakers' Bureau, PTA's, and periodic written reports to the communities. Ironically, the one point of access that has been a stumbling block is the telephone directory and operator. Some directories require an address in order to be listed, and those Hotlines that demand anonymity have been refused a listing. In addition, there is yet no agreement by the phone company as how to list these Centers in the Yellow Pages, regardless of their name.

Training

The philosophy, services, and techniques of crisis intervention are initially conveyed to volunteers through a short training period, of not more than a dozen sessions, which utilizes role-playing, sensitivity groups, outside experts, and real crisis situations. It is necessary to understand oneself before one can help others and make oneself sensitive to the real but unstated and hidden needs of people seeking help, and so the volunteer is placed in situations which reveal his own biases and hang-ups. Authorities on subjects likely to be problems provide the information to answer these needs. Instruction in the content, organization, and update of the referral files is additional input into the volunteer's subject knowledge. The data sheets are a check that his training is consistent with the user population and its problems. Telephone techniques in particular are explained, demonstrated, and practiced through role-playing and actual supervised calls.

The initial training period, during which some volunteers are asked to drop out or do so by choice, is followed by weekly or monthly meetings to discuss problems, unanswered needs, and internal policies. Though written material plays a minor role initially, most crisis centers develop a training manual for future reference. The manuals describe the goals and services and emphasize the importance of follow-through, feedback, and up-date, so that services and resources will reflect community needs.

Is your library manual an adequate reflection of your library's stated priorities? Or does it contain more "don'ts" than "do's"? Would you be uneasy if your public read it?

Resources

Several crisis centers have indicated the desire to establish a resource library in their facilities (for reference by both staff and clientele) made up of handbooks, pamphlets, periodicals, and directories. One newsletter, the Confederation, mailed a questionnaire to crisis centers asking for recommended materials for such a basic collection. Materials so identified would be likely candidates for inclusion in a library's collection. Perhaps the library could provide them on indefinite loan to its local crisis center.

An informal network connects the over 750 crisis centers in the U.S. and Canada. The total number is increasing rapidly, despite the high death rate for new centers. The Exchange has established its responsibility for the production of the <u>National Directory of Hotlines, Switchboards, and Related Services</u>. At the International Hotline Conference, regional divisions were organized. The network also consists of smaller metropolitan area councils, such as in Long Island or Baltimore, and national research centers, all of which publish newsletters or journals and hold conferences and workshops. But there is great resistance to any strong network with regulatory powers. A proposal for national standards and accreditation was defeated in 1971, but the minimum criteria suggested: 24-hour-access, continuous training, justification of need for a service, formal evaluation to include feedback, are an accurate reflection of their importance to the crisis center philosophy.

Summary

In summary, a crisis intervention center is an easily accessible storefront or telephone community facility, counseling, advocacy, information, and referral service feeding into a larger human services network, using paraprofessionals from the community, who are peers of the clientele, with professional back-up when needed, and providing stop-gap crisis services until more comprehensive and preventative services can be found.

When phrased this way, the crisis services image is parallel to storefront library "outreach" programs. Librarians are searching for new and innovative ways to reach the nonuser. Can we learn anything about changes in services, hours, personnel and training, and public relations from a similarly nontraditional service? In addition, several public libraries have gone into the information and referral business themselves, so it is not entirely academic to ask if and how libraries, both school and public, should become a part of this network and cooperate with crisis centers as equals. Third, if we can accept as fact that we will never serve everyone directly and personally, can we perhaps serve our public indirectly by providing information and back-up services to the staff of our local hotline, switchboard, and free clinic, i.e. consciously serving community groups. Fourth, how can we apply the information crisis centers are collecting about the needs of troubled youth in our communities to even traditional library services, e.g. in areas such as book selection or programs.

"Every community needs a police department, a

public school system, a mental health clinic, a welfare agency, a fire department ... and a suicide and crisis intervention service...."[8] Is the library ready to assume its place among these community helping systems?

References

1. Braverman, Miriam. Ph.D thesis in progress at Columbia University School of Library Service.
2. Sebald, Hans. Adolescence; A Sociological Analysis. Appleton-Century Crofts, 1960, p. 24.
3. Bell, Joseph. "Take Your Troubles to the Hotline." Seventeen, August 1970.
4. Kahn, Alfred J. Neighborhood Information Centers. Columbia University School of Social Work, 1966. Reprinted by University Book Service, Brooklyn, N.Y., 1971.
5. Leviton, Dan & Stanley Parey. Proposal for a University of Maryland Crisis Intervention Center, 1970. 8p. mimeo.
6. Kahn, op. cit.
7. Donahue, Joseph. Public Information Center: Final Report. Enoch Pratt Free Library, February 1971.
8. McGee, Richard K. "Toward a New Image for Suicide and Crisis Services." Crisis Intervention, vol. 2, no. 3, 1970, p. 63.

DIRECTORIES OF CRISIS CENTERS--NATIONAL

National Directory of Hotlines, Switchboards, and Related Services. Ken Beitler. The Exchange, 311 Cedar Ave. South, Minneapolis, Minn. 55404. January 1, 1972. 50p. $2
The most complete directory at this time. Arranged geographically, included Canada.

Win with Love! A Comprehensive Directory of the Liberated Church, Including Peace Organizations, Youth Switchboards, National Resource Groups, Immigrant Aid Centers in Canada. Part I, October 1970, no. 4, 63p; Part II, June 1971, no. 5, 63p, Berkeley Free Church, Free Church Publications, POB 9177, Berkeley, Calif. 94709. $1.50
Geographically arranged.

Radical Therapist Rap Center Directory. Radical Therapist,

Hillsdate, N. Y. 12529. June 1971 Supplement, p. 1-7.
50 cents
Does not include hotlines and switchboards and so complements Beitler. Geographically arranged. Indicates type of services provided.

Switchboards and Hotlines. Appendix One in Ambrosino, Lillian. Runaways. Beacon Pr., 1971, p. 109-116.
An example of incomplete directories appended to books which are not updated.

"Directory of Suicide Prevention Facilities." Bulletin of Suicidology. March 1969, p. 47-58.

DIRECTORIES OF CRISIS CENTERS--LOCAL

[If your region does not produce its own directory, your library or librarians' association can offer to create and update it.]

Survey of drug abuse programs for the Washington Metropolitan Area, Information Document. January, 1971. Metropolitan Washington Council of Governments, 1225 Connecticut Ave., N.W., Washington, D.C. 20036. 55p. mimeo.
Free
Arranged A-Z within the regions of Washington, Maryland, and Virginia. Services not exclusively drug-oriented, e.g. Hotlines are included. For each program affiliation, goals, hours, clientele, facilities, and funding are indicated as well as contact person.

New Jersey Drug Help Centers and Hotlines; a Preliminary Working Directory. Jana Varlejs, comp., Montclair Public Library, 1971. 5p. Dist. by the N. J. Librarians for Social Responsibilities, Princeton Public Library, N. J. 08540.
Librarian originated directory.

DIRECTORIES OF COMMUNITY RESOURCES

[Every crisis center (and library!) needs an accurate, up-to-date guide to community resources. Many centers have created these in the form of files. The following are a sample of published directories that show their variety in depth and origin. If your community does not have such a guide, create one.]

Direct Action. Philadelphia Librarians SRRT. October
1970. 2p.
A simple alphabetical list of community organizations with
telephone numbers.

Free for You. Help Center, Univ. of Maryland, College
Park, Md. 20742. Fall, 1971. 8p. mimeo. Free.
From Abortion to Zoo. Aimed at the local college student.

The Golden Goose. No. 1, 1972. Sue Critchfield, Bay
Area Social Responsibility of Librarians Round Table,
Community Resources Committee, 72 Ord St., San
Francisco, Calif. 94114. Bi-monthly.
"The newsletter that intends" to list resources, to find lists
of such resources.

Health Counseling and Crisis Intervention Referral Resources
(for the Washington Metropolitan area). Prepared by
Dr. Catherine M. Miller, Dept. of Health Education,
Univ. of Maryland, College Park, Md. 20742; n.d.
1970? 8p. mimeo.
From Abortion to Veneral Disease, for each service, address,
hours, fee, services, and personal contact are included.

People's Yellow Pages. Vocation for Social Change, 351
Broadway, Cambridge, Mass. 02139. 93p. 75 cents.
A meaty directory, arranged by subject with many "see"
references to the appropriate term used. A model community resource guide for the alternative culture of Boston.

"Phones," **Quicksilver Times**, listed in every issue. Many
of the local alternative presses have similar listings,
e.g. "Frequently Called Numbers," **Los Angeles Free
Press**.
These are the barest of guides, giving telephone numbers
only.

**A Questionnaire to Gather Information for the Interagency
Information Referral Resource Committee.** Sponsored
and supported by the Prince George's County (Maryland)
Health Planning Advisory Council and the Health and
Welfare Council. July 1971. 10p.
An excellent model for preparing a directory.

Social Action Organizations of New Jersey. N.J. Librarians
for Social Responsibility, Princeton Public Library, N.J.
08540. May 1971. 12p.

Communication and Education

PERIODICALS

American Journal of Orthopsychiatry. American Orthopsychiatric Assn., N.Y. Five times yearly, $16

Bulletin of Suicidology. National Clearinghouse for Mental Health Information, NIMH, Chevy Chase, Md. 20015. Spring 1970 special issue commemorating the tenth anniversary of the Los Angeles Suicide Prevention Center. Might be discontinued.

Confederation Newsletter. Main Line, Cornell Univ., Sheldon Court, Ithaca, N.Y. 14858. College oriented.

Connection: Newsletter for New England. Project Place, 37 Rutland St., Boston, Mass. 02118.

Crisis Intervention. Suicide Prevention and Crisis Service, 560 Main St., Buffalo, N.Y. 14202. Vol. 1, No. 1, 1969. Index to 1969 and 1970 in Vol. 3, no. 1. Includes annual bibliographies, 1968-.

The Exchange. 311 Cedar Ave. South, Minneapolis, Minn. 55404. Monthly. $6
"A national newsletter for hotlines, switchboards, and other youth-oriented projects." Ken Beitler, ed.

Free Clinic Journal. National Free Clinic Council, 701 Irving St., San Francisco, Calif. 94122. Annual. $5

Northeast Hotline Bulletin. Hotline, 1355 Northern Blvd., Manhasset, N.Y. 11030.

Radical Therapist. Hillsdale, N.Y. 12529.

Schneidman, Edwin, ed. Life-Threatening Behavior. Avail. from Behavior Publications, 2852 Bdway., N.Y. 10025. Quarterly: $10 (indiv.); $20 (institutions). Official journal of the Assn. of Suicidology.

The Vita. $1
Newsletter of the International Assn. for Suicide Prevention.

Vocations for Social Change. Canyon, Calif. 94516. Bimonthly. $10
Source of information about new services, directories, alternative institutions.

ORGANIZATIONS--NATIONAL

American Assn. of Suicidology.

Center for Studies of Suicide Prevention, NIMH, Chevy Chase, Md. 20015.
A joint sponsor of the Bulletin of Suicidology.

Center for the Study of Crisis Intervention. Univ. of Florida, Gainesville, Fla. 32601.

Los Angeles Suicide Prevention Center. 2521 W. Pico, Los Angeles, Calif. 90026.
Has produced studies on adolescent crises. "Student-packet" of article $3.

National Clearinghouse for Drug Abuse Information, NIMH, Chevy Chase, Md. 20015.
Among its many publications are its Report Series and its Selected Reference Series.

National Clearinghouse for Mental Health Information, NIMH, Chevy Chase, Md. 20015.
Publishes the Bulletin of Suicidology.

National Free Clinic Council. 701 Irving St., San Francisco, Calif. 94122.

Technical Information Section, NIMH. Will provide computer research on crisis intervention.

The International Assn. for Suicide Prevention. Newsletter, The Vida, and conferences.

ORGANIZATIONS--LOCAL

The International Hotline Conference has regional coordinators: Western Region: Myldred Jones, 12100-54 Montecito Rd., Los Alamitos, Calif. Northeastern U.S. and Eastern Canada: Gus Potter, Operation Hotline, 1355 Northern Blvd., Manhasset, N.Y. 11030. Also publishes newsletter, "Northeast Hotline Bulletin." New England Region: Project Place, 37 Rutland St., Boston, Mass. 02118. Newsletter: "Connection." Many metropolitan areas have also formed informal associations, e.g. Los Angeles, Long Island, that sponsor workshops.

Communication and Education 335

CONFERENCE, INSTITUTES, COURSES

First International Hotline Conference, Los Angeles. April, 1970. Dr. Gerald Bissiri, Hotline, Children's Hospital, 4650 Sunset Blvd., Los Angeles, Calif. 90027. Proceedings.

Second International Hotline Conference, Pacific Grove, Calif. May 25-28, 1971. Dr. Gerald Bissiri. See above.
Proceedings and a list of participants. An account of the conference was also prepared by Gus Potter, 1355 N. Blvd., Manhasset, N.Y. 11030. Tape cassettes available from Elaine Lynn and Associates. A movie filmed at the conference, "Crisis Intervention by Phone," 30mm., color, is available from Elaine Lynn and Associates, 1506 S. Bay Front, Balboa Island, Calif. 92662.

Third International Hotline Conference, Carlton College, Northfield, Minn., June 20-23, 1972. Virginia V. Sparling, 1600 N.E. 150 St., Seattle, Wash. 98155.

Eastern Regional Hotline Conference. College Park, Md. June 9-11, 1971. Sponsored by NIMH, Health Suicidology Section. Dan Murphy, Washington Free Clinic, Coordinator. Available from: Dennis Jafee, No. Nine 266 State St., New Haven, Conn. 06511.
Includes lists of participating groups and persons, and a Resources-Publications bibliography.

Midwest Region Hotline Conference. March 19, 1972. Minneapolis. The Exchange.

Sixth International Congress on Suicide Prevention. Mexico. December 1971. Proceedings $4. Avail. from: Los Angeles Suicide Prevention Center.

Radical Therapy Conference. Washington, D.C.
List of participants.

Summer Institute in Suicidology, July 27-August 7, 1970. Also a Winter Institute, January 25-February 5, 1971. A continuing series sponsored by the Center for Studies of Suicide Prevention, NIMH.

American Assn. of Suicidology. Annual conferences. Fifth on March 31, 1972. Michigan.

National Free Clinic Council. Annual Meeting. Washington,
D. C. January 14-17, 1972.

American University. Dept. of Psychology. 57.507. Crisis
Intervention, Theory, and Technique. Dr. Barry McCarthy, Dr. A. Berman.
A course.

Univ. of Maryland. Dept. of Health Education. Crisis
Intervention. Dr. Catherine Miller.
A course to be offered in Spring 1972.

Univ. of Maryland. Dept. of Psychology. Second Annual
Symposium. Current issues in community-clinical psychology: Crisis Intervention, held March 23-25,
1972. Address inquiries to: Gerald Specter, Dept. of
Psychology, Univ. of Maryland, College Park, Md.
20742.

BIBLIOGRAPHIES

Bibliography on Suicide and Suicide Prevention. Prepared
by the Los Angeles Suicide Prevention Center. National
Clearinghouse for Mental Health Information, NIMH,
Chevy Chase, Md. 20015.
3300 items, covering 1897-1967.

Crisis Intervention. Annual bibliographies on crisis intervention.

Drug Dependence and Abuse, a Selected Bibliography.
National Clearinghouse for Drug Abuse Information.
March 1971. 50p. GPO. 60 cents
Arranged by subjects, e.g. socio-cultural aspects, law
and public policy, information resources. An annotated edition is planned.

Student Suicide, a Bibliography. 3p. mimeo. Available
from NIMH.

TRAINING MANUALS PRODUCED BY CRISIS CENTERS

[The following is not a comprehensive list of such manuals.
Virtually every hotline, switchboard, and counseling center
has an in-house manual. All that are listed below have

Communication and Education

been inspected by the compiler. Librarians would do well to compare them to their own policy and training manuals.]

Advocate Guide. People's Free Medical Clinic, 3028 Greenmount Ave., Baltimore, Md. 21218. July 1970. 8p. mimeo.

Berkeley Switchboard Operators Manual. Free Church Publications, BPOB 9177, Berkeley, Calif. 94709. April 1970. 24p. $1

Community Relations. Tom Paine Society, 31 W. King St., York, Pa. n.d. 4p. mimeo.
A practical guide for other centers as well.

Drugs: Information for Crisis Treatment, a Manual. Matthew Lample, Drug Help Inc., POB 366, Ann Arbor, Mich. 48107. 1971. 25p. 75 cents

Drug Abuse: Acute Treatment Manual. California Medical Assn. 1970. 8p. mimeo.
Includes suggested resource directory form.

A Drug Manual. Richmond Crisis Intervention Center. November 1970. 48p. mimeo. Available from Hotline Coordinator, c/o Adolescent Clinic, Box 151, Medical College of Virginia, Richmond, Va. 23219.
Includes a 14-page dictionary of slang drug terms and drug profiles for every drug including usual dose, duration of effect, effects sought, physiological effects, possible ill effects, withdrawal symptoms, etc.

Guidelines for the Establishment of a Hotline Service. Developed by attendees at Conference on Emergency Telephone Service, Children's Hospital, Los Angeles, Calif. February 24 and May 26, 1969. 21p. mimeo.

A Letter to All Telephone Volunteers. Drug Aid Program, Catonsville, Md. 1971. 6p. mimeo.
Their training and policy manual.

Manual. Franklin County Hotline, POB 307, Greenfield, Mass. 01301. n.d. 12p. mimeo.

Moyer, Beth. A Descriptive Analysis of a Personal Emergency Telephone Service Used in Crisis Intervention for Youth in Richmond, Va. Thesis. Write Ad. Clinic.

Richmond Hotline Training Manual. September 1971. 12p.
  mimeo. Hotline Coordinator, c/o Adolescent Clinic,
  Box 151, Medical College of Virginia, Richmond, Va.
  23219.

San Francisco Switchboard Operating Procedures. Haight
  Ashbury Switchboard, 1826 Fell St., San Francisco,
  Calif. 94117. September 1970. 13p. mimeo. Free

Training Manual for Telephone Evaluation and Emergency
  Management of Suicidal Persons. Suicide Prevention
  Center, Inc., Los Angeles, Calif. n. d. 27p. mimeo.
One of the first crisis centers in the U.S.

CRISIS CENTERS

[The following are articles or documents directed toward the public that describe the purpose, services, and history of local centers in the Washington area. Similar documents are available from crisis centers themselves in your community and in articles in your local alternative press.]

"Connection." Harry, March 29-April 8, 1971. p. 8.
  Describes and compares six Baltimore area hotlines.

"A County Mental Health Association's Hotline." School
  Health Review, September 1970, p. 27-30.
  Describes the Montgomery County, Maryland, hotline. The entire issue is on Crisis Intervention.

Hotline, Could an Anonymous Listener Help? Information
  Sheet. Northern Virginia Hotline Inc., Arlington, Va.
  22205. flier. n. d.

McCarthy, Barry & Berman, A. L. "Student Operated
  Crisis Center." Personnel and Guidance J., March
  1971, p. 523-8.
Describes the American Univ. hotline.

"Switchboard--Our Community Headphones Offers ..."
  Quicksilver Times, June 2-16, 1971, p. 5.

Statement of Purpose. Washington Free Clinic, Washington,
  D. C. n. d. 9p. mimeo.
Includes history and services.

Communication and Education

[For articles on other hotlines and crisis centers, see Readers' Guide and Education Index under "Telephone in Counseling" and "Suicide-Prevention"; Psychological Abstracts under "Crisis Intervention"; Alternate Press Index under "Movement Centers"; and from your local crisis center. Documents not found through these indexes include:]

CLARKE, Nancy B. "Help." Youth Magazine, 1505 Race St., Rm. 1203, Philadelphia, Pa. 19102, October 25, 1970, p. 1-10.

JAFFE, Dennis. Number Nine: Responses to Youth Problems at a Crisis Center; an Investigation of a Social Experiment. State Street Center, 266 State St., New Haven, Conn. 06511. August 1971. 106p. mimeo. $10
An extensive description of a crisis center operation, based on survey data. Divided into nine sections that include background in community mental health, telephone and storefront counseling, staff, a survey of community attitudes, a bibliography, and a directory of Connecticut crisis centers.

"Help!" 25 min. color. $265. Avail from: Concept Films, 312-1155 15th St., N.W., Washington, D.C. Describes the Philadelphia Volunteer Youth Crisis Center.

CRISIS CENTERS--THE PHENOMENON

AGEL, Jerome, ed. Radical Therapist Anthology, Ballantine, 1971. $1.25

AGUILERA, Donna. Crisis Intervention, Theory and Methodology. C. V. Mosby, 1970.

BELL, Joseph N. "Take Your Troubles to the Hotlines." Seventeen, August 1970, p. 242-3. Reprinted in pamphlet form by Social and Rehabilitation Service, Youth Development and Delinquency Prevention Administration, HEW, Washington, D.C.

FARBEROW, Norman L. & Schneidman, Edwin S., eds. The Cry for Help. McGraw, 1965.

GARELL, D. C. "Hotline Telephone Service for Young People in Crisis." Children, September 1969, p. 177-80.

JAFFE, Dennis. Number Nine. See section immediately above.

LEVITON, Dan & Stanley Pavey. Proposal for a University of Maryland Crisis Intervention Center. n. d. 18p. mimeo.

PARAD, Howard H., ed. Crisis Intervention: Selected Readings. Family Service Association of America, 1969.

POTTER, Gus. Hotline Story. Paper presented at Hofstra Univ. Symposium, September 9-10, 1971. 17p. mimeo. Operation Hotline, Town of North Hempstead, 220 Plandome Rd., Manhasset, N.Y. 11030.
An excellent summary of hotlines: history, philosophy, services, finances, staffing, callers.

RUITENBEEK, H., ed. Radical Therapy. Bantam, 1972.

AMERICAN CHILDREN'S CLASSICS: WHICH WILL FADE, WHICH ENDURE?*

Sara Innis Fenwick

The would-be commentator on the classics produced for children in the United States finds himself looking back over a period that is a fairly brief one even considering the late emergence of all children's literature written in the English language. If it can be granted that the classic must have shown at least an indication of living to a second generation, then we can, with very few exceptions, set up boundaries of two wars in the history of this country. Most of those books for children that have endured to the second boundary, World War II, were written after the Civil War. This period of eighty years, 1865-1945, marks the development of children's literature in this country, starting out as it did as a serious self-conscious literature addressed to the young, through decades characterized by some outstanding contributions, an increasing number of good but not great writings, and a large output of syndicated cheap books. The post-World War II years have been marked by an explosion of publishing in children's literature, with new themes and subjects and an obvious reflection not only of the rapid changes in the social scene but of the message styles characteristic of the newer media.

Before 1865, there was almost no book written for children that has survived in the reading life of children today. This is not to overlook the fact that children did read and adopt in their own world of literature the novels of James Fenimore Cooper and the legends of Washington Irving; simply to note that, until after the Civil War, there was, in this country, a dearth of truly imaginative literature created for children.

---

*Reprinted by permission from the October 1972 issue of Wilson Library Bulletin. Copyright 1972 by the H. W. Wilson Company.

Having survived the era of writings for spiritual nourishment and the parallel and succeeding decades devoted to literature with utilitarian and moralistic purposes, some first-rate writers in the 1860s responded to the upsurge of new economic, social, and political life and a new freedom, by communicating in individual styles and forms with the imagination of the child reader. Four books published between 1865 and 1876 marked the beginning of the contribution of American writers to what was to become a distinctive modern literature for children. The slow pace at which that literature grew and developed in variety, however, can be judged from a glance at a chronological review of the significant books of fiction which have in the past, and some of them in the present, been considered classics of our literature. Not included here are retellings of traditional literature and invented fantasy in folktale format, picture books, poetry, and books of nonfiction. This is not to say that there are not classics in each of these genres; I omit them merely to allow for a focus on one type of book.

The chronological approach is probably as useful as any other here, inasmuch as the life of a classic is determined by the point at which a book, no matter how many generations have designated it classic, ceases to communicate to a contemporary audience; and the qualities that dictate just when that time will be, are more likely to be changing values of society than any considerations of style, plot management, or book design.

After the Civil War--Huck, Tom, and Hans Brinker

Four surviving books from the first post-Civil War decade, 1865-1876, are Hans Brinker, Little Women, Story of a Bad Boy, and The Peterkin Papers. A re-reading of Hans Brinker makes the adult reader appreciate anew the enduring appeal of the plot--the suspense and the characters who have realistic dimensions of courage, fear, competitiveness, compassion, family loyalty. To re-read, however, is not to experience, as did the first readers in 1865, a detailed and colorful introduction to an interesting foreign country, but rather, offers a step backward into a time when the picturesque features of a country's geography and living customs seem to date the book more than one would expect from the number of years that have passed since the book's writing. This writer has been repeatedly surprised not only at the tenacity of teachers in keeping this title on resource lists for social studies units, but at the accompanying reluctance to treat it as an historical account. A recent revival of a film version on television has demonstrated again the appeal of the narrative, but a narrative shorn of the tedious travelogue sections of the book. It is quite likely that Hans Brinker has been for some years valuable to us chiefly as an historical contribution to our history of literature for children. Its importance here is without question as the most memorable composition of an outstanding literary figure, and as part of the beginning of a new era in the writing of fiction whose didactic characteristics are much less important than the narrative.

Volumes of commentary and criticism have been written about Mark Twain's two enduring boy heroes of this period--Tom Sawyer and Huckleberry Finn--and these need not be summarized here. The Adventures of Huckleberry Finn, written in 1885, fourteen years after The Adventures of Tom Sawyer, is probably one of the best illustrations of the book of multi-level appeal to appear in American literature until fifty or more years later. This lone position is in part due to the fact that most of the books that can be read first for plot action by the younger reader, who can cope best with issues that are clear cut and with recognized solutions, and that can also be read in later years of childhood, adolescence and adulthood for unfolding levels of ideas, language, and theme, are books of fantasy. This genre is represented by few early American contributors, certainly none who ranked with such British writers as Carroll, or MacDonald or even a little later with Grahame or Milne.

Both titles of Mark Twain stand up to the demands and expectations of today's readers: Tom Sawyer for its adventure and deep understanding of boyhood; and Huckleberry Finn for these qualities plus, on a more mature level, confrontation with the conflicting demands of loyalty and justice, of society's demands and personal integrity.

"Little Women" and "Little Men": Didacticism and Humor

Louisa M. Alcott's best remembered and most continuously read novel, Little Women, speaks of a time equally distant in the past but the setting is less a point of interest than is the reader's involvement with the family joys and sorrows of four girls who are very distinctive characters. The warmth of the family strength and mutual support is important, and visible in the rebellions, the triumphs, the mistakes, and the maturing of each of the characters. Even in the most tenderly tearful passages, it is not Victorian sentimentality that comes through in this novel but the ideal of self-control and self-discipline; qualities that together with the saving perspective of humor make the essential morality meaningful to the child reader of succeeding generations.

It is a different story with Little Men. It is true that the young readers--especially the girls--carry over to this sequel their disappointment at not being able to unite Jo and Laurie in marriage and are seldom quick to transfer the good Father Bhaer to the role of romantic lead. The expected formula has been disturbed, but this is a strength rather than a weakness--a good antidote for a surfeit of series stories. A re-reading of this volume, however, brings to light an over-burdening degree of sentimentality and heavy didacticism.

A re-reading made this adult amazed that boys had ever been readers of Little Men, and perhaps they seldom were. So much of the narrative and conversational style, together with the didactic commentary, seem to testify to the hand of the feminine author. The emotions of the characters are natural, however; and the concerns are those in which the young reader of many succeeding generations has been able to participate; the major stumbling block for today's reader is in the author's rhetoric. It is this quality that would seem to retire Little Men to the historical collection, supposing it were possible or even advisable to try to deprive the devotees of Little Women of "what happens next." They will almost inevitably find the reading experience disappointing. It is unlikely that even the special appeal for little girls of the Victorian age of the chapter on "Patty Pans" will continue to hold the current reader.

"A More Child-Like Dimension"

A book that was part of the newly expressed freedom to write about child life was Thomas Bailey Aldrich's Story of a Bad Boy (1870). Fictional boy heroes have been far more naughty and even sinful in other and later writing, but like his contemporary, Tom Sawyer, Tom Bailey was appealing to boys young and old in his everyday adventures and escapades. This fertile condition for satisfying reading

does not, however, exist today, and the small New England
town setting has seemed foreign territory for most boys in
this decade. The title, itself, is looked upon with some dis-
favor and disdain by today's parents. Nevertheless, it
marked an important part of the early development of realistic writing addressed to children and as such it has an honored place in the collection of historical writing.

A surprising and happy re-reading experience from
these years was the Peterkin Papers (1880) by Lucretia
Hale. This was one of the most original pieces of writing
for children in pre-1900 years. Ridiculous situations in the
perplexing lives of the Peterkin family, told in straight-
faced narrative, well honed in style, are still delightful to
read. Admittedly the mechanics of life on which many of
the situations center, e. g. , making a book, or coping with
the salt in Mrs. Peterkin's coffee, may be harder for the
young child today to accept as non-literal reading--or even
better, listening--experience; but the episodes of the Christmas tree and of Elizabeth Eliza's piano are easily recognizable. It can be granted that the appreciative audience has
undoubtedly diminished, but for a few listeners--to one or
two episodes--there is still a good experience here; and it
may be that the reality-cum-fantasy character of these
stories is more child-like in its dimensions and demands
than some of the recent fiction for children in which the
child has difficulty making an acceptable (to him) distinction.

Among these books written just before and after the
turn of the century that merit reconsideration, those by
Frances Hodgson Burnett have a place. An American writer
by early adoption, she made a considerable contribution to
the reading life of boys and girls in this country, although
much of her writing has settings and themes rooted in English life of the last century. Probably unique in its impact
on the American social scene was Little Lord Fauntleroy
(1886); but most read and re-read by children was The
Secret Garden (1910). The former is seldom read in the
present day but adults, at least, still recognize the reference
to a style of costume for boys, and with it the stereotype of
a namby-pamby, over-dressed boy who in all fairness should
not be confused with the straightforward, thoroughly honest
boy of the story. In this case, the plot as well as the
rhetoric does not translate to the 1970s. This is far less
true of Secret Garden, however; for on re-reading it
seemed to have the same elements of plot appeal, and few
obstacles to an identification by modern young readers with

the spoiled, unhappy Mary Lenox. Psychologically well
realized, she is a heroine in a narrative that locates the
major suspense more firmly in the concern as to how the
characters will react than in the hope that a miracle will
happen for all involved. Today's readers of Harriet the
Spy will not find Mary Lenox a strange girl to know.

    A versatile writer and artist who made rich contributions to children's literature in the years at the turn of the century was Howard Pyle. He is still represented well on the shelves of home and institutional libraries by his Merry Adventures of Robin Hood and his series of retellings of the King Arthur legend. The title frequently found on bibliographies today is Men of Iron, but another tale with a medieval setting, although less visible, is as good a story and has a theme that may be even more contemporary: Otto of the Silver Hand, published in 1888. The setting is medieval Germany, and the tension between violence and gentleness, peace and war, is created without sentimentality. Like all of this author-artist's books, the illustrations are as meticulously authentic as research and attention to detail can make them.

    The years from 1900 to 1920 in the U.S. produced many books but few giants among them. The century began with The Wonderful Wizard of Oz (1900) by Frank Baum, who continued to write more books as sequels. He was followed in this endeavor by other writers who continued until halfway through this century to capitalize on the original creation, and on the periodic stimulation of public interest by cries of "repression of freedom to read" leveled at those libraries where the titles, or the majority of them, had disappeared from the shelves.

    The original book by Baum represented a truly original piece of imaginative writing in terms of plot management and fantasy characters. Perhaps it also won an especially appreciative audience because it was a truly American contribution to a genre of writing deservedly dominated by British authors. In any case, whatever the strength of the repressive actions, the titles written by Baum have continued to delight young children. No one has ever claimed literary merit for the writing; the adult has only to try reading a few pages aloud to be quite uncomfortable with the woodenness of sentence structure and generally poor handling of dialogue. Older and more thoughtful readers see some obtrusive authorial rhetoric in the presentation of some of the characters, notably the Tin Woodman and the Cowardly Lion, but children accept them as written.

The extrinsic factors of survival are probably more observable here than in most long-term favorites; but children continue to testify to many intrinsic factors.

Series Fiction, Pioneer Fiction, and Pure Nonsense

The flood of series fiction, many of them Stratemeyer syndicate-promoted, almost inundated these decades with the mediocrity of tailored plots, predictable actions, and characters memorable usually only for their good looks and reliable appearance at the scene of action just in time to save the situation. Actually, when one is re-evaluating all the books of the past (not just the classics) one should pay special attention to the influence of this generation of adventure series and to the materialistic values, stereotypes in character, and social roles portrayed. Here is to be found strong evidence of all-sufficient, all-wise adolescent characters, who can step into adult-centered situations and solve the problems that have defeated the "establishment" or the authority figures. We have recently tended to view this characteristic as a trend in the writing of the present decade but it was evident seventy years ago.

Not even the decade of the twenties can be said to have added much of lasting worth to the list of classics. To be sure, Will James' Smoky was published in 1926, and could still be considered one of the most interesting and realistic cowboy stories ever written. It poses some reading problems for many of the boys who would enjoy it but are discouraged by the colloquial language. It holds an audience if it is read aloud by someone who can give an authentic sound to the language. Unfortunately, even its length marks it as one of the titles that may not survive the present generation's addiction to the television time clock.

Not to be overlooked, however, in these earlier decades of our modern literature is The Rootabaga Stories (1922) by Carl Sandburg. Although this title falls somewhat outside our present discussion of fiction, these delightful and poetic tales of nonsense were outstanding in a literature so barren of created imaginative literature in the modern short story form. Most of these brief stories have kept their charm for modern children, especially if they are read aloud or told. Pony Pony Huckabuck who plucked and plunged to find a shining silver slipper buckle excites the same delighted response to the chimes and rhythms of the language as ever she did in earlier years.

Two of the stories of pioneer America that were written in the thirties and which have now delighted two generations, continue to have the same appeal as when they were new. These are, Caddie Woodlawn, by Carol Ryrie Brink (1935) and The Little House in the Big Woods, together with its several sequels, by Laura Ingalls Wilder (1932). The tomboy Caddie, rebellious at having to assume her expected role as a young lady, strikes a familiar chord in the hearts of many pre-adolescent girls; but it is the family, with the warmth and care, one member for one another, and their struggles to survive in harsh frontier conditions that make the stories of the Wilder family memorable.

It is interesting that these books with a recognized historical setting, are, like the Alcott books, never referred to by children as out-of-date; but that one of the stories published a decade later, The Moffats, (1941) by Eleanor Estes, quite often is dismissed today as old-fashioned. When it was written it had the same appeals of warm, sympathetic family life, delightful childlike humor, the hardships of poverty and the triumphs of making-do in spite of it, that characterize the earlier books mentioned above. Perhaps it is too near in time to be accepted as descriptive of an historical time. The people and the very real problems still mark this first of a series of three titles about the Moffat family as a book that deserves to survive, but it may take another generation to come back to it. Children, until the age of eleven or twelve years, have a tendency to view time in two segments: today and long ago.

Two books of fantasy in the two decades beginning in 1930 that apparently have won a continuing place for themselves are Mr. Popper's Penguins written by Richard and Florence Atwater (1938), and Rabbit Hill, by Robert Lawson (1944). The pure nonsense, with a very straight narration, has no pigeonhole in time to hinder its survival. It seems to this writer that Rabbit Hill might, in addition to the perennial appeal of Georgie and his adventures, speak with a special relevance to contemporary concerns with the natural world. Sharing night on Midsummer Eve might well be observed in one way or another today.

Two adventure books were re-read, both of them from the decade of the forties. <u>Call it Courage</u> by Armstrong Sperry (1940) was a pleasant reward. It struck me as being every bit as much of a personal testament of courage and achievement as it did when I first read it, and in the format of a large-type paperback it seemed much less formidable than the original, albeit much less distinguished in design with the loss of the excellent illustrations and the unusually fine page design. It must be admitted that a disappointingly high percentage of likely readers quietly put the original back on the shelf without reading, possibly because of an unappealing format.

A second book examined for this period was <u>Johnny Tremain</u>, by Esther Forbes (1943). I did not seriously believe that this title was in any danger of being forgotten either by children or by critics, but there was a question as to how the boys' motivation for taking up their guns would read today. The theme that stands out at the close of the book "that a man shall stand up" is so perfectly a bringing together of the struggles and ideals of all the characters that it is right from a literary and an emotional standpoint, and should be recognized as such by the young reader.

During these two decades that actually did see a flowering of American children's literature, there were many other titles that now stand in the way of becoming "classics," and this discussion has noted only a few, in a limited form, and with a very personal commentary. There are, among other books not discussed, a number of picture books from these years that have become seemingly permanent fixtures in children's reading, and have satisfied several generations of the picture-book audience.

The Newbery Medal and Its Influence

A new factor influencing the survival of outstanding children's books--outstanding, that is, at the time of their publication--is the Newbery Medal award, together with the considerable number of other awards that have followed this first recognition of writing for children. Designed to honor a book considered by a committee of librarians and other professionals working with children and books to be the most distinguished contribution to children's literature, the award has been presented annually since 1922 when the first medal was given to Hendrik Van Loon's <u>Story of Mankind</u>. The award has had considerable influence over the years in recognizing and encouraging the publishing of good books for children, and in bringing the books and the standards by which they are judged to the attention of both children and adults, but especially the latter audience. Fifty-one Newbery award winners now stand on the shelf and there are many books that continue to be distinguished in the changing world of literature. It is worth noting, however, that an award does not itself make a "classic"; and that even the most outstanding of these selected titles are subject to the same erosion of changing interests and needs. One of the characteristics sought in the selection of the Newbery Medal books is universality, but the recognition of this elusive quality is not always infallible. The statistical error of assuming that a list of fifty books, chosen one each year by a changing group of people, represents the fifty best books of these years is a not uncommon, but false assumption. Common sense tells us that the fifty best books published since 1921 might very likely include four from one year and none from three other years. Therefore, we do well to honor the award book for what it represents each year, and to rejoice in the good literature that it has recognized over the years; and to re-evaluate these books with the same care that we use for all literature.

As we survey the survival characteristics of books in children's literature it seems a fair statement that very few classics endure lacking the criteria of good writing. Nevertheless, there are some other factors at work in the field of children's books that must be recognized and weighed for their influence.

In today's book business it must be noted that the measures of endurance in terms of number of editions, visible presence on bookstore shelves and publishers' catalogs, on shelves of libraries, in book club offerings are none of them necessarily the measures of a classic book. Two conditions frequently foster the continued life of many titles that are easy of access for reprinting: the nostalgic memories of adults and new cheap reprint editions. Titles continue to be passed on from one generation to the next because they are remembered and bought by adults who recall that adults bought them in their childhood, and so back two, three, and four generations. Unfortunately, these treasures are often passed on without re-reading. The same titles are frequently kept on library shelves, replaced with regularity and preserved on lists of recommended books because they are familiar. Only these factors at work would explain the bright, new editions of The Five Little Peppers series, Rebecca of Sunnybrook Farm, or Anne of Green Gables, among others. It is not the purpose of this article to question the reading pleasures of these books and many other similar survivals from the end of the last century and the early years of the present one. It is the writer's purpose to point out that the mere endurance of a widely sold book is not necessarily due to any of the qualities that mark a literary classic.

If the persistence of books in publishers' series labeled as "classics" and in lists of recommended readings (including those lists of professional associations that are regularly revised) cannot be assumed to be due to an enduring quality of distinguished writing and imagination, then such titles should be regularly re-read for their relative levels of continuing significance and historical importance. The results of such continuous re-examination should be to identify those writings that no longer speak to an audience today. These are books that should be retained in appropriate locations for their historical interest to students of children's literature, but should not be replaced in active library and bookstore collections and should disappear from the bibliographies of recommended books. It would be hoped that they would not reappear periodically in new and reissued editions. Publishers who are considering the commissioning of new illustrations and of type for books that have been on these lists for generations, or which have been out-of-print from other sources, would be making a productive investment in the total reading scene if they re-evaluated the content of the books under consideration, and instead of maintaining long out-dated books kept alive by adult nostalgia, would give new visibility to titles that for a variety of reasons were slow in winning an audience but have continued to give evidence of endurance.

It can be argued that re-evaluation, as well as all evaluation by adults, is an imposition of adult values and a denial of freedom-to-read to the child. Students in professional schools for the preparation of teachers and librarians are particularly sensitive to this argument today.

It seems to this writer that the assumption of some responsibility for the selection, reviewing, and criticism of children's books by adults is justified, but only if those same adults are willing to develop and foster skills of serious literary criticism, to recognize and exercise the highest degree of objectivity, to make themselves familiar with current knowledge about child development and above all, to keep alive channels of communication with children's interests and concerns. Such skills and knowledge continuously exercised with the judgment gained from years of enthusiastic reading are good insurance that adult critics can accept without apology a responsibility for the criticism of children's literature.

The oft-repeated phrase "children know what they like" can profitably be accompanied by the response that they do not always know all the books that they might like, given the availability and understanding introduction which establishes a confrontation between reader and book.

TIME FOR DECISION: LIBRARY EDUCATION
FOR THE SEVENTIES *

Andrew H. Horn

Library schools, if they are not already doing so, must soon make some decisions about their programs; specifically, the master's degree programs. These decisions are of central importance because that degree should articulate with paraprofessional and undergraduate programs as well as with postmaster's and doctoral programs. These decisions cannot be focused upon defense of the status quo; rather the decisions must be directed toward change. All of the institutions and organizations, and all of the people who vitalize the institutions and organizations which impinge upon library schools are themselves in the process of making decisions in response to demands for change--libraries, librarians, professional associations, universities, students, teachers, academic administrators and planners.

One way to start the decision making process is to establish a model or hypothetical program. When it is agreed to accept the model, or some modification of it, it becomes a plan. When the plan is fully implemented it becomes a program. At UCLA about two or three years ago we began to construct a model for a master's degree program. We do not claim that it is ours because it has been shaped and changed by the professional literature; by policies and plans of professional associations; by studies of higher education and the reports of these studies, many of which contain radical recommendations; and by programs of graduate library schools in the United States (especially that of the University of Chicago) and abroad (especially those of Great Britain and Canada). Although there are many aspects of the model which seem only to describe current practice at one place or another, it is unlikely that there

---
*This article was written originally as a speech and is here reprinted by permission from Special Libraries, December 1971.

is any existing program which contains every element and sub-element of the model. If such a program actually did exist, we would no longer be talking about a model, but rather the program itself.

This model for a master's degree program in library and information science consists of seven elements:

1. The statement of the mission and objectives of the school offering the program.
2. The policies, procedures and organization required to operate the program and improve it.
3. Admission requirements.
4. Degree requirements.
5. Means of obtaining competence and evidence of competence.
6. Areas of competence which the degree certifies.
7. Articulation of the degree with formal and informal continuing education programs.

It could be argued that the first two elements are related and supportive rather than actual parts of a degree program, and that they are therefore inappropriate as elements of the model. Yet, a program which is not identified with the mission and objectives of the school which offers it can quickly become irrelevant and arcane. The same will happen to a program which is regarded as separate from the organization, policies and procedures needed to make it operate and improve.

It could also be argued that continuing education is something which follows a master's degree program and is therefore inappropriate as an element of the model. However, it is felt that the master's degree is simply a stage of formal education and really the first part of professional education which must be a continuing process. Further, the master's degree program should provide the focus for two kinds of continuing education programs of library schools: 1) those leading to additional certificates and degrees, and 2) those which simply stimulate mutually beneficial interaction between schools and practitioners.

1) The Mission of the School

Most universities have passed from line budgeting through performance budgeting and have arrived at relating

Communication and Education

planning to budgeting with continuous review and evaluation. At first it seemed difficult to apply PPB to academic situations because the concept was devised for single mission-oriented programs, and once the mission was accomplished the program was finished. Universities are multi-program institutions and most of their programs are open-ended; that is, their missions are really never accomplished. In a library school, instead of setting out to prepare a given number of persons to enter professional practice, our mission has been continuously to prepare such persons for a profession which has changing requirements. It turns out, after all, that neither universities nor library schools can escape defining their missions simply because they are open-ended. The model calls for definition of the library school's mission under several headings:

--To study manpower needs, locally and nationally, in order to determine the kinds of competence needed by professional practitioners, research-teaching personnel, and specialists in libraries, information centers, the information and communication industries, bibliographical enterprises, and training or educational institutions. The school must determine the type, quality, and level or intensity of training required to equip its graduates for effective contributions at the present time, but more importantly, also for predictable changes in our society.

--To recruit, select, and train (i.e., offer the necessary programs of instruction leading to appropriate degrees and certificates) persons to fill the general and specialized manpower needs of the agencies mentioned above. Graduates must have skills in management, research and teaching; and also general professional competence as well as some specialized professional or subject-oriented competence.

--Through research, to contribute to the solution of problems encountered in librarianship, bibliography and information science; through state-of-the-art studies, to provide fresh interpretations or determine areas currently in need of study; and through far-ranging inquiry, to discover new knowledge or new insights and report them in the professional and scholarly literature.

--To provide the opportunity and facilities for continuing education of practicing librarians, bibliographers, and information scientists.

--Through direct participation on the part of its faculty, staff and students, to advise and assist in established, innovative, and experimental programs--local, regional, national, international--which directly or indirectly are related to the information needs of people at all age levels in various social and institutional environments.

--To review and evaluate this mission and measure and analyze the performance of programs established to accomplish it.

A school must also list all of its programs, preferably as a part of the statement of the school's mission, to ensure that each program is directly related to the mission and to show relationships among programs. At UCLA, for example, we have identified five programs of instruction and research which depend almost entirely upon university funding through the school's budget. We have identified five additional programs which depend upon university funding only for stimulation, administration and use of facilities. Extramural grants and paid fees or sales determine the limits of some of these programs; others depend heavily upon volunteered time of the school's staff and of interested practitioners.

2) Written and Codified Policies and Procedures

The model cannot specify policies and procedures because they must vary with the mission of the school and the legislation of the parent institution. My own school, for example, has prepared over 50 formal statements of policy and procedures; several of them have undergone many revisions.

It is in the policies and procedures that one should be able to discover how a school accomplishes or assures certain requirements important to a master's degree program, even though not specified in it. Here are some examples. How does the school attempt to recruit students with a variety of ethnic, cultural, and economic backgrounds? How does the school guarantee the participation of students and staff members in basic decisions such as staffing, academic programs, courses, etc. ? What are the guidelines for evaluating student performance? How does the school provide for evaluation of teaching effectiveness and course quality by students as well as by faculty members and the support and administrative staff? How are the civil rights and academic freedom of staff members and students protected? What machinery is provided for due process and appeal? What evidence is there that the school is making maximum use of up-to-date teaching techniques, of multimedia instructional materials, and of equipment and facilities to promote a stimulating and effective learning environment? How does the school guarantee compliance with its own regulations and those of the university?

Modern society demands responsible administration and management, complete disclosure of activities, protection of individual privacy and civil liberties, and full accountability. A model for professional education cannot disregard these demands.

3) Admission Requirements

Admission requirements are not new. Library schools have always had them, but the model makes clear certain aspects which are frequently obscured.

--A person applied for <u>admission to a program</u>, offered by the school, not merely to student membership in the school. Each program must have objectives, and the program must lead either to a degree or certificate or not. Admission requirements must not be artificial or arbitrary; they must either be directly and demonstrably related to the program, or to the limitation in number of students for which the school has resources and facilities.

--Admission requirements must be enumerated and explained clearly, quantitatively when appropriate. This is essential for the potential applicant to prepare himself to qualify for admission, or to enable him to make a self-evaluation which will determine whether or not he should apply.

--Admission requirements should not be changed capriciously, and they should not be changed without public notice. The effective date of changes must be reasonably set, usually a year following announcement, so that potential applicants are allowed a realistic amount of time to make adjustments in their preparation for admission.

--It must be made clear that admission requirements collectively reflect a standard for admission and that there is a possibility of waivers, adjustments, modifications, weighting, and consideration of qualifications not specifically enumerated.

Formulation of admission requirements is more difficult than it may appear. Universities have broad, minimum admission requirements which all departments, schools and colleges within them must honor. In addition, the university expects each school to determine specific additional admission requirements which must be academically justified, realistically related to programs, and which take into consideration the just claims or demands of minority groups or disadvantaged persons for access to professional training. Practicing librarians occasionally give advice to schools on admission requirements. Sometimes these cannot be legally applied; sometimes they conflict with general standards established by a university.

Most schools have not attained model status in the matter of admission requirements. Some schools announce admission requirements, but are very lax in applying them in order to fill quotas or sub-quotas of students. At the other extreme, schools are sometimes said to be so rigid in the formulation of requirements and in applying them that they deny access to persons of great professional promise. Occasionally there may be injustice, or cowardice, in the enforcement of requirements--as when an applicant is told his GRE score is too low, or that the quota is filled, when in reality the admissions officer may have misgivings about the emotional stability of the applicant, or may employ personal prejudices.

4) The Degree Requirements

So far as I am aware, the master's degree requirements of universities are reasonable, albeit somewhat formal, and present no real difficulties. They usually include: 1) Minimum and maximum length of residence in the university; 2) Minimum number of courses, and specified level of courses; 3) Scholarship standing, i.e., minimum grade point average. Fortunately, there is a growing liberalization, even at the graduate level, in the assignment of pass-fail grades rather than A, B, C letter grades or numerical grades; 4) Formal filing of a thesis or research paper, or of a comprehensive examination, or both; 5) A petition for advancement to candidacy for the degree or certificate.

Universities leave to schools and departments the determination of additional degree requirements, applicable to the specific needs of the discipline or profession for which the degrees provide initial preparation. It is here that the model departs from common practice. In the model, the additional requirements for the master's degree in library and information science are:

--Evidence of competence in specified areas, i.e., the model specifies seven competencies which are necessary for all practitioners in librarianship, bibliography, and information science. The important departure from previous practice is that <u>competencies</u>, not courses, are required for the degree. Roy Stokes (1), a penetrating observer, gave us a brilliant metaphor when he goaded us about the trading stamp mentality which has pervaded American higher education. We, I hope, no longer expect a graduate student merely to accumulate semester or quarter units and grade points as though they were stamps, with the objective of filling his book so that he may go to the redemption center-- the registrar's office--and turn it in for a degree.

Beyond minimum competence in all seven specified areas, a higher level of competence in certain areas is also required, the areas of higher competence depending upon the student's field of specialization. The seven areas of competence are listed in the sixth element of the model.

--The second degree requirement is evidence of specialization in a field within, or closely related to, librarianship, bibliography, or information science. The specialization may be developed almost entirely within the program and courses offered by the library school, but the specialization might be based upon study in cognate academic disciplines or professions. When the specialization is based upon cognate disciplines, its relevance to librarianship, bibliography or information science must be evident in the thesis or brought out by comprehensive examination if a research paper is submitted in lieu of a formal thesis.

Normally, evidence of satisfactory preparation for specialization will be an academic year of post-baccalaureate study in addition to the academic year normally needed to acquire the seven basic competencies. However, experience and/or study in some other discipline or some other university or place may provide a part or all of the specialized preparation. The library school may, when it deems it necessary, require formal testing to prove that experience is actually equivalent in knowledge base to academic study.

--The third degree requirement is a thesis <u>or</u> research paper. If a student has already written a formal thesis or dissertation to fulfill the requirements of an earlier degree he should elect to present his research in format acceptable in the open literature or by a clearinghouse. It is expensive and time consuming to appoint a faculty committee to direct a student's research when a committee is not needed. It is also wasteful to insist upon formal thesis format, spelling out in detail the research methodology, when a student has otherwise proved his research understanding by having already written a thesis or dissertation.

The subject of the thesis or research paper must lie in the student's field of specialization; and if the paper does not directly prove an understanding of the theories, principles and methodology of modern research, there should be a comprehensive examination to prove that understanding and the relationship of the research paper to the broad concerns of librarianship, bibliography, and information science. The research paper or thesis must be of sufficient importance and substance to justify immediate dissemination through publication or deposit in an information clearinghouse which will furnish copies upon request.

--The final degree requirement is the completion of a summary record of competence, a curriculum vitae, and a summary record of performance in the school. These records, compiled by the student and by his faculty program advisor, are prepared for deposit in the student's permanent file.

5) Explanation of What Is Meant by Competence

Competence is acquired through: 1) an understanding of the theory and/or principles underlying a defined area of knowledge, technology, or practice; 2) a familiarity with the literature of a defined area; and 3) demonstrated ability in using the techniques, tools, and methods for effective performance in a defined activity or operation.

Some of the <u>means</u> of obtaining competence and examples of <u>evidence</u> of competence are:

--Formal, organized course work or a program of study. <u>Evidence</u>: transcripts, course grades, scores on examinations, written performance evaluations, papers submitted to fulfill requirements of a course or a program of study.

--Independent study. <u>Evidence</u>: special written or oral examinations, publications, reports.

--Directed individual study. <u>Evidence</u>: written or oral examinations and/or evaluation by the person who directed the study. Most library schools have courses designed to provide directed individual study.

--Working experience. <u>Evidence</u>: written evaluation of the nature of the work and of the performance of the individual doing the work, prepared by the person supervising the work. Self-evaluation is acceptable evidence also, supported by a written or oral examination.

--Internship. <u>Evidence</u>: written description of the program and evaluation of performance in it.

Two points are worth emphasizing in connection with this element of the model. First, it is recognized that competence may be acquired in a variety of ways, both before and after admission to the master's degree program, and in locations other than the library school and its university. Second, it permits--hopefully, even encourages-- transferring part of professional education to libraries or other information agencies, and it will involve practicing librarians in the teaching program. Of the means of imparting competence, internship seems to be one of the most effective and the one in which librarians can be most fully involved in teaching. However, good internships will be difficult to establish because the library providing the facilities for the intern should be paid for its time and effort, and the intern should receive a stipend.

6) Areas of Competence Required for Master's Degree

Here again, the model departs drastically from recent practice, even though schools for several years have been reducing the number of courses specifically required for degrees. Requiring competencies rather than courses also calls upon practitioners to accept new responsibilities in professional education; it even invites them to participate directly in determining degree requirements. This element is related to continuing education which should lead both to and from the school. Practitioners will renew and update their competencies, and in so doing they will renew and update the programs of their professional schools.

The matter of requiring competencies for degrees relates to both accreditation and certification. It is probably necessary in the early stages of a certification program to rely heavily upon two devices: 1) provision of a grandfather clause to certify experienced practitioners who lack paper qualifications, and 2) blanket acceptance of degrees or courses within accredited programs as evidence of qualification for certification. However, if a certification program stops here there will be endless bickering about what courses should and should not be offered in professional schools. At this level, a certification program is quite unrealistic because it implies that one can acquire competence only through degrees, courses, workshops, institutes, etc. It is the old trading stamp mentality again--in the profession rather than in the university. It also, at this level, makes continuing education an option rather than a requirement. Lifelong certification makes no more sense, and is no more in the public interest, than drivers' licenses without expiration dates. One should not be certified or licensed to practice in any profession without periodically proving that he has maintained his competence. Also, certification at this level is something of a "cop-out" because it means that the certifying body and the practitioners for whom it acts have not answered the most important question of all: <u>Exactly what kinds of competence are necessary</u> (and required to protect the public), <u>for successful professional practice in the field of librarianship being certified?</u>

When the profession and the various segments of it are able to tell the professional schools exactly what competencies are needed, the schools will either be able to respond properly, or be compelled to announce that they cannot respond.

Lacking clear definition of required competencies by the profession, the model must rely upon a combination of existing practice and critical comments about the practice which has appeared in the professional literature. The model lists seven areas of competence which the master's degree in library and information science should certify. It will probably be difficult to reach agreement on the list. At UCLA it has taken us over a year to construct a list, and we are not satisfied with it. However, this element is the most important in the model.

The seven areas of required competence are:

1. Foreign languages, mathematics or statistics, and computer programming. Library schools can hardly be expected to teach these competencies. Students should have acquired the minimum competence before entering the program. Higher levels of competence can, of course, be acquired during the program through courses in other departments of the university or through the other means of acquiring competence explained in the fifth element of the model.

2. The philosophy and major problems of librarianship; the roles of librarians, bibliographers and information scientists in society; the social value and educational relevance of libraries, information, and communication systems.

3. Evaluation, selection, and acquisition of materials for libraries and other agencies which provide texts (manuscript, printed, sound recorded, etc.), documents (books, serials, microforms, maps, prints, and other media of recording), and information services for education, research, recreation, and cultural enrichment.

4. Identification, description, information analysis, and bibliographical control (e.g., listing, locating copies, etc.) of documents which record human knowledge (including, but not limited to, printed or written texts).

5. Information resources and services; dissemination of information.

6. Government, organization, administration and management related to libraries and other information agencies; contemporary theory and practice in the use and development of human resources within organizations.

7. The nature and importance of skills which are essential for performance at the professional level by librarians, bibliographers, and information scientists--specifically: a) Theories, principles and methodology of research. (It is a requirement of performance at the professional level to be able to identify problems, investigate them, propose solutions, test the proposed solutions, and communicate findings.) b) Theories, principles, and methodologies of

teaching, supervision, and performance evaluation. (It is a requirement of performance at the professional level to be able to teach others to use libraries, locate and evaluate information, enter and use information systems, etc. and to recruit, train, supervise and evaluate the performance of assistants.) c) Applicability of systems analysis and design, quantification (measurement, costing, etc.), and mechanization or automation in the solution of problems of management, communication and information retrieval.

7) Master's Degree Relates to Continuing Education

In January 1971 The Carnegie Commission on Higher Education published a special report, Less Time, More Options: Education Beyond the High School (2). One of the major themes of the report is stated this way: "Opportunities for higher education and the degrees it affords should be available to persons throughout their lifetimes and not just immediately after high school." Another theme: "Society would gain if work and study were mixed throughout a lifetime, thus reducing the sense of sharply compartmentalized roles of isolated students v. workers and of youth v. isolated age."

A major recommendation of the Report is that a degree or other form of credit be made available to students at least every two years in their careers, and in some cases every year. At each of these points there would be three options: 1) terminate formal higher education, 2) continue formal higher education to the next certificate or degree point, or 3) stopout--not dropout--for a period of time to gain work experience. The Report suggests that the master's degree should represent two years of study after the bachelor's degree.

The master's degree in library and information science represents the threshold of continuing education. At this point the student may enter professional practice and terminate formal higher education; he might continue without interruption to a certificate of specialization or a doctorate; or he might enter professional practice and later return for further formal higher education.

Library schools have failed to be satisfactorily responsive to the demands for more continuing education programs because they usually lack the funds, personnel and other resources to provide the service. But perhaps both the schools and practitioners have taken too limited a view of what continuing education is, or can be. There are ways other than summer sessions and institutes.

The Carnegie <u>Report</u> just mentioned, and others such as <u>A First Report of the Assembly on University Goals and Governance</u> (3) sponsored by The American Academy of Arts and Sciences (also published in January 1971), provide strong indications that universities are becoming, or are planning to become, more involved in open or extended programs which will bring universities into working relationships with the communities and professions they serve. There will be a change in the age levels of entrance, exit, and re-entrance into and out of the university. The result will be a student body mix of younger and older persons, of beginners and experienced practitioners, and of persons with a great variety of backgrounds. This association of differences will greatly enhance the learning process.

Actually, much of this is already happening in librarianship. More and more students are acquiring some competence in libraries, where librarians are the professors. There is some, but there should be greater, use of librarians as part-time or temporary faculty members in the schools. It is less common, but it should become more common for full-time library school faculty members to be granted leaves of absence to return to practice in order to update or extend their professional experience. This also suggests the possibility of exchanges--and I know of none in the United States--between libraries and library schools whereby a librarian and a professor might be exchanged for a year. Any faculty member who has tried it, and been conscientious about it, knows that getting back on the firing line of professional practice is bound to increase his competence which is, after all, what continuing education is about. Professors need continuing education also. Any librarian who has tried it, and been conscientious about it, also knows that preparing and teaching a course for presentation to an intelligent and critical group of students is bound to increase his competence and be a very real exposure to continuing education.

At UCLA we have learned that having one or two librarians in a course or discussion section greatly enlivens it, adds a dimension of reality to discussion, and forces us to relate theory to practice. Perhaps all library school courses should be open concurrently as extension courses in which any qualified practicing librarian might enroll upon payment of a reasonable fee. Conversely, perhaps all organized extension and summer session courses--our traditional devices for continuing education--should be open to students who are degree candidates. The mix of student and practitioner should also appear in institutes, workshops, conferences, special lectures, meetings of faculties, meetings of professional associations.

Conclusion

This model has been developed for the purpose of assisting decision making on professional education for the 1970's and even the 1980's. Any school which adopts it, or some modification of it, for its plan and then begins to implement the plan will probably encounter unanticipated problems or unexpected reactions by students, alumni, practitioners, academic senates, and university administrators. However, if professional associations are able to make decisions about competencies needed and to consider real certification programs, the decisions the schools must make will be better ones and the problems of improving professional education will be greatly simplified.

References

1. Roy B. Stokes. "Trading Stamp Mentality: From Across the Atlantic, a Critical View of American Library Education." Library Journal 92: p. 3595-3600 (Oct. 15, 1967).
2. The Carnegie Commission on Higher Education. Less Time, More Options: Education Beyond the High School. New York, McGraw-Hill, 1971. 8,45p.
3. The Assembly on University Goals and Governance. A First Report. The American Academy of Arts and Sciences, 1971. 51p.

NEW TRENDS IN HIGHER EDUCATION:
THE IMPACT ON THE UNIVERSITY LIBRARY*

Richard W. Lyman

Doubtless there once was a time in which it was logical to look to a college president for prophecies, at least as far as the future of higher learning and its supporting institutions was concerned. The college or university president had time to think, a suitable vantage point from which to see the world of learning, and a well-stocked and, more important, well-perused library of relevant books and essays.

Habits linger long after the conditions that gave rise to them have disappeared. Nowadays the president's time to think is likely to consist of little more than the hours spent on airplanes (and even that will presumably be eroded once telephones are installed in jets), plus the hours provided by insomnia. His "suitable vantage point from which to see the world of learning" is all too much of the time the academic equivalent of a foxhole, and as for his well-stocked and well-perused library he hasn't time to stock it, much less peruse it. Why should anyone expect wisdom, still less perceptive prophecy, out of a person so beset? Yet you were so incautious as to invite me, and I so rash as to accept. Indeed, I could hardly do otherwise, since I firmly believe that the library is the heart of the university, that a healthy university cannot be without a healthy library-- and that not enough university presidents fully and adequately recognize these facts. So here I am.

What can the leaders of research libraries expect as a result of changes in the world of higher education during this decade? Will new groups of library users emerge while

---

*Originally a paper presented at the 78th meeting of the Association of Research Libraries, May 1971, and here reprinted by permission of the American Library Association from College & Research Libraries, July 1972.

others fade from view? What will be the library-related content of higher education, and will it alter in nature or total dimensions? How will society's shifting patterns of life-styles and objectives affect the research libraries? These are the kinds of casual queries put to me by your Program Committee, a group that certainly knows how to seek blood from a turnip. Fortunately, they did not ask me about the effects of technological advances, such as the microfiche revolution, upon higher education. Of the arguments over how soon and how completely these changes will in fact take place, I can only plead ignorance and quote from Richard Brinsley Sheridan's play, The Rivals:

> The quarrel is a very pretty quarrel as it stands; we should only spoil it by trying to explain it.

First, then, the matter of student population. While we are going to arrive at a much-advertised plateau, or even slip into a decline, with respect to the college-age population during the early 1980s, estimates of the U.S. Department of Education call for an increase meanwhile in the number of degree credit students at all levels from the 7 million of 1968 to 10.3 million by 1978.[1] The percentage increases at all levels and of both sexes are expected to be smaller than in the previous decade, but that is scant comfort when one looks at the absolute numbers. In persons filing through the library turnstiles or lining up at the checkout counter with books under their arms, the trend is still dramatically upward.

There are voices to be heard questioning such estimates, and asking whether Americans haven't been oversold on the importance of a college education, and whether we aren't even now trying to send to college many persons who would profit more from vocational training, or immediate immersion in the job market.

I doubt that these voices will prevail. We Americans already have demonstrated a capacity for stretching the concept of a college education to include practically every form of skill or knowledge known to man (and perhaps a few that might better have been left unknown). Our ingenuity in this regard seems unlikely to flag. The growth of the community colleges suggests continuing adaptability, although opinions are mixed as to the success of these ventures in meeting the actual needs of their students.

I happen to believe that some of our difficulties derive from our rather undiscriminating notions of what constitutes "higher education"; people's expectations go unfulfilled because of them, and the tendency to reduce the whole thing to a matter of preparing for participation in the economic life of the nation has made us vulnerable to charges of Philistinism--even though some of those making the charge most energetically are themselves Philistines of a rather blatant sort. But the tendency to regard "a college education" as everyone's birthright will grow inexorably, in my opinion.

In all likelihood the educational "stretch-out," whereby even the Ph. D. does not constitute the end of the line and postdoctoral work grows apace, will continue. It may be-- one must devoutly hope that it will be--the case that the prospect of still more years of preparation before a person can be considered ready to operate as a fully prepared professional will exert additional pressure upon the contemporary doctorate degree, to shorten its duration and lighten its burdens. Too many doctoral dissertations are still attempts to climb Mt. Everest, when skills that could be acquired by a brisk walk in the foothills are all that the toiler will ever need later in life. Too many dissertation directors feel such a sense of personal identification, not so much with the student as with the student's finished work, that they delay unduly the completion of the doctoral exercise while seeking perfection in the doctoral product.

Yet the total impact of all these shifts inevitably is going to be greater and more diversified demands upon research libraries. You are going to have to provide a greater diversity of services, both because they become technologically possible and because your users are going to be more and more diverse--as to age and ethnic, economic and social background. I believe it is not merely a fashionable cliché to suggest that there will be marked increases in the numbers of people dropping in and out and back into institutions of higher learning. All the signs point that way. "Future shock" cannot be contained otherwise. People's skills will become obsolete and will need refurbishing or replacement. And the increases in leisure time, for practically everybody except research library directors and university presidents, will give people both the opportunity and the motive to return to the classroom. Further, the drive for women's rights will continue to exert pressure on all institutions, including those once resistant to all thought of part-time study or over-age students.

The relationships between burgeoning state and community colleges and research libraries have yet to be worked out; we all talk about interinstitutional cooperation but its growth is halting and sporadic. The pressure of an increased and diversified student population will make still more imperative the attainment of significant progress along these lines. If progress is made towards something approaching the British "Open University" the major research libraries will have to play their part, too. The combination of these pressures should (to use a hospital analogy) increase the load upon the library's outpatient clinics, as compared to its inpatient wards. The silver lining may conceivably be a greater awareness on the part of the public and the keepers of the public purse that a great research library is not just a piece of a university, but a community asset in its own right, and therefore worthy of community support.

But now I'm poaching in the game preserves of Roman Numerals II and III on your program, the Governmental and Fiscal Environments. Back to the users.

What will all these people be doing in college or the university? How will changes in what they are studying and how they study it affect the libraries? Here again, what I have to offer is largely conventional wisdom. The loosening of the bonds, once provided by curriculum requirements and by compulsory reading assignments within courses, will doubtless continue, at least for a time and in most institutions. I do detect the beginnings of some backlash already, however. At Hampshire College in Massachusetts, while conventional course requirements and majors are eschewed, there is an emphasis on the need for curricular structure and a degree of diversification from each student that seems to me significant. I doubt if most students really want to be quite as free from requirements, and therefore guidance, as their rhetoric would cause one to imagine--or as the ablest and most independent-minded of them in fact are.

Still, there will be many, many more flowers growing in the catalog garden; that seems assured. The magic phrase, "interdisciplinary course," has not lost any of its appeal. Indeed, linked as it now is to the belief that subjects hitherto kept apart must be joined together in order to enable us to deal with the problems of our complex world, the password, "interdisciplinary," seems destined for still greater things. To some extent this is bound to feed the publishing trade with new categories of titles, although this is perhaps less likely to affect research libraries than the paperback textbook industry. More important for our purposes, the growth of new combinations of subject matter within courses will connect with the tendency to value independent study, and the research libraries can expect a greater usage from students now veering from the Reserve Book Room to the stacks, and a greater need for cross-referencing, both in bibliographic tools and by skilled reference librarians.

Even without the thrust towards interdisciplinary work, the familiar "knowledge explosion" has been raising the costs of bibliographies, indexes and abstracts to dizzy heights, as you all know. Mr. Ellsworth has said that the University of Colorado library now spends more on these items each year than its total acquisition budget fifteen years ago.[2] And with a greater number of students, possessing a greater variety of backgrounds and of preparedness to use sophisticated research tools, no doubt the costs of staffing will continue to increase, so as to make available to the student the help he needs in making effective use of these bibliographic aids.

It is a commonplace also that greatly increased burdens fall upon the library because of the need to reach beyond the confines of Europe and North America in acquiring research materials. Keeping track of publications of all kinds in portions of the world where neither the publishing industry nor the bibliographic skills and services are well organized becomes terribly difficult. I see little likelihood that such pressures will decrease. We may or may not find ourselves tending towards some form of "neoisolationism" following our withdrawal from Southeast Asia--as Mr. Nixon says he fears will be the case. But I doubt that such shifts in the emphasis of public concerns will do much to diminish the scholarly interest in all parts of the world that gives rise to these acquisitions burdens. Proverbially, new academic areas are hard to shut down once they have been opened up. As the late dean of Yale College, Bill Devane, once observed: "The trouble with experiments in higher education is that they never fail." We had little or no scholarly competence in the Southeast Asian area before our disastrous political and military involvement there; we have little enough even now. But what we have we'll probably try to hold, and only the sheer rigors of budgetary shortage are likely to make any of us give up.

Since such rigors are having some effect, however, it might be worthwhile to utter a warning note here. If so-called "exotic" programs are eliminated because they are very expensive, and not least so in respect to their library costs, and if the job is done on an individual basis, each institution thinking only of its own programs and assuming that no one else is contemplating cutting back in the same area of study, the results will be very bad. The same pressures will tend to produce the same results everywhere if there is no effective coordination among institutions. We all agree that there should be greater efforts toward coordination in the building of specialized research collections to avoid expensive overlapping and duplication; I'm now suggesting that there must also be coordination in the dismantling of collections. If Siwash University decides that Balinese studies are too rich for its blood, it had better get in touch with others in the field to make sure that Balinese studies do not simultaneously disappear everywhere in the country. Cooperation in trimming programs could also dovetail with cooperation in building them; the now-to-be-unused publications that comprise Siwash's Balinese collection should go over to Alligator State, whose decision has been to keep its Balinese studies program going, but to cut out Samoan studies, which are being continued at Siwash. And so on.

Much is being said about the need for changes in postgraduate education. If the number of doctoral programs no longer requiring a full-dress dissertation should really increase, one assumes that there would be some lessening of the pressures upon research libraries. But here, as in other matters, it becomes very difficult to distinguish between lip service to a fashionable ideal, and genuine commitment to change. As one of our most experienced college-watchers, Professor Lewis Mayhew, puts it: "There are probably good reasons to wish for a change, but in spite of the fact that 111 institutions (in his 1968-9 survey) predict a new teaching doctorate (by 1980), visits to university campuses do not reveal widespread, active interest."[3] He also notes that despite conflicting opinions as to the need for Ph.D.'s in the coming decade, projects abound for new programs, and not least in those fields most closely dependent upon library resources, the humanities and social behavioral sciences. How the country will respond to the alleged oversupply of Ph.D.'s is perhaps more a function of political attitudes and the resultant availability or unavailability of money than it is of scholarly or institutional

choices and ambitions. Depressingly, there are only a few
signs of progress towards recognition of the fact that no
society can support a full-fledged university at every cross-
roads, nor even a first rate full-fledged university in every
state. State colleges still press for the right to give advanced degrees; universities-in-name-only still strive to
become universities-in-fact. Perhaps we shall see, during
the next decade, a greater readiness to 'see merit in a consciously intended and cheerfully accepted diversity of post-
secondary educational institutions. Certainly we must hope
so, for otherwise we are likely to see more of the tragic
and ironic situation in which universities such as Harvard,
Stanford and Princeton reduce their graduate programs,
while other institutions forge ahead to create new programs
despite their lack of research facilities, such as libraries
strong enough to support high quality work. As a result,
the libraries at Harvard, Stanford, and Princeton will not
feel any significant reduction of burdens, while new and impossible ones will be placed on the shoulders of library directors elsewhere.

Let me now turn to what one might term the personal
and institutional conditions of life, as they are likely to affect research libraries. Presumably the winds of freedom
will continue to blow in a bewildering number of directions.
More students will elect to live like other citizens, scattered
through the surrounding community, rather than in dormi-
tories close to the library doors. More will take part-time
work at all levels, while holding a job or raising a family.
It is probable that research institutes and "think tanks" not
closely connected with any university will proliferate. Indeed, if the campuses continue to be so frequently disrupted,
a great deal of research presently being done in universities
may move to less threatened quarters. That will be a tragedy, in my view, for it will leave undergraduates with fewer
opportunities to learn what research really is (and unlearn
some of the popular myths about it), while leaving university
research libraries in a most anomalous position, bereft of
many of their regular users, but called upon to work out
cooperative arrangements from afar with burgeoning institutional users outside the university. Again, although the pattern of use may alter significantly, the burdens of providing
service seem likely only to grow, never to decline.

Furthermore it is perhaps worth noting that there
are still some fields--one thinks of law immediately--where
the dominant research orientation of the post-World War II

university is only now beginning to take hold. I think you
will see the best law schools moving simultaneously towards
practical work experiences for their students, and the promotion of more serious advanced research for both students
and faculty. Not satisfied with having changed the LL. B. to
a J. D. degree, the law schools can be expected to encourage
postgraduate work to a significantly greater extent--again,
providing only that funding can be found. And if the current
crush to gain admission to our law schools continues, and
if the current preoccupation on all sides with the enormous
needs of our society for trained legal minds persists, even
the funding problem may be solved, or at least ameliorated--
no doubt to the traumatized surprise of law deans and law
librarians who have become accustomed to straitened circumstances while all around them were waxing fat on federal appropriations and foundation largesse.

Against this must be set the perceptible decline in
the prestige of research among many younger scholars in
the humanities. Even if the teaching doctorate does not
materialize to a significant extent, it may well be that the
amount and kind of research which graduate students and
younger faculty are willing to undertake will change, and in
ways that lighten somewhat the strains upon the libraries.
This is far too imponderable to judge as yet; one can only
note the prevalence of disillusionment with the research
mystique, and of attacks upon what the critics consider too
literal an attempt to apply to the humanities the styles and
traditions of research originally developed by the sciences.

It would be rash to conclude, however, that a diminished respect for traditional kinds of research will make the
research librarian's life any easier. For one thing there is
the demand for a whole host of nontraditional materials;
fewer students may wish to analyze the prosody of Ezra
Pound's *Cantos*, using editions of his works and of works
on prosody, but many more will want to listen to tapes or
recordings of the cantankerous old poet himself reading from
the *Cantos*. If, as seems likely, more people take seriously
the idea of lifelong education, and if, as seems very unlikely,
television finally begins to contribute to the cultural life of
the country in a way more worthy of its initial promise, thus
stimulating the appetites of the general public for knowledge,
the libraries will find themselves beset with cries for help
from many outside the universities, and will have to respond.

It may be well at this point to recognize another and

and downright disagreeable result that may come from changing life styles. Heaven knows that we have already seen instances of brutal disregard for the fragility of a great library, and for the rights of other users. Political protests have in several institutions included vandalism directed at the library, and especially at that precious key to its use, the catalog. At Stanford last (1970-71) year, several thousand catalog entry cards were removed, in many cases defaced or destroyed, as part of a campaign of harassment on behalf of a library employee who had been penalized for his part in a campus disruption. There have been cases of arson in libraries that chill any booklover's heart. And politics aside, the general incidence of theft and careless or outright destructive misuse has become serious cause for concern.

It would be bad enough if one could explain such developments by the fact that many persons are now coming into contact with great libraries for the first time, and are doing so with inadequate preparation to respect their value, or to measure the seriousness of damage done to the collections or the catalogs. Unfortunately, this is almost certainly not the cause of the trouble. Rather it is merely one more expression of that pervasive disrespect for cultural heritage and for the authority of established institutions that infects rich and poor alike, but as far as one can judge seems to take more virulent hold of the rich than of the poor. In all too many cases, the new barbarians do not even have the excuse of an inadequate upbringing.

Less dramatically, but still a problem for anyone trying to manage a library, the strong populist egalitarianism of our time, combined with a love of self-assertion, will make it ever harder to devise effective regulations, especially if the thrust of those regulations is in any way to give greater privileges to some users than to others. As the complexity of services and relationships increases, and likewise the variety of materials collected by libraries, the need to keep track of users might seem greater than ever. But the chances of successfully differentiating among users according to seriousness of need are surely in decline. How could it be otherwise, in a time when some faculty (fortunately not many, as yet) seem unwilling to assert even that they know any more than students, still less that they have any legitimate claims to special attention in the library or anywhere else?

Unhappily, the demand for equal treatment generally takes the form of equal immunity for all, rather than equal subjection to rational regulation for all.

But this paper was not intended to be a political polemic, and I would return to the more general topic with one sweepingly destructive observation. It seems to me that when all of the predicting and the extrapolation of trends is done, we are still left with the stark recognition that a few macro-events entirely outside the world of scholarship can and probably will make mockery of all efforts to peer ahead. Professor Mayhew reminds us how suddenly the assassination of Martin Luther King altered the situation with regard to the admission of disadvantaged minority students in all the major universities of the country.[4] Granted, trends were already visible, headed in the same direction; but nothing so dramatic by way of enrollment increases and program innovations would have taken place without this transforming tragedy.

Similarly, the fate of the great issues of our time, from war and peace to the possible invention of breathable air, can produce sudden wrenchings or profound alterations in the course of research libraries. Short of the coming of some new Dark Ages (and how one wishes that some people knew enough human history to recognize that as a distinct possibility!), one can be reasonably sure that the future of the libraries will be shaped by the one word, "more." More materials, more users, more services, more relationships to other agencies, more dependence on advanced technology, more need for managerial and diplomatic skills of a very high order--the list is endless. You must be brave people to occupy the positions you now hold; you are not likely to require less courage in the course of the coming decade.

References

1. Statistics of Trends in Education, National Center for Educational Statistics, U.S. Department of Health, Education and Welfare, 1970.
2. "ACLS Newsletter," 22 (January, 1971): 10.
3. Graduate & Professional Education, 1980: A Survey of Institutional Plans. New York: 1970, p. 29.
4. Mayhew, op. cit., "Introduction," p. ix.

THE SOBERING SEVENTIES:
PROSPECTS FOR CHANGE*

Ellsworth Mason

You may recall one of the great scenes in world literature, a shipwreck scene, in a most remarkable novel by Joseph Conrad. You will remember that the good ship <u>Narcissus</u> encounters in its voyage a tropical storm of everlasting fury, the kind of storm that could be invoked only by a former sea-captain who had felt typhoons in his very body. For two days the <u>Narcissus</u> is relentlessly pounded into a state of helplessness. The ship lies almost on its side. The crew, battered nearly into insensibility, hangs by rope lashed to its upper deck rails, waiting for the ship to slide under the waves, as seems inevitable. Lashed to the wheel and feeling with deep sensitivity the state of the ship, the captain senses an easement in the fury of the storm, and drives with his remarkable will the half-dead sailors to the nearly impossible task of raising a sail, and as the sail is raised with incredible labor, the ship groans and slowly begins to right itself.

For some time now, in a considerable range of librarianship I have noted people looking for all the world as if they, too, were lashed by rope to that upper deck rail waiting for the ship to go down, but I sense that the moment for righting the ship may be at hand, given the leadership and determination to do so. In Conrad's novel, the intimate feeling of the battering storm is equalled only by the profound thrill as the ship begins slowly to right itself.

Let us talk, first, about the meaning of the word "public" as used in the term "public library." In the minds of the populace, the distinction between public and private, once clear cut and sacred, is fast disappearing. Two

---
*Reprinted by permission from <u>Library Journal</u>, October 1, 1972, published by R. R. Bowker Co. (a Xerox company); copyright 1972 by the Xerox Corporation.

central reasons stand out among many. First, the need for
learning materials at all age levels and for a great variety
of reasons, is widespread, especially in urban areas. In
face of the size of the demand for them, the materials are
quite scarce. A good argument can be made for the fact
that, confronted by the potential demand for their use, the
great libraries of New York City are book-poor indeed, and
in terms of service, nearly nonexistent, although their collections are great, and their services tolerable in light of
the small fraction of their potential users that they actually
serve.

The second reason for the blurring of the public-private boundary is that nearly all private libraries now receive to some degree, and increasingly, public funds. On
Long Island, high school students in need of materials lacking in their own school libraries, leap into station wagons in
groups and make a safari from one library to another--they
don't care whether public or private--occasionally being
thrown out, of course, but persisting. Ever since I was a
pup in librarianship, we have been encouraging the reaching
out for books. Now that it's happening we're somewhat resentful of it all.

I therefore want to talk about public libraries, not in
terms of their funding (I don't care where they get their resources), but rather in terms of policy--those libraries dedicated to inclusion as a basis for defining their proper users,
or even outreaching, rather than exclusion, for whatever
good and acceptable reasons. The two most unique public
libraries I have ever known were both privately funded. One
was the Melvil Dui Hose and Library Company Library.

Melvil Dui (the name is, of course, disguised) struck
it really rich in gold mining, and sold out early in the century for seven million dollars. Today, this could hardly get
the doors of your library open, but before the rise of the
income tax, when you made seven million, you could stuff
it all in your pockets in two dollar bills and take every
nickle home. What is more, in those benighted days, for
a dollar you could buy four sporting ladies, ten quarts of
beer, or, if forced by poverty to forego sin, you could feed
a family of six on it for three days.

In the manner of the nouveau riche in all periods of
history, Melvil Dui set out to impress himself on the community by an act of public generosity, and like the nouveau

riche in all periods of history, knowing little about either
the public or about generosity, he followed the prevailing
fashion in such matters. In those days, there was less arson than there is hereabouts these days, but there was much
more wind; and conflagrations were common, often total
conflagrations. This condition gave rise to the Fire Hose
companies, which consisted of a group of 20 stalwart volunteer men (women's rightists take note), who would dash on
signal to their hose company building, to trundle fire hose
and hand pumping equipment on wheels to the scene of the
fire. Since wood frame houses burn fast in a wind, these
companies were numerous, and spread all over town. They
were high-spirited, highly competitive, and enjoyed great
social prestige at the time. Endowment of funds to supply
equipment, buildings, training, and a certain amount of
liquid fellowship to a hose company was considered a great
public good, and therefore began the Melvil Dui Hose Company, whose future direction was surely undreamed at the
time.

In the cruel and inevitable course of change, as people grew less enthusiastic about running, steam pumps replaced hand pumps, and horses proved stronger than men,
the importance of the old hose companies diminished. I am
sure that there must have been the usual indignant complaints
about the evils of automation, the faceless machine versus
stout-hearted men, and the importance of personal attention
and individual devotion in extinguishing fires. Nevertheless,
horse-trucks were followed in turn by motorized fire engines,
and the hose companies ceased. But the return on the endowment of the Melvil Dui Hose Company went right on
flowing in, much to the discomfiture of its trustees, who
were now bereft of Dui's guidance by his death. So they
proposed, through some wild humanistic impulse, to change
the original purpose of the company slightly by turning it
into a library.

When I say changed its original purpose "slightly,"
I recall my original visit to that library, many years later.
I had been working in a library a short distance away, but
had never heard of it because it had no means of getting
out to the public at all. The building, a small, sturdy,
square brick building whose library area was one floor, did
not even smell like a library. But within this tiny building,
the most radical experiments in library procedures since the
time of the Altamira cave drawings were in process.

These experiments consisted mostly in elimination. The organizational confusions inherent in large book collections had been solved by having a collection no larger than 3000 books, mostly worn and dirty paperbacks, shelved solidly on wooden shelves strewn around the room in a free-form arrangement, totally unimpeded by any classification system. This, in turn, eliminated the necessity of labels, and neatly avoided the pitfalls inherent in any technical processing at all. Obviously, under this system it is impossible to have a processing backlog. Acquisitions were further simplified by the fact that few books were bought.

In the floor space freed from what would have been a cumbersome card catalog case (had there been a catalog) was the solitary furniture in the room, one desk and one chair, and at this desk was located the entire library staff, which had also been simplified down to one very intense lady, well in her sixties, who had been appointed to this post by her predecessor. Obviously the governing system of this library had also been simplified. Salaries, too, had been nearly eliminated, since the librarian drew only a nominal salary from the endowment income, using the rest of it for heating and some minimum cleaning maintenance. The circulation procedures made automation unnecessary by the simple expedient of charging out books by handwritten notes, in pencil, on squares of brown paper, torn from kraft bags.

If there was ever a librarian's paradise, this happy little piece of laissez faire was it. No board of trustees to contend with, no one to give her orders, no stupid processing (indeed, no processes at all save writing out charges on brown paper slips and reshelving a few books), no worrying about outgrowing the building, no worrying about budget. That is to say, no worrying about budget so long as a small handful of money and the body of one little old lady sufficed the library as its total resources.

This weird library may not have been in the front of Thoreau's mind when he said: "Our life is flittered away by detail ... simplify, simplify," but it worked, because despite everything against it, this was in a very real sense a good library. It was located in an impoverished and troubled Latin-American minority neighborhood, and the kids were in and out constantly. That little lady knew every book in the place, and what is more, stocked books that these youngsters wanted to read. Her circulation was high, and she constantly scrounged the right kind of books to replace old ones and refresh her stock. She knew those youngsters backward and forward, what they could do and what was new to them and was able to keep them reading actively. This I take is the central purpose of any library.

The second distinctive private library encountered during my early years was run out of the bedroom of a retired male schoolteacher in Kansas, who noted the fact that, in the Rocky Mountains, there often are lightly-populated areas of three-thousand square miles without a library. In fact, one of the great untapped publics for reading books is the wheat country in Montana, where the farmers are reasonably leisured for seven months of the year, and subscribe to numberless magazines of dubious value to keep their minds occupied.

This schoolteacher took the initiative, and his own meagre lifetime savings, to buy a collection of about 500 books, mostly on western history, including some fiction, which he arranged to ship in footlockers to remote pinpoint centers in the Rockies--general stores, gas stations, Indian agencies--anywhere he could be assured of a potential reading public, for a period of six months to a year. He had a back-up collection in his home which he lent, on mail request, directly to the requester. His materials had become known throughout this vast country, and were considerably in demand.

Let me draw from these two libraries one of the simple truths that we have forgotten, that when any activity grows beyond the scope of a single person, it suffers. Whether it is a family, or a gas station, or a crap game or a library, only on this small a scale is it possible to provide fully human response, and even on this scale, it takes an unusual person to provide it well. Beyond the scope of a single person, which is where the whole world dwells these days, we begin the process of dehumanization, and the more we multiply the number of people through whom a process must work, the more dehumanized the response becomes.

Every evil that besets us these days, though we generally blame some other surface phenomenon, is caused in one way or other by multiplicity. During the War (World War II, to be precise) while I was a CB in the Central Pacific, the natives of the Gilbert Islands, who were remarkable people in many ways, knew our central difficulty. Though they liked the friendly, informal American GIs, they made no attempt to conceal the fact that they thought us amusing. "Americans too much," they would say frequently. "Too much men, too much clothes, too much jeeps, too much work. Too much." And here we are 25 years later hung up on all the too muches that one could think of. When people scream for greater humanization of everything, they should recognize how inevitably small the fund of humanity actually is in a society grown so big, too big to have a heart.

On the other hand, it is clear that we have not really begun to tap what is available. The public library is suffering all the ills of contemporary society--over-organized, over-crowded, inconvenient, directionless, unable to get rid of its trash. We tend to substitute organization for personal effort, to keep our chain of command straight rather than our humanity straight. We confuse Randtrievers and computers, and other machines, with libraries, which they are not. We confuse buildings with libraries. We confuse book collections with libraries, and even book collections are not libraries.

The best example of this fact is the central library of the New York Public (the Reference Division, as it is named), which contains one of the greatest book collections in the contemporary world and more than four million volumes of periodicals. It is, in fact, an international treasure hoard. But, with the best efforts of the staff, this treasure cannot begin to be mined because of its sheer size. A recent seven-month fellowship enabled me to study ten major academic research libraries to see how they were solving a range of problems into which Hofstra's library is rapidly emerging, and after seeing the imbalances caused in libraries by massive research collections, I am nearly at the point of thinking that they should be remote from the library.

But still I remember the director of a prominent urban public library stating to me his conviction that a public library had to build research collections to distinguish itself, though at the time I knew that his library contained a virtually complete collection of William Morris' great Kelmscott Press which was virtually unused.

Priorities, then. Aims. What is wrong with public

libraries, to the degree that they fail? They simply have the wrong books, which are kept in the wrong library locations, divided in complex ways that are difficult to understand, and with too little guidance through the maze.

A few years ago I wrote an article that called libraries "unnatural places and practices," and argued that to the majority of users libraries are maddeningly hard to use. Let's begin with the collections. Shortly after Sputnik was launched over our heads, I began to get the uncomfortable feeling that public librarians were teetering their noses at the public. There was deprecation of reading for pleasure, and much pride in the great increase in serious books in their collections for serious readers. I had always thought that a serious reader was one who read seriously, no matter what he read, but I got the feeling from such remarks that public librarians had begun to think that the public good was increased by one who read a book on the of Sputnik, but not by one who read a novel by Louis Auchincloss, who was guilty of writing best-sellers (and whom I am assiduously collecting).

This marvelous switch to every library becoming its own Ph.D. factory is still with us, and it is no wonder. We still haven't the slightest idea of what goes on in the mind in the learning process, and we still, in the academic world at all levels, are probing to find out how to make it happen. I grew up in a laborer's family, in a town that had no public library, and formed the habit of reading during one summer when I devoured pulp magazines--Romantic Western, Argosy--two or three a day. I simply couldn't get enough of Hopalong Cassidy, but there is evidence that I was not literarily maimed for life. I went on to take a Ph.D. in English literature at Yale, with my dissertation on James Joyce. My older daughter, who is now a good young scholar, waded in her time through every one of the Nancy Drew novels, which I am informed by teeter-nosed librarians is pretty inferior stuff, and they try not to stock it. Who in the world can tell at what age, or by what book, anyone is going to get hooked with an interest in anything under the sun?

The trouble with collections, then, is that they are selected by librarians, who construct a range of mechanical criteria that often have nothing to do with public needs, that is to say, the needs of each of the multifold, constantly changing publics, who are available, and largely untapped, as library users.

Take children's books, for instance. My two-year old son knew the minute he set eyes on the first one given him that Scarry is one of the greatest geniuses who ever wrote for children. I would have said that Scarry is lousy, but, you see, I'm an adult librarian. My son is a much better judge of his own reactions than I am. I consequently recommend that you get my son, or his counterpart, to help you select his level of children's books. Never mind those Newbery-Caldecott items, written and illustrated with half an eye to parents and the other half to graying librarian judges.

I think that you should have on your paid staffs, as aids in book selection, intelligent members of any definable segment of the public that you're interested in luring. Don't make them stick to the book reviews, or publishers' blurbs, or Publishers Weekly. Have them go wandering in stores, watch them and listen to them, and try to see what they see in their selections, and why they think it important. We know that blacks understand black thoughts and attitudes because of their common, unique experience. But if an influx of immigrants arrived from Kenya, even speaking English, American blacks would not do as their interpreters. Involve the blacks of your city, and not just black librarians, in selecting books that you hope will reach blacks. And use as your measure of success the intensity with which the materials are used, and not whether you think the frontal lobes of the brain are growing. The function of a library is to get people reading and to keep them coming back.

Some time ago, I heard a most delightful informal talk by two reporters for Newsday who were the guiding brains in generating the best selling novel written under the conglomerate pseudonym, Penelope Ashe. Their title was at first Stranger in the Valley, because "stranger" was a popular word in recent titles. It changed to Naked Is the Stranger to sex it up, and when one writer complained that it wasn't dirty enough, they called it Naked Came the Stranger. The manuscript was assembled from 12 different reporters who wrote one chapter apiece (one was written in two and a half hours), then was levelized and edited, and submitted to a publisher. When he accepted it for publication, the editors thought that they had to admit the hoax, and the publisher was delighted with the revelation. But when they asked him if he really liked it, he said that he hadn't read it. He never reads manuscripts submitted to him, he said, but hands them to his 12-year-old-son. If his son likes them, he publishes them.

Now let us come to buildings. The grand old public library buildings early in the century--the New York Public, the Boston Public, the Enoch Pratt--were carefully designed to elevate the soul. The grand staircase, the marble, the grand (if not great) paintings, the noble (if not distinguished) sculpture, all were to make you, the public library user, awesomely aware that you were holding culture, with a capital K, by the tail, and that it was wagging you. The ambition of these early libraries is illustrated in William Poole's aim, when the Newberry Library opened in 1893, to build a collection in 25 years of one million volumes, an unimaginable figure at a time when there was no library at all in the United States of research strength. Consequently, these libraries were built large, and stable to the point of near-indestructability. They, of course, were provided with very little illumination, since our ancestors seemed not to have needed any. And they were built on the edge of, or adjacent to parks, with relaxed space around them. They have now been freighted with books to the degree that a mass removal of the collection would require the entire Soviet army. They now are jammed in, and very far from dwellings, but there still is current the belief that the central public library of a city should be built on the busiest central traffic artery, that is to say, at the peak of city congestion.

Joyce describes the growth of the city of Dublin, in terms of human reproduction, in a lyrical passage of <u>Finnegans Wake</u>, a weird book that holds a central view that humanity, although lovable, is, and always has been, and always will be, more or less in a mess.

> Dear Dirty Dumpling, foostherfather of fingalls and dotthergills. Gammer and gaffer we're all their gangsters. Hadn't he seven dams to wive him? And every dam had her seven crutches. And every crutch had its seven hues. And each hue had a differing cry.

This is the history of your libraries. As cities expand, branches are flung out to keep pace with the direction of population growth. But the population keeps shifting in numbers, in composition, in education, in wealth. Nothing will stand still, except the library buildings, and these are rigid and largely unmovable. We are going to have to do away with the idea of a great, fixed-location central library, with large collections and reading rooms, and with fixed branches, and begin to think more of a central warehouse for the collection, a storage and issuing point, and fluidly moving, constantly changing, much smaller branch libraries, whose central function will be to get readers interested, and serve as substations for the central warehouse that will have become a pumping station.

There is nothing new about this idea, except perhaps the proposal that it become total. Most of you are aware of the remarkable job done by Len Freiser at the Central Board of Education Library in Toronto, supplying in photocopy materials needed by children in the school system, with no library collection at all. They hated him in the surrounding libraries, but loved him in the schools. The bookmobile, of course, has long been the totally fluid library unit used throughout the country, and the floating, battered sound trucks from the Brooklyn Public Library, setting up at likely points in the inner city, is the same kind of thing. But we ought to develop an infinite variety of sizes of units throughout the city.

We could begin by distributing in endless corners, in clearly recognizable crypts, Books in Print and the Subject Guide, with a phone to the nearest library service unit. The very first thing students see facing them, as they walk into our reference area is a set of Books in Print, and we get endless use of it there from people who have never heard of it. We need small substations, buildings to house one to four librarians, small enough to be moved on a truck and set down and picked up, as use dictated that they change location. We need buildings something like small branch libraries, prefabricated to fold up for easy removal, that could snap together in modules to vary their total size for different purposes. These would contain some books, but not permanent collections, packaged on shelving designed to be quickly packed and moved. Of course, the collection, drawn from the central warehouse, would change as often as different needs were detected at various facilities.

The emphasis in buildings should change from the idea of the importance of large units in limited numbers, except as warehouses and sub-warehouses, and toward the idea of multiple, movable, contact point units spread all over the city, and constantly changing. If Muhammed won't come to the library, we must bring the library to Muhammed.

Communication and Education

With this change will come changes in the nature of the service provided by the library system. To a great extent this will involve changes in the nature of the staff supplied <u>at the contact point</u> in the small units, where the prime emphasis should be on humanity, and congenial, obvious helpfulness, rather than on professional skills--on personality rather than intellect. If your hair raises at this, it ought to raise even more stiffly if you take a good look at what you now have and its future. I do not denigrate the highly professional and intellectually demanding skills necessary to probe a wide range of materials and library needs. But these will be located back at the ranch, in the larger storage libraries, which will be reached by the contact points once readers are hooked into action.

Service will involve infinite production of photocopied materials--the photocopier is the only revolutionary machine in the entire range of technology; everything else is a chimera. Service will involve an endless variety of means to get materials out to contact points quickly by bicycle, motorscooter, motorcycle, taxicab, bus, truck, subway, helicopter, or simple backpacks. The methods are infinite, the organizational demands intricate, but variety is the heart of the answer.

Service will involve a great range of book purchase on demand, for immediate processing and issuing. And let us talk about processing, which will now become part of the service system. It should be simple and as completely designed to be humanly acceptable as possible. I suggest that for a whole range of public libraries, the use of classification is already minimal, and its use will decline further under a system of central storage libraries with little access by the user. It has been completely useless for the bulk of the collection at the New York Public Library for a very long time. This sacred cow, I think, will succumb to common sense in the future, and classification will become a location symbol. Technical processes too will become humanized as time goes on.

So much for a brief view of some changes that I think are bound to occur in basic library operations; now for a consideration of one overriding present problem, and a foreview of what might come up in the future. The problem of serving minority groups is the public library's most pressing concern at present, and I want to look at that word "minority" for a minute, because it is one of the cliches that keeps getting us into trouble, by conditioning us to mono-vision where we should have multi-vision. "Minority," to most librarians, probably means blacks and Puerto Ricans (although, from watching them move I am convinced the Puerto Ricans will probably be our most quickly successful immigrant group since the Irish). However, minority groups shift rapidly. In Chicago at the turn of the century, according to Mr. Dooley, it was the Irish, who, in turn looked down on the Germans because they couldn't organize into power groups. Right now, throughout the country, minority groups vary enormously. In the southwest, the worst off are likely to be the Spanish-Americans; in the Rocky Mountains, the American Indians; in San Francisco, the Chinese; in Ithaca, New York (according to a scrawl on the wall), the Italians; in Salt Lake City, perhaps the Episcopalians.

But we really are not concerned about the fact that they are minorities. In New York, we have a small minority of Indian Sikhs, and no one worries about them because they are doing well. On the other hand, in Mississippi, blacks are not a minority. We are really concerned with opening up economic mobility, the safety valve that has allowed the United States to absorb an incredible range of people churned up by upheavals throughout the rest of the world, and has, within my lifetime, allowed the standard of living of the most massive group of workers in history to rise from the bare necessities or less to a shamefully indulgent level. We are really concerned with economically blocked groups, not minorities.

You must expect these to keep changing. You can gear up intensively for the blacks only to find suddenly that they have moved to suburbia, or somewhere else, and that you have entirely different groups with entirely different problems on your hands. And there are convection currents in social mobility. When I see unions in this area settling for a virtually guaranteed salary of $30,000 a year, I'm looking at the blue nouveau riche. On the other hand, my coevals (most of whom grew up poor) have spawned offspring who are hell-bent on getting down into the lower economic class as fast as possible. Believe me, they will make it, and we will have WASPS among the economically blocked groups.

We will undoubtedly have repeated surges of immigrants

fleeing pressures around the world that will tax the hardiest in the next half century, and they will probably flock to the cities and be public library patrons. Here again, flexibility, and the ability to fold the tents of one's programs and build new pavilions overnight will be required.

I should anticipate a large influx of people from Vietnam, Indonesia, and India as the Chinese overrun their borders, which they are bound to do sooner or later. We will get non-Moslems from African Mediterranea, where even now Christians, as well as Jews, are doing poorly. Whites will sooner or later be driven out of Middle and Southern Africa. From Latin America will come the starving with a wide spectrum of backgrounds. And in your lifetime, you are likely to see another bust in Russia that will produce another generation of emigres.

Indeed, looming above all the problems of our time is the great waving phallus of mankind, spouting semen like Mt. Aetna in eruption, or like the explosion of a hydrogen bomb. The great hordes of babies leaping from well-cared wombs, like spiders from an egg-sac, or like armed men from dragons' teeth, are likely to absorb most of the earnest attention of your lifetime.

We can expect, in addition, vast decentralization of everything, in demographic shifts that will involve institutions as well as populations. The large cities will shrink in size, while smaller cities throughout the country will grow larger--Cedar Rapids, Iowa; Lancaster, Pennsylvania, for example--and your loads will shift considerably. Industry will disconglomerate, and decentralize far more than at present. Large universities will grow smaller, smaller universities will grow larger, and new universities will be added. Giant libraries will be decentralized, or perhaps, recentralized, in great collection warehouses, while the active library service units themselves will be relatively small. The myths of economy of size, or the satisfactions derived from large unit experiences, have now exploded, as far as quality of result is concerned.

As our priorities shift, and they are shifting, albeit slowly, we will see a general decline in the prestige and importance of the world of technology, although certain socially beneficent technologies will thrive. Here I differ with Buckminster Fuller who would achieve Utopia by turning all of the work over to computers and redistributing all the resources. It has become clear that the claims for computers are enormously exaggerated, even for industry, and especially in applications to library operations. It is clear that our technological culture has produced the most inconvenient of all centuries, and has led to war, pollution, serious depletion of resources, and a trash problem that only a planned obsolescence economy could generate.

For some time there has been a slowdown in the flow of new talent into technology. For three years we have slowed scientific research to the extent that in a recent visit to one of our most prestigious universities, I found new Ph. Ds. in physics, chemistry, and electrical engineering having great difficulty finding jobs. As the consumer movement gains headway, and we choke tighter in our own debris, planned obsolescence will be sharply curtailed, together with its monster handmaiden, the communications industry, which is the really vicious poisoner of our entire culture. All of these factors will shift radically the public's focuses of interest, and will reemphasize the values to be found in the kinds of materials to be found in libraries.

As technology slows and we begin to pick up the enormous arrears of our unpaid debts, to nature, to life, to ourselves, our material standard of living will decline, but we surely can afford to cut off the useless fat from fathead ways of living and greatly benefit from slenderizing.

We can expect within the next ten years a decline in the general prestige of formal education as it becomes clear that it cannot perform the miracles we daily demand of it. With this decline will come a new realization of the possibilities in self-education, and an increase in the number of responsible adults seeking education by whatever avenues they can get it.

I think, in sum, that we have been suffering a national hangover from self-indulgence, and as we recover from it, we will become more humane, more satisfied, and less important on the international scene. We can have either our image or our humanity, but not both.

THE QUALITIES OF A BOOK, THE WANTS OF A DISSERTATION*

Robert Plant Armstrong

Between scholarly writers, especially new ones, and sensitive readers who demand specific qualities in the works they read, there often exists an abiding state of warfare. The reader is the aggressor and the new writer the enemy; the battleground is the editor's overcrowded desk, for the editor is the reader's ombudsman. The issue is the written page, involving clear differences of opinion concerning the level, the demeanour, and the forms of serious discourse. The discrete casus belli is the dissertation; and it is the chief object of this paper, in putting the issues forthrightly, to bring about the dissertation's defeat and achieve a creative discursive peace.

Pedantry has been scorned for centuries by those who, equally as serious as, if not indeed more serious than, the pedant, have ever been more humane in their work, seeking to relate the subjects of their investigations and the learned discourses which embody them to the affairs and the ends of man. In the past several generations, however, pedantry has ceased to be a subject for jest and has instead been hallowed by tradition and institutionalized. It is indeed the curse of much contemporary scholarship; but because it is a complex structure it is difficult to attack, even though it is comprised of carefully learned and utterly wretched attitudes. It has therefore flourished relatively undisturbed. Thus had pedantry been enabled to effect a qualitative jump, and instead of being a sportive vagary it has become a ponderous modus vivendi. That splendiferous emptiness men once rejected with derision, their descendants have mutated into a discursive anomaly they call the dissertation.

It is a regrettable irony--indeed even a tragic one--

---

*Reprinted by permission from Scholarly Publishing, January 1972. Copyright 1972 by the University of Toronto Press.

that the means by which a scholar in every real sense
<u>creates</u> himself as scholar is so little studied, so little
understood. Far from being simply "information transference," a book is a finite estate of being. To create such
a work requires both conviction and art. The art of writing
is perhaps the most important skill the scholar ought to acquire, and it ought to be the subject of faithful attention and
practice. But the student does not acquire it; he learns
instead the honoured forms of drab discourse, the arid
niceties of documentation, and the simple-headed regimens
of a proper bibliography. All that he might learn of a
really profound and meaningful kind about the nature of the
discourse whose exercise will be a large part of his life is
relegated to accident. As a result he fails to discover the
book as a viable and independent context for man.

    The book is, first of all, a humane work which the
writer intends to be taken seriously. That the book is humane means that its writer is at all times keenly aware
that his book is <u>him-thinking</u>, and that therefore the <u>him</u> is
not only ineradicable, it is the essence of the book. The
best work, therefore, will be humanized by virtue of the
explicit presence of an estimable man brooding through the
work. That the book is humane further implies that in the
final analysis its chief importance lies in its relevance to
man and his estate. In the most profound sense therefore,
a book, by virtue of being a humane work, is a work of
human context, an existential event, a potential encounter.
The humane book possesses a centre of gravity which is
within man.

    A book then is a fabric <u>in</u> and <u>of</u> consciousness.
Now, one can hardly for a moment pretend that this distinguishes the book from the dissertation, and expect anyone
to believe that the dissertation must not also have the same
characteristics with respect to consciousness! What I have
in mind is quite different. Since a book is a fabric in and
of consciousness and since it becomes an existential context
for the reader who enters into it, it follows that the book's
rootedness in consciousness must be fully and richly exploited
as the sub-stratum of all the rest if all the rest is in fact
to be achieved. That challenge to roundedness, that wholeness which is of all attributes most subject to the critical
examination of the consciousness, must be met. This requires not only all the writer's knowledge but all his fancy
as well. To make <u>an</u> <u>estate</u> of the work--a viable and, to
the probing consciousness, a veritable and existent estate--

is the heavy charge placed upon the author of the book.

This view of the book is based upon many assumptions which will become manifest as we proceed. But one of the most basic tenets is an unshakeable belief that language is a human activity and that it has no more honourable function than to present man-thinking. Man-thinking is at every constituting moment of the book mediator between his reader and the world he perceives and incarnates into his own words. Language is a tool only in the sense that it makes man instrumental. That language is a precision instrument with its own objective existence apart from man is the premise which informs the worst dissertations--and for that matter the worst books; that it is a structure of being is the premise of the fully realized book.

A further critical feature of the book results from the model the author adopts for himself and his work. He may fancy himself as the writer of a dissertation, which is highly specialized and often therefore of little consequence, or he may regard himself simply as a writer, a certain kind of man--one who through his written prose, with serious dignity and with respect for language and discourse as a mode of being, does a human work and establishes an aspect of the world. Further, the writer can view his work either as a dissertation, which as a highly specialized form is also a highly restricted one, or he can regard it as an attempt at organic creation through language, different from the greatest books in the language perhaps only by virtue of the fact that it may flow from a lesser man and is devoted to less profound and stirring issues. In both these pairs of alternatives, those choices pertaining to the dissertation involve the acceptance of specialized models; the second choices do not. The writer of the dissertation sees himself as involved in the execution of a complex and erudite ritual for a cohesive, erudite, and minimal audience, and he sees his work as conforming to certain requirements of structure and levels of discourse. The writer of the book on the other hand consciously sees himself as existing within the tradition of his language and literature and regards his work as directed to every man possessed of the requisite wit, learning, and taste to appreciate it. The writer of the dissertation hounds his points to the ground with packs of footnotes while the writer of books, using footnotes, when inescapable, with neither bravado nor timidity, treats his ideas and his evidence as straightforwardly and honourably as he can. He does so out of respect for his work, for his readers, and for himself, not out of a base desire to please his committee or to flatter his director.

At the outset, then, the writer must decide whether his work is to be organic or artificial, humane or academic, an end or a means, and whether he, as author, is to be civil or dull, whether he is to place himself and his work within the mainstream of the viable literary traditions of his culture or to journey the tortuous by-way of the dissertation. Further, he must determine whether he is to write a _natural_ form or an unnatural one. In making up his mind on these points, the writer should bear in mind the fact that few scholars, once released from the disciplines of the graduate school, would of their own free will choose subsequently to write a dissertation. Unhappily, of course, there are some senior scholars to whom the form seems to be a natural means of expression. It is such people, one suspects, who invented the form and do the most to perpetuate it.

As a further aid to defining the book, I point to the fact that a book is in daily discourse distinguished from what is called a nonbook. Nonbooks are of several kinds; but their differences notwithstanding, they all share two common features: they tend to be written for market rather than for intellectual reasons, and they are all means rather than ends. Since their centre of gravity is external to man it is difficult, no matter what their pretensions, to regard them as humane, serious, or dedicated to creating a context in and of the full stuff of consciousness. Of all nonbooks, the most conspicuous example is the "coffee-table book." The latter usually find their market by virtue of their decorative assets rather than from any literary or intellectual merit, or for that matter--since such works are often art books--by significantly serving important aesthetic or historical purposes. Although such books are phenomena of the age of self-improvement, they seem to be of little effect, and in the final analysis they appear to serve much the same purpose as the frilly lampshades one so often sees conspicuously gracing certain front windows.

Another type of nonbook comes into being from giving expression to the desire to gather together bits and pieces of literary materials. Whether such collection is done around a common theme or around a constellation of such themes, it gives strong evidence of the simple desire to collect. The abundance of anthologies and readers attests to this. Perhaps the strength of this drive to anthologize owes much to the lucrative textbook markets, but if this is so, then in this respect we live now at a fortunate time. The abundance of relatively inexpensive paperback books seems to have ended the heyday of the big and expensive classroom reader. Whatever the case, the fact remains that the anthology is perhaps the most common form of the nonbook, and its rationale is identical to that of the coffee-table book, which appears to be that there is justification and indeed even some virtue in the snippet approach to the study of the long progress of human achievement.

There are other nonbooks which are also alien to the notion of book as humane, though these, by and large, are without attractive markets, thus making the motives for their compilation less comprehensible. I have in mind both the symposium and the festschrift. At their worst, these two nonbooks are empty forms of flattery; and even though at their best they may constitute major contributions to knowledge, yet publishers have grown wary of them. Like the coffee-table book, some symposia and festschriften are dedicated to vanity; like the anthology, their parts are often disparate; like both, they are in general mundane and without interest to any save the specialist with a marked tolerance for the dull, the inane, and the inconsequential. Still, both the festschrift and the symposium are published, even fairly bad ones. Vanity and the amazing support vanity can generate sometimes constitute so powerful and insistent a force that the publisher finds it difficult to resist; he accepts the work unenthusiastically, and brings out a small printing.

There are more profound traits than market and vanity, however, which the genres of nonbooks have in common, and these are the features which perhaps distinguish them most significantly from the book. The coffee-table book is likely to be deficient in thoughtfulness and in coming to grips with a problem, though it may be both synthetic and programmatic. The anthology often rates somewhat higher in thoughtfulness but again fails to grapple with the issue. The symposium and the festschrift at their best can exhibit thoughtfulness and thoroughness, but common emphases, perspectives, values, and judgements are absent.

In short, nonbooks are marred by the absence of probity, of unity, and of responsibility. Each of these terms, save perhaps responsibility, is clear enough. <u>Probity</u> designates that quality of being at once both significant and illuminating, and <u>unity</u> is the coming-togetherness of the work into a whole. Responsibility is in one respect the obligation to treat the subject in the fashion it deserves, which the word ordinarily means. But it implies more than this, for the proper way of treating a subject is thoughtful, analytic (or synthetic), programmatic and exhaustive, fully rounded, taking hold of a problem. Works so treated achieve that marvellous three-dimensionality characteristic of the good book. Each of these three terms--probity, unity, responsibility--is an important criterion of the book and must be present; if one or another is absent, a nonbook results.

The dissertation may lack any or indeed all these characteristics; thus it is clear that the dissertation is another genre of the nonbook. It is in all probability for failure to honour the criterion of probity that dissertations most commonly fail to be books. The dissertation never achieves that quality of being historically, socially, conceptually, aesthetically--humanely--significant. The reason does not lie solely in the fact that the writer has written a dissertation instead of a book. There are some writers who deserve no greater challenge than the dissertation. I am concerned here, however, rather with that person who could achieve probity but who is precluded from doing so by the requirements of a system committed to a form to which probity is alien--because the work is usually carefully kept minimal, cut off from any but the most apprentice-like intellectual pretensions or achievements. Its mass is thus limited, and it is dedicated to embodying certain conventions of purpose and procedure.

The dissertation is likely, under even the worst of circumstances, to exhibit some unity of concept, owing to the fact that phenomena have been selected, an inquiry conducted, and data organized in relation to the "problem" which is the core of the dissertation. But it is the rare dissertation that does not fail when it comes to unity of address. "Address" involves a complex of factors--the strategy compounded from both the consideration and the demonstration of the question; the attitude toward the subject of the work as well as toward its hypothetical readers (who should be ever present in the writer's mind during the act of composition); and the surface of the book, by which I mean the text and its condition as a prose continuum.

The strategy of consideration in the dissertation is not only likely to be acceptable, but is often in the vanguard of its field with respect to methods, values, and objectives.

Coherence of demonstration, however, is usually found wanting. Most dissertation directors doubtless are dedicated chiefly--or at least earnestly--to the education and the success of their students, but it is nonetheless true that often the writer is never permitted to act as a free agent, blessed with the ability to perceive a condition of man or the world and trained to disclose it in a professional fashion. Accordingly, alongside a virtuosity in the use of advanced techniques of demonstration, he is often likely to exhibit an unnatural reliance upon such supports as the skilful hedge, the evasive footnote, and the demonstration of the inconsequential or the obvious. The example of a recent dissertation of more than ordinary interest will demonstrate this point. In the context of a fresh and insightful study of a certain people, the writer of the dissertation, when it came to the point where he wished to write of their religion, was required to go back through the literature, reviewing all the attitudes of anthropologists toward religion in general before he was free to make his own points. This is not an extreme case. The experiences of many editors will provide additional instances where it has appeared that the writer of the dissertation felt he had to demonstrate the obvious before he could invoke the concepts whose existence clearly implied the basic facts or earlier work. Let the dissertation writer beware who abandons his prerogatives of choice to someone else. Even the noblest research director may push a student into digging about in recondite corners of the area of his own concern. To abdicate one's responsibility of choice to another risks the failure to achieve probity. The student faces for a time the opportunity to choose what he will write; at some point he arrives at the best of all motives, which is to say that he wants to write on a given subject _because_ it is significant; the failure to seize this chance and instead to let pressures of time or power coerce him into a project because it is easy or because someone else wants it is in all probability to deliver himself and his work over to a poverty of pertinence.

Attitude toward subject, which is also a function of unity, varies greatly in the dissertation--whether because the subject itself is trivial, or because the writer's relationship to it is. In a book the writer is more likely free to go where interest and the logic of inquiry take him. To the extent that the dissertation-writer may be coerced into alien directions, to that same extent is his interest likely to flag and his attitude toward the subject to fluctuate. Further, it is sometimes difficult for the dissertation-writer to visualize that hypothetical and ideal reader whom, in the fullness of his pertinence and intellectual originality, he ought to address. Instead, he is ever aware of his all too certain actual readers--his committee. He must write for them, a minimal and often--in any real sense--his least important audience.

In the dissertation again, as for that matter is true of the bad book as well, unity is often violated with respect to surface, notably in the level of discourse, the level of diction, and the level of rhetoric. It is the mastery of these which further distinguishes the writer who can write from the one who cannot, and the dissertation from the good book. For the best writers, these surfaces require little attention; for the worst, little attention is possible. But for the majority of writers, who are placed between these two poles, assiduous reworking, whether alone or with the help of an editor, will induce such unity.

In the book responsibility is reflected in that intellectual attitude which respects both the thesis, treating it ever seriously, and the spirit of inquiry whose sole interest is to disclose all relevant analysis and synthesis. Dissertations frequently either regard the thesis with a seriousness it may not merit, which is a kind of intellectual sentimentality, or, more rarely, undervalue the proposition, betraying cynicism.

It is in the adequacy and clarity of demonstration, which are functions of responsibility, that most writers of dissertations fall into serious and often terminal error. In the dissertation phenomena may be overanalyzed, underanalyzed, inappropriately analyzed, and irrelevantly analyzed. This last error eventuates from the misapprehension of the nature of the thesis, and is not as uncommon as one might suspect. And while clarity of inquiry is largely a function of positive and creative solutions, it is also an independent quality of mind that abhors cant and abjures passing fashions in the disciplines.

There are other traits which, while they do not inevitably characterize the book, almost never mark the dissertation. They may be considered secondary characteristics of the book. The most notable member of this secondary cluster is what I shall call the presumption of authority. The writer of the book and the writer of the dissertation both have sought to master the facts of one area of human concern. But the treatment of the data is markedly different in the book from that in the dissertation. The writer of the dissertation is tyrannized both by his facts and by his discipline (although the rise of interdisciplinary studies is somewhat ameliorating this latter condition). The writer of the book, on the other hand, while respecting his data, yet is liberated by them. He is at ease with facts, using them adroitly in support of his argument. This difference in attitude, deriving from different initial estimations of one's role with respect to one's project, makes different end products. There is no easy reckoning of the transformation when a writer regards himself as virtuoso of evidence, thesis, field, and expression. A corollary to the presumption of authority is the generation of freedom to depart from slavish reliance upon the citation of the facts and views of predecessors and to range creatively and with confidence over the domain.

In the best books, there develops from this freedom a sense of urgency which seldom blesses the dissertation. It comes also from the prerogative allowed the author under such circumstances to presume both his own authority and the importance of his work. This, then, is the second element in that cluster of secondary characteristics that distinguish the book.

A third item in this cluster is the presumption of the value of the expression of one's self when defining an idea, a judgment, or a fact. At the same time, this presumption entails the recognition of the privilege of invoking and making operative this value. It stresses recognition of the importance of one's self as ground for one's views, thus opening to the author the opportunity to engage on that voyage of simultaneous self-discovery and phenomenon-discovery which provides the foundation for his presumption of the importance of his work and his presumption of authority. The implicit assumption in the writing of a book is that the author himself is important. The assumptions concerning the writer of a dissertation, it need hardly be said, often appear to run quite contrary to this view. This presumption of the importance of one's self to the inquiry, besides having profound onto-logical implications, has more readily apparent and exceedingly attractive consequences as well, for it permits the expression of the writer's own personality in his prose to the limits of his ability to work in the language.

I am writing here about the worst dissertation and the best book. But not all books, not even all good books, are of the kind I have been discussing. While the book which is humane, which establishes a significant human context, which in roundedness and credibility creates a field of consciousness--extending the reader's consciousness by adroitly, trenchantly, and creatively directing it toward new phenomena or to new perspectives on old ones--is in my judgement the best book, its number represents perhaps but a small percentage of the books published each year. Most works are either aimed in the same direction as the best book, but are notably deficient in some respects, or else they are of a quite different sort. The book we have discussed so far is the thesis book. There is also, however, the non-thesis book, and many terminal graduate discourses are likely to be of this type for the plain reason that it is in most respects an easier kind of project to undertake.

The thesis book is primarily creative, establishing through originality of concept and argument a position which has not previously existed or is not generally accepted. A non-thesis book, on the other hand, is content to describe or to explain that which already exists. Non-thesis books are exemplified by some archaeological studies and certain histories and biographies, which are intended to do no more than record the verifiable events of the life of a period or of a man. Now we know as a matter of fact that no presentation of history or biography proceeds without selection and that that selection invariably betrays the presence of value as a principle of selection. This value is a point of view. The non-thesis book therefore is one which, while it is indubitably written from a point of view, yet exists within an unquestioned intellectual tradition and does not specifically argue a case or offer distinctively new or importantly modified points of view. The non-thesis book is inherently conservative, and the non-thesis dissertation is the safest kind of dissertation to write.

The ontological nature of the non-thesis book is as unlike that of the thesis book as a photograph of Cézanne is different from one of his self-portraits. The non-thesis book is a sketch or a profile of what incontestably exists; unlike the thesis book, it does not have as its objective the establishment of an aspect of reality. The only structures the non-thesis book must incorporate are the immanent ones of the phenomenon or process with which it is concerned, as these structures are traditionally accepted to be, within the author's own tradition. By definition, therefore, there is unlikely to be any major disputation over the nature of those structures or their interrelationships or their significance. This is not to say that there may not be scalding controversy over the details as represented. But unless the whole premise of observation is rejected by virtue of an opposing thesis, this controversy is certain to be restricted to a question of the adequacy or the reliability of the account.

So much, then, for a brief overview of the most striking inherent differences which distinguish the book from the dissertation. But there are other distinguishing factors which are not inherent but which often--even though extraneous--have a determining influence upon the work, for they can be insidious and insistent. They amount to a concerted power which often prevents the young scholar from producing a book in his first extended job of professional writing. Wholly external to the writer, this power is the combined product of tradition, the nature of graduate education, and the role and personality of the dissertation director. Tradition has it that rather than being the first act of the scholar, the dissertation is the last act of the student. The dissertation is viewed therefore as the work not of a professional but of a pre-professional. Thus the writer of the dissertation is forced by tradition to resort to the writing of a form that is dysfunctional, because in its primitive form the dissertation will be read by few and because no publisher will in all probability consider publishing it as it stands. At the same time, tradition places a great value upon publication, with the result that the young writer finds himself caught in a vise between forces, being required to remain a student, presenting what often amounts to little more than an underwrought and overextended term paper for his dissertation, and at the same time being required to publish as a means of advancing his professional career.

The agency of tradition is the graduate school which, after the model of the rest of the university, treats the graduate student as student. The graduate school seldom conceives of its scholars in any way profoundly different from that in which undergraduate schools think of their freshman students. It therefore permits the perpetuation of tradition by approving the research of a trivial proposition and its incorporation into what, in the world of "real" communication, can only be called a dysfunctional form. We may consider ourselves blessed that there is, here and there, some evidence of the weakening of this system. At one university recently the Ph.D. candidate, having been examined on his research, was discharged with the degree promised and no dissertation required. He was instructed rather, and quite simply, to produce a book based upon his research. The system that generally prevails, however, is but another instance of the great pains American society takes to postpone the maturation of its young.

There is every reason why, in this day of Ph. D. overproduction, the requirement to write a dissertation should be dropped and the requirement to write a book substituted. Such an action might impede Ph. D. production enrich scholarship, take young scholars in the serious terms the great majority of them deserve, and give them early acquaintance with that viable form of communication they will use throughout their productive lives. There can be little doubt that this more creative and worthwhile use of human energies would constitute its own reward. In addition the economics of learned book publishing, which militate against the publication of the dissertation owing to its negligible market and the subsequent high cost of publication, would be affected, I believe for the better, in view of the fact that labour would be saved and better and more marketable works would eventuate.

Under some circumstances, such as the presence of an intellectually imperialistic director of research, one of the worst faults of the dissertation is perpetrated. In the good dissertation, as in the book, the genetic principles of the work's growth are inherent in the field, the thesis, the data, the inquiry, and above all the writer. But in the unfortunate circumstances provided by the aggressive director, the genetic principle is an external one. Instead of conducting research after his own interests and in his own fashion, the student investigates some minor area of the research director's field of interest. His research thus becomes but a footnote to the research of his professor, and the sole achievement may well be only that the senior man will not have to conduct some research for which he himself had little time and perhaps even little inclination. Under such circumstances there is practically no possibility of a book, and the whole project of the dissertation, once the degree has been granted, had best be broken down to some simple stage at which the parts may be studied, reassembled, and permitted to grow after their own dictates, perhaps into one or two papers. Inevitably and wastefully some large part of the work will have to be abandoned.

If the writing of dissertations is to be discouraged

and the writing of books encouraged, it is obvious that profound changes must come about in the requirements for graduate degrees. The graduate schools must revise their ideas and expectations regarding that major writing project upon which the awarding of the degree in large measure depends. Further, steps must be taken to insure the complete intellectual freedom of the candidate, perhaps by distinguishing his research director from his dissertation director. As an added step it might be well, as often as possible, to include a professional editor as a full member of the candidate's committee.

All that is wrong with graduate school writing as it tends to be practised today is symbolized by the existence and extraordinary popularity of A Manual for Writers of Term Papers, Theses, and Dissertations by Kate L. Turabian (University of Chicago Press). While undeniably useful within its limited terms, this manual, in wide use among dissertation writers, makes no mention of the fact that the dissertation is, or ought to be, a form of discourse. On the contrary, sole attention is given to the mechanics of presentation. That this is so reflects the staunch prevailing attitude toward the dissertation, namely that it is not expected that the doctoral research or the extended statement of that research and its arguments will be of consequence. All that matters is that the work be written in a scrupulously traditional fashion. Footnotes, most often the curse of the dissertation as far as the publisher is concerned (for they are overused to the point not only of vice, but, worse, to utter dependence of mind), are treated in thirty of the manual's 103 pages--an amount considerably greater than that directed to any other topic. In contrast, the discussion of the physical presentation of the body of the text itself is accomplished in twelve pages. While on its own terms the manual is reliable and beneficial, its existence without the concomitant existence of another manual devoted to those vastly more important dimensions of the thesis in terms of its nature as an achievement in extended and serious discourse is profoundly revealing. The attentions of the writer must early be fixed upon the humane and genetic nature of the book as the consummate form of mature discourse.

Part IV

THE SOCIAL PREROGATIVE

THE GREAT EAST HAMPTON LIBRARY MESS*

Dwight Macdonald

EAST HADLEYBURG?

East Hampton
December 16, 1971

Dear Editor:

  In the Dec. 9 Star Lloyd Tennenbaum expresses concern about "the secrecy-shrouded dispute" over the library board's recent dismissal of Mrs. Joan Ford, their head librarian for over three years, without presenting charges and giving her a hearing on them. He complains that, aside from its initial report, the Star "has kept an unwonted silence in both its news and editorial columns" and has provided "no chronology of events."

  As a cosigner of the letter in your Nov. 11 issue that began it all (publicly, at least), [There was a story on page one, Nov. 11 issue] may I remove a few shrouds from this enigma wrapped in a mystery and attempt a chronicle, w. commentary, of The Great East Hampton Library Mess? A tempest in a teapot, perhaps--but I think the tea leaves can be "read" for larger meanings about our town's present atmosphere.

  Especially since it has been followed by two larger storms: the police commando raids on the Beale-Bouvier ladies' untrimmed property (charge: reactionary eccentricity) and on Mrs. Johnson's untrimmed nursery school (charge: progressive eccentricity). Three scandals in a month each

---

*These two letters appeared originally in the East Hampton (New York) Star, on December 23 and December 30, 1971. They are reprinted here by permission of the Star and of the American Library Association, which published them in American Libraries, September 1972.

The Social Prerogative 407

arising from an abuse of authority that could be described, depending on how moderately you use adjectives, as "arbitrary," "antiquated," "reckless" or just plain "kooky." Quite a record for one small town!

Ominous fissures, malignant lesions are suddenly appearing in this pleasant community to which I retired to end my career in a half-acre cottage about the same time Mrs. Ford arrived to begin hers.

Is East Hampton another Hadleyburg, whose corruption under its respectable veneer, in Mark Twain's story, was so unexpectedly uncovered by the stranger's little test? (We've flunked three big ones in a month.) Or worse-- assuming any sensible American town would rather be exposed as wicked than ridiculous, better Sodom than Sauk Center--are we beginning to resemble Kipling's "The Village That Voted the Earth Was Flat?" It didn't really--those provincials were victims of a practical joke by hostile outsiders, press lords and show-biz moguls ("flat as your hat/ flatter than that").

But we're our own victims: the practical jokers are our (unelected) library board. The outside press is merely an accomplice after the fact appreciative of that curious little retrograde enclave in the boondocks that provides such amusing copy. Cf. the New York Times front page report on the Beale ladies' travail, also the p. 4 feature story on the library mess, in Newsday, which lately (Dec. 14), followed it up with a column of light-hearted comment by Stan Isaacs that didn't do much for our town's image either.

It all began (privately) with a longhand note Mrs. Ford received on Oct. 20 from Mrs. Mary (Russell) Hopkinson, president of the board of managers of the East Hampton Free Library ("free" I now take in a Pickwickian sense re. our library, likewise "public"). It read:

> In March 1969 three members of the board met with you to discuss the relationship of the librarian and the board. The meeting was called because even at that time there had been considerable friction between you and the board concerning the policies by which the board chose [a Louis XIV word! DM] to have the library operate. This friction has increased to the point that the board feels you would be much happier to resign and find a position where you and your

board can be more in accord. We therefore request that you send in your letter of resignation subject to our contractual rights.

The board's legal right to dismiss their librarian without a hearing is clear, by the way; two months' notice, with pay, is all that is stipulated in the agreement. It's their moral right--by standards generally accepted in U. S. A. 1971 (though not U. S. A. 1897 when the library was founded) as to firing professionals like teachers and librarian--it's that we question.

On Oct. 22 Mrs. Ford replied: "... I request a hearing before the entire library board ... wherein the reasons for my dismissal may be presented in detail and where I will have an opportunity to answer the charges." To which on Oct. 30 Mrs. Hopkinson replied with a typewritten letter whose operative sentences were:

"There have been no 'charges' [why the quotation marks? slang? irony? nonce word? vulgar term?--DM] on which your dismissal was based. The board ... feels that you have been disinclined to carry out its decisions and that friction will continue as long as you are director.... Since the board has definitely determined that you are not to continue as an employee and the reasons for this decision are sufficient in the opinion of the board to justify such action taken, no useful purpose would be served by holding such a meeting. The action of which you have been advised is final. Your position will terminate as of Nov. 1, 1971." Louis XIV hell--the Politburo!

At this point David Ignatow chanced to learn of Mrs. Ford's dismissal--not from her but from a distressed assistant--and called up Arthur Roth and myself because he was disturbed, as were we, by this unexpected (to us outsiders who merely use the place, as against the board ladies who actually run it) dismissal of a librarian we'd thought East Hampton lucky to have: alert, helpful and knowledgeable about books.

We met with Mrs. Ford who gave us her side, including the above correspondence. We felt that even if the board had good reasons for dismissing her, she was entitled to know what they were and to a hearing at which she could defend herself as best she could. Also we were curious, given the collision between our and their estimates of

Mrs. Ford, to know what they had against her, specifically.

So we called up Mrs. Hopkinson and requested a meeting with her and some of her board ladies (by a quirky--and in 1971 possibly illegal as discriminatory--fiat of the founding fathers, and mothers, the board excludes males) to get their side. Her first reply was negative: the board wasn't obliged to justify its decision to outsiders who lacked their "background" of experience with Mrs. Ford, nor did she admit there were two "sides." But later she changed her mind and agreed to receive us.

So, on Nov. 1, as our letter in the Nov. 11 Star stated, David Ignatow, Arthur Roth and I met with Mrs. Hopkinson and two other board ladies in her home on Windmill Lane (not the Amagansett one but the posh East Hampton one near the Maidstone Club) and tried to find out why they had fired Mrs. Ford. They listened patiently to our increasingly desperate questions and we listened to them (mostly Mrs. H., with supporting crowd-murmurs from her colleagues) though less patiently as the hour-and-a-quarter nondialogue nondeveloped.

A confrontation in a heavy fog. After Mrs. H. had read the sections of the library's bylaws defining the mutual obligations of board and librarian, we tried to get down to business. We learned that fourteen of the sixteen board members had attended the meeting at which it was decided to dismiss Mrs. Ford without a hearing and that the vote was unanimous. (We forgot to ask whether some had dissented and if so whether, as often happens, the minority had agreed, in the interests of unity, to make the vote unanimous.)

Was Mrs. F. incompetent? we asked. Heavens no, what an idea--nobody could question her professional ability. (We felt a bit guilty for being so suspicious.) Did the board object to her selection of new books and magazines, then? Not at all. Maybe there had been complaints from library users--discourtesy, slackness?

Well, a couple about allegedly late openings, but nothing substantial, really. Toward the end a few life-style issues loomed vaguely through the fog: the no-bare feet notice Mrs. Ford wouldn't put up and the posters she did put up; also a running obbligato of pianissimo murmurs about her "attitude." But when we pressed them--"Is that it, then?"--the ladies were amused by our masculine simplicity: "You couldn't think those were our reasons, much more serious issues were involved." "What, for instance?"

(That male lust for definite answers--"cross examination" my wife calls it, inaccurately; it's direct examination.) "What right have you to ask us such questions? The board knows the situation after three years of Mrs. Ford, you don't. It's been a very distressing problem--do you think all of us could be totally wrong about it?"

Supressing the obvious reply, I again asked--or maybe it was David, this is a reconstruction from memory, it was not an occasion for taking notes: "But what were the serious issues?" "She refused to follow board policies."

"Couldn't you give us some specific instances?" "Mrs. Ford knows perfectly well what they were." "She says she doesn't." "Well really--we've told her often enough." But --" etc.

The dialogue was hardly Socratic. The ladies seemed to be dummying up--they wouldn't even admit they disliked Mrs. Ford, personally, that is--it was just her strange (or at least unexplained by them) "disinclination to carry out board decisions" on many also unexplained occasions that bugged them. Perhaps they had bound themselves by a Mafia oath of collective silence--omerta? Or maybe they were standing mute on advice of counsel.

If so, their legal adviser was more cautious than sagacious. If you're stonewalling, it's a tactical error to expose yourselves to questions even if--and especially if-- you don't answer them.

We were about to draft a letter to the _Star_ after this meeting which seemed to leave us no alternative short of dummying up like the board, when we learned from Mrs. Ford that a board member was sounding out her colleagues on possibly giving her a hearing, after all. So we held up our letter, hoping sweetness and light (and common sense) would prevail and it could all be settled quietly, inside the family, so to speak.

I sent Mrs. Hopkinson an inscribed copy of my anthology of parodies--no crack intended, just have some around--with a view to fraternizing across the battlelines,

The Social Prerogative

also I'd liked her and her husband personally, and I'm sure the other fifteen board ladies are nice people, personally, which makes it more depressing, and significant--with a note:

"We appreciated your courteous willingness to hear us out. Here's hoping some rational--if not amicable--solution can be arrived at without public fuss." Our hopes were disappointed. The maverick board lady's demarche was not successful. So, after waiting a week, we wrote the letter.

I hope my old friend, Jean Stafford, with her jibes in her Dec. 9 letter at "protest people" who jump on Juggernaut "bandwagons" and set them in motion to crush helpless library boards--she pulled herself up just short of calling us "trouble-makers"--will read at least the above paragraphs. I was puzzled by that testy footnote to her brilliant farrago of the previous week that seemed to endorse our notion that the board should grant Mrs. Ford a hearing.

My bother wasn't her change of mind, and heart--I've done that myself, often, though her track time must be a record--but the way she explains it: (a) "no reason the board's actions should have been made public in the first place"; (b) her intention was not to "question" the board's decision but only to urge them "after the issue became a noisy brawl ... to defend themselves"; and (c) "They did not start the ruckus. It was the Protest people, the Cause people, the climb-on-every-bandwagon people."

Now really, dear Jean, let's consider. (a) The only way the affair could have been hushed up ("not made public") would have been for Mrs. Ford to leave quietly, as they asked her to (what glowing references they would have gladly given her!). But she thought she'd done a good job and even, I'm afraid, that in the "frictional" disagreements she'd been right more often than they; so she asked for a hearing.

However private it might have been--and nobody asked for a townhall meeting--if the board didn't rescind her dismissal and was unable to convince her their decision was reasonable, both possibilities being not unimaginable, then, unless she lost her memory or agreed to join the board ladies in their omerta vow of silence, which would be masochism beyond the call of duty, she might be expected to spill a few beans in public, if only to protect her professional reputation. Only when both sides are satisfied, can (or should) such hearings be kept private afterwards.

(b) Likewise, the only way the board could have "defended itself" and avoided "a noisy brawl" (or even a quiet brawl as this one has been right up to this unquiet chronicle) would have been to grant a hearing, a modest concession that is all Mrs. Ford and her supporters have asked for, indeed what you recommended in your first letter (J. S. I)--though your latter postscript (J. S. II) doesn't mention "hearing" not even in the quotemarks Mrs. Hopkinson used to disinfect that other dirty word, "charges."

(c) Of course the board "didn't start the ruckus." The last thing authorities want when they're trying to put over a fast one on the Q. T. is a ruckus. Peace, harmony, brotherhood--on their terms--is their sincere wish. "This was such a nice friendly town and we were all so proud of our library, why do you want to tear it apart?" a board lady asked me plaintively.

Or, as Mrs. Hopkinson told a reporter (<u>Riverhead News Review</u>, Nov. 25) in a rare, perhaps unique, interview she may now regret: "We had no idea she was going to do this." By "this" she meant Mrs. Ford's taking her case, after weeks of getting nowhere, to the New York Library Association (more on this later). The board president was genuinely shocked.

Simple example of displacement of unconscious guilt feelings onto victim who was here especially threatening because she defended herself. If dubious about Freud, see Marx for explanation on the conscious level. A similar displacement appears in J. S. II's blaming us critics for the mess initiated by the very board action we criticize. In ancient despotisms the bearer of bad news was executed but this is nice little old East Hampton, isn't it? Or is it?

Those abusive epithets J. S. II showers on us are mystifying because the tone of our letters in the <u>Star</u>, protesting the board's action and asking many reasonable questions the board hasn't answered--reasonable (and unanswered) questions, was more temperate--and civil--than the agitated rhetoric with which J. S. II denounces them. "Noisy brawl" is utterly baffling.

It takes two to tango, or to brawl, and the board has refused to mix it up, maintaining what you might call an

The Social Prerogative

undignified silence. As for noise: our decibel count is a polite murmur compared to J.S. II's shouting. Come back little J.S.I!

The Newsday feature mentioned above included an attractive photo of Joan Ford (will she become the Angela Davis of librarians? the board is doing its best) plus the two posters some board members have objected to, unofficially. One is "No Silence," an effort to liven up the mausoleum atmosphere of the traditional library, an atmosphere the board values more highly than does the H. W. Wilson Co., which distributes the posters; I might add H. W. Wilson is to library business as McGraw-Hill is to business business, and about as wildeyed; also that the sign is behind the circulation desk and not in a reading room (where even I would object to it).

The other poster, lettered by Ben Shahn, reads: "To Sin By Silence When They Should Protest Makes Cowards of Men--Abraham Lincoln." Not terribly inflammatory, in fact a mealymouthed platitude compared to remarks by Jefferson and other founding fathers a librarian might have tacked up. But a Mr. Malcolm Aldrich--Newsday calls him "a New York philanthropist who oversees the library's finances"--did complain to Mrs. Hopkinson and she passed it on to Mrs. Ford, making the matter quasi-official.

Mrs. F. says Mrs. H. told her Mr. A.'s beef was that the poster "encouraged dissent" (w. is what I'd consider books are for, among other things--I wouldn't buy a used library from that man). But maybe this is unfair to Mr. A. Mrs. H. admits he complained to her and that she relayed it to Mrs. F. but she denies he said anything about "encouraging dissent."

"So what was in his mind?" I asked (here we go again), curious why an innocuous truism (and by a Republican!) could have disturbed their financial adviser so much he wanted it deleted from his/our library's wall. (One thinks of financial advisers as level-headed.)

Mrs. H. replied, a bit crossly, that she didn't know what might have been in Mr. A.'s mind since she wasn't a psychoanalyst. (I didn't dare press her on the implication that he hadn't given a reason and she hadn't asked for one.) The usual stalemate.

How did it all happen? (1) Why did the board dismiss their head librarian as unceremoniously as an unsatisfactory housemaid? (2) Why did it take them so long to get rid of her although they insist the "friction" began soon after they had (rashly) hired her? (3) Why didn't they give her a hearing on charges when they finally did act--and why do they still refuse this elementary justice after weeks of flak, protest, mess and scandal? And (4) did they really think as of A. D. 1971, they could get away with it?

The last answer is Yes--my impression is they had no idea what they were getting into, a sincere miscalculation. The other answers are more complicated. They'll be in Part II next week.

Dwight Macdonald

HADLEYBURG--II

December 22, 1971

Dear Editor:

To resume (and conclude) from last week: (1) Why did the board dismiss their head librarian like an unsatisfactory housemaid? (2) Why did it take them three years? (3) Why have they refused to give her a hearing?

(1) The board ladies fired Mrs. Ford like a housemaid because that's how they thought of her--or perhaps, to be fair, an upper servant, a housekeeper. Not a lazy or sloppy housekeeper--they don't question her professional abilities--but still a servant who "didn't know her place."

They seem to think of the library as an extension of their living rooms--a restful, tasteful retreat that was being "ruined" by their librarian-housekeeper.

"All those tacky posters ... and 'NO SILENCE' if you please ... and now bare feet, really! ... If I've told that girl once...." These aren't real quotes nor is there any hard evidence that the board ladies confuse their library with their living rooms or their librarian with a housekeeper, in fact I'm sure they'll be sincerely shocked and surprised at such an accusation--so many shocks and surprises lately!

The Social Prerogative   415

But it's a reasonable inference from their behavior. Parodic license: inventions that are true to life.

The housekeeper assumption was reinforced by a private-property syndrome: "We do as we choose with our own." The board feels no obligation to defend, or even explain, their policies to outsiders. (Or so I infer from their collective silence in the face of weeks of public protest.)

Even if the library were wholly supported by private endowment, this baronial attitude would be anachronistic: in the big world outside East Hadleyburg the barons in charge of the great private foundations recognize their public accountability for the way they administer their fiefdoms. But our library is no longer private in any sense.

Of its 1971 estimated budget of $56,000, nearly half comes from public sources: a $20,000 subsidy from School District taxes (next year it will be $25,000, due to Mrs. Ford's not the board's enterprise--see below) plus $4,000 in overdue fines and $2,300 from nonresident fees (the library is "free" only to "residents" and the library's map is not extensive).

When we asked Mrs. President Hopkinson if we might meet with some of the board to learn why they had fired Mrs. Ford, her first reaction was: "What business is it of yours? By what right do you ask us to explain our decision to outsiders who can have no idea of the long, painful experiences that forced us to make it?" Parodic license-- Mrs. Hopkinson was more courteous and less succinct--but that's what she meant.

Our explanation that we were library users who'd found Mrs. Ford excellent (also that we wanted precisely to get some idea of those experiences) impressed them enough to grant the meeting, but only, it was made clear, as a concession not as a recognition of any outsiders' rights. Their business was to run the library, ours was to use it, and their librarian's was to do as she was told and no back talk. Proprietor, customer, employee--in that pecking order.

(2) One awkward question, among many, is why the board took so long to rid themselves of an employee they found "difficult" almost from the start. A very slow burn, considering that per contract they could have fired her at any time on two month's notice with pay.

Were they soft-hearted? ("Let's give that awful little woman a chance.") But hardly a kindness to let a young wife with two small children and a (currently) unemployed husband settle in here for three and a half years and then suddenly, long after she'd survived any reasonable probation period and had become attached to the library and the community, to uproot her and throw her on a job market that's not so fat these days. No, I can't see them as softhearted. Nor as hard-headed, either.

To put up for so long with a head librarian who was, they allege, chronically "disinclined to carry out the board's decisions" indicates either collective masochism or administrative ineptitude. Either way, they don't seem the practical types needed to run a serious institution.

My guess is that neither kindliness nor masochism was involved, though ineptitude certainly played a part--what a laugh, to have them firing her, an East Hadleyburg joke. The simplest explanation that fits all the facts--always the best one, cf. Sherlock Holmes--is that the sixteen board ladies delayed so long because they couldn't think of any formal charges substantial enough to wash in public. So they endured their unladylike but horribly competent librarian until they just couldn't stand it any more and then they fired her.

The immediate spur to action may have been that the library-owned "Purple House," actually pale lilac, between the library and the Star's office became vacant last fall and that Mrs. Ford asked to rent it as rather more convenient than Sammis Beach and that the board realized they would be totally--as against only 80 percent--committed to keeping her on if they let her move in--in short, that it was now or never. Their foolish hope was for a quid pro quo backstairs deal.

Quid: you resign quietly and "voluntarily." Quo: we give you good references, sincerely stressing your professional talents and insincerely glossing over the "friction" that made us fire you; caveat emptor.

Or, as President Hopkinson put it in her initial (Oct. 19) demarche: "The board feels you would be much happier to resign and find a position where you and your board could be more in accord."

When Mrs. Ford, expectably, refused to be a good, dishonest sport and insisted on a formal hearing, they must have realized they had mistaken their woman--and after so much experience! But they still hadn't thought up anything that would wash in public.

So in her second letter (Oct. 30) Mrs. Hopkinson denied there were any "charges" as there weren't and merely reiterated that "friction will continue as long as you are director." Perhaps true, perhaps not--perhaps a self-fulfilling prophecy; but in any case an evasion of the real questions: Why the friction? Which brings us to:

(3) Why hasn't the board given Mrs. Ford a hearing despite all the protests and scandal, why do they continue to stonewall when they could get off the hook by a modest concession to justice and good manners? My informed guess is: because they felt, rightly, that their objections to Mrs. Ford, like certain wines, wouldn't travel well.

That is, the friction was caused by (a) her professionalism, which they thought unduly aggressive, and (b) her life-style, which they found alien if not downright repellent, politically and culturally.

Perfectly sound, or at least humanly understandable, private reasons for getting rid of her, but not so convincing to the library-using public which, judging from their letters in the Star, seems to approve of (a), aggressive or not, and to be undisturbed by (b).

(a) At the Nov. 1 meeting, Mrs. Hopkinson read, as an example of Mrs. Ford's "disinclination to carry out board policies," a memo she (Mrs. H) had written about a disagreement that arose in the first months of Mrs. F's tenure. Mrs. F asked the board to draw up a definite salary schedule for its employees for the first time in its history.

The board refused, stating it couldn't predict future income. I thought her proposal reasonable: granted unforeseen contingencies might force alterations in the schedule (though is the library's income that chancy?) still it would have been a step towards regularizing things, one that is in fact common library practice; also a benefit to the employees if a bother to the board. At the end of her first year, Mrs. F raised a really painful question.

She pointed out that the 3 percent automatic annual pay increase for the professional staff established by the board before she arrived was by then about half the actual annual increase in the B. L. S. cost-of-living index and she asked it be doubled. This request--or demand, depends on where you sit--was also not warmly received.

But she kept pressing, as was her irritating and admirable habit, and after some dignified stalling the board yielded most of what she has asked for, their reluctant largesse even spilling over onto the nonprofessional part-timers.

After all, she had a pretty good case. Both episodes seem to me to show Mrs. F's insistence on running a library by professional standards. But to a board accustomed to more recessively gemütlich housekeepers they may have seemed evidence of insubordination. (Certainly Mrs. Hopkinson brought up the first as such at our meeting with her.)

As also may have seemed to them--who knows?--Mrs. F's pushing them in her first year to ask the School District to kick in another $5,000. Town won't, can't give it, taxes too high already, said they as solid taxpayers.

No harm trying, and we need the money, said she as solid librarian. Finally they gave in and asked for it and got it, about the time they fired her.

When board members talk about "friction," they always assume Mrs. Ford was the abrasive element--"We really tried to get on with her, but she was so difficult!" But maybe she had to be "difficult" to keep her professional self-respect in dealing with such a board.

(b) A kulturkampf, too--a clash of life styles, social values, generational cultures that was probably the chief frictional element. The one official directive which, both sides agree, Mrs. F ever refused to carry out, flatly, was their order last summer that she post a sign: "No Bare Feet." Both parties intransigent on this trivial point of etiquette--no surrender!

Absurd--but kulturkampf, hence not absurd. It was this trivial-deep issue, for instance, that finally broke up the Nov. 1 meeting at Mrs. Hopkinson's in disorder, blowing away the polite fog and revealing the bleak confrontation.

The Social Prerogative

Our argument was that bare feet are not per se repulsive, that they can't infect the books, and that children, hippies and adult bathers who drop in from the beach shouldn't be discouraged; in sum, that use should precede decorum in library priorities.

Theirs was that bare feet lower the tone (I guess they do, really), that they are "dirty" (are shoes cleaner? Moslems and Japanese wouldn't agree), and that if Bohack's and the A. & P. have outlawed bare feet, can the East Hampton Free Library lag behind in hygienic good taste? Maybe I didn't get their full argument--we were all suddenly talking at once. Or maybe I did.

There's something explosive about the issue I don't understand. It arouses intense passions--especially among the no-bare-feet partisans--as inexplicable to me as was to Gulliver the deadly political strife in Lilliput over whether to break the big or the small end of a breakfast egg. Maybe some sexual nuance that escapes me?

The great bare-feet showdown (for once Mrs. F was on the conservative side: from time immemorial, or 1897, no anti-bare-feet sign has disfigured the library and she didn't propose, at her age, to buck tradition) was one of many, misty flaks. About posters, as noted in Part I.

About the (all too) lively book column she wrote, on her own time, for the <u>Star</u>--especially the one on Attica with Eldridge Cleaver's <u>Soul on Ice</u> among the Suggestions for Further Reading (great prose style though not so sure about its politics); and the "shit detector" one (OK, a quote from Hemingway but still--That Word).

Even her personal appearance was criticized: "But she doesn't look like a librarian" was one gripe quoted to me, and so she doesn't, thank God--for a long time I thought her just another cheerful, pony-braided part-time girl, a very helpful one.

Kulturkampf. She's in her early 40s, they're in their 60s, average age 65, or so I'm told. No objection to that-- it happens to be precisely my age--but they shouldn't hold her youth, and the style and values proceeding therefrom, against her. It's none of their business as a library board.

Last month Mrs. Ford submitted her case to the

intellectual freedom committee of the New York Library Association. On Nov. 30, two delegates from the committee met with the board--fourteen members were present but not of course Mrs. Ford although it's customary in such meetings. It was a nondialogue like our little Nov. 1 rump session.

The delegates can't say they weren't warned. "There is not going to be any hearing for Mrs. Ford," President Hopkinson firmly and (indiscreetly) told the Riverhead News Review five days in advance. "We will explain our position to the association."

They did, for two hours. Two weeks ago the association asked President Hopkinson if the board would agree to a closed hearing--just the two parties and their lawyers, the record to be made public later. She said maybe they could meet and decide sometime next month.

It is most unlikely they will change their minds and most likely the NYLA will impose the only "sanctions" it commands--it's not a trade union, alas--a public censure of the board for violating due process. (Another black eye for E. Hadleyburg.) Even this will be a new departure in militancy.

Finally, some modest proposals: (1) The present charter (granted by the State Board of Regents in 1911) should be amended (a) to break up the female sex monopoly (which may well be illegal in a state-chartered institution anyway) in future appointments to the board; and (b) to immediately add seven new members, not chosen by the board: three selected by the officials of the East Hampton School District (which now provides almost half the library's annual budget-- no taxation without representation--Mr. Eamon McDonough, the high-school librarian, would be an obvious representative) and four by vote of registered book-borrowers.

This enlarged board would have one indisputable superiority to the old one: it would have an odd number of members, making tie votes impossible; like practically all boards except our library's.

(2) Contracts for future head librarians, including Mrs. Ford's brave successor when and if those want ads in the Sunday Times turn up one, should include a formal hearing before dismissal if the dismissee so requests.

(3) The head librarian should be allowed to stay through the whole board meeting, with vote. Mrs. Ford asked to stay (though not vote, there are limits to her boldness) but she was firmly dismissed after she had made her administrative report on grounds her job was running the library, not eavesdropping on matters of finance and general policy. She thought she could run it better if she were clued into the larger picture--one more "frictional" issue on which I agree with her.

(4) The board should redefine the limits of their authority over their librarian. More definitely and, I suggest, more narrowly: give her a free hand if she's doing a good job, or fire her if she isn't, but don't vaguely, unofficially meddle in her professional sphere: running the place.

Sometimes I wonder if a library really needs a board --but strike that out, these are practical proposals.

Dwight Macdonald

REVEALING HERSELF*

Janet Sternburg

> When the endless servitude of woman is broken, when she lives for and by herself, man--heretofore abominable--having given her her release, she too will be a poet! Woman will find some of the unknown! Will her world differ from ours? She will find strange, unfathomable, delicious, repulsive things; we will take them, we will understand them!
>
> Rimbaud

I want to share with you my conviction that women are now experiencing a surge of creative power that issues out of the very fact of being a woman; that this current is working to reshape the landscape of imagery, relationships, and choices that have been the accepted province of male, and until now, cultural sensibility. The source of the outpouring is deeper than anger, wider than discontent. Unzoned, how it _feels_ to be a woman has welled up to the surface of expression, to the fact of art.

Arriving at this discovery has been an intrinsic and heady element of my own commitment to the women's movement. I have been talking with friends, listening to their voices and to my own; concurrently I have been reading books and seeing films made by women. Notes that initially seemed personal and idiosyncratic began to merge into a common chord.

This article is a kind of note-taking in process, a reflection of several of the specific guides--a film and a quartet of novels--that have been instrumental in my coming to understand the contours of this new and emerging landscape. I am writing about film and fiction--apples and oranges--not because this grouping forms a watertight unit

---

*Reprinted by permission from Film Library Quarterly, 5:1 (Winter 1971/72).

The Social Prerogative

of programmed comprehension, but rather because these works all happened to intersect my path at roughly the same time, and so suggested to me interrelationships that might otherwise not be apparent. No film or novel can or should be the quintessential expression of femaleness; what is exciting to me is the suggestion of a dynamic cross-fertilization, a way of using diverse sources across media lines in order to find mutually complementary voices.

The film Growing Up Female: As Six Become One is the first major documentary about the experience of being a woman in America, and because it is persuasive and honest, fills a vast gap in what has previously been available to us. The filmmakers, Julia Reichert and James Klein, explore the process of socialization that molds a woman as she grows into an image suited to the needs of media, of business, of jerry-built myths concerning the nature of her fulfillment. Asking women to bear witness to the quality of their lives and to their options for self-definition, the film derives much of its painful authenticity from its structure--a series of encounters with six females whose ages range from four to thirty-five and whose backgrounds vary from poor black to upper middle-class white. Out of these portraits, each in a dialectic relationship to the others, emerges a cumulative portrait of the condition of womanhood; not an abstract symbol, but a composite woman, partly her own self, partly a creature concocted out of conditioning.

Strong, single-focussed, sometimes harrowing in its picture of self-contempt, the film emphasizes an analytic presentation of its case. The filmmakers have wisely allowed us to meet real women, not merely cases in point. However, they have not, in the interest of the clarity of their logic, allowed the highly charged, personal revelation to find its way into the fabric of their argument. Growing Up Female outlines the new terrain, defines its parameters and co-ordinates. We catch glimpses of the inhabitants behind their masks.

It is, however, the women novelists who are sending us letters from the interior, telling us how it feels to live there. Let me introduce you to a cast of characters. First: Margaret Reynolds, heroine of Anne Richardson Roiphe's novel, Up the Sandbox, the only book of the quartet to explicitly treat the issue of a woman's role. A Manhattan housewife married to a Columbia University professor, and mother of two small children, Margaret is a modern Red

Riding Hood, tracing a delicate, finely wrought path through
the woods. On one side of her lie the quiet pastures of
domestic life, biologically fulfilling, intellectually stultifying;
on the other side looms the jungle of glamour and career,
an undergrowth of self-images which are fraught with danger
even as they are seductive. Her attempt to resolve her
ambivalences is the core of the novel.

Next: Diana Balooka, the thinly disguised autobiographical voice of poet Sandra Hochman's novel about divorce, Walking Papers. Talented, rich, neurotic, Diana has lived out what Margaret has fantasized, proving in the process that a woman's will to cancel out herself can operate as effectively in Tanzania as on Riverside Drive. Diana's second divorce is the trigger for the first-person reflections of the novel, a series of quick takes infused with the sense that womanhood is the cutting edge of despair.

Meet: Claudia, the pre-pubescent, black heroine of The Bluest Eye, a first novel by Toni Morrison. Miss Morrison has recently written a piece for the New York Times in which she presents the reasons why black women find the women's movement irrelevant; she may, in fact, resent her novel's inclusion in an article about aspects of that movement. But what is striking about Claudia is her precarious balance on the fence of her girlhood. Still anarchic and restless, she ponders the mysteries that await her on the other side of adolescence.

And lastly: An unnamed teenage heroine, the "I" of An American Girl by Patricia Dizenzo. Daughter of an alcoholic mother and a dispirited, failed father, she yearns desperately for what she conceives to be normal family life of the Fifties, a world banded by "Strike Me Pink" lipstick, semi-classical music, and Bulova "Miss America" watches conferred on graduation.

These women, joining metaphoric hands with the women we encounter in Growing Up Female, are invaluable guides to the rapids of woman's consciousness. How have their stories altered the old wilderness and illuminated the new?

Self Images

When a woman gazes in the mirror, what is the

The Social Prerogative 425

source of her reflection? And when she looks inside herself, what does she see? The makers of Growing Up Female focus on the way in which a woman is manipulated to discard her early, intuitive self and to identify with a learned, preconceived notion of her sex. They equate socialization with inauthenticity, an estrangement from the true self.

We are presented with a cool, calm, but ultimately horrifying look at a nursery school. In the playground the little boys urge their swings to go higher, the challenge of body against space defeating the natural condition of gravity. Inside the nursery school, the little girls hover around the oven like dwarves in a miniaturized environment. Growing Up Female quietly observes the behavior of children at an age when conventional wisdom would assure us that no sex differentiation had yet taken place. Why are the girls at the arts and crafts table, in de facto segregation from the boys playing with their trucks? The off-camera voice questions the teacher about the nature of the line the children dare not cross; she replies that "girls tend to fritter their time away ... their attention span is shorter." As the teacher continues to reveal her bias against little girls, it becomes clear that her female charges are caught even now in a bind; they are being programmed to act in accordance with an approved collective identity, but even when they act like little girls, they fail to please! Their female teacher has been infected with the plague of contempt for her own sex, and she passes it on to her pupils by disapproving of what she conceives to be the ineradicable nature of little girls.

Growing Up Female presents us, in the person of Ginelle, a recipe for getting a boy to like you: "You drop your books. You say, 'oh, my.' He'll say 'oh, hello.' You say, 'oh my, my books.'" At age eleven, Ginelle is sensible enough to know that this advice, offered by a seemingly sage friend, is nonsense. But whether she will be able to retain that perspective is moot. Ginelle, pegged by her teacher as going through a transitional year in which interest in the opposite sex will out, is caught between two images, each equally irrelevant to her. To her parents, she is now the "tomboy" who will soon grow out of it to become a "little lady." Her mother wants her to wear dresses; she, who revels in football, can see no point in them. But in her bedroom, where she is interviewed by the filmmakers, she is surrounded by her parents' choice in room decorations

--peacock feathers, engravings of girls in curls--and by what are presumably her own choices--"Love" comic books. The commercialization of the biological pull has begun to divert the expression of her sexuality into the accepted channels of feminity.

In Ginelle, we come to know a girl who has so far eluded the pressures to exchange her instinctive self for a factory model. It would be natural for her to search for prototypes after whom to pattern her desire for freedom. But if she were to look to older women, she might well find that they have merged their self-image with a collective identity which equates approval with femininity, and femininity with being attractive to men.

Commercial America's Consumerism

"The goal of commercial America ... is to maximize sexual stimulation and minimize sexual availability--in this way an infinite number of products can be inserted in the resulting gap." This comment by sociologist Philip Slater might well be the motto of a man whom we meet in Growing Up Female; mustached, vested, and seated in wristflick proximity to his stereo, he is the new, hip image of the advertising executive. His comments about the manipulation of women as consumers are so blatantly outrageous that his presence on the screen frequently evokes from an audience the boos and hisses reserved for the villain in the silents who ties girls to the railroad tracks. And in fact, this particular villain is figuratively performing a similar function, only the bondage that he is perpetrating is far more subtle. With glee at his cleverness and implicit loathing for his victims, he regales us with his creation of a "new group of consumers, the hip woman.... The illusion of freedom is what we sell them. Then they all get married, and we sell them on the mother and wife image."

Surrounded everywhere by images of what she should be, it becomes increasingly difficult for a woman to retain a core of self-determined identity. The consequence is sometimes an overwhelming desire to merge herself into the accepted norm: the heroine of Patricia Dizenzo's novel recalls that she wanted "to avoid God and be the typical American girl. I wanted to just eat a lot of junk, be normal, laugh and drive around in a convertible when I was seventeen...."

But the sheer impossibility of even measuring up to the variety of selves thrust at a woman takes its toll in self-contempt. She is repeatedly exhorted by the media to assume a new persona, but of course, being human, cannot shed skins so gracefully. This repeated "failure" is internalized as a self-image of degradation. When Diana Balooka, the heroine of <u>Walking Papers</u>, attends a luncheon, she finds that--"Mayor Lindsay ... addresses all the outstanding women." He says, "My favorite ideal woman would sing like Callas (applause), cook like Julia Child (applause)--." What does one do with such an implied mandate? Perhaps, like Diana, one turns her cosmetician into a god, capable of bleaching her hair into a halo. "She must angelize me-- creating the aura, the ring around the body. Rona gets rid of my black roots."

Or she can try to rebel by turning the giver of the mandate into an object of intense hatred. Cursed with the annual gift of a blue-eyed baby doll cast in the image of Shirley Temple, Claudia finds herself at first merely uninterested in "pretend" motherhood; but disinterest turns to repulsion when she discovers that she cannot love it, even though, mysteriously, "adults, older girls, shops, magazines, newspapers, window signs--all the world had agreed that a blue-eyed, yellow-haired, pink-skinned doll was what every girl child treasured." Enraged at the stereotypical insult to both her race and her femaleness, Claudia turns her anger in upon herself, at first destroying the dolls with a "disinterested violence." Then, guilty at the depths of her hatred, she transforms that emotion into a thwarted love for the image she can never be, and so affirms again the capitulation of self to a false ideal.

The identification of oneself with a doll, the ultimate symbol of powerlessness, is another curve ball on the trajectory of self-definition. Twenty-one year old Tammy in <u>Growing Up Female</u> prides herself on her independence. Interviewed in her room strewn with poster images of male freedom in the persons of Peter Fonda and John Lennon, she casually fondles a Raggedy Ann doll. When the heroine of <u>An American Girl</u> dreams of her relationship with her father, she pictures a "little doll that looked exactly like me that he kept in a hidden room inside his head and that he was twisting out of shape in there." That the doll identification is associated with a loss of self worth is evidenced by Sandra Hochman's description of her heroine's abortion. "Did I know I was risking my life--did my life mean so little that

I would allow myself to be driven, blindfolded, in a car through the streets of Newark?.... Suddenly I became a tiny Japanese doll, a performer in the doll theater. I was being manipulated by the nurses."

Providing us with a conceptual spine, <u>Growing Up Female</u> documents the pressures applied by schools, parents, and media to the vulnerable point of self-image. Elaborating from this center, the novels suggest the passage from natural self through acceptable image to self-loathing and powerlessness. It is hardly a pretty journey, but one of the characteristics of the new landscape is that it must please no one but the speaker, and so is free to reveal the pain beneath the cosmeticized mask.

Mothers and Daughters

If a woman sees herself as incurably damaged because of the fact of her sex, how then does she relate to other women? What has she learned as a daughter, transmitted as a mother? The bonds between women, especially those between mother and daughter, have been eclipsed by a culture whose prevailing religious iconography portrays a mother cradling in her lap a Divine Son, and whose prevailing concept of mind stresses the primacy of the oedipal tie between son and mother. Isolated from the communal functions of initiation, further estranged by the merchandising of competition between older and younger women, mothers and daughters have only just begun to reveal the unbidden feelings of a relationship that outreaches biological fact to become a <u>condition</u> of a woman's life.

Out of the diverse voices, mothers and daughters all, that are speaking through film and fiction, the dominant chord is best sounded by the opening image of <u>Growing Up Female</u>. A screen door opens onto a porch, and a mother and a daughter emerge. Holding hands, they walk down a shaded street. At first I found myself strongly drawn to that vision of an earlier time when I too had been protected by that unfolding warmth. But when I looked back at the film, I jumped out of the skin of nostalgia by the recognition of an unobtrusive visual fact--the pair on the screen were wearing "mother/daughter" outfits, the same material clothing the unformed body and the heavy, maternal one. The power of that image exceeds repugnance at middle-class values that praise the cuteness of a xeroxed child; it lies instead in the mystery of the alternating current of response, a push towards closeness and biological continuity, a pull away from the imposition of false identification, and the social forces that serve to manipulate and distort the relationship.

Transmitting and Mimicking Inadequacies

Between these poles is the tenuous, unexplored balance of genuine connection. Watching her daughter in the playground, Margaret of Up the Sandbox reflects on the nature of their knot. "It is something perhaps in the secret sticky protoplasm out of which I molded her--myself now devoted to a replica of myself, now slave, now master, caught in a bind; not pleasant, certainly nowhere happy, predictably bound for clashing of wills, disappointments, expectations, unmet pride, hurt--all that I know will happen between a mother and a daughter, between me and Elizabeth.... Elizabeth is marred because she is mine and each waking hour I transmit in a thousand unconscious ways the necessary code for her to absorb my personality, to identify with my sex, and to catch like a communicable plague, all my inadequacies and mimic them or convert them to massive ugly splotches on her still young soul." In her role as a mother, Margaret sees her sex as virtually a contagious infection; and yet, full of self-doubts, she finds consolation as a daughter yearning for her own mother: "Dreadful to confess, unfashionable point among my friends, too terrible to admit to anyone, I loved my mother and still would comfort myself on any number of occasions by nestling close to her, big and aged as I am, but of course I can't even covertly show her I am still available." Margaret's emotions transcend the ordinary notions of maturity, the prescription to shed parental ties, to replace love objects with their surrogates. She goes to the root of feeling and recognizes there that a primary relationship has been dehumanized, aborted, and that she has been an unwitting agent of its death.

Margaret speaks to a two-edged bond whose conflicts are at the core of my response to the opening image of Growing Up Female. Focused and enlarged in proportion to the degree of socially encouraged estrangement, the relationship between mother and daughter is a kind of double exposure in which images of maternal suffocation are superimposed upon images of maternal closeness. The novels reveal a composite woman, a picture of the mother within the daughter, the daughter within the mother.

In one telling scene from An American Girl, the teenage daughter who recounts her life to us returns home from school to find her mother drunkenly ordering virtually the whole array of beauty products offered by the visiting Avon lady. Full of maternal concern for the household budget, she disengages her childish mother from the situation. Her role-reversing solicitude, the expression of a damaged intimacy, moves her mother to start "talking about her childhood," saying she was always miserable when she was young because she could never live up to her mother's ideals.... She started crying, calling her mother's name, saying "Mother, Mother, help me, help me get out of this."

Daughter of a thwarted, alcoholic mother, the heroine of An American Girl can define herself only in terms of this essential relationship. Where her mother is dirty, she is neat; where her mother acts out her destructive rage, she withdraws into passive forms of achievement. At the same time that her actions are defensive attempts at carving out a niche of personality, they are also an expression of her need for her mother's approval. But the tragedy of the relationship is that her virtues are met with competitive derision by her mother, who interprets them as devices to highlight her own inadequacies. An American Girl gives us two women locked in the terror of their bond: a mother who vents the spleen of her failure upon her child and a daughter whose authentic self has been lost by the need to react in either accommodation or opposition.

If the forces of religion, psychology and economics have combined to deny women the experience of organic connection with their own sex, then perhaps an additional factor--the transfer of a woman's dissatisfaction onto her female child--has furthered the alienation of daughter from mother. The last sequence of Growing Up Female introduces us to the mother whose image opens the film. In her thirties, with several children, she leads the suburban life of material comfort. The occupation of her adult years has been the care and feeding of her family. As we watch her perform the routine tasks of her day (feeding the dog, tucking a child into bed), we hear her voice-over, ready to explode with domestic frustration: "I just can't go on dusting, picking up after other people!" Counterpointing her discontent, however, is her assertion that it is important that she be at home in order to be the "controlling force in my children's life." Because her scope of operation has been so confined, she has rationalized her custodial function into a noble purpose. Controlled and limited herself, she uses the apron strings that oppress her to bind her children. Writing of the American housewife, Philip Slater has said, "In most societies the impact of neuroses and defects in the mother's character is diluted by the presence of many other nurturing agents. In middle-class America the mother tends to be not only the exclusive daytime adult contact of the child, but also a contact with a mission to create a near-perfect being. This means that every maternal quirk, every maternal hang-up, and every maternal deprivation will be experienced by the child as heavily amplified noise from which there is no respite." And when the message is transmitted to the image of a woman's self that is her daughter, it is apt to be all the more deafening in its cacophony of internalized prohibitions and anger.

In the novels, the women experience their mothers as both larger and smaller than life, as the only person who can unlock the mysteries of rites of passage and the only person who can utterly fail them by refusing to meet their waiting daughters' need for truth. One of the most moving sequences in Growing Up Female concerns a group of prepubescent little girls rambling through woods, full of energy and curiosity. As they leap across a stream, the filmmakers freeze the motion of one girl midway between two banks; they ask us, what will happen to her in her passage to adolescence? Although the film does not deal with the onset of sexuality except as it manifests itself in social behavior, it suggests the vital questions of the transition to womanhood. Traditionally women have passed on the secrets of their sex; what is the experience for a woman growing up in America?

"We talked about the facts of life, and my mother kept repeating over and over, 'What a wonderful thing it is to be a woman....' I wanted at that very moment to escape from my inevitable role of woman and remain a child forever. I tried to explain this, but it was impossible to put it into words. So I just lay on the comforter listening to my mother's soft voice reminding me of the importance of washing myself properly and brushing my teeth regularly and saying 'What a wonderful thing it is to be a woman.' " In Walking Papers, Diana Balooka is visited at summer camp by her mother; it is time for the ritual of initiation, but what is described is neither knowledge nor comfort. In their place is unreality, a stereotyped image tailored to the needs of evasion. Earlier we have come to know Diana's mother as a partner in a bad marriage and a woman with deep ambivalence about taking care of a child. And yet her legacy at a crucial time in her daughter's life is only an empty panegyric, leaving her daughter to giggle competitively with her friends at boarding school about who will be the first to 'Fall Off the Roof.'

The heroine of An American Girl described a subsequent initiation. Embarrassed by a trip to Woolworth's for her first bra, she makes a pact with her mother that the latter will do the actual buying; she will pretend to be totally uninvolved with the whole transaction. But at the last minute, her mother breaks the trust and displays her daughter's vulnerable sexuality by holding up the bra, talking loudly, and implicating her in the purchase. We are presented again with a mother who proves to be false guide, a saleswoman of unreality.

New Frontier of Women's Feelings

Relayed from this new frontier of women's feelings, comes news of a stirring--the emerging expression of female sexuality, its beginnings and possibilities. In The Bluest Eye, the onset of a friend's menstruation is greeted with a measure of compassion by Claudia's mother. But neither biological fact nor mother warmth can answer the question voiced by the little girl who that day had begun her cyclical bondage.... "'Is it true that I can have a baby now?' 'Sure,' said Frieda drowsily. 'Sure you can.' 'But ... how?' Her voice was hollow with wonder. 'Oh,' said Frieda, 'somebody has to love you.... Then Pecola asked a question that had never entered my mind. 'How do you do that? I mean, how to you get somebody to love you?' But Frieda was asleep. And I didn't know.'"

It is as if generations that have been brainwashed have descended upon a single little girl, as if all the strands gather into one life. The questions asked by mothers and daughters are just now being posed; we are all pressing for damages on grounds of willful exploitation, imposed isolation, and a need to deny the texture of experience. The tangled skeins are just beginning to be unravelled, suggesting through film and fiction a condition to be understood and a new relationship to be appreciated.

Choices

What then are the choices available to a woman? If she has learned to accept a self-image of worthlessness, will she then have a choice? If she has lost part of herself by following false mandates, where does she find it again? How, from the territory of relationships and self-definition, does a woman create life roles?

At root, these questions are the explicit theme of the film and the implicit direction of the fiction; the former treats the sociology of choice, while the novels deal with the internalizing of values that determine choice. <u>Growing Up Female</u> begins by pointing out that American society says that we are free to choose our life when we reach the age of twenty-one. Examining the choices open to a woman when she comes of age, the filmmakers demonstrate the fact that women do not have access to the universal promise of the American myth.

The film introduces us to Terry, who is sixteen years old, black, and attending a vocational high school where she is being trained as a cosmetician. We are taken on a tour of classes offered to women at her school, past the secretarial class and pausing in the keypunch room. A male teacher tells the interviewer that a female is more adept at keypunch operations because she is more "sedate"; however, he "uses men for anything beyond keypunch.... The nature of woman is that she wants to get married." In Terry's class, we hear her teacher define the role of a cosmetician as "helping a woman to be feminine by artificial means." The camera pans past the bald heads of mannequins lined up to receive their crown of imitation fibers, and comes to rest on Terry, passively absorbing the precepts that to be feminine is to be beautiful, and to be beautiful is to be attractive to men. As I was watching Terry's unchanging face--sleek hair all but covering the shy edges of her profile--I suddenly realized that her look reminded me of photographs of Vietnamese peasants, their faces seemingly passive beneath the bombardment of their culture, while the mannequins' heads with their seemingly depilated hair evoked thoughts of defoliation and destruction inflicted upon an inwardly suffering victim.

If Terry is being molded by her regular classes, how much more insidious is her required course in marriage, taught by her guidance counselor, in which she learns that "the husband should make the major decisions" and that "a wife should not expect her husband to do any of the housework.... Leave time for his education to help his later life ... you do want your husband to be a success." At age sixteen, she has come to accept the division of sex roles; submissively, she explains to the interviewer her relationship to her boyfriend--"It's like a marriage. He strives to be dominant."

What are the choices facing Terry? She hopes to escape her small town, but the odds are stacked against her ever escaping the pervasive value system she has learned. She will tease the offending hairs, and may even come to embrace the mythology that limits her options. One might be tempted to feel that as a black woman from a commercial high school, Terry is an extreme example of a woman's possibilities for choice. But the same sexual stereotyping is apparent in the white middle-class high school of <u>An American Girl</u>, when the heroine who has excelled academically reads "Right Job for Judith," a career orientation for would-be secretaries. Also a victim to the pressures of high school popularity, she decides not to compete for the cheerleading squad, but is thrown into a panic when, on the eve of the tryouts, she dreams that God talks to her, telling her that this is her last chance. The fear of missing out on whatever small option is possible informs the inauthentic choice of taking whatever is offered. The suburban mother of <u>Growing Up Female</u> has the guts to admit that if she had her life to live over again ... "If I hadn't married, would I live it the way I'm living today? Oh boy ... I doubt it."

<u>Women Confronting Basic Assumptions</u>

Sometimes the illusion of choice produces the actuality of intense compulsion; the poor, broken child of <u>The Bluest Eye</u> is ultimately driven mad both by the violence done her by her father's rape and by the cultural rape of her selfhood, but also by her immediate desire, beyond all reason, to be beautiful, to possess "the bluest eye." At other times the failure of options is far less dramatic, choice having translated itself into the struggle to be taken seriously on the domestic battleground. The dimensions of the trap are articulated by Margaret of <u>Up The Sandbox</u>: "I am doing what every peasant woman has always done. I am nurturing. Paul sits in the library, in his classroom, and he tries to find some sensible thread, some explanation for bloodshed, revolution, poverty ... and while he reads and traces similarities and disparities from Plato to Freud, I repeat each day the sameness of everything." Margaret, however, does not question her assumption that in "America, of course, any mobility is theoretically possible, so I have only myself to blame if I have not passed from Paramus High School to the Princess Borghese's inner circle." As with many women, she has difficulty confronting the basic assumptions that govern her life, that make her fantasize about a life she could have led had she exercised those supposedly free options. For Margaret's life is divided between the daily round of her familial duties and the imagined adventures of her liberated alter ego whose activities range from winning a scoop on Castro's sex life, to paddling down the remote reaches of the Amazon in search of a primitive tribe, to plotting to blow up the George Washington Bridge as an act of revolutionary terrorism. But cutting through the dreams of glory is anxiety about her imminent life when she must come face to face with the implications of the role for whose creation she assumes single responsibility: "--but what will I do, when I have no special chores, no one demanding my approval, requiring my attention? I will fall like a disinherited meteor and crash on some unimportant bit of ground." Margaret is caught in the bind of the educated woman who has gleaned hints of what the world might offer, whose sensibilities are always honed and at the ready, and yet, in spite of her gifts, has found herself opting for the urban variation of Adam's rib.

And what of Diana? Diana, whose life is the very paradigm of Margaret's dreams, has casually run through several successful careers, several not so successful marriages, and has accumulated the money and credentials to move with mobility across the world. But Diana cannot move at all, except to howl in pain. Movement to her is despair, a clock ticking away a message of something gone awry. Sexually free, Diana has allowed herself to be tied to men who are conveniently able to mesh with her masochistic demands for unhappy love affairs. In a world of presumably unlimited options, Diana has made it necessary to continually take her own measure, and finding it of course wanting, has chosen to cast herself in the last available prison, the cell of disappointed love.

What is overwhelming about experiencing the novels and the film is that through a number of women we encounter the major institutions of society, and so begin to catch glimpses of the paucity of choice offered to women by the schools, by media, by love, by marriage and the family. By the end of Growing Up Female, the women met, the choices examined, we are moved to realize that "six" have become "one," that we have experienced a shared, essential truth of what it means to be a woman in America. Formerly buried under the divisions of class, race, and dogma, that universal core now lies unconcealed. The final image of the film comes full circle to the mother and daughter we met at the beginning; although we have come to know the boundaries circumscribed around several generations of women, what of this young daughter whom we see at her mother's side? The filmmakers tell us that "in the end, a woman emerges, her future uncertain, her identity unknown."

If we look to the newly opened territory whose landscape is being carved by the expression of women's sensibilities, we can, I believe, see signs of the emerging woman. For at the center of her liberation is this very move towards finding a public voice for the discoveries of self-exploration. This film, these novels, are early steps towards self-definition--they will continue to be joined by others. Knowing that their landscape need not justify itself by pointing to towering figures of individual genius, women are creating out of the same dynamic, anarchic and democratic impulses that underlie the entire women's movement. Past the prohibition against talking about their bodies, women are realizing Diana's truth that "out of my womanhood is my madness woven," and are finding in themselves a new impulse to transmute that womanhood into art. Woman is only now revealing herself.

References

Film
Growing Up Female: As Six Become One. 60 mins., b/w, price apply. Producers: Julia Reichert and James Klein, 1971. Distributor: New Day Films, 267 W. 25th St., New York, N.Y. 10001.

Books
An American Girl, by Patricia Dizenzo. Holt, Rinehart and Winston, 1971. $4.95.
Walking Papers, by Sandra Hochman. The Viking Press, 1971. $6.95.
The Bluest Eye, by Toni Morrison. Holt, Rinehart and Winston, 1970. $5.95.
Up the Sandbox, by Anne Richardson Roiphe. Simon and Schuster, 1970. $4.95.

Also, much recommended:
The Pursuit of Loneliness, by Philip Slater. Beacon Press, 1970. $2.45.

SENIOR POWER!*

Peggy O'Donnell

> Old age should burn and rave at close of day
> --Dylan Thomas

Perhaps, but most older Americans are too tired just trying to exist. As a minority 10% of the population they lack glamour in a culture devoted to youth. Of the 20 million Americans over 65, 25% live below the poverty line, while 40% of the single older adults have an income of less than $1500! Pensions, social security, old age assistance funds remain low, while costs spiral. Many older people who own their own homes are hit hard by increasing property taxes. Others are unaware of the income tax exemptions that would lower taxes. Financial conditions are worst among the aged in minority groups.

Contrary to popular belief, most older Americans are not in poor health, though they are more likely to be victims of chronic diseases, such as arthritis. Only about 18% of the aged are actually disabled. Yet they pay a quarter of all health costs. Despite Medicare, which covered only about 43% of their medical costs in 1969, older people on reduced incomes are less able to pay medical bills.

However, their mental health may suffer as isolation grows. Friends and family die or move away. Lack of any kind of transportation segregates the rural aged. In the urban ghettos, where a substantial portion of the elderly reside, fear of street crime and an inability to cope with the transit system may keep the older person a virtual prisoner. As isolation increases the older adult may be subject to depression. If mental illness occurs, psychiatric help is less available, since often there is a feeling that it would be wasted. Loneliness may be complicated by the fact that sexual desire does not disappear with age, though old people

---

*Reprinted by permission from Synergy, 37 (summer solstice 1972).

may feel ashamed when these urges occur. Potency may decrease, but the major problem is the lack of a suitable partner. The suicide rate is high among older people. In San Francisco, one-third of all suicides are committed by people over 60.

Even when an older person is active and mobile, he may feel invisible. He has become a victim of agism, ("not wanting to have ugly old people around"). This is a form of prejudice that infects all of us, since most people hate to think about aging. We somehow hope it won't happen to us-- but every elderly person we see reminds us that it will. Such rejection causes an older person to believe he is as worthless as the younger generations say. He conforms to the stereotype and becomes increasingly unable to cope.

Older people who feel needed are mentally just as healthy as the young. But how to feel needed when there is nothing to do? As one sociologist said, "Old people haven't a damn thing to do and nothing to do it with," and they face many years in this condition of social insecurity, since "medicine has kept them young but technology has made them obsolete."

The situation will worsen with the increased emphasis on earlier retirement as an even greater number of people must live on smaller incomes. Gerontological advances allowing many to live to their nineties will result in a large population that faces 35 or 40 years as "old people," with little money, and nothing to occupy their time.

But with increased awareness, the picture may not be so grim--for the affluent oldster, volunteer groups are available, and these are becoming more eager to welcome the older experienced person who can provide valuable skills. Retired executives counsel small businessmen through SCORE. Doctors, lawyers, librarians and many other professionals donate their expertise to community action projects. VISTA and the Peace Corps have also welcomed older adults.

Increased efforts are being made not only to prevent job discrimination on the basis of age, but also to create salaried positions for older citizens. A few of the programs that enable older people to help others while helping themselves are "Green Thumb," which allows older men to work on public landscape projects, "Foster Grandparents," which enables low income old people to provide support and love to

The Social Prerogative

institutionalized children, and "Project FIND," which utilizes elder senior aides to search out old people living in poverty and neglect, and put them in touch with agencies that could help them. An activist role is espoused by California Rural Legal Assistance Senior Citizen Project. Here older people are trained to act as lay advocates for other old people who may be too insecure or unable to handle a welfare hearing or to beat down bureaucratic walls to find services they need.

However, older adults are not just waiting around for others to take care of them. As 17% of the voting population (and more apt to vote than younger citizens) older activists are spearheading movements to force legislators to meet their demands for housing, tax relief, and health care. Senior power groups are springing up all over the country. Here, the righteously militant California Legislative Council for Older Americans, led by Rev. Edward Peet, has lobbied for increased social security and Medicare payments, and lower transportation costs. Working for material benefits gives a feeling of achievement to people who too often are told their usefulness is over.

The government is becoming more aware that the aging have problems, and an attempt to discover the real situation of the older adult was made by the recent White House Conference on Aging. The older people considered their single most important need was to be allowed to remain in their own home. To do this, the elderly will need adequate income, and in some cases supportive services, such as homemakers, nurses, and transportation. Public housing and nursing homes are not the answer.

The public library can help here not only by book deliveries to those older people who are shut-in, but by being aware of the relevant services in the community for referral purposes. Library service to older adults, in the past, has consisted mainly of shut-in programs, deposits in senior centers, and film or book programs. All are passive forms of recreation--which in the view of many authorities are just what the older people don't need. What they want is active involvement in projects, a chance to exercise the talents that have been "retired," and a renewed feeling of purpose that will provide a sense of self-worth. At the same time, they need vital information that will help them live more adequate lives. Library service must meet these needs.

Ira Philips, the ALA delegate to the White House

Conference, noted there was little concern with libraries
either before or during the conference. He felt since the
meeting dealt with real survival issues like income, health,
and housing, that libraries--considered as purely recreational
resources--did not assume much importance to the participants. Libraries must relate their services to these major
issues. "To accomplish this task the whole question of
information-referral centers should be examined by appropriate ALA divisions ... and recommendations should be
made as to how libraries can become involved in alleviating
the survival problems of the aged."

This of course, means more staff and money. It
seems that money may be forthcoming. S. 3196, The Older
Readers Services Act of 1972, was launched in February
which could appropriate $50 million for services, materials
and employment in libraries for older people. But in the
meantime, what resources can we as reference librarians
provide, and what programs might we encourage?

Referral services are needed--each report stresses
the need to connect the elderly with the hundreds of state,
federal, and local programs that might help them. In no
case do they discuss that the public library might fulfil this
function, but what place could be more natural? Many older
people spend a great deal of time in the library. A library
in a community should be aware of the programs available
there--what services they offer and who can apply. Updating
material and making it accessible should be combined with a
welcoming attitude so older adults feel it is safe to ask for
help. In doing the latter job well, the library might provide
its most vital single service to lonely older persons.

Researching your community for relevant agencies can
be done in a number of ways, but the most important step
will be taken when you become aware of types of organizations that are active in this area. Contacting them in person, by phone or mail to determine just what their services
are will lead to discovering new agencies. A list of agencies
sponsoring programs for older adults appears at the end of
this article. Your community may have local offices of
these programs.

In addition, how about some positive attempt to truly
understand aging? Sponsor programs that involve older adults
in the planning and participation, and focus on gut issues
rather than entertainment. If possible, hire older people for

The Social Prerogative 441

part-time work, or as volunteers. Use them as library assistants on special projects such as local history or oral history collections, using their memories, old scrapbooks, pictures and other ephemera. Start a shut-in service using older adults to deliver materials. See if you can have a representative from Social Security or Medicare regularly available at the library to answer questions. Promote what the library does and keep older adults informed through a brochure or a spot announcement on TV or radio.

Libraries in the last few years have been reaching out vigorously to many minorities, but unfortunately most have lagged behind in this field. If your social conscience won't prod you to become actively involved, think about the fact that you too will be old some day....

AGENCIES THAT PROVIDE SERVICES OR PROGRAMS FOR OLDER ADULTS
(The list is selective--full info on each agency and its programs should be obtained from local branches.)

FEDERAL   Administration on Aging--330 Independence Avenue S.W., Washington, DC 20201
         Conducts national programs for the elderly. Primarily responsible for planning, research and publications.
Dept. of Health, Education & Welfare--330 Independence Ave S.W., Washington, DC 20201
         Social Security and Medicare information.
Dept. of Housing & Urban Development--1451 7th St., S.W. Washington, DC 20410
         Sponsors low rent housing projects for the elderly, with applicable research on housing, transportation, medical facilities and health.
Dept. of Labor--Constitution Avenue & 14th N.W., Washington, DC 20210
         Many of its manpower programs are specifically designed to include older workers. There are older worker's service units in many cities.
Office of Economic Opportunity--1200 19th N.W., Washington, DC 20506
         Innovative programs in employment, housing, and transportation. Best known is

its "Project FIND," used to locate old poor people and turn them onto agencies that can help them. OEO projects may be part of Model City or Community Action; most communities are involved one way or another.

NATIONAL
The National Council on Aging--1828 L St., N.W., Washington, DC 20036
Non-profit organization active in all fields, involved in programming and publishing. Works with government and private agencies. Maintains the most comprehensive library on aging.

STATE
Many states have a Commission on Aging which works with the federal Administration on Aging.
Health Care Services--May include adult day care centers, health and nutrition education, home nursing programs.
Social Welfare Department--Welfare benefits, food stamp program.

LOCAL
Large cities sometimes have an "Office on Aging." Also Welfare Departments and Health Departments sometimes have programs for older citizens. The public library should also provide access to any local equivalent of:
American Association of Retired People--
Many social activities and special benefits. Monitors relevant legislation.
Friendly Visitors Programs--Volunteers who visit elderly, do errands, etc. Usually church sponsored.
Homemaker Services--Light housekeeping, shopping, cooking. May be volunteer or available at low cost.
Meals on Wheels--Delivery of hot meals to the home. May be free or small charge.
Senior Citizens Clubs--Though many are simply recreation centers, some provide counseling and referral service.
Telephone Reassurance--Goes under many names; all provide that the older person will be called once a day at a set time. If he does not answer caller will check immediately to see if he's all right.

Know how to help in these areas:

<u>Emergencies</u> (financial, food, shelter, clothes)
Charitable organizations
Churches
Social Welfare Departments

<u>Employment</u> (Agencies such as Salvation Army
often make employment referrals)
Goodwill Industries
Government sponsored programs such as
"Foster Grandparents" and "Green Thumb"
"Mature Temps"

<u>Housing</u>
Nursing and Convalescent Homes
Public Housing
Retirement Communities
Senior Hotels

<u>Medical</u>
Dental clinics, medical schools offering free
or inexpensive care
Hospitals with special geriatric clinics
Suicide prevention groups

RESOURCES

California. Commission on Aging. <u>A Design for Action to Improve State and Local Programs for the Aging</u>. Institute for Local Self Government, Hotel Claremont Bldg., Berkeley, CA 94705, 1971. $3.

Directory of all major programs with full descriptions of particularly successful ones in California. Other states may have similar program directories.

California Rural Legal Assistance. Senior Citizens' Project. <u>Advocate's Handbook</u>. CRLA, 942 Market St., San Francisco, CA 94102. $1.50.

This handbook is a result of CRLA's project to train laymen to become advocates for old people who are unable to fight for their rights. The project emphasizes the use of older adults in the advocate's role. The first section describes the problems of the elderly poor. The rest of the manual is devoted to training the would-be advocate.

The following National Council on Aging publications may be ordered from their publications office at 1828 L St., N.W., Washington, D.C. 20036:
Publications 1971-72.   Free.
   Listing of books, periodicals, pamphlets, films produced by NCOA. Particularly useful are the SOS (Senior Opportunities & Services) technical assistance monographs. Each item is devoted to a specific problem of older adults or programs that can aid them.
The Golden Years ... A Tarnished Myth.   1970.   Free.
   Report on the conditions of the elderly poor. Emphasizes need for referral to helpful agencies. (The Project FIND Report.)
A National Directory of Housing for Older People.   Rev. ed., 1969. $5.50.
Older Americans: Special Handling Required. By Marjorie Bloomberg Twin. Prepared for U.S. Dept. of HEW and U.S. Dept. of HUD.   Free.
   An excellent source of information on older adults which covers their role in society, specific problems and sources of help available to them.
Resources for the Aging: An Action Handbook.   2nd ed. NCOA for the Community Action Program, OEO. Single copy free.
   Catalog of national resources which can provide financial and other assistance to community programs for the aging.

Office of Economic Opportunity. Region IX. Directory of Projects for Older Adults. 100 McAllister, San Francisco, CA 94102.   1970.   Free.
   A description of the Senior Opportunity Service Projects sponsored by OEO in Region IX (California, Arizona, Hawaii.) The Directory is currently being updated and should be available soon.

Townsend, Claire. Old Age: The Last Segregation; Ralph Nader's Study Group Report on Nursing Homes. N.Y., Bantam Books, 1971. $1.95.
   Nader's task force of young students took jobs as aides in nursing homes to back up their research. Focuses on the problems, but also makes recommendations. Appendices include laws relating to the aged and questions to ask when visiting a nursing home.

   The following may be ordered from the individual agency or the Superintendent of Documents, U.S. Government

Printing Office, Washington, DC 20402:
U.S. Department of Health, Education and Welfare. Social and Rehabilitation Service, Administration on Aging. <u>Publications of the Administration on Aging.</u> Free. Superintendent of Documents #FS17.311:P.96.
> <u>Senior Centers in the United States--A Directory.</u> $2. (HE17.302:Se 5/3)
> <u>Transportation and Aging</u>, $1.75. (HE17.302:T68)
> <u>Words on Aging; A Bibliography.</u> <u>More Words on Aging--Supplement, 1971.</u> 75 cents, 55 cents. (HE17.311:Ag4)
>> Subject index to books, magazine articles and documents.

U.S. Department of Housing and Urban Development. <u>The Built Environment for the Elderly and the Handicapped</u>, 50 cents (HH1.23:EL2/2)
> Bibliography on all types of housing available to older adults.

White House Conference on Aging. National Planning Board. <u>Background and Issues.</u> Washington, DC 20201. 1961. Nominal fee for each. (Y3.W 58/4:2 ---)
> 16 reports prepared for the White House Conference on Aging. Titles include:

Education	Physical and Mental Health
Employment	Planning
Facilities, Programs and Services	Research and Demonstration Retirement
Government and Non-Government Organizations	Retirement Roles and Activities
Housing the Elderly	Spiritual Well-Being
Income	Training
Nutrition	Transportation

PERIODICALS

<u>Aging.</u> U.S. Department of Health, Education and Welfare. Social and Rehabilitation Service. Administration on Aging, $2.50/yr.
> News of national organizations, state and local projects, and information of federal developments. Includes a review section on literature on aging.

<u>Current Literature on Aging.</u> National Council on Aging, 1828 L. St., N.W., Washington, DC 20036. Quarterly, $3/yr.
> Subject arrangement of recent books and articles, prepared by the library staff of the National Council on Aging.

The Gerontologist. Gerontological Society, 1 Dupont Circle, Washington, DC 20036. Quarterly. $10/yr.
"For the professional who keeps abreast of new developments in the aging field." Excellent articles and reports on all aspects of aging.

NOTES ON CONTRIBUTORS

ROBERT PLANT ARMSTRONG is the director of Northwestern University Press.

R. H. BLACKBURN is the chief librarian at the University of Toronto.

MARGARET C. BROWN is chief, Processing Division, the Free Library of Philadelphia.

WILLIAM COLE is an editor and anthologist.

W. G. K. DUNCAN was former President of the Australian Library Association, was professor of history and political science at the University of Adelaide, 1951-1968.

WILLIAM R. ESHELMAN is editor of the Wilson Library Bulletin.

SARA INNIS FENWICK is a professor at the Graduate Library School, University of Chicago.

CAROLYN FORSMAN is a doctoral candidate at the School of Library and Information Science at the University of Maryland.

D. E. GERARD is senior lecturer, Department of Bibliographical Studies, College of Librarianship, Aberystwyth, Wales.

HILLIS L. GRIFFIN is the librarian at the Argonne National Laboratory, Argonne, Illinois.

ANDREW H. HORN is dean of the School of Library Science, University of California, Los Angeles.

BETTE HOWLAND is a writer living in Chicago. Her essay is part of a larger work.

HERMAN W. LIEBERT is librarian of the Beinecke Rare Book and Manuscript Library, Yale University.

RICHARD W. LYMAN is president of Stanford University.

DWIGHT MACDONALD is an author and critic.

ARCHIBALD MACLEISH is a poet and playwright, formerly Librarian of Congress.

ELLSWORTH MASON is director of the University of Colorado Libraries in Boulder, Colorado.

ERIC MOON is president of the Scarecrow Press.

PEGGY O'DONNELL is a Virgo with Gemini rising. She conducts workshops when not writing for Synergy and cheering on BARC's good works.

HUIBERT PAUL is the serials librarian at the University of Oregon Library, Eugene.

ARTHUR PLOTNIK is associate editor of the Wilson Library Bulletin.

SAMUEL ROTHSTEIN is a professor at the School of Librarianship, University of British Columbia.

PATRICIA GLASS SCHUMAN is associate editor of School Library Journal.

F. A. SHARR is the State Librarian of Western Australia.

RALPH R. SHAW was the founder of Scarecrow Press, as well as a librarian and professor.

GERALD SHIELDS is the editor of American Libraries.

JANET STERNBURG is a writer, filmmaker, and an associate producer for NET in the area of film and drama.

HANS WELLISCH is the head of the Documentation Centre of TAHAL Consulting Engineers Ltd., Tel Aviv, and has published widely on classification and indexing.

THOMAS WEYR is a senior editor at the Research Institute of America and a contributing editor to Publishers Weekly.

Z
671
L7024
#3
1972

JAN 9 1974